Governing Metropolitan Regions in the 21st Century

Cities and Contemporary Society

Series Editors: Richard D. Bingham and Larry C. Ledebur,
Cleveland State University

Sponsored by the
Maxine Goodman Levin College of Urban Affairs
Cleveland State University

This series focuses on key topics and emerging trends in urban policy. Each volume is specially prepared for academic use, as well as for specialists in the field.

Governing Metropolitan Regions in the 21st Century

Don Phares
Editor

Routledge
Taylor & Francis Group

LONDON AND NEW YORK

First published 2009 by M.E. Sharpe

Published 2015 by Routledge
2 Park Square, Milton Park, Abingdon, Oxon OX14 4RN
711 Third Avenue, New York, NY 10017, USA

Routledge is an imprint of the Taylor & Francis Group, an informa business

Library of Congress Cataloging-in-Publication Data

Governing metropolitan regions in the 21st century / Don Phares, editor.
   p. cm. — (Cities and contemporary society)
Includes bibliographical references and index.
ISBN 978-0-7656-2088-0 (cloth : alk. paper) — ISBN 978-7656-2089-7 (pbk. : alk. paper)
1. Metropolitan government—History—21st century. 2. Municipal government—History—
21st century. 3. Comparative government—History—21st century. I. Phares, Donald.

JS241.G67 2009
320.8'5—dc22   2008053552

ISBN 13: 9780765620897 (pbk)
ISBN 13: 9780765620880 (hbk)

Contents

List of Illustrations

Tables

Figures

Maps

Acknowledgments

The genesis of this volume was a two-day working session held at the University of Missouri–St. Louis. There were participants from several metropolitan areas in the United States and also from Canada and Mexico. The focus of the session was to discuss issues pertaining to various facets of "metropolitan governance."

I want to acknowledge the involvement of the Public Policy Research Center at the University of Missouri–St. Louis for its financial and logistical support and for its participation in this working conference. I especially want to recognize the Center's director, Dr. Mark Tranel, for his support and participation.

This conference would not have been possible without the many participants who prepared and presented papers and who were involved in two days of in-depth discussion of metropolitan governance issues. Finally, I want to recognize those colleagues who have joined the project by working with an original participant or preparing a new chapter. Each of these individuals is, in part, responsible for this volume, *Governing Metropolitan Regions in the 21st Century*. My thanks to each of you for your time, effort, and professional involvement in an important public policy issue.

Prologue

On Metropolitan Government and Governance

Don Phares

An Overview

How metropolitan areas govern themselves is a topic that has permeated the academic and professional literature for decades. It has also received regular attention from both the print and visual media. The coverage has gone in cycles, sometimes being very much "in vogue," sometimes nearly dormant. At present, governing metropolitan regions is a very hot topic that is receiving a great deal of academic and professional as well as media attention. The focus, however, has shifted from the "reform" approach that looks at government structure to the so-called new regionalism that emphasizes a more informal governance approach.

Two variants of this issue have been addressed—metropolitan government and metropolitan governance. The government variant focuses on the development of new formal government structures to handle the existing and emerging issues in metropolitan areas; this has often been referred to as the reform movement, for which there is an extensive literature covering several decades. The parameters of governance are somewhat more obscure in focus and diverse in content. Governance looks to dealing with metropolitan issues with a variety of means but not through a formal metro government structure. The approach is much more informal and less "global." Tables 1.1 and 1.2 in Tranel's Chapter 1 provide some idea of the diversity that has evolved to deal with metropolitan problems, both state enabled and informal arrangements. It should be noted that this is far from an exhaustive list.

There are many facets to the government/governance "debate" but two broad, overriding aspects cut across both approaches. The first looks at the geographical scope of coverage. How encompassing should this spatial coverage be? An entire Metropolitan Statistical Area (MSA)? The most populated portion of an MSA? How does the coverage change to accommodate growth, decentralization, and the associated sprawl? Population expansion or movement and sprawl can render an existing "governance" arrangement, formal or informal, obsolete over time.

So a first matter to be confronted is what is, or what should be, the geography of governing metropolitan regions?

The second aspect deals with the scope of coverage for service delivery from the trivial, such as animal control, to the significant, such as planning, infrastructure development, environmental concerns, and waste treatment, to the myriad other issues that presently exist and that will come into existence as metro regions expand, decline, or otherwise change. How much and what should be regional? How much and what should be left to a more local level of decision making? How important is coordination among these metro functions? How do citizen/taxpayers view the situation?

Neither of these issues can be addressed and answered with absolute finality given the (often rapidly) shifting nature of metro areas, evolving national circumstances, and the ever-changing global environment. However, something must be done. Metropolitan issues and problems will not go away and should not (cannot) be ignored. They remain, expand, and sometimes fester.

The Plan for This Volume

This book examines specifically what has occurred in thirteen major metropolitan regions in the United States, Canada, and Mexico. It also contains two overview chapters that look at governance in the United States and Canada (Chapters 4 and 12) and one that examines Mexico's two largest metro areas (Chapter 14). In addition, two chapters discuss the governing issue—one from a formal government perspective (Chapter 2) and one from an informal governance perspective (Chapter 3).

Given the sheer number of metro areas in the United States, some 360 plus, obviously no volume can pretend to cover all that has taken place, is taking place, and will take place. In point of fact most of the metro areas are small enough so that the major metropolitan issues do not affect them, or, if they do, not very much. They may be metro by formal definition but not in terms of function, size, scope, or the weight of issues and problems they confront.

The metro areas dealt with in this volume cover an array of "approaches" to governing. They cover a spectrum in the United States, Canada, and Mexico that provides a glimpse into what has been done across North America. As a working framework, the work done by David Walker (Walker, 1987) is useful in that it shows the array of governance approaches that have been employed. It is summarized in Table P.1.

Walker characterizes the governance approaches from "easiest" to "middling" to "hardest" in terms of their achievability. The easier ones tend toward the "governance" options such as various types of informal cooperative agreements to legally binding arrangements to private contracting. They may be the easiest, but they can also be the weakest link in the governance chain. They may accomplish, and, in fact, have accomplished a specific task at hand at a given point in time, but there is no "formal" structure to guarantee their continuance. There is usually no

Table P.1

Regional Governance Approaches: Walker's Classification

Approach	Summary description
Easiest	
Informal Cooperation	Collaborative and reciprocal actions between two local governments
Interlocal Service Agreements	Voluntary but formal agreements between two or more local governments
Joint Powers Agreements	Agreements between two or more local governments for joint planning, financing, and delivery of a service
Exterritorial Powers	Allows a city to exercise some regulatory authority outside of its boundary in rapidly developing unincorporated areas
Regional Councils/Councils of Government	Local councils that rely mostly on voluntary efforts and have moved to regional agenda-definer and conflict-resolver roles
Federally Encouraged Single-Purpose Regional Bodies	Single-purpose regional bodies created when tied to federal funds
State Planning and Development Districts	Established by states in the 1960s and early 1970s to bring order to chaotic creation of federal special purpose regional programs
Contracting (private)	Service contracts with private providers
Middling	
Local Special Districts	Provides a single service or multiple related services on a multijurisdictional basis
Transfers of Functions	Shifting of responsibility for provision of a service from one jurisdiction to another
Annexation	Bringing an unincorporated area into an incorporated jurisdiction
Regional Special Districts and Authorities	Regionwide districts for providing a service, for example, mass transit or sewage disposal
Metro Multipurpose District	A regional district to provide multiple functions
Reformed Urban County	Establishment of a charter county
Hardest	
One-Tier Consolidation	Consolidation of city and county
Two-Tier Restructuring	Division of functions between local and regional
Three-Tier Restructuring	Agencies at multiple levels of government that absorb, consolidate, or restructure new and/or existing roles and responsibilities

Source: Adapted from Walker (1987).

coordination, and their existence is predicated on shared local cooperation, which in some of our fragmented metro areas can be tenuous.

The "middling" group looks more to versions of formal special districts (local and regional) and annexation. This category is, of course, heavily influenced by available state-enabling legislation for special districts of any type and for annexation procedures. In some states these are easy to accomplish, and in others difficult or nearly impossible. Special districts are the only form of local government that has grown over the past more than fifty years. As Hall's chapter (Chapter 4) shows in Table 4.1, special districts have more than tripled in number since 1952, going from 12,340 in 1952 to 37,381 in 2007, while municipal and township governments have remained about constant in number. The special district approach has been the one favored for dealing with metro problems. They are, however, often not truly metropolitan in geographical coverage and deal with a single metro issue such as transportation, wastewater treatment, or tourism and recreation. Most often there is little, if any, coordination among them at the regional level.

The "hardest" of Walker's groups is the one that has been used the least in the United States. There is really only one "metro" government in the United States—Portland, Oregon. The options in this category have been used much more widely in Canada, due to strong provincial pressure and incentives, but with varied outcomes ranging from the Toronto example, which has "evolved" to the more stable Vancouver case (see Chapters 12 and 13). The results in Mexico are more mixed and limited due to the prevalence of strong private sector involvement in Monterrey and the ever-changing political environment in Mexico City, the country's capital and largest city with more than 20 million people (see Chapter 14).

A very recent case where movement toward metro government might well be appropriate is New Orleans in the wake of one of our nation's worst natural disasters, Hurricane Katrina. Whelan (in Chapter 11) points out the strong case that can be made for a regional approach to dealing with the devastation from Katrina. He notes, however, that things remain pretty much the same with little or inadequate coordination and cooperation among governments (federal, state, and local) and no metropolitan context with which to "fix things."

Perhaps the most "successful" approach in Walker's "hardest" category is consolidation as discussed for Louisville in Chapter 9 and Indianapolis's UniGov in Chapter 8. However, beyond these two examples, success should be qualified by the small number of consolidations that have actually occurred. Table 4.2 in Hall's Chapter 4 lists the successful city-county consolidations since 1805. The number is rather small given the more than two hundred-year time span. The Louisville case has been characterized as "uncertain" in terms of outcomes (see Chapter 9), and the Indianapolis UniGov as more successful (see Chapter 8). Perhaps this can be accounted for by the thirty-year time span (1969 vs. 1999) between these consolidations and by the fact that matters have settled in UniGov but are still settling in Louisville.

What Is on the Government/Governance Horizon?

Looking to the future of governing metro areas in North America is a daunting and, obviously, speculative task. However, some points seem to stand out as relatively clearly defined. The following are some thoughts looking into the twenty-first century.

First, federal or national involvement in metro issues will vary among the three countries under examination here. Canada already has a history of some national involvement working with or through provinces. Mexico will most likely continue to be driven by an ever-changing political context, especially as it affects the nation's capital and largest metro area, Mexico City, with its population of more than 20 million and growing. In the United States, formal federal involvement in metro concerns has not been there. The United States has never had an urban policy let alone a metro policy, despite the fact that these areas contain the vast majority of its people, businesses, commerce, and so on. Federal involvement has been virtually entirely financial. Federal funds are placed in select programs but without much, if any, thought or planning for functions on a metropolitan scale. Given the extreme pressures now on the federal government, a national "metropolitan policy" seems to be at the very bottom of the queue or off the list entirely, if, in fact, it has ever been considered seriously.

At the state or provincial level things vary among the three nations covered in this volume. Canada has a long tradition of involvement in metropolitan area governance (see Chapter 12 for a thorough discussion). Beginning in a major way with Toronto, provincial involvement has been present in metro areas throughout Canada. This is likely to continue but perhaps soften a bit. The trade-off between broader scale metropolitan government and local accountability is becoming more problematic. Smith points this out in Chapter 13 with respect to Vancouver, which has been one of Canada's more outstanding examples. In Mexico the situation is less clear and is heavily driven by politics in Mexico City and strong private-sector involvement in Monterrey (see Chapter 14).

The United States is the clearest case. States generally do not become involved in local metropolitan issues. While implicit, there is almost a universal "hands off" policy, despite the fact that local governments are legal creatures of the state. Any state involvement usually assumes either the form of enabling legislation that allows local governments, which collectively are our metro regions, to "do something," or the form of just ignoring the problem. State participation may take the form of permissive legislation on annexation and consolidation, the establishment of special districts, or other subtle nuances on local prerogatives. In many cases states provide legislation that fiscally supports localities. There are few, if any, legislative incentives for localities to have a regional focus. In point of fact, the incentives that states provide to localities may actually support focusing more locally, not regionally, for example, through tax increment financing (TIF), unequal tax revenue distribution schemes, ignoring disparities in taxable property wealth, or protecting the local zoning and land use powers.

One thing that seems crystal clear is that metropolitan government in the United States is not likely now, or perhaps ever. This is discussed in detail in Chapter 2. The literature surveyed here on regional governance is not focused in a comprehensive metropolitan context. It tends to look at specific aspects (e.g., transportation or economic development) but not at the whole. Another part of Chapter 2 outlines the numerous reasons why this is, and probably will continue to be, true. Unlike the United States, the situation in Canada is quite different. It has a long tradition of metro government and provincial involvement in promoting and even mandating it. This is summarized in Sancton's chapter (Chapter 12). The situation in Mexico is less clear. Monterrey has evolved toward metro governance through an interaction of the public and private sectors. Mexico City, in contrast, has been subject to political nuances that have affected the development of metropolitan governance (see Chapter 14). Thus, the three countries vary in their approach to metro governance—from virtually none in the United States to considerable in Canada to somewhere in between in Mexico.

What is the likely path for metropolitan governance? In Canada, while still evolving, things are relatively clear. Sancton (Chapter 12) has presented four situations.

1. No metropolitan level of government but various single-purpose authorities and strong provincial involvement in metropolitan issues (Toronto).
2. A multifunctional metropolitan-level institution covering all or most of the metro area such as in Montreal, Vancouver, and Quebec City. (See Chapter 13 for detail on Vancouver.)
3. A federal-government institution (the National Capital Commission) with multifunctional capability in the National Capital Region, which straddles the provinces of Ontario and Quebec.
4. A single municipality that covers all or most of a census metropolitan area (CMA), making another level of government unnecessary.

In Mexico the status is the least clear. Monterrey's metro governance is a collaboration between the private and public sectors and has been relatively stable. Mexico City, in contrast, is torn by being the nation's capital, by pressures for more programs to deal with a large and growing population, serious social and infrastructure problems, and the constant presence of a complex nexus of national, regional, and local politics.

The United States in many ways occupies a position at one end of the spectrum, in contrast to Canada with its history of metro governance and Mexico with its evolving status. Metro governance in the United States is following an incremental approach to achieve this goal, one step at a time. As Chapter 2 indicates, no formal metro government is likely. The more likely path is the one that has played out, for example, in St. Louis (see Chapter 5). After more than eighty years and six attempts to achieve formal metro government, only one attempt has been successful, while the rest have failed. The Metropolitan Sewer District was formed to deal with a very severe and expanding public health problem in the region. The last metro government attempt was voted down in 1990.

What has occurred instead is an incremental approach to metro issues, geographically involving various parts of the region and functionally dealing with specific areas of concern (see Table 5.1 for detail on governance approaches). Metropolitan government has evolved into regional governance, moving, albeit slowly, one step at a time, over the past five-plus decades.

As Rosentraub and al-Habil point out in Chapter 3, the expansion of governance is growing but it needs to be flexible or "elastic" in nature not formal in structure. They argue that such an approach is much more likely to meet the requirements and expectations of taxpayers. This corresponds to the findings in Chapter 2 on the possibility of formal metro government. The incremental approach is happening, the formal metro is not.

Finally, it should be stated that there seems to be no single or easy solution to the problems and issues confronting the governing of metro regions. Formal structure "works" in Canada, is less successful in Mexico, and has not, with one limited exception, come into existence in the United States. Given the incredibly complex and often conflicting problems and issues, a constantly changing social and economic status, the pressures of the global environment, local politics, and citizen perception, and so on, each region must form its own arrangement to deal with metropolitan governance, especially defining what it means for the area.

The following chapters detail what has been outlined in very general, summary terms in this prologue.

Reference

Walker, David B. 1987. "Snow White and the 17 Dwarfs: From Metro Cooperation to Governance." *National Civic Review* 76, 14–28.

Governing Metropolitan Regions in the 21st Century

1

Introduction

Contextual Factors Affecting Who Will Govern Metropolitan Regions in the Twenty-First Century

Mark Tranel

Framing the Topic

Metropolitan governance is trapped in a vortex of competing values. In twenty-first century metropolitan regions, local entities must consider banding together to respond to these abstract issues ranging from the global economic reality of competition for knowledge workers to such disaggregate everyday life issues as who picks up the trash. These are very different tasks, and academics have yet to reach a consensus on how they recommend the public sector be organized. The historic values of democratic access, a structure with checks and balances to protect against tyranny, and a free-market system of property ownership conflict with current needs to respond to international competition among metropolitan areas for mobile capital and workers, are part of the debate. Yet how to plan for, finance, and deliver programs and services in metropolitan areas is not clear. To be centralized (in a formal governmental sense) or not to be centralized (in a governance sense) is the question that continues to push forward the discussion of what values to optimize and how to optimize them.

Collectively the authors in this volume provide abundant detail on structures and processes in twelve cities as well as a historical and theoretical context on government versus governance. Their consensus starting point for "who will govern" is "who does govern." Although they agree that informal governance arrangements can be distinguished from government (for example, the only true formal government in the United States is Metro Portland) in contemporary urban regions, the chapters that follow catalogue a wide variety of characteristics of governance. Structurally, the most frequently mentioned characteristics are:

- regional—between the local government level (municipal and county) and the state, there is a gap at the metropolitan regional level not provided for in the U.S. federal system.

- democratic—beyond the formal institutions, the people and the civic community of a metropolitan area have rights and responsibilities in creating the arrangements that will fill the regional gap (this is done using a variety of options combined in a variety of ways).
- organizationally inclusive—formal government organizations, nonprofits, the private sector, and the community must all be included in the informal regional arrangements.
- municipal focus—other authors place the emphasis on municipal governments working with and through a regional institution.
- voluntary cooperation—perhaps the most frequently repeated word in describing the regional structure is cooperation manifested in interlocal contracts in such areas as first responder communications and training, sharing personnel for code enforcement, joint purchasing of supplies, and soliciting bids for street improvements.

Three purposes for some form of regional capacity are generally repeated throughout the descriptions:

- planning—this has both geographic and temporal aspects. Geographically the individual municipalities, counties, and special districts cover only a fragment of the region. No one is responsible for the whole, but the case is made repeatedly that someone should be. At the same time, the persistent pattern of expansion experienced over the past fifty years in metropolitan areas requires an institutionalized capacity (or some other way to deal with it) to consider regional needs and impacts well beyond the current fiscal year. Economic development planning and transportation are frequently cited as principal regional needs.
- production—there is a persistent argument that some services, for example, transportation infrastructure, should be administered by a regional body.
- regulation—environmental issues, in particular, cross local jurisdictional boundaries, making regional action on air quality, for example, the only effective level of regulation.

Underlying these three purposes is the assumption that there exist a common set of concerns and a common goal by which the structure (formal or informal) can be guided in responding to metro "needs," and for which it can be held accountable.

While the exact definition of governance remains flexible, five themes permeate the discussion among the twenty authors contributing to this volume.

1. In response to a variety of economic and social causes, metropolitan areas have grown spatially, and as they have grown, a multitude of governments and governance arrangements have developed. These decentralizing forces are inherently focused on the short term and at the narrow local level, not on the long term and the metropolitan area (Paytas, 2001). Despite the prospect of long-term high

Table 1.1

State-Enabled Tax-Based Jurisdictions

County	Municipal
Bridge commissions	Bridge commissions
Common road districts	Business districts
Common sewer districts	Health districts
Convention facilities authorities	Homeless assistance program
Emergency planning districts	Industrial development corporations and authorities
Emergency management agencies	Land reutilization authorities
Drainage districts	Municipal Redevelopment Authority
General health districts	Neighborhood improvement districts
Homeless assistance programs	Planned industrial expansion authorities
Industrial development corporations and authorities	Port authorities
Neighborhood improvement districts	Public Building Authority
Port authorities	Rapid transit commissions
Road districts	Sewer districts (sanitary and storm)
Senior citizens' services boards	Sheltered workshop boards
Sewer districts	Special improvement districts
Sheltered workshop boards	Tax increment financing commissions
Solid waste management districts	Tourism commissions
Tourism commissions	Union cemetery board
Transit systems	
Tuberculosis control units	
Veterans Service commissions	

Source: U.S. Census of Governments (2002).

energy and food prices, suburban expansion will continue and the prospect remains for continued formation of new local governments and governance arrangements in newly populated areas.

An aspect of the extant structure that should perhaps receive more attention is the role of the state in enabling not only decentralized but also extremely specialized local government structures. While the Canadian chapters recount the assertive role provinces play in establishing regional government, a sampling from the *Census of Governments* for the state governments of the U.S. metropolitan areas discussed in this volume (see Table 1.1) shows a bewildering array of local authorities and one of the consequences of the geographic expansion of urban development into formerly rural counties. While the states may have had just cause to authorize these many and varied single-purpose agencies in outstate areas, their multiple applications in a single metropolitan area is a significant contributor to public sector fragmentation.

At the same time, state constitutions enable local jurisdictions to enter into cooperative agreements or relationships so informal that they do not require authorization. Table 1.2 shows the wide range of categories and even more numerous specific areas where local governments can work together to enhance efficiency and effectiveness without collapsing into a formal unified jurisdiction.

2. *Metropolitan areas are economically and socially significant and will likely become more so over the coming decades.* Bruce Katz specifies five qualities of urbanization—scale, speed, diversity, complexity, and connectivity—which continue to evolve and to which the governance/ment structures must adapt and respond (Katz, 2007). The productivity and creativity in national economies is based in metropolitan areas. Moreover, the scale of the problem is expanding. Two-thirds of the U.S. metropolitan population lives within ten "megalopolitan" areas.

3. *A toolbox of reforms exists.* There are in fact no novel concepts for governmental reorganization proposed in this volume. While consolidation of many, if not all, of the multitude of regional subgovernments into an effective, comprehensive entity is still proposed by some, a plethora of other formal and informal options is discussed. These include the arrangements suggested by the new regionalists such as shifting to nonprofit organizations, intergovernmental contracting, service delivery agreements, regional authorities, and regional special districts.

4. *Neither academics nor voters have developed a consensus as to how metropolitan regions should be structured.* It is noted in general for metropolitan areas over the course of the twentieth century and in detail in Chapters 2 and 3, that proposals for centralization of the structure of government in areas have generally not been supported. Long lists of obstacles to regional reform are presented. Even metropolitan areas that approve some type of regional structure often balk at expanding the authority of regional bodies and that where extensive intergovernmental cooperation exists, approval of a consolidated government is overwhelmingly rejected.

5. *Local context is paramount.* From structural vetoes and Mardi Gras mentality to minutely fragmented ward politics and stymied economic elites, the authors provide abundant detail on local context. Some metropolitan areas are described as moving incrementally, and perhaps unintentionally, toward regional governance but not government. Others have regional authority imposed upon them. Whether at the level of an individual metropolitan area or comparing the experience in Canada, Mexico, and the United States, the local context in which regional governance is discussed significantly influences its prospects.

Local Applications Across North America

These themes emerge from the thirteen case studies presented in this volume. In the Prologue, Don Phares sets the tone for the issues to be dealt with in the volume. In Chapter 2, Donald F. Norris, Don Phares, and Tonya Zimmerman work from two definitions of governance to discuss why there has been limited adoption of formal metropolitan government schemes in the United States. In an extensive literature review, they organize articles on the topic of metropolitan government into ten categories. While there is no consistent methodology or message across the

Table 1.2

Informal Governance Arrangements

Council and Policy Making Operations
Legislative review
Common by-laws, policies, and job
    descriptions
Governance structures
Training and professional development
    initiatives
Information technology—research, systems development, etc.
Lobbying and advocacy

Overall Management
Management functions—i.e., CAO or
    joint directors
Financial systems
Procurement practices and policies
Purchase or sale of services
Use of assets
Human resource management and benefit packages

**Public Works, Transportation,
    and Environment**
Water testing facilities
Water utilities and water supply
Equipment
Technical expertise
Sewer collection and treatment
Street paving
Crosswalk painting
Snow clearing
Solid waste management
Electric utilities
Public transit
Watershed protection plans

Economic Development and Planning
RDAs/chambers of commerce/boards of
    trade
Industrial parks
Planning and economic development staff
Marketing/promotion/sales/and revenue
    sharing
Development and/or sharing of infrastructure

Recreation, Culture, and Tourism
Staff training initiatives
Equipment purchase and sharing
Municipal recreation facilities
School board facilities for municipal recreation purposes
Tourism associations
Recreation programming
Trails development
Community events and festivals
Marketing/promotion and revenue generation
On-line scheduling of courses, registration, and revenue collection
Information sharing and links to web sites

Protection and Enforcement
Inspection services
By-law enforcement
Policing
Fire protection
Dispatch services
Civic addressing
Detention facilities
Equipment sharing
Training

**Information Technology and
    E-Commerce**
Web site development and maintenance
Systems and software review, development, and maintenance
Records management
Technical expertise
Alternate service delivery—private sector

**Training and Professional
    Development**
Needs identification and delivery
Open enrollment training
Program and research development fund

Source: Union of Nova Scotia Municipalities (2002).

articles, Norris, Phares, and Zimmerman are able to extract an inventory of political and economic/financial challenges sufficient to conclude that formal metropolitan government in the United States is no more likely in the twenty-first century than it was in the twentieth century.

Mark S. Rosentraub and Wasim al-Habil argue in Chapter 3 that the theoretical case for a unified formal metropolitan structure is passé. Regional governance as a "web of organizations" will, however, expand. Using Greater Cleveland as an example, they describe the flexibility of informal collaborations among public, nonprofit, and private organizations as they create a governance response to local needs and issues.

In Chapter 4, John Stuart Hall acknowledges the challenges to regional governance, but he describes how regional actors rise to action, whether or not they are the leaders authorized through the democratic process. He cites Wallis's finding that there are new regional capacity factors (engagement of the private and nonprofit sectors, new leaders interested in metropolitan community, and processes for facilitating regional vision and consensus) as well as new demand factors (global economic competitiveness, service concerns, and fiscal disparities).

Using St. Louis, Missouri, as a case study in Chapter 5, E. Terrence Jones and Don Phares find regional governance emerging incrementally. After recounting the historical record of failed formal government restructuring proposals, they trace the development of incremental regionalism to service a broad range of areas including education, parks and open space, public safety, and transportation. While the roots of incremental governance do not go back as far as the proposals to restructure government, Jones and Phares show how multi-county governance structures have been accepted and used for over fifty years.

St. Louis is also the location used by Dennis R. Judd and David Laslo in Chapter 6 to focus governance issues on the redevelopment of a downtown area. They trace the roles of the players involved in downtown redevelopment over the span of the second half of the twentieth century. The challenges of the fragmented structure of local government ultimately are overcome by the efforts of the civic elite and the mayor and other full-time policy entrepreneurs.

To test whether less governmental fragmentation means more metropolitan governance, Donald F. Norris, Carl W. Stenberg, and Tonya Zimmerman examine Baltimore, Maryland, in Chapter 7. After delineating the arguments made in the literature for the harmful effects of local government fragmentation, they describe the structure in Baltimore, with only a central city government and five county governments. There are three governance structures—the Metropolitan Planning Organization (MPO), a nonprofit economic development marketing corporation, and an ad hoc committee of large businesses that advocate for regional cooperation. The authors find that while governments in Baltimore are few, they are enabled to act autonomously and often do, thus complicating the potential for metropolitan action.

Suzanne M. Leland and Mark S. Rosentraub add additional empirical evidence in Chapter 8 to examine the claims for regional impact of consolidated government by comparing and contrasting four metropolitan areas. They observe that regional governance was both accepted and rejected depending upon the issue, in fragmented as well as consolidated governments. From their analysis of Charlotte, Cleveland, Indianapolis, and Wyandotte/Kansas City, Kansas, they conclude that fragmented government structure is not a predictor for absence of regional action and existing regional governance is not a predictor for supporting additional regional activities.

The 2000 consolidation of the city of Louisville and Jefferson County, Kentucky, provided Hank V. Savitch, Ronald K. Vogel, and Lin Ye the opportunity in Chapter 9 to study governance before and after a change in government structure. While they are able to document some of the benefits promised by a regional government, such as a reduction in expenditures for the combined jurisdiction, and a concomitant reduction in the municipal workforce, they also report mixed or negative results on other measures. A variety of types of crime increased, air quality did not improve, and out-migration from the area increased.

The Phoenix case study in Chapter 10 by Rob Melnick and John Stuart Hall expands the geographic analysis from the previous chapters to include an examination of government/governance interaction in a metropolitan area of the Sunbelt with a rapidly expanding population and economic development. What started as largely a "private city" model with government in service of economic development has an evolving governance structure with new cooperative and cross-sectoral community building.

In another before-and-after study, Chapter 11 by Robert K. Whelan compares governmental structure in New Orleans based on the impact of Hurricane Katrina. He proposes theoretical, historical, policy, and human reasons why a restructured government could be expected after such a massive natural disaster. Through a detailed political, structural, and cultural analysis, Whelan finds that despite the various reasons for expecting movement toward metropolitan governance, the traditional approach to government in New Orleans has largely survived intact.

Andrew Sancton moves the governance analysis to Canada in Chapter 12. In addition he expands the scope of the analysis from specific metropolitan regions to describe the role of the national and, in particular, the provincial governments that have direct responsibility for municipal government structure. He notes the four types of institutional arrangements found in Canada's ten largest cities. While each metropolitan area has some form of province-imposed regional government, Sancton discusses their strengths and weaknesses from the perspectives of democratic decision making and control of sprawl.

In Chapter 13, political accountability is the focus of Patrick J. Smith's examination of the impact of British Columbia's Regional District system on Vancouver. To strengthen metropolitan Vancouver's capacity to complete regional projects, address regional service needs, compete effectively in the global marketplace, and negotiate from a position of strength with the provincial government, Smith posits the need to shift from the Greater Vancouver Regional District governance structure to a formal Metropolitan Vancouver Authority, a decade-old proposal that has not been acted on. This would give direct control to Vancouver stakeholders rather than diluting it through a government structure that reserves authority to the provincial level.

In the last case study in the volume, Mario Bassols Ricardez recounts Mexico City's transition over the past several decades from authoritarian to more democratic regimes, emphasizing the linkages between a fragmented economic and social structure to competition among political parties and their various leaders. He describes the tensions that exist among the municipal government and the state and national governments and resulting implications for both long-term public works projects and daily local services. He contrasts this with the more stable government in Monterrey, which has had a persistent political elite. Despite their very different governmental forms and governance problems, both cities experienced rapid growth in the later twentieth century.

Future Direction for Research

The question that remains is who governs and to what effect? In a 2000 policy brief, the Organization for Economic Cooperation and Development (OECD) identifies five characteristics of a successful urban area that reinforce the importance of discussing who will govern metropolitan regions in the twenty-first century:

- economic diversity in the manufacturing and services sector
- a supply of skilled human capital
- the right institutional networks
- the right environment
- good communications (OECD Observer, 2000).

The authors of the chapters in this volume provide keen insights into the forces shaping the public provision of goods and services for North American metropolitan areas but they do not identify such a set of benchmarks against which structure and purpose can be measured. The next symposium on governance in metropolitan areas should perhaps focus on such output measures.

References

Katz, Bruce. 2007. "A Blueprint for National Prosperity." Brookings Council, New York, May 23. Available at www3.brookings.edu/views/speeches/katz/20070525.pdf.

OECD Observer. 2000. *The Reform of Metropolitan Governance.* Paris (October).

Paytas, Jerry. 2001. "Does Governance Matter? The Dynamics of Metropolitan Governance and Competitiveness." Carnegie Mellon Center for Economic Development, December. Available at www.cmu.edu/ced/publications/governancematter.pdf.

Union of Nova Scotia Municipalities. 2002. "Handbook on Inter-Municipal Partnership and Co-operation for Municipal Government." Available at www.gov.ns.ca/snsmr/muns/workshops/PDF/MunicipalCooperation_Seminar/Intermunicipal_report.pdf.

U.S. Census of Governments. 2002. "Individual State Descriptions." Washington, DC: Bureau of the Census, vol. 1, no. 2.

2

Metropolitan Government in the United States?

Not Now . . . Not Likely

Donald F. Norris, Don Phares, and Tonya Zimmerman

Despite what many American scholars, practitioners, and observers believe to be strong theoretical and empirical evidence supporting the adoption of metropolitan government in the United States, for the past fifty years or so there has been virtually no movement in this direction. This is true despite the fact that the academic and professional literatures are rife and robust with arguments for metropolitan-wide governmental solutions.

The sole example that stands out as approaching metropolitan government is the Metropolitan Service District (or Metro as it is called locally) in the Portland, Oregon, metropolitan area. Metro is a multifunctional metropolitan governmental structure (the only one in the United States), and it serves more than 1.3 million people and encompasses three counties and twenty-five cities. It provides a range of services such as regional transportation planning, waste recycling, green and open space programs, and addresses an array of environmental and growth concerns. But, even here, Portland falls short of a true metropolitan government—a government that is geographically broad enough to encompass area-wide problems and issues and a government that provides the typical range of local government services within that area-wide geography. And, even more telling, no other metropolitan area in the United States comes close to achieving the scope of Portland's Metro.

The obvious question, and the one that we address in this chapter, is why this lack of meaningful metropolitan governance is true and whether it will continue to be the case.

Before proceeding, however, it is important to provide a definition of the otherwise malleable term metropolitan or regional governance. Without a common understanding of metropolitan governance, it is difficult to proceed analytically in this arena. After providing such a definition, this chapter reviews the recent academic literature on metropolitan governance in the United States. This review seeks to determine whether the recent literature on regionalism provides either theoretical or practical guidance to scholars and governmental officials for advancing a regional or metropolitan government agenda.

This is important because the literatures that underpin the writing of the metro reformers, the public choice school, and the New Regionalists are internally consistent and cohesive and support these schools' policy recommendations. Is the contemporary literature on regionalism consistent and cohesive and can it be said to support a common set of policies toward regional governance?[1] Then, based on the definition of metropolitan governance provided herein, the recent scholarship in the field, and other relevant literature, this chapter suggests reasons why metropolitan government has not, and probably will not, come into existence in the United States despite strong arguments in its favor.[2]

Defining Metropolitan Governance

There are at least two competing definitions of metropolitan governance among U.S. and North American scholars. The first is the more traditional definition and emphasizes governmental structure. It essentially says that metropolitan governance requires some form of metropolitan or area-wide government in order to control and regulate behavior and provide services within the governed territory. Scholars who hold this view argue that without the regulatory and service provision capacity of government, hardly anything meaningful will be accomplished to address the issues for which metropolitan governance is said to be needed (e.g., Norris, 2001).

The second definition is the one advanced by a group of scholars who advocate what has come to be known as the new regionalism. Their position is that metropolitan governance does not require a unique governmental structure but can be achieved through voluntary cooperation among the major players (governmental and nongovernmental, including the private sector) in the metropolitan area (e.g., Savitch and Vogel, 2000a). Studies by new regionalist scholars show that a good deal of cooperation does, indeed, occur among governments and other organizations in American metropolitan areas (e.g., see Chapters 5, 7, 8, and 9 in this volume).

However, what the new regionalists' studies do not show (and this is where they are vulnerable to criticism from scholars who hew to the more traditional definition of metropolitan governance) is that cooperation functions as effectively as governments do. Here, two limitations to cooperation are quite evident. The first is that local governments simply will not voluntarily surrender their autonomy, especially around "lifestyle" issues (Williams, 1967). In the absence of area-wide authority to overcome local autonomy, not much can be done to address the really thorny area-wide problems or issues.

This has been clearly demonstrated in Maryland's Smart Growth program, which does not touch county zoning authority. As a result, more than a decade later, Smart Growth has had virtually no impact on containing sprawl in Maryland (Knaap and Frece, 2007).

The second limitation is that of the "least common denominator." This means that it only takes one or a few local governments within a metropolitan territory to refuse to cooperate over an issue to effectively scuttle any effort to address that issue for the metropolitan area as a whole. Moreover, because of their autonomy, local governments cannot be forced to cooperate with one another. As Anthony Downs (1992) has observed, voluntary cooperation is the "least satisfactory type of arrangement . . . because it cannot compel local governments to coordinate their behavior or to monitor and adjust that behavior" (p. 130).[3]

Regardless of which of these definitions is more nearly correct, the history of metropolitan government in the United States over the past fifty-plus years clearly demonstrates that although the subject has been widely researched, and written and talked about, there is very little to show for it.

Recent Literature About Regionalism in the United States

The recent literature on metropolitan government, metropolitan governance, and regional governance and regionalism (hereafter referred to as regionalism) in the United States covers a wide spectrum of issues and employs a variety of research methodologies. This diversity, however, means that little has been written on any single subject and that there is little consistency or coherence among articles across the spectrum. For this chapter, an extensive review of the literature was conducted using various library databases and also the bibliographies of published works. We found forty-five articles about regionalism in the United States published in refereed journals between January 2000 and April 2007. After review, these works were placed into ten functional categories (see Table 2.1). Only three of the categories have more than four articles published within them. Each category of this literature is discussed below.

Three articles were written on the subject of regionalism as a means of regional economic development. One article (Olberding, 2002b) described the results of an empirical study about voluntary regional organizations that are focused on economic development. Olberding found that most of the organizations she studied were relatively new. She discovered that the members of these regional organizations were derived mostly from the business community. She also found that some metropolitan areas had more than one organization devoted to regional economic development, and she questioned this duplication. In another article, Olberding (2002a) examined the relationship of cooperative norms, economic need, and a regional lifestyle to the formation of regional partnerships. She concluded that cooperative norms, economic need, commuting across jurisdiction lines (a lifestyle measure), and the strength of an existing Council of Government (COG) each played a role in the formation of these regional partnerships. She found that despite the importance of cooperative norms in the partnership's formation, these cooperative norms had little impact on the structure of these regional partnerships.

A third study compared the literature about regional cooperation in Western Europe and the United States, particularly regarding cooperation for economic development (McCarthy, 2003). McCarthy concluded that the local context is important in developing this type of cooperation. She claimed that it is not neces-

Table 2.1

Articles About Regional Governance, 2000–2007

Category	Articles
Regionalism as economic development	Olberding, 2002a, 2002b McCarthy, 2003
Equity concerns	Bollens, 2003 Hughes, 2003 Orfield, 2003
New regionalism	Savitch and Vogel, 2000a Wheeler, 2002 Parks and Oakerson, 2000 Scott, 2007 Jonas and Pincetl, 2006
Interdependence	Levine, 2001 Post and Stein, 2000 Hamilton, Miller, and Paytas, 2004
Open space/smart growth/sprawl	Howell-Moroney, 2004 Pastor, 2001 Gainsborough, 2002 Katz, 2000
City-county consolidation	Steinacker, 2001 Carr and Feiock, 2002 Mead, 2000 Fleischmann, 2000 Swanson, 2000 Rosentraub, 2000 Savitch and Vogel, 2000b, 2004
Regional cooperation	Gainsborough, 2003 Probsdorfer, Ruchelman, and Richman, 2003 Wood, 2006
Transportation	Alpert, Gainsborough, and Wallis, 2006 Hubler and Meek, 2005 Vogel and Nezelkewicz, 2002
Theory	Hamilton, 2000, 2002, 2004 Mitchell-Weaver, Miller, and Deal, 2000 Brenner, 2002 Jonas and Ward, 2002 Basolo, 2003 Feiock, 2007 Lowery, 2000
Miscellaneous	Collin, Leveillee, and Poitras, 2002 Visser, 2004 Basolo and Hastings, 2003 Steinacker, 2004

Note: Full citations of all reviewed works are found in the references section of this chapter. Articles are listed approximately in the order in which they appear in the text of this chapter.

sarily possible to transfer a successful program from one area to another. McCarthy also noted several difficulties in studying the effectiveness of these cooperative efforts including such issues as scale, context, causation, spillovers, time, and the availability of indicators.

Another three articles examined whether regional governance can or should play a role in social equity. Two of the articles were responses to the initial article. In the initial article, Bollens (2003) examined whether "metropolitan governing bodies" encourage equity policies. In particular, he examined single-service regional agencies, regional agencies developed as a result of federal transportation and air quality policies, councils of governments, state action leading to regionalism, metropolitan governments, and coalitions working for regional goals to discover whether equity policies were being produced at the regional level. Bollens claimed that regionally focused equity policies do occur through the actions of states, coalitions, regional agencies created through federal policies, and other regional agencies. He noted seven different types of equity policies that developed through these types of organizations, for example, fair share housing, policies about growth, and economic development policies. He argued that the multiple types of regional equity policies that he described in this article showed that there are more types of equity projects at the regional level than previous literature indicated. However, he claimed that such equity policies generally occur in response to state and federal influence (e.g., federal housing or transportation policy).

In one response to Bollens, Hughes (2003) argued that state and federal government involvement may actually harm regional equity. He provided examples, such as a case of fair share housing in New Jersey, a reverse commuting policy, and policies associated with the Workforce Investment Act, to show how state and federal action may harm regional action. He concluded that federal and state policies merely create the possibilities for cooperation. However, he argued that these policies do not necessarily mean that equity will occur.

The second response (Orfield, 2003) did not directly address Bollens's argument regarding equity policies at the regional level that are supported by the federal and state governments. Instead, Orfield focused his reply on the lack of attention that regionalism discussions give to the issue of segregation and concentrated poverty. Orfield discussed the progress that has occurred in developing regional equity policies surrounding the issues of taxes, transportation, and planning. However, he voiced concern about the limited progress and lack of attention toward the reduction of segregation and concentrated poverty in regionalism efforts. He argued that this lack of attention resulted from a poor understanding of the problems associated with segregation and concentrated poverty. A second reason, he claimed, for the lack of attention to these two issues was that the current solutions to problems of segregation and concentrated poverty were not direct enough.

Articles in the next category addressed issues around the new regionalism. Savitch and Vogel (2000a) discussed the reasons for its growing importance, in particular mentioning issues of sprawl, declining cities, growth concerns, and economic competition. Focusing on the issue of governance versus government, their article was fairly brief as it was a preface to a special issue on new regionalism in a journal.

An article by Wheeler (2002) focused on new regionalism as it relates to regional planning rather than government-governance. Wheeler described what he called the five key characteristics of new regionalism. Several of these characteristics focused on types of planning and approaches to it, and one characteristic concerned growth and fragmentation. Wheeler concluded the article by describing the limited progress toward regional planning, but he encouraged strengthening of the existing regional structures.

Next, Parks and Oakerson (2000) related findings from research projects conducted for the U.S. Advisory Commission on Intergovernmental Relations about local public economies to the new regionalism. First, the authors argued that the local public economies approach is a useful way to understand metropolitan areas. They claimed this is a result of its ability to focus on different types of provision and production arrangements. They also argued that governance in a metropolitan area could occur without a metropolitan government. By metropolitan governance they were referring to the ability to affect the rules that govern the operation of local governments, including, for example, the creation of local governments and tax and expenditure rules. They also discussed the importance of a "nested" provision of services. They described a "nested" provision as a provision of services that develops at different scales of government depending on the scale that is efficient for that service. These provision areas may overlap for different services. In this way, they argued that regionalism and localism both need to be included in the discussion of service provision and production. Parks and Oakerson also argued that fragmented areas were able to work out solutions to regional problems. They encouraged, as a result, increased flexibility in the structuring of service production and provision in metropolitan areas to help address problems.

Scott (2007) argued that the concept of smart growth has become a significant example of the type of policies advocated by the new regionalist movement. He then examined policies adopted under the smart growth rubric in the San Francisco Bay Area to determine whether smart growth (and, by extension, the new regionalism) had produced new models of regional governance in this area. For his study, Scott chose to focus on transit-oriented development (TOD) as the particular policy representing smart growth. Curiously, he did so after admitting that "public transport is not a viable transit option for the vast majority of commuters" (p. 24). After a brief overview of the processes leading to the adoption of TODs in this region, Scott concluded that smart growth had become a "politically operationalized form" of the new regionalism, and had indeed contributed to the "development of new governance models and mechanisms" (p. 31) that were consistent with the new regionalism.

Jonas and Pincetl (2006) examined the new regionalism in California to determine whether the new regionalism is part of changing global processes, referred to in other literature as the "new politics of scale," or part of a local movement. These authors argued that local and historical context were important in attempting to understand the regionalism efforts in California, as compared with focusing on the larger economic conditions typically discussed in the new regionalism literature. To emphasize this point, they discussed the history of regionalism efforts in California.

The next category, on interdependence, includes articles that discussed economic competitiveness as an argument for regionalism. An article by Levine (2001) reviewed literature on regionalism and economic theory to determine the effect of regional planning on economic growth. Levine examined the literature surrounding metropolitan reform, public choice theory, city-suburban economic interdependence theory, new regionalism, and urban economic theory to explain the development of regionalism as it relates to economic development. Using these literatures, she discussed three factors important in regional economic development: quality of life, quasi-governmental, and economic. She concluded that the literature showed that regional planning could be important in regional economic development.

Post and Stein (2000) examined the interdependence of cities and suburbs through the use of per capita income measures, as well as the role of the state economy and governmental fragmentation. These researchers found a relationship between central city and suburban economies that was separate from the state economy. However, Post and Stein were not able to discover whether the city economy influenced the suburban economy or vice versa. They also found that governmental fragmentation did not play a direct role in the interdependence of cities and suburbs.

Hamilton, Miller, and Paytas (2004) argued that understanding metropolitan regionalism requires an understanding of "authority relationships" (p. 151) between and among state and local governments in regions. Therefore, they examined both vertical (state-local) and horizontal (local-local) relations in America's metropolitan areas. To do this, they used a variety of measures of local and state government authority as well as a measure of governmental fragmentation in regions. Hamilton, Miller, and Paytas also employed a measure of regional competitiveness. Their purpose was to determine whether different varieties of state-local relations affected competitiveness. On the vertical dimension, they found that state centralization (essentially, strong state governments) had a slight negative association with regional competitiveness. On the horizontal dimension, they found that decentralization (essentially, local governmental fragmentation) had a significantly negative association with regional competitiveness. This led the authors to conclude that the structure of government in metropolitan areas matters to regional economic competitiveness.

Works about open space, smart growth, and sprawl as they relate to regionalism constitute the next category of papers examined. Three of these articles claimed that open space and smart growth policies were an impediment to regional government. In a study of Philadelphia, Howell-Moroney (2004) found that higher socioeconomic communities, fast growing communities, and more recently developed communities were more likely to adopt open space policies. As such, these communities, which would be needed for a regional coalition, would not be interested in regional solutions because they had chosen to deal with their problems on their own.

Pastor (2001) discussed the problems of developing new regionalist and smart growth movements in Los Angeles. He explained that Los Angeles should be more likely to have new regionalist and smart growth types of movements than other areas. He argued that this should occur because of the smaller disparities in terms of economic conditions and more similar racial compositions between the central city and suburbs than exist in other metropolitan areas. However, he claimed that despite these similarities these movements did not actually happen. Pastor argued that differences on the dimensions of economic conditions and racial compositions occurred at other levels within the Los Angeles region, for example, communities within Los Angeles not reflected by the formal municipal boundaries. In particular, he studied these different types of communities based on the designation of an inner city area and different levels of ethnic change. Pastor argued that these differences may be what prevents the types of new regionalist efforts expected of an area that on the surface is so similar. As a result, he argued for a focus on a "community-based regionalism," using community development groups as a strategy for regionalism, which he claimed was occurring in Los Angeles.

Gainsborough (2002) examined public opinion in New York and Los Angeles regarding growth, in an attempt to understand whether the issue of growth could be used to build regional action. She found that opinions differed about the issue of growth between city and suburban residents and among demographic groups (e.g., race-ethnicity, age, education, income). She found that stronger connections to the central city of the region (e.g., visiting the central city for recreational purposes) made support for slow growth policies less likely, whereas local connections (e.g., involvement in local activities) made support for these policies more likely. In addition, she discovered that even those groups that saw growth as a problem were not necessarily supporters of slow growth policies. Gainsborough concluded, as a result, that it would be difficult to form regional coalitions around this issue. One article (Katz, 2000) discussed the role that the federal government could or should play in limiting sprawl, including a suggestion about encouraging both formal and informal metropolitan action in areas such as transit, housing, workforce, and economic development.

The next group of articles examined city-county consolidations. Steinacker (2001) indirectly looked at city-county consolidation through a discussion of the Miami dissolution vote. She used the urban politics literature and theories about the agenda setting process, especially Kingdon's (1995) model, to determine which better explained the outcome of the Miami dissolution vote. She argued that the urban politics literature, which focused on issues such as the efficiency of services, accountability, participation, satisfaction with taxes and services, minority group power, and equity, would have predicted a positive outcome for this vote. By contrast, she argued that Kingdon's model, which focused on factors that explain how issues get on public agendas and ultimately are adopted or rejected, would have predicted the vote to fail. After examining the history of the Miami dissolution vote, she concluded that the Kingdon model did a better job than the urban politics literature in explaining the outcome of the vote, because the vote, in fact, failed.

Using survey data, Carr and Feiock (2002) examined the actors involved in the process of consolidation. They found that newspapers, the Chamber of Commerce, mayors and county executives, developers, and civic organizations were very frequently supporters of city-county consolidation. Local government employees, city and county commissioners, taxpayer organizations, and constitutional officers were frequently among those opposed to it. Carr and Feiock noted that the key issues in determining support and opposition to consolidation were fragmentation in planning, growth management, fear of taxes and spending, size of government, and the responsiveness of government. Finally, they concluded that for the most part the supporters of consolidation were not very likely to get consolidation referenda passed.

Mead (2000) examined the Charlotte-Mecklenburg area to understand whether the consolidation process had led to New Regionalism. He also discussed the prospects of new regionalism. He found that while formal consolidation had not been successful, new regionalism existed to some extent. Mead argued that this was a result of annexation and functional consolidations. However, he claimed that both annexation and functional consolidation had reached their limits in usefulness because some issues involve multiple counties and not all issues are seen as regional. Because some of the regional issues involve multiple counties or are not seen as regional issues, Mead concluded that there are limits to what new regionalism can accomplish in the future.

In a study of Louisville-Jefferson County, Savitch and Vogel (2000b) examined the history of the area's regional service compact or agreement. They also compared the situation in Louisville under the compact to the potential for benefits with consolidation. Savitch and Vogel claimed one benefit of the compact was less competition. They explained that the region's position had improved since the 1970s on several indicators of urban distress such as number of families below poverty, educational attainment, housing conditions, and unemployment. Furthermore, they claimed that the region's position on indicators of prosperity such as business profits and payroll, property value, income, and revenue improved during this same time period. They argued that consolidation would not create any additional real improvements in these indicators, only the appearance of them by masking the urban problems with suburban affluence. Savitch and Vogel concluded that expanding the cooperative effort would be more beneficial than further consolidation attempts (see Chapter 9 in this volume).

Fleischmann (2000) used a case study of four city-county consolidation attempts in Georgia to examine whether city-county consolidation led to regional problem solving. He concluded that in order for consolidation attempts to succeed, issues surrounding services, taxes, race and "governmental 'turf'" (p. 224) had to be addressed in the campaign. Most of the people he interviewed believed the consolidation attempt impacted the issues that were addressed by the government after the attempt. In particular, some of the interviewees explained that there were issues addressed after the consolidation attempt that would not have been addressed without it, for example, types of land use planning. Similarly, some of the interviewees felt that there were issues not addressed after the consolidation that might have been without it, for example, annexation. Fleischmann concluded that consolidation can help regional problem solving to occur, but that state support is very important. He argued that without state support little regional problem solving will occur.

The final studies of city-county consolidation focused on its impacts on the government, service delivery, and the population. A study of Jacksonville-Duvall County (Swanson, 2000) used literature to examine the reasons for consolidation, who supported consolidation and in what ways, and the effects of consolidation. Swanson reviewed the issues that various reform groups, media and academic, used to encourage consolidation. In particular, Swanson examined the issues of the benefits of consolidation in terms of jobs, taxes, accountability, and efficiency that were used to support consolidation. He also discussed several governmental problems that reform groups used to support the case for consolidation, such as inability to meet service demands, qualifications of workers, and efficiency. He then reviewed several studies of the impacts of consolidation, focusing on such impacts as economic efficiency, equity, accountability, and effectiveness. Swanson did not come to any real conclusions about the impacts of consolidation. Instead, he mentioned the different views of it, issues about consolidation that he felt needed to be addressed, and questions that he felt should be addressed in future reform.

In a study of Indianapolis, Rosentraub (2000) discovered some positive effects of consolidation. In particular, he claimed that consolidation led to some downtown development, stabilized the population and employment, and reduced sprawl after consolidation. However, he explained that the additional downtown development imposed costs on certain areas of the city while residents of other areas benefited. He also explained that despite Indianapolis's having a consolidated government there were still multiple tax and service districts of different sizes within the consolidated city. He cautioned other governments to create a financial arrangement different from the one in Indianapolis when consolidation occurs, to limit the problems that Indianapolis experienced in terms of costs and benefits to different areas of the consolidated city. Another problem, Rosentraub noted, was that much of the growth in the region remained outside of the new government boundaries (see Chapter 8 in this volume).

Savitch and Vogel (2004) discussed the changes in power in Louisville-Jefferson County that occurred as a result of consolidation. They focused on issues of territory, management, and political rules. They found that consolidation tended to benefit the wealthy residents of suburbs and to hurt minority and working class city residents, in terms of power. Savitch and Vogel also noted that the consolidation strengthened the power of the mayor and limited the pool of candidates eligible to become mayor in the new consolidated area. They also argued that consolidation changed the types of policies produced. In particular, the authors claimed that the new government focused on development in the suburban areas and failed to maintain previous city positions on issues of police review, wages, housing, employment, and gay rights (see Chapter 9 in this volume).

Another group of articles used case studies to examine the existence and extent of regional cooperation. Gainsborough (2003) discussed the role of business organizations in informal regional cooperation in Los Angeles and Houston. She found that, in both cities, businesses saw regional cooperation as important. However, she noted that the reasons were different between cities. She claimed that the local context (e.g., history, structure of other institutions, and the relationship between the city and the suburbs) made the role of business in promoting regional cooperation different in the two areas she studied.

Probsdorfer, Ruchelman, and Richman (2003) studied cooperative efforts by regional organizations in the Newport News/Norfolk/Virginia Beach metropolitan area. They found nine regional efforts that were implemented during their study period. They concluded that having an external funding source was a key factor of each success. They claimed that external funding sources limited the discussion between areas in the region over who would have to pay for the project and who would benefit from it. As a result, external funding allowed projects to move forward. Probsdorfer, Ruchelman, and Richman also claimed that the use of some type of cooperative networking model allowed the projects to be implemented. By contrast, they found ten proposals that had not yet been implemented. They argued that this failure to implement resulted from a history of distrust and competition. They also claimed that the projects that failed to be implemented each used a scattershot networking model, a model where there is little cooperation. Finally, these authors noted that regional efforts did not have a clear base of support, which inhibited the development of these types of efforts.

Wood (2006) examined the extent of metropolitan governance in Kansas City. Using interviews with city leaders, he discovered that the regional COG, the city of Kansas City, Missouri, networks of actors, and community wealth were important in developing intergovernmental agreements for service delivery. Using a regression analysis, Wood found that the socioeconomic status (e.g., wealth) of the community also contributed to the development of these arrangements. In addition, he found a negative relationship between the per capita size of the city budget and the development of intergovernmental arrangements. In contrast to what would be expected, Wood discovered that these intergovernmental agreements were just as likely to occur for lifestyle as for systems maintenance issues. He also found that most leaders perceived benefits of some sort (e.g., economies of scale, costs, etc.) to these intergovernmental agreements.

The next category of articles examined transportation in relation to regional governance. Alpert, Gainsborough, and Wallis (2006) examined the South Florida Regional Transportation Authority to discover how regional governance develops. Using network analysis, the authors argued that the strength of the existing policy network was important in the development of regional cooperation. This was particularly true because there was a history of distrust between the communities. One type of network analysis allowed Alpert, Gainsborough, and Wallis to determine some of the key actors in the network. They discovered that several groups, such as local governments, businesses, and the South Florida Regional Planning Committee, were in positions to help make connections between relevant actors in the region. They particularly emphasized the role of the business community in regional cooperation for transportation. Alpert, Gainsborough, and Wallis also explained that there were limitations in using the network analysis model because of, for example, outside actors, such as the state government, who were not part of the network but had impacts on the outcome of policies.

Hubler and Meek (2005) examined four joint power authorities and COGs in transportation in the San Gabriel Valley of California. These authors referred to the San Gabriel Valley as a subregional level. They were particularly interested in whether subregional governments (e.g., COGs at the subregional instead of regional level) could be effective in coordinating regional action. They concluded that subregional organizations, such as the COGs under study, could be effective in implementing various regional programs, for example, transportation projects. They noted that subregional projects had been successful in areas even when full-scale metropolitan governance had not. However, they explained that due to limited funding only so much work could be done through subregional organizations.

Vogel and Nezelkewicz (2002) examined the Metropolitan Planning Organization (MPO) in Louisville to evaluate the usefulness of MPOs as a tool of new regionalism. The authors focused their case study on a decision about whether or where to build a bridge across the Ohio River. Vogel and Nezelkewicz found that some metropolitan-wide coordination occurred, but the MPO was not an example of metropolitan governance. This was because the MPO did not always lead to thinking with a regional perspective. For example, they argued that the MPO was not able to coordinate region-wide land use planning with transportation planning. They concluded that new regionalist goals were not met in this case because the process did not focus on regional growth.

Several articles contributed to the discussion of the theoretical frameworks around regionalism. Hamilton (2002) argued that regime theory could be used to examine regional governance. He then applied regime theory to the Chicago metropolitan area and concluded that the Chicago metropolitan area does not have a regional regime. Despite this, he discussed several attempts to create regional thinking, for example, with the Metropolitan Mayors Conference and Chicago Metropolis 2020, a civic agency designed to implement the recommendations of a report. He indicated that a regime could develop in the Chicago metropolitan area with some changes to these existing organizations. However, he felt that there could be problems in creating a regime because of historical issues between the cities and suburbs and a lack of any agency with authority at a regional level.

Hamilton (2004) developed a framework of factors that he believed were important in the development of regional regimes, including the capacity of government and private actors to work regionally; the existence of a crisis; the opportunity to work regionally; and environmental factors such as, history, politics, culture, and economics. Hamilton then applied this framework in a comparison of the Pittsburgh and Chicago metropolitan areas. He found that the Pittsburgh area had a higher capacity to work regionally in both the government and the private sectors than the Chicago area did. In addition, he discovered that the private sector in Pittsburgh began its involvement with regional cooperation in a time of crisis, unlike in the Chicago metropolitan area where the involvement did not begin in a crisis. Hamilton argued that a crisis allowed actors to develop a rallying point for support for regional action. Finally, he found that the Pittsburgh metropolitan area had environmental factors more conducive to developing a regional regime than Chicago. Specifically, Hamilton argued that Pittsburgh was smaller in terms of physical size than Chicago and thus did not have as diverse an economic base as Chicago. Hamilton argued that such factors made it easier to create a vision for the region seen as beneficial to all. Given that these two factors were important in his framework, he unsurprisingly discovered that the Pittsburgh metropolitan area had a regional regime, while the Chicago metropolitan area did not. As a result of this finding, he concluded that his framework is useful in understanding what is important in the creation of regional regimes.

Two articles examined the development of regionalism. In one, Hamilton (2000) developed a framework, based on literature, to understand the factors that affected whether regionalism occurs, and the type of governmental structure (i.e., government or governance) that occurred. His framework centered on the following factors: government policies, civic sector involvement, business community, media, philosophy, taxes, services, reform, and developers. He used the history of the Pittsburgh region to show how this framework applied to real cases. He concluded that the framework could be useful in understanding how regionalism develops.

In the second article, Mitchell-Weaver, Miller, and Deal (2000) claimed that in the 1990s regionalism returned to the political agenda in the United States. They further argued that during this period a "regional coalition" based on central city and environmental concerns had developed. These authors claimed the two key tenets of this coalition focused on the negative consequences of fragmentation and the emptying out of the metropolitan centers. Mitchell-Weaver, Miller, and Deal discussed the "regional coalition agenda" using an article by Walker (1987), two reports by the Brookings Institution Center on Urban and Metropolitan Policy (1998), and the U.S. Department of Housing and Urban Development (1999) as well as Portland's Metropolitan Service District and the Minneapolis-St. Paul area. They concluded that in the 1990s there was a movement away from ideological arguments for metropolitan reform and toward an analysis based on data.

Brenner (2002) emphasized the lack of one singular argument about metropolitan reform. He began the article by discussing previous metropolitan reform efforts. He then explained that, instead of there being one single type of metropolitan reform, such reforms were specific to the local context within which they developed. Next, he discussed more recent debates about metropolitan reform. In this section, he concluded that the most recent round of reform efforts in the United States was dominated by multiple interests and actors aiming to control the process and outcomes of what he referred to as a "metropolitan rescaling" process. He further argued that this was part of a struggle between neoliberal and progressive forces over the very meaning and content of metropolitan governance in order to address such key progressive issues as accountability, segregation by class and race, sustainable development, and a more equal distribution of resources.

Jonas and Ward (2002) examined recent debates about regionalism and regional governance in the United States and the United Kingdom and found what, at first glance, appeared to be three notable similarities. The first similarity was that globalization was used on both sides of the Atlantic to explain " . . . changes in the spatial context of urban policy" (p. 378). The second was the inclusion of nongovernmental actors in the concept of regional governance. The third similarity was the argument that city-regions were now the appropriate spatial scale for aggregating social, economic, and political interests, especially for the purpose of global economic competitiveness. However, after two mini-case studies of regional governance activities and structures in Southern California and the northwest of England, Jonas and Ward rejected the idea that urban policy had somehow converged (i.e., were more alike than different) between the two countries. Indeed, they argued that their examples showed that there was no " . . . uniform understanding of globalization, urban governance, and the city region" between the United States and the United Kingdom (p. 396). They also observed that, to better understand urban policy in the two nations, it was necessary to understand the specific national and subnational contexts out of which the policies arose.

The next group of articles examined regionalism in terms of public choice theory. Basolo (2003) examined the theories of local autonomy, rational/public choice, and collective action as they related to explaining the failure of regionalism to occur. She argued that self-interest underpinned each of these theories. She further argued that, as a result of this commonality, policies about regionalism resulting from each theory should be like one another. Basolo explained how all three theories led to the conclusion that voluntary regionalism was not likely to occur. She emphasized Olson's notion from his 1965 piece that coercion and incentives were needed for collective action to happen. Basolo concluded, however, that more research was necessary, using a different version of rational choice to understand whether voluntary cooperation can occur.

Feiock (2007) also examined rational choice theory, specifically what he called the second generation rational choice model. He argued that this model focused more on context than the original model. Feiock then developed a framework, and propositions to go with the framework, about how various factors related to goods, the community, and local politics affected transaction costs and, as a result, cooperation and voluntary regionalism. This article drew no specific conclusions, but suggested further study of this type of rational choice model.

Lowery (2000) reviewed the differences and similarities between the public choice school and what he called the new consolidationists over the issue of metropolitan governance. He concluded that negative social, political, and fiscal consequences had occurred in metropolitan areas for reasons other than those posited by the public choice school. In particular, high transaction costs, themselves a result of fragmentation and attendant political boundaries, prevented metropolitan-wide policies to address said consequences from being adopted. Lowery argued that in the 1990s the scholarly literature produced considerable evidence to support the position of the new con-solidationists. This was especially true for evidence supporting their concerns about inequity and the need for redistribution. At the same time, however, the public choice school was largely silent in response to criticisms from the consolidationists.

The remaining articles focused on a variety of issues about regionalism. Col-lin, Leveillee, and Poitras (2002) examined thirty-five U.S. and Canadian cities to describe institutional reform and metropolitan fiscal strategies. They found that fragmentation was still the dominant type of metropolitan form in the United States. They claimed that voluntary institutions, such as regional councils, played a larger role in the United States than the imposed solutions more frequently found in Canada in reorganization efforts. Collin, Leveillee, and Poitras also discussed the ways that metropolitan areas had developed metropolitan-wide fiscal strategies. In particular, they discussed income taxes, sales taxes, and user fees to finance some costs, the role of state government in distributing funding, and infrequent cases of tax base sharing. They concluded that while cooperation did occur, most of the cooperative efforts for fiscal purposes and institutional reforms they examined had occurred as a result of actions required by other levels of government.

Visser (2004) explained the ways in which the effectiveness of a regional council of government (COG) was impacted by the need for members, civic support, its willing-ness to work with other organizations, and the local historical context. He then discussed the outcome (whether the COG was effective in producing regional action) of two regional COGs in Michigan using the issues of membership, support, cooperation, and context. He concluded that the factors of membership and capacity to provide services were important in determining whether the COG was effective in producing regional action. He also argued, as a result of his analysis, that trust was important in whether the COG was effective in producing regional action. Visser concluded that collaboration could occur, but that collaboration did not replace regional government.

Basolo and Hastings (2003) discussed regionalism through housing policy in Portland, Minneapolis-St. Paul, Louisville, and New Orleans. The authors concluded that there was some degree of regionalism in the cities they studied. However, they noted that the degree of regionalism differed in each city, and that, regardless of the level of overall regionalism in these cities, there was a limited amount of regionalism in their housing policies. Basolo and Hastings discovered that local context and NIMBY (not in my backyard) attitudes that focused on issues such as race and regional growth as well as economic strength were important causes of the limited degree of regionalism in housing policy.

Steinacker (2004) tested Orfields's concept that state legislatures can be used to promote regional policy. He focused on Orfield's discussion of district characteristics that could predict voter support for issues. Steinacker examined seven propositions about regional issues in California to test Orfield's model. She found that there was a relationship, although not always significant, between district characteristics (e.g., socioeconomic characteristics, poverty, growth, tax capacity, and city need) and voter support for these propositions about regional issues. However, she discovered that some relationships were not as Orfield proposed. In addition to Orfield's factors, Steinacker concluded that district type (urban, suburban, and rural) and racial composition were important in understanding support for regional policies. Based on her results, Steinacker concluded that the prospects for regional coalitions through state policy were limited.

This examination of the recently published literature on regionalism and metropolitan governance demonstrates at least the following about this field:

- no consistent story is being told about regionalism;
- no consistent approach to issues relating to regionalism has been developed or appears to be evolving;
- no consistent methodologies are employed to examine issues around regionalism;
- no consistent message is being provided about regionalism; and finally
- few, if any, studies have critically examined the need for or desirability of regionalism from the broader perspective of the entire metropolitan area.

Unlike the literatures that have emerged previously in this field and have provided theoretical and/or empirical support for the metro reform, public choice, and new regionalist schools, the recent literature on regionalism in the United States lacks coherence, cohesiveness, and consistency. To use a contemporary metaphor, it is "all over the lot."

The absence of a more coherent, cohesive, and consistent scholarship that clearly delineates the need for and desirability of regionalism (and metropolitan governance) may help to explain why such little progress in advancing regionalism has been made in the United States in recent decades.[4]

Factors Affecting the Adoption of Metropolitan Government and Governance in the United States

The next section of this chapter addresses the principal factors that explain why only one metropolitan area in the United States has taken serious strides in the direction of metropolitan governance. These factors are grouped into two categories: political considerations and fiscal factors.

Political Considerations [5]

A Dislike for More Government

In the United States, there is a historical and clearly stated dislike for more government, despite the fact that the country has 89,476 local political jurisdictions (Census of Governments, 2007). A concern usually associated with metropolitan government is often stated as: "What? another level of government?" Given the already vast proliferation of local governments, most of which are located in the nation's 360-plus metropolitan areas, this argument standing by itself makes little, if any, sense. Nevertheless, it is a strong element of the American political culture.

American Local Government Ideology

Americans strongly believe that local government, the government closest to the people, is the best government. This rhetoric is in part an artifact of American history and in part an expression of everyday experience. At least since Thomas Jefferson, a central theoretical view of American government has been that of the sovereignty and autonomy of the individual in his or her local community (e.g., Syed, 1966.)

At a practical level, Americans live in local communities and experience government and governance there. They receive most of their governmental services, particularly the ones that affect them most significantly (e.g., police and fire protection, public education, land use regulation, etc.) at the local level. Citizens are also the most able to make their views about governance and service delivery known with the greatest impact at the local level. Indeed, the historic and prevailing local government ideology is an important part of the reason why local citizens oppose nearly anything that would threaten the existence, powers, services, or autonomy of their local governments.

Movement of Power Away from the Existing Local Political Base

There is a prevailing fear that metropolitan government would rearrange the local power base away from the fragmented array of existing local governments and concentrate it in the hands of a new metropolitan government. Many would lose power and some, but likely fewer, would gain. Political control over territory and resources, some or much of which now is very local, would be lost. Such power and control is highly guarded and prized no matter how small the locality. Surrendering it to a metropolitan government is most often not viewed as an acceptable option.

As we indicated above, the prevailing view in the United States is that "the more local the better" and even the smaller the better when it comes to government. This view translates further into the belief that in a smaller community residents tend to feel more involved in what is happening in their community. They may know the mayor, police chief, and members of the city council personally and feel that they can call on them if an occasion arises. Metropolitan government would potentially lessen or even eliminate this feeling of closeness to "my government" or "my politician."

Constitutional Status of Local Governments

Constitutions for the fifty states provide explicitly for local government formation and also for the roles and functions of elected local officials. Granting this constitutional and legal status to localities in a state is of fundamental importance. While these constitutional provisions do make up a legal framework for local government, they rarely, if ever, provide a comparable framework for regional governmental structures. Throughout the United States, it is much more difficult to establish a truly regional form of government than it is to incorporate a new municipality or create a special district. Tradition, inertia, and a variety of diverse specific interests form around the existing local government structures; they operate to favor the status quo over governmental change and reform. These constitutional powers once established create a power base that goes largely unchallenged. Furthermore, the existence of numerous local governments helps to preclude the establishment of other (new) governmental structures within the purview of the existing localities.

Political Territorial Imperative

The constitutional and legal status of general-purpose local governments gives them unique territory over which to exercise sovereignty and provide services. At best and in nearly all regions, the territories encompassed by regional organizations (e.g., regional planning councils and councils of government) include already existing local governments, and the latter are decidedly not interested in giving up either territory or powers to the former—nor can they be compelled to do so. As such, regional bodies are at a serious disadvantage when compared with local governments that inhabit the regional territory. The former have no independent hold on the territory while the latter clearly do.

Additionally, in the animal kingdom, turf is protected at almost any cost. This territorial imperative (Ardrey, 1966) can be applied to the realm of local politics as well. Whether mayor of a large city (or a small village) or council per Random House person for a very small city, political turf is coveted and protected. Hence, existing local governments often bitterly oppose any kind of metropolitan structural reform.

Legal Status of Local Government

State constitutions in the United States expressly provide a legal basis for the creation of local governments and for the roles and functions of elected local officials. This grant of constitutional and legal status to local governments is fundamental. Not only do state constitutions provide the legal basis for local government, these documents also rarely provide a comparable basis for the existence of regional governmental structures. Due to these legalities it is way more difficult to establish regional government than to incorporate a new city or create a special purpose local jurisdiction. Both legal/political inertia and particular interests develop around extant local government structures, and they strongly favor the status quo rather than governmental change and reform. Constitutional and legal status, thus, mean that local governments exist in law; are accorded structure, functions, and powers; and, once established, beget an existence that is largely unchallenged. The existence of local governments and the associated legal provisions helps to preclude the establishment of other alternative or supplemental governmental structures.

Lack of State Leadership or Intervention

While state governments in the United States are heavily involved in setting the framework for local government operations—local governments are legal creatures of the state in which they are incorporated—with very few exceptions, states have avoided the political quagmire of governmental reorganization in metropolitan areas. States have more often been reactive to narrow and specific local issues and problems rather than proactive in terms of broader issues and problems that go beyond local boundaries and cut across an entire metropolitan region. This is in contrast to Canada (see Chapters 12 and 13 in this volume) and also Mexico (Chapter 14) where provinces and the national government have played an active role in encouraging or mandating local restructuring and to the UK where the central government has been quite active in local government restructuring and reform.

For the most part, state officials in the United States also do not meddle in local affairs without ample reason because they know that to do so would create an unenviable backlash by local voters.

State Electoral Structure

An important reason why state governments rarely intervene in local governmental affairs has to do with state and local electoral structure. Many state elected officials have come up through the lower elective ranks beginning in local government. They have a healthy respect for local government, and they know that their constituents do as well.

Additionally, state legislators are elected from local districts that encompass all or parts of one or more local governments. This means that local governments and their residents bring problems and issues and express their policy preferences to their state legislators. This reinforces the legislators' knowledge of and respect for local government and local affairs.

Finally, state legislators are fully aware that if they act, especially without good cause, to intervene in the affairs of local governments (particularly to do anything that adversely affects the territory, finances, or powers of local governments), the legislators will almost certainly be opposed at the next primary or general election by local elected officials or local citizens who take serious exception to their actions.

Ease of Incorporation and Annexation

Constitutional provisions and/or legislation in many states allow for the incorporation of new cities with relative ease (e.g., Krane, Rigos, and Hill, 2001). The ability of cities to annex surrounding, unincorporated territory varies considerably around the nation. Cities in the Northeast and Midwest are largely precluded from annexation, while those in the South and West have a greater legal ability to annex. Throughout the country, with some exceptions, it is also relatively easy to form special districts to deal with specific issues or problems (e.g., water, wastewater, refuse, air pollution, public transport, etc.). The current political environment in the United States encourages an "incremental" approach to dealing with local concerns. Make your city larger by annexing territory, incorporate a new city, or form a special district to address a particular problem, obviating the need for a more comprehensive approach.

Race, Class, and the Protection of Enclaves

The development of many metropolitan areas has been characterized by enclaves often defined in racial, ethnic, or socioeconomic terms. Such a sorting out by race and class has come about in large part through local zoning and land use prerogatives and/or the incorporation of new municipalities. Evidence shows that, in recent decades, racial and class distinctions have become even more extreme between central cities and suburbs (Lowery, 2000). A metropolitan approach would, almost necessarily, threaten at least the more well-off enclaves. Hence, those who benefit from the present existence of enclaves and the future ability to create new enclaves oppose metropolitan government. Additionally, residents of suburban enclaves (almost without regard to the racial or class makeup of these enclaves) would oppose metropolitan efforts to "bail out" central cities.

The Residential Bias of the American People

Nearly every public opinion poll on the subject shows that large majorities of Americans prefer to live either in suburbs, small towns, and/or rural areas (see, for example, "Where We'd Live," 1989). Additionally, and dating back at least to Jefferson, there is a strong anticity bias abroad in the land. Americans generally profess to dislike large cities. In combination, these attitudes mean that, ceteris paribus, Americans not only will move out of and away from cities to suburban and fringe areas, but they will not be kindly disposed to participate in efforts (especially those involving their tax dollars) to help central cities. This is true regardless of the merits of such campaigns or the dire needs of central cities. Moreover, for at least the past fifty years, the suburbs are precisely where Americans have moved, and when they got there they showed virtually no interest in either assisting the central cities that they left or surrendering the autonomy and independence of the suburbs and rural communities into which they moved.

Lack of Federal Leadership

As we noted above, state governments rarely enter the domain of metropolitan or government governance. Neither does the federal government. To begin with, unlike the American states and some European nations, the U.S. federal government has no constitutional authority over local governments. More important, except for a brief period from about the mid-1960s until the late 1970s, with a short interval of very limited impact in the 1990s, the U.S. federal government has had little or no policy, presence, or interest in things urban or metropolitan. Indeed, the federal government has provided no significant or sustained leadership to help achieve metropolitan or government governance at virtually any time.

The Strength of Pro-Sprawl and Pre-Fragmentation Forces

This is a game, in the sense of the term as employed by Long (1958), that pits developers, builders, real estate organizations, suburban residents, and suburban elected officials against academics and "goo-goos" (e.g., the good government groups such as leagues of women voters, chambers of commerce, and editorial writers).

In nearly any contest between pro-sprawl and pro-regionalism forces, the staying power is clearly with the former, who have strong and immediate financial interests at stake and who are organized and well financed. The latter, by contrast, are mostly amateurs and volunteers who may have strong intellectual and emotional reasons for involvement, but who are usually poorly organized and financed. As George Washington Plunkitt said about the municipal reformers of his day, they "were only mornin' glories—looked lovely in the mornin' and withered up in a short time, while the regular machines went on flourishin' forever, like fine oaks" (Riordon and McDonald, 1994, p. 57).

The Difficulty of Implementing a Metropolitan Government

Putting in place a metropolitan government is a difficult and complex undertaking. It involves complex arrangements between and among existing local governments and the layering in of the metropolitan unit. Governmental structure will be altered as will finances, not to mention local politics and myriad legal considerations. It can also be hard to maintain.

As we have previously noted, the one example closest to a metropolitan govern-

ment in the United States is found in Portland, Oregon. Planning for this metropolitan arrangement actually began in the late 1950s. Although Metro was initially
approved by popular vote in 1978, it required a number of years of incremental
movement to achieve its current form, which came about via another popular vote
in 1992. From planning to implementation it took almost forty years.

The most recent city-county merger, Louisville/Jefferson County in Kentucky,
was put before voters who said "no" three times starting in 1956 until the merger
was finally approved in 2000 (see Chapter 9 in this volume). Again it took several
decades from "start to finish." In fact, efforts to achieve some form of metropolitan
governance usually begin (and almost always end) with easier, albeit limited and
partial, alternatives rather than a true metropolitan government.[6]

Uncertainty

Just as markets do not like uncertainty, neither does the political system of a metropolitan area. Discussion of metropolitan government introduces an unacceptable
level of uncertainty about what the political countryside will look like in the future,
raising questions such as:

- How will the change be implemented?
- How long will it take?
- What is the implementation process going to entail?
- Who will be affected and how?
- Who will be in charge of the changes?

These are questions that engender uncertainly and thus great reluctance to venture
very far from the status quo.

Local Government Autonomy

Local government autonomy—or the ability of these governments to exercise their
police powers ("the power to regulate private activities in order to protect the public
health, safety and morals," Gray and Eisinger, 1997, p. 365) broadly within their
territories—is sacrosanct in the United States. There is absolutely nothing new
about this conclusion; it has been well known for over one hundred years (Danielson, 1976; Teaford, 1979). Indeed, local autonomy is the single most important
reason that American local governments are unwilling to enter into arrangements
for regional governance.

Arrangements for regional governance that would have "teeth"—that is, would
involve local governments' ceding authority to regional entities to address certain
matters now under their exclusive control (e.g., land development and public education) would directly threaten local autonomy. As Williams (1967) pointed out over
three decades ago, although local governments may be willing to cooperate on mat-

ters of systems maintenance (essentially housekeeping and infrastructure matters), they are highly unlikely to give up control over lifestyle issues. Nothing much has changed in this regard in the thirty-plus years since Williams wrote this.

Although local governments are creatures of their respective states and although state governments have constitutional and legal rights to control local governments, for the most part everyone acts as if local governments are autonomous. And local governments and their citizens continually guard their autonomy. Local autonomy becomes especially salient politically when lifestyle issues are involved (e.g., schools, law enforcement, zoning, and other land use powers, etc.). The fear is that in addressing area-wide issues and concerns, metropolitan government will erode local autonomy—and to be effective it would have to.

A recent example is found in the state of Maryland, which is being widely touted as the "Smart Growth" state. However, because state government has taken no action to curb local governments' almost exclusive local land use planning and zoning powers, smart growth legislation has had virtually no impact on sprawl. Another example comes from England where, ten years after the abolition of true metropolitan government, local governments remained adamantly opposed to metropolitan government in any form.

Economic and Financial Considerations

Protection of Financial Base

The fragmentation of local governments in metropolitan areas produces a disparity among jurisdictions where available resources are not geographically consistent with public service needs. Often the disparity is very large. This leads to a situation of have and have-not communities. While the have-nots might prefer a redistributive metropolitan resource base, they usually lack political and economic power to move metropolitan government forward. The have communities generally possess the power and resources to protect their financial bases. As is true in most human pursuits, money matters. It is no different in this context.

Interjurisdictional Economic Competition

One thing that a metropolitan government might do well is to promote an entire region for economic development purposes and worry about specific locations within the region as a second stage in the process. Theoretically, everyone benefits if new economic development is attracted to a metropolitan area even if it does not fall within a specific locality.

Resources, structure, and local energy and power would be focused on the region as a whole. In a milieu of fragmented local governments, which characterizes nearly all of metropolitan America, such an approach would tend to lessen interjurisdictional competition. It would be much less likely that a municipality within the metropolitan area would be able to promote just itself effectively and, thus, it would lose the associated benefits from its own self-promotion to those derived from an area-wide economic development strategy. In essence self-promotion is perceived as giving a greater advantage to a local community than regional promotion. This advantage would be lost, or lessened, with metropolitan government.[7]

Fear of New Taxes

"No new taxes" is a mantra that has played out in recent years over both the national and state countryside. It also is very much in play at the local level. A fear associated with metropolitan government is that it would entail new taxes, often viewed as significant, to support metropolitan services. Local residents already feel overburdened with the local taxes they are paying—city property taxes that grow with increasing housing prices, sales taxes levied for general and increasingly for specific purposes, and property taxes associated with schools and special districts all contribute to this view.

Even with the suggestion that metropolitan government would be "revenue neutral" in keeping with a "no new taxes" mantra often voiced in a metropolitan reform context, there would still be a redistribution of resources across the area, perhaps considerable. Some residents would lose and some would gain. Overriding concerns are: who gains, who loses, and how much is gained or lost?

Conclusion

This chapter presented two competing definitions of metropolitan governance, reviewed the recent literature on metropolitan governance in the United States, and discussed a number of factors that have kept, and will keep metropolitan government and governance from occurring in the United States.

Regardless of which definition one adopts—governance through governmental institutions with the power to coerce or governance through voluntary cooperation—there is no true metropolitan government and precious little metropolitan governance (at least on tough and controversial issues) in American metropolitan areas. The recent literature on the subject lacks coherence, cohesiveness, and consistency and provides little guidance to scholars or advocates seeking solutions to metropolitan problems.

Finally, as demonstrated by the sixteen (and there may be more!) principal factors affecting metropolitan governance, the very structure of the American political system and many of the values and attitudes underlying it strongly bias that system against either metropolitan government or governance. Certainly, the political system is biased against metropolitan government. There are no such governments in the United States today, despite more than fifty years of calls to establish them. There is a bias against metropolitan governance, if by that one means coordinated actions among all or nearly all of the local governments in a region to address the tough issues facing the region or substantial parts of it (e.g., crime, drugs, poverty, education, housing, fiscal disparities, etc.). Nowhere in the United States does such governance exist, either.

Consequently, in conclusion we offer a quotation from an article on regionalism written eight years ago by one of the authors of this chapter:

> Based on current trends, . . . a reasonable forecast for regionalism in the U.S. 20 years or more hence would be that it will closely resemble the state of regionalism today. Economic imperatives will not overcome the political impediments to regionalism and regions will continue as governmentally fragmented entities resistant to nearly all efforts to achieve regional governance. (Norris, 2001, p. 569)

Notes

1. The literature reviewed here consists of all articles on regionalism (and related topics) published in scholarly journals from January 2000 to April 2007. This selection was chosen in order to understand the contribution of the contemporary literature to a common understanding of regional governance and whether that understanding, should one emerge, might lead to consistent policy recommendations or implications. The year 2000 was chosen as the starting point for reasons of time and other scarce resources. The literature review ceased with April 2007 when the initial draft of this chapter was completed.

2. This chapter is an extension and expansion of a paper presented at the 2006 Conference of the European Urban Research Association, Warsaw, Poland, May 2006.

3. Although Downs was writing about methods available to reduce traffic congestion, his observation holds across the range of metropolitan issues and problems.

4. Not that scholarship alone can produce regionalism. Were this the case, the metropolitan reformers of the 1950s, 1960s, and 1970s would have been far more successful. But a consistent and cohesive scholarship can at least provide a theoretical underpinning and empirical evidence to support regionalism.

5. Several of the points that follow were originally referred to in Norris (2001). They are revised and reprinted here with permission from Wiley-Blackwell Publishing, Ltd.

6. For excellent discussions of the options available leading from small and incremental up to comprehensive metropolitan reform, see Walker (1987) and National League of Cities (2007).

7. Many regions do, indeed, have regional economic development organizations. But economic development is a largely noncontroversial systems maintenance issue, unless participating jurisdictions begin to feel like losers because new economic activity is located within their competitor jurisdiction's territory, not theirs.

References

Alpert, Lenore; Juliet F. Gainsborough; and Allan Wallis. 2006. "Building the Capacity to Act Regionally: Formation of the Regional Transportation Authority in South Florida." *Urban Affairs Review* 42, no. 2: 143–68.

Ardrey, Robert. 1966. *The Territorial Imperative: A Personal Inquiry into the Animal Origins of Property and Nations.* New York: Atheneum.

Basolo, V. 2003. "U.S. Regionalism and Rationality." *Urban Studies* 40, no. 3: 447–62.

Basolo, Victoria, and Dorian Hastings. 2003. "Obstacles to Regional Housing Solutions: A Comparison of Four Metropolitan Areas." *Journal of Urban Affair* 25, no. 4: 449–72.
Bollens, Scott A. 2003. "In Through the Back Door: Social Equity and Regional Governance." *Housing Policy Debate* 13, no. 4: 631–58.
Brenner, Neil. 2002. "Decoding the Newest Metropolitan Regionalism in the USA: A Critical Overview." *Cities* 19, no. 1: 3–21.
Brookings Institution. 1998. "The New Metropolitan Agenda." *Brookings Review* 16, no. 4: 2–38.
Carr, Jered B., and Richard C. Feiock. 2002. "Who Becomes Involved in City-County Consolidations? Findings from County Officials in 25 Communities." *State and Local Government Review* 34, no. 2: 78–94.
Census of Governments. 2007. *Government Organization.* Washington, DC: Department of Commerce.
Collin, Jean-Pierre; Jacques Leveillee; and Claire Poitras. 2002. "New Challenges and Old Solutions: Metropolitan Reorganization in Canadian and U.S. City-Regions." *Journal of Urban Affairs* 24, no. 3: 317–32.
Danielson, M.N. 1976. *The Politics of Exclusion.* New York: Columbia University Press.
Downs, Anthony. 1992. *Stuck in Traffic.* Washington, DC: Brookings Institution.
Feiock, Richard C. 2007. "Rational Choice and Regional Governance." *Journal of Urban Affairs* 29, no. 1: 47–63.
Fleischmann, Arnold. 2000. "Regionalism and City-County Consolidation in Small Metro Areas." *State and Local Government Review* 32, no. 3: 213–26.
Gainsborough, Juliet F. 2002. "Slow Growth and Urban Sprawl: Support for a New Regional Agenda." *Urban Affairs Review* 37, no. 5: 728–44.
———. 2003. "Business Organizations as Regional Actors: The Politics of Regional Co-operation in Metropolitan America." *Polity* 35, no. 4: 555–72.
Gray, Virginia, and Peter Eisinger. 1997. *American States and Cities.* 2d ed. New York: Longman.
Hamilton, David K. 2000. "Organizing Government Structure and Governance Functions in Metropolitan Areas in Response to Growth and Change: A Critical Overview." *Journal of Urban Affairs* 22, no. 1: 65–84.
———. 2002. "Regimes and Regional Governance: The Case of Chicago." *Journal of Urban Affairs* 24, no. 4: 403–23.
———. 2004. "Developing Regional Regimes: A Comparison of Two Metropolitan Areas." *Journal of Urban Affairs* 26, no. 4: 455–77.
Hamilton, David K.; David Y. Miller; and Jerry Paytas. 2004. "Exploring the Horizontal and Vertical Dimensions of the Governing of Metropolitan Regions." *Urban Affairs Review* 40, no. 2: 147–82.
Howell-Moroney, Michael. 2004. "Community Characteristics, Open Space Preservation and Regionalism: Is There a Connection?" *Journal of Urban Affairs* 26, no. 1: 109–18.
Hubler, Paul, and Jack W. Meek. 2005. "Sub-Regional Transportation Initiatives: Implications for Governance." *International Journal of Public Administration* 28, 1081–94.
Hughes, Mark Allen. 2003. "Comment on Scott Bollens: 'In through the Back Door: Social Equity and Regional Governance.'" *Housing Policy Debate* 13, no. 4: 669–74.
Jonas, Andrew E.G., and Stephanie Pincetl. 2006. "Rescaling Regions in the State: The New Regionalism in California." *Political Geography* 25, 482–505.
Jonas, Andrew E.G., and Kevin Ward. 2002. "A World of Regionalisms? Towards a US-UK Urban and Regional Policy Framework Comparison." *Journal of Urban Affairs* 24, no. 4: 377–401.
Katz, Bruce. 2000. "The Federal Role in Curbing Sprawl." *Annals of the American Academy of Political and Social Science* 572, 66–77.

Kingdon, John W. 1995. *Agendas, Alternatives and Public Policies.* 2d ed. New York: Longman.

Knaap, Gerrit-Jan, and John W. Frece. 2007. "Smart Growth in Maryland: Looking Forward and Looking Back." *Idaho Law Review* 43: 445–73. Available at www.smartgrowth.umd. edu/research/pdf/knaap-frecefinaldraft.pdf.

Krane, Dale; Platon Rigos; and Melvin Hill, eds. 2001. *Home Rule in America: A Fifty-State Handbook.* Washington, DC: CQ Press.

Levine, Joyce N. 2001. "The Role of Economic Theory in Regional Advocacy." *Journal of Planning Literature* 16, no. 3: 184–201.

Long, N.E. 1958. "The Local Community as an Ecology of Games." *American Journal of Sociology* 64, no. 3: 251–61.

Lowery, David. 2000. "A Transaction Costs Model of Metropolitan Governance: Allocation versus Redistribution in Urban America." *Journal of Public Administration Research and Theory* 10, no. 1: 49–78.

McCarthy, Linda. 2003. "The Good of the Many Outweighs the Good of the One: Regional Cooperation Instead of Individual Competition in the United States and Western Europe." *Journal of Planning Education and Research* 23, no. 2: 140–52.

Mead, Timothy D. 2000. "Governing Charlotte-Mecklenburg." *State and Local Government Review* 32, no. 3: 192–97.

Mitchell-Weaver, C.; D. Miller; and R. Deal Jr. 2000. "Multilevel Governance and Metropolitan Regionalism in the USA." *Urban Studies* 37, no. 5/6: 851–76.

National League of Cities. 2007. *Guide to Successful Local Government Collaboration in America's Regions.* Washington, DC.

Norris, Donald F. 2001. "Prospects for Regional Governance under the New Regionalism: Economic Imperatives versus Political Impediments." *Journal of Urban Affairs* 23, no. 5: 557–71.

Olberding, Julie Cencula. 2002a. "Does Regionalism Beget Regionalism? The Relationship Between Norms and Regional Partnerships for Economic Development." *Public Administration Review* 62, no. 4: 480–91.

———. 2002b. "Diving into the "Third Waves" of Regional Governance and Economic Development Strategies: A Study of Regional Partnerships for Economic Development in U.S. Metropolitan Areas." *Economic Development Quarterly* 16, no. 3: 251–72.

Orfield, Myron. 2003. "Comment on Scott Bollens: 'In through the Back Door: Social Equity and Regional Governance.'" *Housing Policy Debate* 13, no. 4: 659–68.

Parks, Roger B., and Ronald J. Oakerson. 2000. "Regionalism, Localism, and Metropolitan Governance: Suggestions from the Research Program on Local Public Economies." *State and Local Government Review* 32, no. 3: 169–79.

Pastor, Manuel Jr. 2001. "Looking for Regionalism in all the Wrong Places: Demography, Geography, and Community in Los Angeles County." *Urban Affairs Review* 36, no. 6: 747–82.

Post, Stephanie Shirley, and Robert M. Stein. 2000. "State Economies, Metropolitan Governance, and Urban-Suburban Economic Dependence." *Urban Affairs Review* 36, no. 1: 46–60.

Probsdorfer, James A.; Leonard Ruchelman; and Roger Richman. 2003. "The Pursuit of Regional Cooperation: Networking Hampton Roads." *Virginia Social Science Journal* 38, 7–85.

Riordon, W.L., and T.J. McDonald, eds. 1994. *Plunkitt of Tammany Hall: A Series of Very Plain Talks on Very Practical Politics.* Boston: Bedford Books of St. Martin's Press.

Rosentraub, Mark S. 2000. "City-County Consolidation and the Rebuilding of Image: The Fiscal Lessons from Indianapolis UniGOV Program." *State and Local Government Review* 32, no. 3: 180–91.

Savitch, H.V., and Ronald K. Vogel. 2000a. "Paths to New Regionalism." *State and Local Government Review* 32, no. 3: 158–68.

———. 2000b. "Metropolitan Consolidation versus Metropolitan Governance in Louisville." *State and Local Government Review* 32, no. 3: 198–212.

———. 2004. "Suburbs without a City: Power and City-County Consolidation." *Urban Affairs Review* 39, no. 6: 758–90.

Scott, James Wesley. 2007. "Smart Growth as Urban Reform: A Pragmatic 'Recoding' of the New Regionalism." *Urban Studies* 44, no. 1: 15–35.

Steinacker, Annette. 2001. "Prospects for Regional Governance: Lessons from the Miami Abolition Vote." *Urban Affairs Review* 37, no. 1: 100–118.

———. 2004. "Metropolitan Governance: Voter Support and State Legislative Prospects." *Publius* 34, no. 2: 69–93.

Swanson, Bert E. 2000. "Quandaries of Pragmatic Reform: A Reassessment of the Jacksonville Experience." *State and Local Government Review* 32, no. 3: 227–38.

Syed, A. 1966. *The Political Theory of American Local Government.* New York: Random House.

Teaford, J. 1979. *City and Suburb.* Baltimore, MD: Johns Hopkins University Press.

U.S. Department of Housing and Urban Development. 1999. "The State of the Cities." 1999: Third Annual Report. Washington, DC. June.

Visser, James A. 2004. "Voluntary Regional Councils and the New Regionalism: Effective Governance in the Smaller Metropolis." *Journal of Planning Education and Research* 24, no. 1: 51–63.

Vogel, Ronald K., and Norman Nezelkewicz. 2002. "Metropolitan Planning Organizations and the New Regionalism: The Case of Louisville." *Publius* 32: 107–29.

Walker, David B. 1987. "Snow White and the 17 Dwarfs: From Metro Cooperation to Governance." *National Civic Review* 76, 14–28.

Wheeler, S.M. 2002. "The New Regionalism: Key Characteristics of an Emerging Movement." *Journal of the American Planning Association* 68, no. 3: 267–78.

"Where We'd Live." 1989. *National Journal* 2602 (October 21).

Williams, O. 1967. "Lifestyle Values and Political Decentralization in Metropolitan Areas." *Southwest Social Science Quarterly* 48, no. 4: 299–310.

Wood, Curtis. 2006. "Scope and Patterns of Metropolitan Governance in Urban America: Probing the Complexities in the Kansas City Region." *American Review of Public Administration* 36, no. 3: 337–53.

3

Why Metropolitan Governance Is Growing, as Is the Need for Elastic Governments

Mark S. Rosentraub and Wasim al-Habil

For some students of urban governance the consistent infatuation with calls for consolidated governments and more regional cooperation among local governments from numerous community leaders generates wry smiles. With a consistency that has become predictable, metropolitan regions experiencing stagnating economic conditions, those suffering through a decline, and even those experiencing rapid growth are peppered with proposals calling for the consolidation of local governments. While economic conditions might vary, a recurring consistency is the view that fewer governments and a concentration of political authority will lead to more effective responses to economic development and the management of congestion and growth-related environmental issues. Indeed, some proponents of consolidated government seem convinced that within regions with fragmented governments there is a virtual absence or a scarcity of programs, institutions, and linkages cutting across cities to advance the development of a region. It is as if, without consolidation, community leaders and voters would be unable to understand or act on efforts to advance a region's development.

To be sure, in some regions—as is illustrated in other chapters in this book—political culture and history left areas with fragmented structures but with examples of extensive regional cooperation for service delivery and economic development. For example, in St. Louis (see Chapter 5) there were waves of interest in restructuring government—far more than would emerge in Greater Cleveland, another area with fragmented local governments—but, as took place in northeast Ohio, local governments remained independent and forged numerous regional agencies and initiatives. In neither area—as will be argued here—did fragmentation thwart regional cooperation and the building of needed institutions for regional governance in addressing specific problems, challenges, and efforts to advance the region's economy. While economic development in Greater Cleveland and metropolitan St. Louis is still less than is desired, the lack of growth cannot be attributed to fragmented governments unable or unwilling to form regional governments, agencies, and programs. And as is detailed elsewhere in this volume, Baltimore (see Chapter 7), with but six governments, has found it no less complex to build cooperative relationships.

In stagnating and declining areas the frequently touted goal is a unified voice and plan for advancing a region's economy. This perspective assumes that fragmented local government structures assume some of the responsibility for changing economic conditions, globalization and its impact on regional economies, tax structures, or other factors that have led a region to fall behind faster-growing areas. A related assumption is that fractionated governments cannot coordinate activities for economic development. In faster-growing areas there are frustrations with the rate at which congestion and environmental threats arise and vacant land vanishes. Consolidation advocates believe a unified government will be better able to curtail sprawling development patterns that threaten the quality of life and that fragmented governments have additional incentives to pursue more narrowly defined self-interests that mitigate against regional and longer-term land use policies (Leland and Thurmaier, 2005).

What is the irony in these proposals that brings a wry smile to the face of some students of urban governance? Around what and when does metropolitan cooperation occur? For more than twenty years, teams of researchers have expanded the study of the governance of urban areas and looked to the roles assumed by the large numbers of nonprofit organizations in the delivery of social services (see, e.g., Smith and Grønbjerg, 2006); the expanding level of intergovernmental contracting and service delivery agreements to reduce costs and achieve economies of scale (see, e.g., Thompson, 1995; Thompson and Elling, 1999); and the roles played by regional authorities, planning organizations, and other metropolitan organizations created by governments and other groups to deliver services at a regional level or across many cities (see, e.g., Foster, 1995; Hooghe and Marks, 2003; Oakerson, 1999).

These assessments illustrate substantial levels of regional activity and cooperation for service delivery to take advantage of efficiencies of scale and regional cooperation for economic development and the management of externalities. The nonprofit organizations, the interlocal contracts, and the numerous special districts that exist each span the boundaries of several if not all cities in a region. In terms of governance, then, these organizations and agreements are regional cooperation without a city-county consolidation, the merger of cities, or the consolidation of a set of governments. St. Louis provides a vivid illustration of this framework even after defeats to consolidation (see Chapter 5). So too, as will be documented, local governments in the northeastern Ohio region have cooperated after movements focused on county consolidation collapsed or just evaporated. In short, in areas in the United States with a multiplicity of local governments there is far more regionalism taking place in the governance of urban regions than advocates for consolidation want to acknowledge. (See Chapter 2 for a discussion of reasons why formal metro government is unlikely in the United States.) As will be argued here, this pattern of creating special arrangements and districts will continue to grow, meaning more not less regionalism in the future. Further, it will be argued that extensive and extended regional cooperation will continue to occur outside of efforts to consolidate local governments. Consolidation is not the only route to achieving higher levels of regional cooperation. What will be suggested here is that flexible governance systems are as likely, if not more likely, to develop regional agencies, organizations, and programs. It is even possible that consolidated systems—less able to provide effective and efficient neighborhood-level services—might find less interest in and success with regional programs. It is possible that consolidation could work against the interests of citizenship by failing to provide residents with a sense of local control over those services delivered at the neighborhood level.

Why do fragmented local governments agree to cooperate with one another? When does self-interest for cooperation overcome the self-interest or desire for independence or "bowling alone"? When is the short-term self-interest benefit of isolating wealthier communities from the liabilities of association with communities that must redistribute tax dollars to provide services to lower income households replaced with longer-term benefits from activities that benefit a region (see Chapter 2)?

Few empirical studies examine why local governments cooperate (and why they do not) and too few assessments make it difficult to find meaningful patterns. To be sure, fiscal factors are important and the attraction of avoiding extensive redistribution costs is a lure that has created independent cities. There is evidence that suggests tax levels, fiscal capacity, and the ability to deliver public services at competitive rates are prevalent concerns (Leroux and Carr, 2007). There is also evidence that higher tax rates can be sustained if the quality of services is seen as being highly desirable. Following on this logic, Feiock (2007) explains that interlocal cooperative governance occurs where there are collective benefits and private interests that unify different local actors to achieve individual and collective economic benefits. This means that political opportunities exist to engage wealthier enclaves if some services are excluded from cooperative agreements. For example, communities might engage in extensive revenue sharing and cooperative agreements for environmental planning, environmental remediation, parks, and water and sewer services while insisting that education remain excluded and more local in nature. Indeed, some excluded services could be justified by management principles in that economies of scale do not exist. More to the point, however, is the need for political agreement between jurisdictions that allow some level of neighborhood or community-level provision of services while encouraging interlocal agreements and revenue sharing for other services.

Feiock (2007) notes that voluntary agreements of cooperation and coordination emerge from a dynamic political contracting process in which all partners achieve benefits that exceed the transaction costs of bargaining a contracting agreement. However, this may be possible only if those services that communities need or want delivered at a local level are excluded from agreements. The political process must recognize the cost savings and internalized benefits from all services and the resulting need for flexible designs. The essential point may be to recognize the environment of the decision setting; the characteristics and benefit radii of services; the economic, social, and political characteristics of community populations (demographic homogeneity); and the networks of existing relationships. All of these factors play important roles in determining and shaping preferences for public services and the potential gains and transaction costs of interlocal cooperative governance.

The analyses and overviews of the role of nonprofit organizations, interlocal contracts, and regional authorities and organizations could lead some to conclude that regional governance models are both being tested and utilized with increasing regularity in virtually all large urban areas. Indeed, whether one thinks of the highly fragmented New York City, San Francisco, Dallas/Fort Worth, or Atlanta metropolitan areas—each characterized by large numbers of units of local government—there are still examples of regional transportation authorities and planning agencies in each area.

Metropolitan Cleveland, with fifty-seven cities in its central county and several suburban counties, has instituted an extensive income tax-base-sharing program that transfers not less than $201 million to the center city each year. The total amount of money moving between cities in Cuyahoga County each year is more than $538 million, giving this highly fragmented local government landscape one of the nation's largest regional tax-base-sharing programs. In 2008 the Mayors and Managers Association of Cuyahoga County led the effort to create a regional tax-base-sharing program modeled on the one used in the Minneapolis-St. Paul region. Beginning in 2009, 40 percent of property tax and income tax growth will be shared and distributed by a formula involving the number of households in a city and the age of housing.

The earnings tax program was created by state law and did redistribute wealth. However, Cuyahoga County's new program was a voluntary interlocal government agreement motivated by the need to expand efforts to help the region's central and older cities meet their needs. While it could be argued that the earnings tax was externally imposed—but required the support of suburban legislators—the new tax-sharing program was completed motivated by wealthier suburban areas identifying their self-interest in sustaining older central cities. Contrary to what some might have expected, these are examples of a sacrifice of short-term financial self-interest for anticipated or hoped for longer-run economic returns. And these programs were made possible at the same time by recognizing that consolidation of all or other services was not feasible. The focus on flexibility achieved substantial fiscal sharing that in other circumstances, where some level of fragmentation was not sustained, would be impossible.

Examples of regional governance may well abound where one did not expect to find it if the analysis focuses only on the number of local governments that exist. Indeed, what is important is not the number of local governments that exist, but the ways in which those local governments have organized themselves for cooperation, the number of nongovernmental organizations involved in regional governance that participate in the delivery of services, and the tax-base-sharing efforts that exist. If the correct framework for analysis is used, one might be led to conclude that far more regionalized governance systems exist in urban America than are found from an enumeration of consolidated systems. When one enumerates only the consolidated governments, a very incomplete picture of regionalism and regional governance is produced. There may well be more regional cooperation in metropolitan St. Louis and Greater Cleveland than in metropolitan Baltimore, even though there are but six governments in the Baltimore area and ten times that number in both Greater Cleveland and metropolitan St. Louis.

Calls for consolidated city-county governments or expanded levels of regionalism might actually seem "behind the times" or passé in the sense that: (1) scale and scope issues for urban governance have been actively debated in the United States, Canada, and Western Europe for more than three decades, and (2) models of and experiments with different types of regionalism for service delivery are being repeatedly implemented, refined, and modified on an ongoing basis.

Regionalism is a dynamic and actively evolving process in virtually every urban center. Regions without significant special districts, planning authorities, intergovernmental agreements for joint service delivery, or tax programs with the potential for redistribution across the boundaries of individual local governments, if they exist, would be the exception, not the rule. Cooperation for improved efficiency and service delivery balanced by a desire for appropriately sized and flexible local governments are taking place despite siren calls that there is no regionalism. Indeed, when one considers interlocal government contracts for service delivery, new revenue-sharing programs among fragmented governments, and all of the other forms of regional cooperation taking place, regionalism seems to be on the rise, even when consolidated governments are absent or regions vote not to consolidate.

While the form of consolidation for service delivery efficiency varies, the concept of regional level cooperation or, at a minimum, joint government cooperation involving varying numbers of communities seems wedded to every region's operations and development. Greater Cleveland and metropolitan St. Louis, typically described as fragmented regions, boast extensive sets of examples of consolidated service delivery and, in the case of Greater Cleveland, substantial levels of regional tax-base sharing involving property and income taxes.

Local government officials—regardless of the level of fragmentation that exists—also frequently recognize that cost-effective ways to manage the financing of infrastructure can lead to lower taxes and more competitive positions for their region. Different factors, including substantial scale economies, large initial costs, and the high asset specificity of these services make local governments adopt the interlocal government's strategy and become involved in shared service delivery without consolidation.

In this environment, calls for consolidated governments or more regionalism miss the point that the process or use of some forms of consolidated service delivery takes place everywhere and expands and contracts in response to issues and the local culture. Flexible governments—not regional or countywide governments that are rigidly defined—are required to meet the governance needs of the twenty-first century. To assume that there is no regionalism or service consolidation in the absence of structural change is not only inaccurate but misreads what citizens prefer. It will be posited here that regionalism and regional cooperation are increasing, and much as Hooghe and Marks (2003) noted, the active debate taking place is over the types of structures for different service delivery systems as: (1) the number of challenges for local governments spans individual city boundaries, and (2) authority is devolved from state-level institutions, leaving regions and cities to fend for themselves.

Flexible governments within regional governance are the new institutional arrangements that have the greatest potential to meet the needs and expectations of taxpayers and voters. The experimentation and debate within each region to find the right mix of service delivery structures is taking place almost independently of the repeated calls for consolidation and in spite of an urban myth that such cooperation, experimentation, and redesign of aging governmental structures is not taking place.

The last factor that cannot be overlooked in the discussion of the emergence of regional governance systems is the value of having local control at the city and neighborhood level for services that not only are efficiently delivered at that level but also enhance a sense of citizenship. Increasingly large organizations create a scale of participation that is difficult to effectively manage. It is not unreasonable to note that in these larger-scale organizations and governance systems individuals might find it more difficult to participate in decision making. However, in a hybrid system, one that identified the services that are best delivered at the neighborhood level, opportunities for participation and citizenship are actually enhanced. Those that focus their attention solely on consolidated frameworks may well sacrifice laboratories of citizenship where people learn about and participate in local government and governance. That is an asset that should be protected and enhanced. What is suggested then by a flexible governments approach to governance is that neighborhood or community-level services are delivered best by smaller local governments.

The special districts that have been created to handle large-scale issues (e.g., transportation, water and sewer services, health care for those without insurance, environmental issues, and economic development) clearly indicate that fragmented governments are capable of responding to local and regional issues. It must now be determined whether a theory of governance emerges from the observations of extensive cooperation among fragmented governments, and why.

Governing Urban Space: Myth and Reality

Warren, Rosentraub, and Weschler (1988), building on an earlier essay by Warren and Weschler (1972), discussed the urban governance conundrum that confronted many areas and predicted it would define some of the issues for cities in the 1990s.

For myriad services that define the quality of life for citizens, from police patrols to neighborhood parks, the scale of service delivery should be the smallest unit of government possible. For other services—indeed, the majority of those impacting citizens in a region and increasingly dominating the agenda of mayors—from economic development to environmental management to transportation and land use planning, a larger scale is needed. Indeed for many of these services or issues a regional scale is highly appropriate, or at least a scale that includes several communities or cities in a single service delivery unit. However, these different scale operations for service delivery could be achieved through interlocal agreements and compacts that leave the independence and structure of local governments intact. Indeed, given the importance of neighborhood service delivery for the quality of life, the argument might be made that a maximum effort should be expended to ensure that local and neighborhood service level provision or production for some services be maintained and strengthened.

The economic decentralization and global competition that are having a substantial impact on the Midwest's industrial centers also mean that central cities in that part of the United States are becoming fiscally challenged in their ability to deliver needed urban services to increasingly poor residential populations. This again underscores the need for regional frameworks for the structuring of tax bases to support local services and for the development of strategies to reverse the decline. For example, by 2005, Cleveland among other Midwest central cities would have 25 percent or more of its households classified as poor. Warren, Rosentraub, and Weschler (1998) were suggesting that governance systems would need to be flexible and able to respond to regional and local challenges simultaneously, and not be lured into a framework of thinking that one governance structure—consolidation, fragmentation, region, or neighborhood—would address the governance needs of any city or region.

Earlier research by the same three authors (Warren, Rosentraub, and Weschler, 1988) pointed to the roles of the various governance institutions at work in urban regions. Identified as a "community services budget," the line of reasoning suggested that in looking for the correct scope and scale of institutions, one needed to consider the inputs from nonprofit organizations, governments, businesses, and citizens themselves (co-production) to understand the range of activities and organizations that produced desired levels of services in communities, cities, and a region. Some of these inputs might have been delivered or made available as a result of resources provided by regional or international institutions at the same time that neighborhood associations and individuals themselves were involved in producing or delivering services. At each level and for many services, municipal and county governments were also involved. In that setting, coordination of service delivery inputs might have been required, but considerable thought also had to be given to the appropriate scale of governance institutions. However, this work clearly pointed to the need for extreme flexibility in the approach to designing urban governance systems and cautioned against the possibility that any region would or could be effectively and efficiently managed by a single consolidated government, or for that matter, fragmented local governments acting independently without interlocal agreements or regional cooperation compacts and associations. A later statement of Thompson and Elling (1999), "let them eat marblecake," may have been more prophetic than they imagined. Whether or not a government is consolidated or not, whether a region is characterized by fragmentation or not, what will emerge in any region's governance system are a number of regional or special government agencies or authorities and organizations as well as myriad local government and neighborhood social and urban service delivery systems. Indeed, this work suggested that urban governance is a complex amalgam of governments, institutions, organizations, and citizens engaged in service provision and production. To think that any single scale of government at the local level could or would control, manage, or direct the wide-ranging set of services and activities that are described as local ignores the reality "on the ground."

Governance, as the term is being used in this chapter, refers to the full range of public, private, and nonprofit organizations created by residents of a region to pursue collective goals. Many nonprofit and other private organizations serve an entire region. As a result, even in a region with no metropolitan governments or a consolidated service delivery unit there are numerous regional organizations providing services. Across the past several decades, scholars focusing on the nonprofit sector have noted its complex scale and scope (Saloman, 2003; Smith and Grønbjerg, 2006). These organizations serve an entire region and work with various governments to address economic, environmental, and social issues. In addition, chambers of commerce and other organizations with regional constituencies often work to advance the economic development of a region. As a result, when communities consider the merits of consolidated or fragmented local governments to address economic, social, or environmental issues, while also focusing on the delivery of services and enhanced neighborhoods, it is important to remember that the scale of the required organizations will vary.

There is an understandable desire to conceive of a simplified if not unified local government structure to deal with all services and issues in a metropolitan area or county. That desire perhaps emanates from a hope for a simple package design for local governments and governance. However, the realities of people's preferences, the scale and scope of issues that impact a region, city, and neighborhood, coupled with the need for management efficiencies, mean that the scale of governance units will change and be dictated by those realities for each service. Those realities or pressures change dramatically by service function, which means that a maximum flexibility in organizational design is a necessity for any realistic discussion of urban governance. As will be discussed later, the range of regional-level issues is actually increasing, thus necessitating the development of new flexibilities. A longing for a unified structure is simply passé.

A new wrinkle, an element that has to be included in any discussion of flexible governance and governments, is the rise of private governance structures sanctioned by cities. This is an example of local governance at the neighborhood level within the context of cooperating with the larger city while focused on issues specific to a local neighborhood. The private governance or government movement is filled with examples of people who are willing to pay higher taxes to focus on local solutions without negating their responsibilities to the city or region. While neighborhood or homeowner associations might serve as examples, more recently business improvement districts (BIDs) have been permitted that allow corporate neighbors to enhance the quality of public services in designated areas (Mitchell, 2008).

Special assessments are made and enforced by local governments, and the fees collected do not replace any local tax responsibilities. However, the funds are used to provide specific public services in the designated BID geographic area. In many ways, these organizations are structurally and fiscally similar to homeowner associations that assess fees to deliver specific services in small geographic areas.

Baer and Feiock (2005) argue that these organizations are private governments delivering services to members and have not only had a long history (homeowner and neighborhood associations have existed in some cities for more than a century) but are becoming increasingly common. However, these organizations function within the boundaries and rules of existing local governments and have not led to calls for the dissolution of cities or de-annexation. Hence, they are just another example of flexible governance and governments that are responding to challenges and opportunities. These organizations are responses to very local problems for which a collective response is necessary. Baltimore's community-based district (CBD) is not purely voluntary; citizens who voted against its formation are still required to be members of the CBD and pay additional assessments to it even if they are dissatisfied by its performance or service delivery. However, the formation of the Baltimore CBD is not necessarily permanent, as the Baltimore mayor and city council organize one or more public hearings every four years to decide whether the district will be terminated or continued for a new four-year period (Baltimore City Department of Legislative Reference, 2004).

The criticisms of business improvement districts and other forms of private governments involve concerns with inequities in service levels that might exist between parts of a city. This has led some to consider these private governments as undemocratic and discriminatory even though they are constituted by votes to serve a specific geographic area. Some might see BIDs and even homeowners' associations as violating Garreau's (1991) theory that such organizations, because of the limited area over which they deliver services, are antidemocratic (as all citizens are not served). These organizations, to some extent, do represent governments or collective activities that could be described as "one-dollar, one-vote democracy" (Garreau, 1991, p. 200). Baer and Feiock (2005) argue that the Baltimore CBD did in fact apply a principle of one citizen having one vote. For example, a kind of interdistrict social inequity might well occur if lower-income owners are unable to pay the additional property taxes and fees to form their own local associations. Consequently, they will likely receive fewer services than property owners in areas where residents can afford the higher fees. That drawback to a flexible design has to be weighed against spillover benefits from the economic integration of a city.

Returning to the regional level, Laslo and Judd (2006), investigating the civic leadership of St. Louis since World War II, point to the unification of civic activity across numerous independent cities to facilitate the revitalization of downtown St. Louis (see also Chapter 6). That action—which is often overlooked in discussions of regionalism—fits Stone's definition of civic capacity as "a scheme of cooperation through which the members of the governing coalition align their contribution to the task of governing" (Stone, 2005, p. 329). Constrained by a focus on formal governments, some who argue for consolidation have underestimated the level of civic capacity that has emerged and is at work in many regions. In greater St. Louis that civic capacity has recently sustained important urban development projects through the creation of a constellation of quasi-public governments and special districts. With the leadership's ability to forge political coalitions, mobilize resources, and make decisions that transcend general-purpose governmental jurisdictions, Laslo and Judd (2006 and Chapter 6) emphasize that the constellation of quasi-public governments and special districts is now transforming the local state in St. Louis. A flexible governmental structure exists that is providing and delivering needed services in a system that enjoys widespread political support.

The future of urban governance will be a flexible web of organizations—some public, some in the nonprofit sector, and some in the private sector—dealing simultaneously with regional issues and local urban service delivery. Expertise in coordination with a particular emphasis on intergovernmental relations and the building of networks between organizations in different sectors of the economy will be needed to govern urban areas. These skills will be at a premium and will be a prerequisite for all urban managers.

From this perspective it is easier to understand some of the wry humor from the debates over fragmentation versus consolidation. Current debates ignore a far more central point. At the same time that there are concerns about the quality of life at the neighborhood level, regional cooperation to enhance the quality of life, economic development, transportation, and environmental management are increasingly needed. Before using some material that will be discussed in depth in a later chapter (Chapter 8), we now turn to a discussion of the reasons for the increased need for regional activity and flexible organizational structures.

Moving the discussion from the theoretical to the practical plane, Greater Cleveland again provides some valuable lessons. As noted, the region is mired in the restructuring of the manufacturing sector, which has led to automation and far higher levels of productivity but also to a shrinking demand for labor. The decline in the fortunes of northeastern Ohio has led to the creation of several regional organizations including the Fund for Our Economic Future that unites the region's foundations in a common strategy for investing in new initiatives. Separate organizations focused on new and emerging companies were established by a series of public–private partnerships involving several cities, foundations, and business associations. At the same time, the region has focused on building community development corporations to concentrate on development with cities and neighborhoods, and these organizations are financed and supported by cities, regional foundations, and local institutions of higher education. Thus, regional and local organizations are forming to respond to initiatives and efforts to change the local economy, and these have taken place without the creation of a consolidated city-county government. Further, to help redevelop downtown Cleveland, the county has agreed to use its tax base for several projects while the new tax revenues created from these projects accrue to Cleveland. That too is a form of regional cooperation or governance without a consolidated government.

Regionalism and the Extension of Urban Space

Regional and cross-jurisdiction alliances will increase—as they have in Cleveland (see Chapter 8) and in St. Louis (see Chapter 5) without a consolidated government—simply as a result of the changes in spatial relationships within urban areas. Over less than a hundred years, challenges and development patterns that were largely contained within the boundaries of individual cities now routinely span across cities and counties. Even when the first suburbs began to emerge in the World War I era, central cities were the appropriate scale at which regional issues were addressed.

Today, the situation is quite different. People want a quality of neighborhood life with parks, schools, and safety services delivered to them in an efficient manner, but in a way that emphasizes local control. At the same time, citizens expect governments within a region to coordinate approaches and resources to address regional problems. That is the "new" demand from citizen-consumers who now vote with their feet between regions as they choose where they wish to live. Special districts, seen as local governments and formal institutions, have adopted strategies that promote regional cooperation. They deal with the boundary design from the perspective of public problems and may achieve greater efficiency in providing local public services to their citizens. Many scholars have also emphasized the flexibility of special district boundaries once established, arguing that this flexibility helps local governance systems to adapt to and easily adjust to changing resource constraints and patterns of demand.

And there is now a broader array of services that transcend the boundaries of any community in the regional city-state in which citizen-consumers live. From traffic control to environmental quality, from strategies to assist with economic development and human capital development to public health and the cost of uncompensated care, the range of regional issues continues to expand. While public safety was once truly limited to one's neighborhood, today the possibility of politically motivated attacks of unprecedented scale requires regional coordination beyond the simple synchronization of communication systems. A single individual or a small group can produce scores of casualties and major disruptions to a region's operations.

Indeed, disruptions of food or water supply systems—not to mention the release of infectious materials—require regional responses and coordination with statewide and national authorities. The citizen-consumer demands that level of regionalism coupled with local control of neighborhood-level services.

As large as those challenges are, and even given the increasing number of issues that regional city-states must address, students of urban governance cannot forget that citizens' everyday lives revolve more around services they consume at the neighborhood level than around services that are regional in scale or that dwarf the boundaries of any individual city. To that end, what is needed is a commitment to flexible governance systems that permit regions to develop regional institutions and compacts for those problems that require a regional or multi-city response. But for neighborhood-scale services, about which citizens want the ability to speak to local mayors and councils, we should be wise enough to ensure that the aspect of the quality of life is protected and enhanced.

This line of reasoning seems to confound many community leaders who today call for regionalism as the appropriate scale for urban governance. Those individuals need to consider the logic advanced by Tiebout (1956) more than a half-century ago, which was more clearly articulated in a subsequent article (Ostrom, Tiebout, and Warren, 1961). Ironically, the leaders looked to fragmented structures as keys for the efficient production of local services that would or could generate the capital necessary for regional responses to regional issues. Not lost in the discussion of a model that ensures competition to create an environment for efficient production strategies that matched the demands of local residents is a political structure that gives residents the chance to either "vote with their feet" or directly become involved in altering the array and quality of neighborhood services. Tiebout (1956) originally envisioned a system in which citizen-consumers exercised their vote, participation, and evaluation of the quality and quantity of local services through their residential choice. In this manner people voted with their feet by moving to areas with the desired mix and quality of services. As extended in later years by Warren, Rosentraub, and Weschler (1992), if there is sufficient local control over local services, then residents can still vote with their feet or get involved directly in changing the array and quality of services. That participation is integral to avoidance of the syndrome so aptly described by Putnam (2000) as "bowling alone."

In essence, what cannot be lost in the discussion of consolidated governments and the overwhelming trend toward a need for regional governance organizations is an equal commitment to protecting ways for residents to directly participate in government. If this were lost, the fear is that "bowling alone" tendencies could lead to a substantial disruption in what are described as the components of a civil society.

Continuing along these several different lines of reasoning, Ostrom and Parks (1999), Parks and Oakerson (2000), and Savitch and Vogel (2000) each produced important publications in a more recent wave of analyses that sustained the logic of flexible organizational structures to meet the varying scale of services required in urban centers. These studies are representative of a body of work suggesting that competitive markets for public services could be more efficient in terms of costs (taxes) and opportunities for participation than a corporate view of decision making that places too much value on centralized authority. The focus on centralized authority is frequently advocated by business elites who prefer single points of contact and more immediate decisions to the time-consuming process usually associated with fragmented governments. However, the supposed efficiencies in terms of lower taxes and the higher costs in fragmented systems are frequently not sustained. Further, the issue of the reduced opportunities for participation in the affairs of governments is too often ignored in calls for consolidation. It should not be assumed that those costs are negligible.

Conclusions

The answer to the central issue addressed in this volume—governance of regions in the twenty-first century—involves recognition that flexible systems will be required. As the number of regional issues increases, local government officials will be expected to develop regional and intraregional associations to address those concerns. Some issues will require the involvement of all units of local government in a region; others will require the cooperation of a few governments, and, of course, one can easily imagine the need for interregional associations for some issues. The effective creation of flexible systems will also require the recognition that some services are more efficiently provided at the local level and that local politics will require that some services are not placed within the confines of consolidated or larger-scale governments.

As a result, while the regional agenda is expanded—and it will be as problems and challenges continue to cross local boundaries—attention cannot be diverted from the services that can and should be delivered at the local level. That level of service delivery is needed to realize the efficiencies created through competition between local service providers, but also to ensure that citizens remain connected and involved with neighborhoods, neighbors, democracy, and local governments. Governance systems must focus as much on combating the "bowling alone" syndrome as on ensuring that services are delivered efficiently and effectively. Local governments will need to act collectively in the future in order to manage transregional problems, and interlocal agreements may be useful because they assist in establishing the principles for cooperative norms that contribute largely toward achieving efficiency and effectiveness in public service provision (Leroux and Carr, 2007).

This framework requires elastic and flexible governments and governance. Governments will need to engage with other governments and organizations for service delivery. That flexibility means the elasticity to stretch to include nongovernmental organizations and private governments in future governance systems. The twenty-first century—unlike its predecessors—will challenge community leaders to create opportunities to build community and experiment with democracy at the neighborhood level while forging partnerships to address regional issues. Perhaps that challenge did exist when suburbs became a reality in the latter part of the twentieth century. Regardless, what is clear at this point in time is that the regions that will grow and prosper are those with sufficient flexibility, that neighborhood services are controlled at the neighborhood level and regional problems and challenges addressed with a coordinated effort that convinces citizen-consumers their preferences for efficiency and efficacy are being met.

References

Baer, S., and R.C. Feiock. 2005. "Private Governments in Urban Areas: Political Contracting and Collective Action." *American Review of Public Administration* 35: 42–56.

Baltimore City Department of Legislative Reference. 2004. http://www.ci.baltimore.md.us/government/legislative/index.php, accessed February 2, 2009.

Feiock, R. 2007. "Rational Choice and Regional Governance." *Journal of Urban Affairs* 29, no. 1: 47–63.

Foster, K.A. 1995. *The Political Economy of Special-Purpose Governments.* Washington, DC: Georgetown University Press.

Garreau, J. 1991. *Edge City: Life on the New Frontier.* New York: Doubleday.

Hooghe, Lisbet, and Gary Marks. 2003. "Unraveling the Central State, But How? Types of Multi-Level Governance." *American Political Science Review* 97: 2 (June) 1134–67.

Laslo, D., and D.R. Judd. 2006. "Building Civic Capacity through an Elastic Local State: The Case of St. Louis." *Review of Policy Research* 23: 235–55.

Leland, S., and K. Thurmaier. 2005. "When Efficiency in Unbelievable: Normative Lessons from 30 Years of City-County Consolidations." *Public Administration Review* 65: 475-89.

Leroux, K., and J.B. Carr. 2007. "Explaining Local Government Cooperation on Public Works: Evidence from Michigan." *Public Works Management & Policy* 12: 344–58.

Mitchell, J. 2008. *Business Improvement Districts and the Shape of American Cities.* Albany: State University of New York Press.

Mullin, M. 2007. "Do Special Districts Act Alone?" and "Exploring the Relationship Between Flexible Boundaries and Intergovernmental Cooperation." Papers presented at the annual meeting of the Midwestern Political Science Association, pp. 1–35, no date.

Oakerson, R.J. 1999. *Governing Local Public Economies: Creating the Civic Metropolis.* Oakland, CA: ICS Press.

Ostrom, E., and R.B. Parks. 1999. "Neither Gargantua nor the Land of Lilliputs: Conjectures on Mixed Systems of Metropolitan Organization." In *Polycentricity and Local Public Economies,* ed. Michael McGinnis, 284–305. Ann Arbor: University of Michigan Press.

Ostrom, V.; C. Tiebout; and R. Warren. 1961. "The Organization of Government in Metropolitan Areas: A Theoretical Inquiry." *American Political Science Review* 55: 831–42.

Parks, R.B., and R.J. Oakerson. 2000. "Regionalism, Localism, and Metropolitan Governance: Suggestions from the Research Program on Local Public Economies." *State and Local Government Review* 32, no. 3: 169–79.

Putnam, Robert. 2000. *Bowling Alone: The Collapse and Revival of American Community.* New York: Simon and Schuster.

Rosentraub, M.S.; R. Warren; and L. Weschler. 1988. "The Production of Urban Services: A Community Services Budget Approach." *Urban Affairs Quarterly* 23: 414–31.

Savitch, H., and R. Vogel. 2000. "Metropolitan Consolidation versus Metropolitan Governance in Louisville." *State and Local Government Review* 32, no. 3: 198–212.

Smith, S.R., and K.A. Grønbjerg. 2006. "Scope and Theory of Government-Nonprofit Re-
lations." In *The Nonprofit Sector: A Research Handbook,* 2d ed., ed. W.W. Powell and
R.S. Steinberg, 221–42. New Haven, CT: Yale University Press.
Stone, C.N. 2005. "Looking Back to Look Forward: Reflections on Urban Regime Analysis."
Urban Affairs Review 40: 309–41.
Thompson, T. L. 1995. "Strategies of Service Delivery in a Fragmented Metropolitan
Area." *Proceedings of the American Political Science Association.* Washington, DC:
The American Political Science Association.
Thompson, L., and R.C. Elling. 1999. "Let Them Eat Marblecake: The Preferences of
Michigan Citizens for Intergovernmental Service Provision." *Publius* 29: 139–54.
Tiebout, C. 1956. "A Pure Theory of Local Expenditures." *Journal of Political Economy*
64: 416–24.
Warren, R., and L. Weschler. 1972. "Governing Urban Space." Unpublished paper. Los
Angeles: Center for Urban Affairs, University of Southern California.
Warren, R.; M. Rosentraub; and L. Weschler. 1988. "Building Urban Governance: An Agenda
for the 1990s." *Journal of Urban Affairs* 14: 399–422.

4

Who Will Govern American Metropolitan Regions, and How?

John Stuart Hall

Governance in the Metropolitan Context

Public policy, governance processes, and economic development work together in complex, debatable, and dynamic ways. Because of the democratic context, rich variety, and sheer number of U.S. local governments and communities, it is particularly tricky to understand and to generalize about these relationships at the local level. This task becomes even more complicated when attempting to discern the interconnection of these factors in American metropolitan regions (*metroregions*), despite the fact that global economic reality and geopolitical change calls for analysis and action at precisely that level.[1]

There are strong practical and theoretical grounds for more and better research about regional governance in the United States. Contemporary governance is government and more. Governance refers to the way public decisions are actually made; the patterns of civic life derived from the interaction of structure and the process of politics (Campbell, 1995, p. 7). The literature on urban governance reveals far more about the workings and responsibilities of formal units of government—cities, counties, special districts, and so forth—than it informs about the real and potential effects of the actions of these many governments on the regional economy and society. Furthermore, the literature focuses more on the effects of formal authority, as opposed to the more informal, nonauthoritative "partnerships" that increasingly characterize the real mechanisms for regional governance and decision making. Compared with the literature on cities, there is far less systematic research about who actually governs regions.

Intergovernmental Factors in Regional Metropolitan Governance

Analysts know far more about pieces of the regional metropolitan governance puzzle than they do about what it should look like when it is completed. Many researchers have carefully enumerated the independent value of formal units of local government. Budgets, responsibilities, and services of U.S. local governments have been described in classic case and comparative studies (e.g., Banfield and Wilson, 1963; Lineberry and Fowler, 1967; Peterson, 1981). But the rich literature focusing on American local government has paid much less attention to describing total contributions of regional metropolitan public policy efforts. With few exceptions, there has been little investigation about how discrete efforts and budgets of separate local governments in metro-regions are allocated and totaled. Without double counting, what do the efforts of any region's local governments in any particular policy or service area total? Even less is known about the comprehensive roles and resources of major private nonprofit and for-profit institutions in regional service delivery, problem solving, and decision making.

The complexity of the American intergovernmental system is such that few have any idea about the true size, shape, and operation of the public sector for any metropolitan region. In short, for most metro-regions, analysts are far more informed about the fractions of government than they are able to derive the governance whole number.

From a policymaking perspective, this focus on fractions is tied directly to local politics and the semi-sovereign nature of American local government. It is partially justified as a simple reflection of reality, of both the power and problems of pluralism. But thoughtful critics such as Gardner see real danger in focusing on fractions because this approach tends to blur the value of efforts toward collaborative governance. Gardner believes that extending the "war of the parts against the whole" submerges attempts to find the common good. As he puts it: *"Pluralism that reflects no commitments whatever to the common good is pluralism gone berserk. A primary task of our dispersed leadership is to achieve a workable level of unity within society"* (Gardner, 1990, p. 97, original emphasis). It is with these practical and theoretical themes in mind that focus on the governance of U.S. regions seems justified.

Governing American Metropolitan Regions: Who and How?

U.S. democratic governance is by design a patchwork of institutions and people, checks and balances. But some would argue that the Achilles' heel of the much-heralded American experiment in democratic governance is regional. Illusive, frequently lagging behind evident region-wide problems, sometimes sharply focused, often totally absent, less formal and more complex than other hot spots of American federalism, governance of U.S. metro-regions has been practically and theoretically neglected. The short answer to Dahl's (1961) classic question "Who governs?" when applied to most American metro-regions is, "Often many and sometimes no one."

But as these places ascend in importance and are better understood, questions about regional governance become more urgent. U.S. metro-regions are changing in ways and at a pace that makes corollary changes in regional governance and American intergovernmental affairs seem inevitable. But what will be the form and function of new regional governance? Who will lead metropolitan America to solve regional problems, cope with urban issues, and meet the challenges of global economic competitiveness? When the status quo is inadequate, how will regional futures be shaped? In short, who will govern American metro-regions?

Why This Question About Metropolitan Regions?

Because Metropolitan Regions Have Enormous and Increasing Economic Clout and Social Consequence

America's 300-plus metro-regions contain major shares of the country's wealth, economic activity, population, amenities, and arts and culture. Many of these metro areas are becoming more closely connected to form "megapolitan areas"—clustered networks of metropolitan areas that exceed 10 million total residents (or are projected to pass that mark by 2040) (Lang and Dhavale, 2005). Megapolitan regions (megas) are "super" urban regions that combine two, and frequently several, major metropolitan areas and demonstrate increased economic interdependence. Megas represent a significant recent change in metropolitan form with important implications for governance. Metropolitan areas that were previously viewed by insiders and outsiders as separate and distinct are becoming more interdependent, merging into larger metros despite historical patterns and legal boundaries. Will these new "super regions" demand some kind of super governance?

Based on current and projected population and commuting patterns, fitted to the U.S. Census Bureau's definition of a Combined Statistical Area (CSA) there are twenty emerging mega areas in the United States. Megas exist in all sections of the nation, cover over one-half the states, contain more than 60 percent of the U.S. population—yet account for only one-tenth of U.S. land area, produce 70 percent of the nation's gross domestic product, and are projected to receive 60 million new residents by 2040 (Lang and Nelson, 2007).

As hubs of global economic competition and centers of international immigration, creativity, and innovation, megas offer much hope and opportunity. Yet the expanding urban metropolis underscores the old adage, "you can't have your cake and eat it too." For these places are also major magnets for many of the "wicked," seemingly intractable human problems of urbanization. You name it: traffic congestion, environmental degradation, homelessness, violent crime, gangs, drugs, poverty, children with children, school dropouts, and much more are part of the metropolitan/megapolitan package. These regions are at the epicenter of economic and social earthquakes that stimulate and challenge our progress as a civilization. Analysts of all sorts, and people who simply want to be involved in shaping a positive and sustainable future for generations to come, increasingly realize the need to focus on both the problems and potentials, the assets as well as the deficits of evolving metro-regions to reconcile the costs and benefits of current trajectories of metropolitan development and change. All concerned have many good questions about trade-offs, assets, visions, futures, and outcomes. Yet despite the very critical importance of these regions and issues, the U.S. and state constitutions say nothing about metro-regions or about how they should be governed. And in the first decade of the twenty-first century, Savitch and Vogel's observation of regional governance remains accurate: "rarely do we see regional legislatures, chief executives, or judiciaries" (1994, p. 2). This profound ambivalence underscores the need to ask: Who governs American metro-regions?

Because "Who Governs?" Is Elemental to Understanding Democracy

In a democracy it is said that "the people" govern. But beyond this truism lie many debates and legitimate concerns. Many have claimed that the highest form of democratic governance was achieved by Greek city-states such as Athens around 450 B.C. Who governed this democracy? Certainly not all its residents. At that time, Athens was made up of approximately 280,000 people. Subtracting 100,000 slaves and additional women and children, left around 50,000 "freemen" who directly governed the city-state (Davies, 1968).

Modern expansion of the vote through representative democracy is an important component of democratic reform but does not resolve all governance issues. Dahl emphasized the complex nature of the voting–governance relationship when he asked, "In a political system where nearly every adult may vote but where knowledge, wealth, social position, access to officials, and other resources are unequally distributed, who actually governs?" (1961, p. 1). In the contemporary U.S. context, the questions "Who governs and how?" and "Why do some seem to have more to say about public policy than others?" as well as a host of related questions, point to the well-plowed but still fertile grounds of democratic theory and community power. Different coalitions, interests, regimes, and elections make for dynamic, fluid governance and enhance the importance of different perspectives and the claims of those who play the game. Certainty is hardly the hallmark of democracy.

"Who governs?" has been asked often in different settings but infrequently applied to metro-regions. The community-power debate focused on cities and flourished for a time before being put mercifully to rest by thoughtful logic and analysis. Bachrach and Baratz (1962) initiated this reconsideration in their classic article "Two Faces of Power," in which they concluded that sociologists consistently found community power to be shared by a few elites and highly centralized, and political scientists regularly found community power to be diffused among many groups and individuals depending on the issue. Bachrach and Baratz said that this consistent difference in findings was a function of different assumptions and methodologies resulting in "two faces of power, neither of which the sociologists see and only one of which the political scientists see" (p. 947).

Ironically, an early answer to the community-power debate was provided by Dahl after his brief but brilliant discussion of the evolution of conflicting theories attending to the "Who governs?" question: "If we ask, 'Who governs?' the answer is not the mass nor its leaders but both together; the leaders cater to mass tastes and in return use the strength provided by the loyalty and obedience of the masses to weaken and perhaps even to annihilate all opposition to their rule" (1961, p. 7).

But is this "governance together" explanation, indeed the entire community-power debate, passé? Has the hypothesized elite/mass interaction over governance lost its relevance at a time in history of well-discussed "disconnect" between people and politics, documented by polls showing increased lack of trust and perceived ineffectiveness of the political process (Yankelovich, 1991)? Perhaps, however, the fluid nature of American local governance that features the passing of power and influence from coalition to coalition, from formal authority to informal compromise, from issue to issue, from amateur to professional (Ehrenhalt, 1991), and from "old" to "new" leadership styles (Svara, 1990) suggests the continued importance of the question and that the answer to "Who governs?" is still "Depends." In this sense, "Who governs?" cannot be separated from "How does metropolitan governance work?"

A related and pressing reason for retaining a focus on "Who governs?" is the challenge embedded in one stream of urban scholarship, to the effect that for big cities, no one governs—or at least no one *governs well.* The genesis of this theme was reaction to urban disorder, social unrest, and indicators of increasing human and social hardship in the cities seen by many observers in the 1970s/1980s. One of these observers, Douglas Yates, answered the question, "Who governs cities?" this way: "The American city is fundamentally *ungovernable* in its present form. Only a compulsive optimist could overlook the distress signals emanating from city hall, which strongly suggest that the city has become the sick man of American government" (Yates, 1978, pp. xiii–xiv; original emphasis). Growing out of a reaction to urban unrest and problems of the 1960s and 1970s, this became a dominant theme of the urban politics literature for at least three decades. This vision of a breakdown in urban governance has been reflected and reinforced in the work of many scholars since the 1960s. They have put emphasis upon the limitations of cities and their citizens in handling local affairs (Warren, Rosentraub, and Weschler, 1992).

Despite these warnings, cities do govern, daily. And, because of the diversity that marks American local government, the nation's cities are governed in many different ways. In fact, research of the past two decades emphasizes the resilience of cities, the ability of cities to cope with complex and changing demands, while delivering standard services with fewer resources. Bahl, Duncombe, and Schulman suggested "urban governments have become *more able to cope* with the realities of limited resources. They have lived better within their fiscal means in recent years and have managed to do this while providing an adequate level of public service" (1990, pp. 54–55; original emphasis; for a similar conclusion see Stein, 1990).

In addition, it is clear from research and observation that the city has over the long haul been remarkably resilient. The profound story and importance of resilience is told by Vale and Campanella: "Although cities have been destroyed throughout history—sacked, shaken, burned, bombed, flooded, starved, irradiated, and poisoned—they have, in almost every case, risen again like the mythic phoenix" (2005, p. 3).

As one study of city resilience demonstrated, between the years 1100 and 1800, only forty-two cities were permanently abandoned following such crises of destruction (Chandler and Fox, 1974).

Despite these abundant capacities and reasoned defenses of the strength of community and local government, there is ample need to evaluate the quality of American urban governance and government continuously. More important, when one looks more broadly at the work of multiple independent local governments in metro-regions and at the bigger list of regional issues, services, and problems, it is difficult to dismiss easily the challenge posed by the "Who governs?" theme. Who is responsible? Is anyone in charge?

Because in the American Intergovernmental System, Governance and Government are Different

In part, past conclusions about, and general neglect of, regional governance are drawn from existing paradigms and models that do not fully reflect reality or the potential of regions to serve as centers for mobilizing resources and solving critical problems. Dodge (1992) has thought carefully about this problem of lagging governance models and concluded that Americans are organized to think about issues at the federal, state, and city/county level. However, he asserts that the important *challenges* of the times are not at that level—they are at the international, regional, and neighborhood levels.

Using the familiar federal system as a starting point, analysts have tended not to focus on these centers and to think of government and governance as close synonyms. Actually, at the community level, the United States has always relied heavily on networks and partnerships of institutions to solve community problems. Tocqueville provided early and important description of this unique American approach to community governance, and contemporary scholars have found communities continuing to solve problems by forming partnerships among governments, businesses, churches, nonprofits, citizen organizations, and other institutions (Boyte, 1989; Salamon, 2003).

But many political scientists and other analysts have been inclined to look first at formal governments and elected officials for clues concerning "Who governs?" If, as Dodge (1992) and others argue, government and governance are increasingly separate spheres, analysis that centers on the former is increasingly limited. Certainly, community governance during the devolution and downsizing decades has changed and, by most standards, expanded. Current fear concerning public reaction to *government* as opposed to *community* and what might be perceived as another layer of government affects practicality of regional reform such as Gerald Frug's (2002) bold and carefully articulated proposal that state legislatures create regional legislatures and establish regional citizenship akin to that of the European Union.

This concern about public perspectives of "new layers of government" is not new, however, and has always played a part in distinguishing regional government and governance. As expressed by Ostrom, Bish, and Ostrom:

> We need to recognize that the local government in a democratic society cannot be confined only to what transpires in particular corporate entities or agencies identified as units of government. This is why it may be more useful to refer to "governance structures" than "governments." We can then appreciate that something viewed as a process of government (governance) requires reference to a much larger universe of discourse than do units of government as such. (1988, p. 212)

The need to focus on governance and not government in the regional discussion was also Dodge's premise: "Governance now encompasses the roles and relationships of all community leaders and citizens—and the organizations they represent—that guide and empower the design of strategies to address common concerns as well as the delivery of services to provide for the common good" (1992, p. 404). Dodge also recognized cross-cutting challenges inherent in modern regional intercommunity governance, which includes interactions among adjoining suburban governments (such as joint agreements to deliver public services); public and private agencies in central cities and surrounding communities (such as collaborations to foster economic development); and public, private, academic, civic, and other community interests region wide (such as collaborations to develop regional visions and strategic plans).

In short, U.S. metropolitan areas are in flux. The economic and social systems of these areas are under significant pressure and changing rapidly. At the same time, citizens are told that government is being reinvented. Certainly, intergovernmental relations are changing, as are perceptions of community, government, governance, and roles in the governance process. The time seems right to examine the full dimension of metropolitan governance, and that process requires a brief examination of the trends and facts of regional governance.

Who Governs Metropolitan Regions and How Has the Governance Process Changed?

Formal Governments in Urban Regions

Currently, American metro-regions are governed in large part by many semi-sovereign jurisdictions that make up the intergovernmental system of any given region. They can be described as semi-sovereign because many of these public entities are governed by independent, elected boards and commissions, with significant policymaking and taxing authority and autonomy. Yet the sovereignty of the many local jurisdictions of the United States is limited, usually by state constitutions, state legislation, or court decisions. American government in a time of devolution, reinvention, and decentralization is increasingly about weaving together the fragments of many semi-sovereign American state and local governments. Metro-regional governance has become more important under these conditions. In most American regions, significant shifts in metro-regional governance will proceed from a history and culture of independent local government decision making, the strongly held U.S. value of "local control."

Table 4.1 depicts the size of the U.S. intergovernmental system and historical trends in the total number of governments from 1952 to 2007. The 89,000 governments found system wide in 2007 is a large number, but it is also, because of school district consolidations and closures, much smaller than the 1952 total, which exceeded 116,000 governments, and it is far removed from even higher depression-era totals.

There are multiple meanings and definitions of key concepts associated with metro-regional governance. What is a region, a metro (urban) area, or for that matter, a neighborhood or community? For example, over thirty definitions of region are found in the classic text *American Regionalism* by Odum and Moore (1938, p. 2). Other, more contemporary, lists of definitions similar in their mix of subjective and objective meaning can be derived from texts covering urban, community, and neighborhood affairs. So "Who governs?" the metro or urban areas of the United States depends in part on how such regions are identified and defined.

To gain some preliminary and general understanding of formal government contributions to the governance of U.S. urban regions, we look to the U.S. Census Bureau for definitions and data. The Census first officially designated Metropolitan areas in 1949 to show functional economic relationships (Anderson, 1988, as cited in Lang and Dhavale, 2005). Census Bureau metropolitan categories and definitions have changed since that time, making comparisons over time difficult. As of the latest census (2000) and population estimates from 2005 and 2006, the Census classified 363 regions of the United States as "Metropolitan"—as opposed to 254 in 1990—and 126 as Combined Statistical Areas a new transmetropolitan regional category[2] that links existing metropolitan areas based on economic relationships (as defined by commuting patterns) (Lang and Dhavale, 2005; OMB Bulletin 08–01). These categories describe growth in urban population that parallels and is accounted for by overall population growth in the United States.

Meanwhile, as we see from Table 4.1, despite the nation's great population growth, there has been insignificant change in units of government from 1992 to 2007. The number of major local general-purpose governments, cities, towns, and counties remains virtually unchanged. Nationally, only the category of "Special District" shows a modest increase over the past two decades, although that government category has increased steadily from 12,340 in 1952 to 37,381 in 2007.

Table 4.1 demonstrates the diversity and range of American governments as well as substantial stability over fifty years of the intergovernmental system. Earlier analysis (Hall, 2004) based on 1992 data demonstrated the enormous range of numbers of governments involved in the governance of the nation's

62

Table 4.1

Trend in Number of Governments in the United States, 1952–2007

Government type	2007	2002	1992	1987	1977	1952
Total governments	89,527	87,576	85,006	83,237	79,913	116,805
Federal	1	1	1	1	1	1
State	50	50	50	50	50	48
Local						
County	3,033	3,034	3,043	3,042	3,042	3,052
Municipal	19,492	19,429	19,279	19,200	18,862	16,807
Township	16,519	16,504	16,656	16,691	16,822	17,202
School District	13,051	13,506	14,422	14,721	15,174	67,355
Special District	37,381	35,052	31,555	29,532	25,962	12,340

Sources: Census of Governments 2002, vol. 1, no. 1, and Census of Governments 2007.

metropolitan areas. Although the numbers have changed slightly, the pattern remains the same.

Between the extremes of the Miami-Dade model of centralization, with less than 100 total governments, and the Chicago metro prototype of public choice in action, with almost 1,700 multiple governments, there is clear evidence of diversity in governance preferences and patterns.

Changing definitions of the urban region, such as the Census Bureau's Combined Statistical Area, the Citistate, and Megapolitan regions, change the number of governments operating within regions, but huge diversity, range, and stability of governments is still the rule. Arizona's Sun Corridor Megapolitan region incorporates parts of 6 Arizona counties and 57 cities or towns, which appears significant until it is compared with the Northeast Mega-Region encompassing parts of 14 states, 405 counties, and several thousand cities and towns (Berman, 2007; Hall, 2008).

The diversity of U.S. intergovernmental systems in metro areas has significant implications for our big question of who will govern metro America and how. A multitude of governmental entities is involved in some way in the business of metropolitan governance or, more precisely, numerous jurisdictions are involved in governing geographic and/or functional parts of each region. Yet lists of governments in metro areas provide only tip-of-the-iceberg information for understanding regional governance. They do not include the many metropolitan-level activities of national and state agencies, the public problem-solving and service-delivery efforts of hundreds of nonprofit organizations in each metro-region, or the semiautonomous activities of numerous boards and commissions affiliated with local governments and special districts. Many of the shadow governments and edge cities portrayed by Garreau (1991) as having enormous consequences for regional development and governance are not captured by these numbers. Most important, when it comes to governance, lists of formal governments do not help one to understand vast differences in accountability, focus, and political power that good case studies of metropolitan-wide governance reveal (e.g., Nelkin, 1974).

Close examination does confirm, however, that in much of urban America, regional governance is parceled and partitioned and is becoming even more so over time. Only seldom does one find exceptions to the rule of piecemeal and specialized governance in the form of one government responsible for most regional public policy. Over time, many reformers and critics have called for the establishment of strong, centralized metropolitan governments. Table 4.2 provides a short list of successful city-county consolidations in U.S. history. This reform is the most difficult to achieve, because of politics. Although hundreds of proposals for local government consolidation have reached the referendum stage, only thirty-four have been enacted since the New Orleans case in 1805 (Leland and Thurmaier, 2005). For the most part, these proposals fail because they involve boundary changes and new power and resource relationships. Those few examples of success in modern times such as Nashville, Jacksonville, Indianapolis (UniGov), and Louisville have

Table 4.2

Successful City-County Consolidations

Year approved	Local jurisdictions involved, state	Means employed
1805	New Orleans, New Orleans Co., LA	LA
1821	Boston, Suffolk Co., MA	LA
1821	Nantucket Town, Nantucket Co., MA	LA
1854	Philadelphia, Philadelphia Co., PA	LA
1856	San Francisco, San Francisco Co., CA	LA
1874	New York, New York Co., NY	LA
1898	New York, Brooklyn, Bronx, Staten Island, Queens, NY	LA
1904	Denver, Denver Co., CO	LA
1907	Honolulu, Honolulu Co., HI	LA
1947	Baton Rouge, East Baton Rouge Parish, LA	REF
1952	Hampton, Elizabeth City Co., VA	REF
1958	Newport News, Warwick Co., VA	REF
1962	Nashville, Davidson Co., TN	REF
1962	Virginia Beach, Princess Ann Co., VA	REF
1962	South Norfolk, Norfolk Co., VA	REF
1967	Jacksonville, Duval Co., FL	REF
1969	Carson City, Ormsby Co., NV	REF
1969	Indianapolis, Marion Co., IN	LA
1969	Juneau, Greater Juneau Borough, AK	REF
1970	Columbus, Muskeg Co., CA	REF
1971	Holland and Whaleville Towns, Nansemond Co., VA	REF
1971	Sitka, Greater Sitka Borough, AK	REF
1972	Suffolk, Nansemond Co., VA*	REF
1974	Lexington, Fayette Co., KY	REF
1975	Anchorage, Greater Anchorage Area Borough, AK	REF
1977	Anaconda, Deer Lodge Co., MT	REF
1977	Butte, Silver Bow Co., MT	REF
1984	Houma, Terrebonne Parish, LA	REF
1990	Athens, Clark Co., GA	REF
1992	Lafayette, Lafayette Parish, LA	REF
1995	Augusta, Richmond Co., GA	REF
1997	Kansas City, Wyandotte Co., KS	REF
1999	Louisville, Jefferson Co., KY	REF
2000	Hartsville, Trousdale Co., TN	Not reported

Sources: Wallis (1994); Leland and Thurmaier (2005); National Association of Counties, available at www.naco.org.

Notes: LA = legislative action; REF = referendum.

*Suffolk initially was a county, but became a municipality prior to consolidation.

been responses to crises, corruption, and/or perceived need in suburban areas for new and improved service levels.

In their close analysis of city-county consolidation attempts over the past three decades, Leland and Thurmaier (2005, p. 475) find that traditional campaign arguments based on increased efficiency and greater suburban/central city equity are generally unsuccessful. Instead, the model of a successful consolidation is a group of civic elites who define the economic development vision for the community, determine that the existing political structure is incapable of supporting and implementing that vision, and convince voters that city-county consolidation is the key to economic development that will benefit the whole community, not just the elites.

A handful of other metropolitan areas of the United States have adopted compromises in which limited regional functions of government are provided by a metropolitan-wide government while many more localized functions remain the purview of existing cities, towns, and counties. The best examples of this approach are Miami, Portland, and Minneapolis-St. Paul.

It is important to note that the vast majority of U.S. metropolitan areas have avoided a metropolitan government solution to the challenges presented by local government fragmentation. This does not mean that most metropolitan areas have not used many different strategies and approaches to enhance region-wide problem solving and governance, but as emphasized earlier, government is not the sole instrument of governance in American metro-regions.

Compared with other national systems, even federal ones, there are important and frequently discussed governance differences accruing from the presence of many, at times overlapping, governments in each region. These governance differences include greater diversity of focus and purpose; an increase in fragmentation of authority and accountability; greater choice, at least for some residents of the region, of bundles of goods and services and tax price of those bundles; genuinely shared sovereignty; an increase in competition among jurisdictions for industry and tax resources; and an increase in cooperation among some jurisdictions to solve some regional problems—sometimes. But most important for this chapter, there is greater difficulty in confidently answering the question "Who governs?" Many trade-offs are inherent in this system. There are enough governments doing enough things to suggest a high degree of access, checks and balance, and accountability. Yet by some standards of economic and problem-solving efficiency, this system seems baroque and fragmented.

Metro-Governance Is Much More Than Governments

But before jumping to conclusions about the governance of metropolitan America based on these broad contours, one needs to look beyond formal governments—to investigate governance in its current form and as it is evolving, not as it is limited by formal public authority. Mercifully for generations of readers and for his own health, Tocqueville did not construct his assessment of American government through Census Bureau categories. He visited communities and found the people of those regions working through various institutions to solve community problems. Tocqueville could not have predicted the number, shape, size, and precise responsibilities of the local governments that have evolved and probably would not have forecast the degree of distrust and disconnect (Bellah, 1991; Cisneros, 1993) that seems to color much current discussion of urban governance.

It also seems very likely, based on his early evaluation, that he would not be surprised by systems of shared responsibility and governance, public–private partnerships, or church and other nonprofit organizations extending community governance to meet emerging community needs. According to a Kettering Foundation–sponsored series of focus groups (Kettering Foundation, 1989, 1990), many Americans who are dissatisfied with governments and politicians are still optimistic about potential contributions to *community* problem solving. In every major metropolitan area, there are hundreds—sometimes thousands—of nonprofit organizations providing significant public services with combinations of public and private resources. These organizations and other community institutions form service-provider and interest-group networks and coalitions that are increasingly active partners with specific governments and their agencies and departments.

Do the People Govern?

Recent reports warn of decline in personal associations, involvement in civic-minded groups, and resultant diminished public power in urban governance. One is frequently cautioned about the very real threats to democracy associated with increased suburbanization, sprawl, edge-city and cul-de-sac subdivision development, and other forces of separation and isolation in urban regions (Downs, 1994; Goldsmith and Blakely, 1992).

Perhaps most influential in this stream of commentary is the work of Robert Putnam, particularly his classic work *Bowling Alone* (2000). In this book, he documented the fact that since 1980, people are bowling more than ever, yet bowling leagues have shrunk by 40 percent. More important, Putnam documented parallel declines in attendance at public meetings and in membership of a wide range of community groups such as parent–teacher associations, League of Women Voters, Elks clubs, and many others. Combined with well-documented erosion of trust in government and political officials (Yankelovich, 1991), these trends and their causes—television is Putnam's favorite culprit, but various other sources of social isolation enter in—may be viewed as general barriers to public participation in metropolitan governance. But there are good reasons not to dismiss quickly either the force of public will in regional development or the potential of increased public involvement in the future of regional governance.

First, there is evidence of increased and more personalized volunteer involvement through some nonprofits and neighborhood groups (Kettering Foundation, 1989). In his reports from around the nation, Peirce (1996) described an increase in civic work, particularly in proliferating neighborhood organizations and development corporations, urban and youth self-help ventures, and regional strategic planning efforts.

Putnam's thoughtful concerns about the erosion of civic and social capital that may be signaled by declines in some forms of personal involvement and association are serious and worth more investigation. Yet these concerns should not overshadow the emergence of new forms of public involvement and civic association "from Internet discussions to hospice support groups to citizen crime control patrols to building friendlier, more walkable neighborhoods" (Peirce, 1996) that suggest far greater potential for public participation in changing regional governance. Particularly impressive increases in civic capacity that could apply to regional governance issues are found in the expanding neighborhood movement and visioning efforts of groups around the country that Berry, Portney, and Thompson (1993) have called evidence of a new "people powered" urban democracy.

Second, many boards and councils responsible for these governments are elected. Even though participation in local elections is often low and many such boards are obscure, they do provide multiple and proximate points of potential access. In addition, as a part of several recent trends, including response to taxpayer revolt sentiments, intergovernmental mandates, and the customer satisfaction emphasis of the reinventing government movement, many local governments are beginning, however grudgingly (Berry, Portney, and Thompson, 1993), to acknowledge the inevitability and desirability of greater public involvement. Research by Henderson (1990) showed an increasing diversity in regional councils of governments (COGs) that parallels empowerment in local governments of traditionally underrepresented populations. In his survey of the nation's COGs, which are sometimes criticized as regional planning bodies lacking the clout of the individual governments they represent, Henderson found increased citizen-oriented task forces and committees; wide variation in the extent to which such devices were integral to the decision making of COG political and technical leaders; a substantially civic, suburban, male, professional, and white participatory profile of COG citizens; and a strong but changing emphasis on demographic, environmental, transportation, and urban and economic development issues.

Finally, substantial research and commentary suggest that in these changing times, within this current U.S. context, reasoned regional change must come from the bottom up. Policy gridlock and not-in-my-backyard (NIMBY) power block change. Metropolitan partnerships need the added strength of incorporation of diverse views and constituents. According to Frug, a regional citizenship like that of the European Union should be cultivated to foster a regional consciousness that can encourage broadening of the regional agenda (Frug, 2002, p. 1766).

Changing Trajectories of Metropolitan Governance

In short, the superficial diagnosis that metro-regions are not governed or not governable is wrong. There is more to governance than government, and there is plenty of both in most urban regions. Over the development of most metro-regions, many important regional public decisions have been made, people have battled city hall and interest groups, and institutions have at times made courageous decisions in the best interest of their regions (see the classic discussion of the evolution of "Government in the Metropolis" in Bollens and Schmandt, 1975). Regional governance is simply not as sustained, coherent, complete, and competent as it could be—a conclusion reached by reformers for some time.

Allan Wallis has provided an excellent historical overview of the evolution of metropolitan areas and attempts to govern them. Most important, he characterized the overall evolution leading to the present state of metropolitan regionalism as pragmatic and incremental, "the triumph of the possible over the theoretical" (1994, p. 9). Change has been step by step, modest, and connected to differences in regional cultures and histories, which explains vast differences in regional governance arrangements. Nevertheless, in his documentation of regional cases, Wallis identified three "waves" of distinct but overlapping reform that correspond to three stages in the evolving social and economic structure of metropolitan areas.

First Stage: Consolidation and Annexation

In the first stage, the region was economically dominated by the central city, and governance patterns followed institutions and issues of big-city politics during the nineteenth and early twentieth centuries. During this period of economic industrialization, a major strategy was territorial expansion and annexation to build large, competitive city-regions. As Table 4.2 shows, it was during this period that some major metropolitan unification and consolidation was initiated and accomplished.

When annexation/unification strategies became limited and less desirable, other options evolved to meet metropolitan governance needs. Primary among these was the development of single-purpose and special districts. Other major governance developments during the latter part of this first wave involved the development of administrative capacity among suburban and small jurisdictions adjacent to central cities and discussion and experimentation with the regional planning commission idea.

Second Stage: Fragmentation

In Wallis's second stage, metro-regions evolved into polycentric structures with certain economic activities dispersed into specialized centers. Arguments from the public-choice school (e.g., Bish and Ostrom, 1973) were employed to rationalize the polycentric (or "balkanization") development and defend fragmentation as a tool for competition and hence better public service. Critics of public choice pointed to severe problems associated with exclusionary zoning, suburban free-ridership, and, as Gulick (1962) emphasized, lack of capacity to deal with region-wide problems. In an interesting comment on the political context of the 1960s, defenders of the polycentric status quo found allies in some minority leaders whose energies were focused on gaining central-city political power. This was despite the segregating consequences of suburban governance of land use and other related zoning-enforcement issues (Wallis, 1994, p. 14).

Thus the second wave of reform was marked by a paucity of major regional government reform and characterized instead by mandatory requirements emanating from federal and state governments. The laws and regulations of this wave focused on procedural approaches aimed at comprehensive planning and coordinated actions. Effects included an increase in the scope and number of COGs, which became a tacit fourth layer of government. By the end of the 1970s and the beginning of federal government withdrawal from urban domestic governance, these initiatives of the second wave seemed to be losing power and focus.

Managing Fragmentation

But withdrawal of many national government incentives has in many regions been replaced by "management of fragmentation" efforts, including reform of strategy and structure of some COGs and planning organizations (see Chapter 6); a modest increase in regional special districts and authorities; and among jurisdictions of regions, continued development and refinement of various forms of informal and formal cooperation including interlocal service contracts, joint powers agreements, and contracting with the private sector (Walker, 1987, p. 16). These and other cooperative arrangements have been adopted by jurisdictions within regions to cope with regional issues in the face of fragmented governments and other institutions. They serve to bridge the second and third waves described by Wallis (1994), and at times—like 911 emergency services and joint use of high investment capital facilities—have proved highly effective.

Third Wave: Responses to New Realities

New realities have fueled the third wave, which is in progress. Wallis (1994, p. 20) cited examples of these new realities from around the United States (including Cleveland, Seattle, Atlanta, Philadelphia, Houston, Denver, Minneapolis-St. Paul, and Phoenix), which are made up of new *capacity factors* and new *demand factors*. The major new *capacity* realities include:

- significantly increased and direct involvement of the private and nonprofit sectors at a regional scale (Lester Salamon's metropolitan studies from the Urban Institute Nonprofit Sector Study, 1987),
- a new type of elected leadership that is more willing to negotiate and partner in efforts to build a metropolitan community (Judd and Parkinson, 1990), and
- increasing use of facilitated decision-making processes to help establish shared visions, resolve conflicts, and develop consensus regarding regional issues.

Demand factors are also a part of the new realities identified by Wallis (1994, p. 22) as enhancing the call for better regional governance. These fall into three strategic areas:

- economic development, specifically within the context of global economic competitiveness;
- allocative concerns related to service delivery, infrastructure development, and now, most urgently, environmental protection; and
- redistributive issues, particularly as aggravated by municipal fiscal disparities.

Regionalism reform in the third wave is seen as driven by these capacity and demand forces, and most were present to some degree during the previous two waves. The difference is in the actual form of regional governance, which is increasingly a function of cross-sector alliances or coalitions, made up of public- and private-sector interests concerning a particular demand.

Major Challenges to Regional Governance Reform

What, if anything, is wrong with the governance arrangements just described that boil down to a system in which an increasing number of individuals and institutions share responsibility while cooperating to develop and sustain networks for governing metroregions? Those who value democratic and pluralistic decision processes can find much value in dispersion of centers of power and responsibility and in processes that bring the contributions of diverse interests and groups together for regional action and policy.

There are signs of a new regional governance process, far more inclusive of institutions beyond local government and their close service—providing nonprofit allies, including universities, media, health institutions, businesses big and small, and regional civic groups. Despite these very positive changes in process and in the expanded universe of "Who governs?" the informed observer (or casual skeptic) must raise at least two questions. Is there still far more conflict than cooperation in regional governance? Are regional governance changes sufficient or occurring at a rapid enough pace to cope with the large-scale, long-range economic, social, environmental, and human problems that threaten to overwhelm many urban regions?

Conflict and Cooperation

Voluntary cooperation and policy networks are often described as key components of regional governance. In most regions, evidence of cooperation abounds *within* some functional areas, such as public safety, and increasingly over certain region-wide problems, including air and water quality, economic development, mass transit, and waste disposal. Voluntary, ad hoc governance has many advantages, including bringing multiple stakeholders into governance and limiting the spread and development of new bureaucracies and is therefore in sync with prescriptions for *governance light* (Melnick and Hall, Chapter 10 of this book). Yet there are real concerns about the link between public accountability and authority that are connected to governance light. Perhaps more fundamentally, how realistic are prescriptions to cooperate and collaborate across the many issues, including such

tough ones as education, housing, social services, and job training and development, facing U.S. regional political systems?

Although the New York region is unique (they all are), many regions may
resonate to the conclusions of Berg and Kantor's (1994) study of the New York
region's 1,700-plus government jurisdictions. Despite more vocal support for
regional cooperation to meet pressing regional needs, including the restructuring
of the economy and its social character, the region continues to be dominated by
the politics of avoidance and conflict, intergovernmental fragmentation, competition, and rivalry. Compared with avoidance and conflict, cooperation has had
limited impacts unless the number of players in the action is limited and the issue
is confined to a single policy area, such as some of the region's mass transit issues
(Berg and Kantor, 1994). Similarly, in a recent examination of cooperation in the
governance of the much different Fort Wayne, Indiana, region, Helmke, Rosentraub,
and McFadden (1994) concluded that intergovernmental cooperation appears to
happen only to achieve clearly specified goals and objectives.

It may be risky to expect too much of intergovernmental cooperation. The
promise and pitfalls of intergovernmental problem solving of regional issues have
been outlined, but this is not easy work and success is often elusive. Perhaps more
important, it is good to remember that conflict in a democracy is not all bad. Conflict
resolution *is* problem solving. The real problem pointed to by Berg and Kantor
(1994) is avoidance of some of the issues most critical to regional development.

Avoidance is an understandable political response in the formal governance
of most regions. First, elected officials of individual jurisdictions are accountable
only to the voters of those jurisdictions. Not surprisingly, they see little advantage
in promoting (much less using precious resources for) regional issues that do not
accrue direct benefits for their jurisdiction. Political parochialism is a major, but not
the sole, culprit. Even those elected officials who seek to advance more far-reaching
and regionally coherent policies often face structural barriers and difficulties.

COGs with rules like "one jurisdiction, one vote" are perfect examples of the structural problem facing regions. Despite the fact that these organizations come closest to
being a region-wide policy voice, they often must avoid the most pressing problems
of the region, particularly those that are most severe for central cities. No matter what
their organization and voting rules, regional organizations with memberships from
area general-purpose governments must choose their battles carefully. The Baltimore
Metropolitan Council, which replaced the Baltimore COG as the premier regional
machine, is viewed as a qualified success by Norris, Stenberg, and Zimmerman (see
Chapter 7 in this book) because it is limited (by decision of its board of executives)
to *those initiatives around which there is unanimity of interest.*

Current Governance Capacity in Metropolitan Regions

Beyond conflict avoidance is the second critical question. Are new regional governance processes and leaders sufficient or developing at a rapid enough pace to

cope with the large-scale, long-range economic and social problems that threaten to overwhelm many regions? Is it reasonable to expect that current coalitions and networks and patchworks of special and general-purpose governments have the capacity to cope with the following three overarching problem areas:

1. *Separate societies and increased segregation.* Much discussed new studies challenge the noble ideal of American egalitarianism by demonstrating growing economic inequality and concentration of wealth and income and wider disparities between highest and lowest income categories (Goldsmith and Blakely, 1992). This problem of increased income and social separation is apparent in many urban regions and fundamental to the "wicked" problems that afflict these centers. The regional governance of the past has had little effect on the creation of "separate societies" within metropolitan America. Changes in the social and economic fabric of many regions have only led to further fragmentation and possibility of conflict. These forces of fragmentation and separation work against the economic demands for regional interdependence articulated by the important contributions of Savitch and Vogel (1994), who, in work supported by Rusk's (1993) book *Cities Without Suburbs,* concluded that self-sufficiency of suburbs "is an impoverished idea."

2. *Changing economic boundaries, markets, and forces.* What is the role of the market in generating and solving regional problems? Is it the hero or villain in the metropolitan movie? To begin, consider the following paradox. Existing local governments have been very responsive to market forces, creating benefits for many individuals, but some contend, also leading to regional conditions that erode U.S. competitiveness in the global economy.

According to Downs (1994), since World War II, America's metropolitan areas have grown and developed in response to widespread personal goals. Downs contended that the American pursuit of these goals over the past fifty years has resulted in a dominant and common vision that has guided metropolitan growth best described as unlimited low-density sprawl. The achievement of the goals Downs described carries a high cost in the form of growth-related problems such as traffic congestion, air pollution, rising taxes for infrastructure, loss of open space, and separation and segregation of the poverty-stricken in inner-city neighborhoods. Downs and others contend that these metropolitan dynamics are the result of natural market forces meeting parochial and limited local government growth management and land-use policies.

Not everyone agrees with this assessment. Some, like Salins (1993), assert that the problems of metropolitan structure and spatial urban sprawl pointed to by Downs are largely due to *market-distorting government* policies and more easily reversed by less intrusive government. Yet either interpretation presents a serious challenge to most metro-regions. To some degree, according to Downs, most American metropolitan areas now face tough choices because of these dynamics.

3. *Policy voids.* Many contend that the most dangerous long-term consequence of prevailing patterns of metropolitan government is that major problems and high-stakes investments are ignored in a perverse pattern that Berg and Kantor have called "the politics of avoidance." In the nation's largest metro-region, New

York, they found the result to be "a system filled with huge policy voids where critical problems of inequality and problems of regional concern remain unattended" (1994, p. 25).

Are regional governance systems able to meet the critical policy needs of the future with shrinking support from national and state governments? Two additional forces affecting all U.S. governments appear to be working toward further fragmentation of metropolitan public policy, the "contract culture" and increased reliance on special districts (Clark and Steward, 1994). Intergovernmental turmoil will affect all metropolitan government options in the near future. One option for states seeking to pursue the goals of economic health and efficient government is substate regionalism. Recent economic problems and political pressures have created renewed interest in this option (Florestano and Wilson-Gentry, 1994; Frug, 2002). These and other big-picture challenges face America's regions. There is good and bad news associated with likely response and resolution. The good news is that all signs point to the increasing importance of mobilizing the significant potential resources of regions to focus on fundamental issues and problems. The bad news is that old patterns of politics and business are slow to change.

Metro-Regional Futures

Regional Metropolitan Reform: What Will It Take?

Because of these forces of change, there is more involved in strengthening metro-region governance than suggested by deliberations about reinventing and/or *restructuring governments*. Recent global economic dynamics combined with examples from Wallis's (1994) third wave of regional reform illustrate significant change and potential for revamping metro-regional governance.

Because of the importance to the national economy of megapolitan regions, which account for over 70 percent of gross domestic product, significant voices urge a new and more effective alignment among the megas and the national government. The America 2050 platform of the Regional Plan Association and its many allies develop specific strategies and formulas for rebuilding megas' infrastructures, developing new energy sources, reducing carbon emissions, and building mega-region rapid rail systems up to world standards (www.America2050.org). Similarly, a recent Brookings Institution report (Katz, 2007, www.blueprintprosperity.org) urges a new "21st Century Compact" between the federal government and large urban regions that reflects "realities of our moment—fast-moving, super-competitive, unpredictable, tumultuous, and metropolitan-led."

Because of the way politics and intergovernmental relations in the United States work, it is likely proposals such as these will not be adopted in total. Yet an effort to move from traditional "silos of public policy" to realign and develop national–local–regional policy collaborations to meet twenty-first century megapolitan, and therefore national economic needs is under way.

It was not many years ago that more significant public issues in regions were settled within jurisdictions by a small but powerful group of businessmen and elected officials who "called the shots" for the region. In contrast, there is now a new and broader leadership that is able, at least some of the time, to retreat from the parochial city competition games and collaborate. New leaders, processes, and old and new networks are fusing with global economic trends and the declining importance of the nation-state to change most American urban regions fundamentally. But what form will change take? How rapidly will the change occur? What effects might the people living in these regions have on its future, on forging genuine self-governance? How will these new urban regions be governed?

Evolution may take too long. The principle to begin with is that locally based *actions* consistent with these larger trends are needed to shape the future and surmount major barriers to development of U.S. urban regions, and build competitive, resilient regions. For many metropolitan areas, this includes overcoming three great disabilities described in *Citistates* (Peirce, Johnson, and Hall, 1993):

1. *A torn social fabric*—illustrated by immense economic and social disparities between a region's affluent suburbs and struggling areas, intensified by differences of race. This condition has worsened in recent years, with severe consequences for the urban economy and society (Goldsmith and Blakely, 1992; Ledebur and Barnes, 1992; Savitch et al., 1992).
2. *The sprawl aftermath*—illustrated by the environmental and economic costs of physical sprawl and the cost of separating jobs from people who need them. Regions have developed without coherence or planning and are now struggling with requirements of the Clean Air Act and the Intermodal Surface Transportation Efficiency Act.
3. *The governance gap*—illustrated by a prevailing lack of coherent regional governance (formal or informal) and the U.S. urban pattern of decision making for the short term, not the long term.

For regions to overcome these hurdles, to be competitive economies, and to become healthy social entities, Peirce, Johnson, and Hall (1993, chapter 8) urged more specific actions. Based on case study examples, they provided a list of guideposts for building cohesive and strong urban regions:

- Recognize the indivisibility of the urban regions.
- Reaffirm the importance of the historic center city.
- Focus on the link between social deprivation and workforce preparedness.
- Spurn defeatism; focus on grassroots community.
- Plan for a multicultural future.
- Build a sense of regional citizenship.
- Remember quality of life issues, including the environment.
- Fight hard for fiscal equity.

- Create work for everyone—even if public money is required.
- Make governance work.
- Undergird governance with a strong citizen organization.
- Plan for a profitable niche in the new world economy.

Downs (1994, chapter 10) also called for regional action. He contended that each metropolitan region needs to follow a series of steps toward new visions of growth and new regional decision-making processes that closely resemble *Citistates'* guideposts. The lists in neither *Citistates* nor *New Visions for Metropolitan America* are intended to be inclusive, fixed formulas for regional success. In both books the authors urged regions to embark on a genuine, inclusive, and long-term visioning process that no doubt will generate different targets, priorities, and governance structures.

These calls for action within general frameworks that redefine—beyond existing political/legal boundaries—the scope and locus of decision making while making participation broader and better are different and new enough to be called paradigm shifts. But the action called for under these general guidelines does not seem as radical in today's regional, economic, and social context as it would have a short time ago. As has been shown, new cooperative and community-building efforts and important changes in regional strategies are under way, which, if sustained, seem headed in the direction of more coherent regional action.

Who will govern American metro regions? The answer to this question extends far beyond legal-constitutional documents and organization charts of governments. "Who will govern?" requires answers to tough questions such as: Who will site regional landfills? Who will match training and education to job development needs? Who will renew the health of regions by focusing on quality-of-life and human development needs? Answers to these questions seem to be, with the thunderous implications for democratic theory, not elites or masses, not one person not one government, but many who understand the power and promise of collaborative regional action. Who will govern? Increasingly, the answer is those who perfect and sustain processes and actions to solve regional problems and build regional community, collaboratively.

Notes

1. The author is grateful to Billie Sandberg for her usual exceptional research assistance and thoughtful counsel. Naturally, the article is the sole responsibility of the author.

2. The Census Bureau makes distinctions between Core Based Statistical Areas (CBSAs), Metropolitan Statistical Areas (MSAs), and Combined Statistical Areas (CSAs). CBSAs are statistical geographic entities comprised of the county or counties that are associated with at least one urbanized area or cluster (the "core") and have a population of at least 10,000 people, plus the adjacent counties, which have a high degree of socioeconomic dependence on the core. MSAs are CBSAs that have at least one urban area that holds a population of 50,000 individuals or more. The Census Bureau considers CSAs as geographic entities consisting of two or more adjacent CBSAs with employment interchange rates of at least fifteen (OMB Federal Register, vol. 65, no. 249, p. 82238).

References

Anderson, Margo J. 1988. *The American Census: A Social History.* New Haven, CT: Yale University Press.

Bachrach, P., and M. Baratz. 1962. "Two Faces of Power." *American Political Science Review* 56: 947–52.

Bahl, R.W.; W. Duncombe; and W. Schulman. 1990. "The New Anatomy of Urban Fiscal Problems." In *The Future of National Urban Policy,* ed. M. Kaplan and F. James, 32–57. Durham, NC: Duke University Press.

Banfield, E.C., and J.Q. Wilson. 1963. *City Politics.* Cambridge, MA: Harvard University Press.

Bellah, R. 1991. *The Good Society.* New York: Knopf.

Berg, B., and P. Kantor. 1994. "The Politics of Avoidance and Conflict: The New York Region." Paper presented at the annual meeting of the American Political Science Association, New York, September, no date.

Berman, D. 2007. "Governance in the Sun Corridor: Where Are We? What Do We Do?" A report for the Morrison Institute, Arizona State University.

Berry, J.M.; K.E. Portney; and K. Thompson. 1993. *The Rebirth of Urban Democracy.* Washington, DC: Brookings Institution.

Bish, R.L., and V. Ostrom. 1973. *Understanding Urban Government: Metropolitan Reform Reconsidered.* Washington, DC: American Enterprise Institute for Public Policy Research.

Bollens, J.C., and H.J. Schmandt. 1975. *The Metropolis, Its People, Politics and Economic Life.* New York: Harper and Row.

Boyte, H.C. 1989. *Commonwealth: A Return to Citizen Politics.* New York: Free Press.

Campbell, B.C. 1995. *The Growth of American Government: Governance from the Cleveland Era to the Present.* Bloomington: Indiana University Press.

Chandler, Tertius, and Gerald Fox. 1974. *3000 Years of Urban Growth.* New York: Academic Press.

Cisneros, H.G., ed. 1993. *Interwoven Destinies: Cities and the Nation.* New York: Norton.

Clark, M., and J. Steward. 1994. "The Local Authority and the New Community Governance." *Regional Studies* 28, no. 2: 201–19.

Dahl, R. 1961. *Who Governs? Democracy and Power in an American City.* New Haven, CT: Yale University Press.

Davies, H.A. 1968. *An Outline History of the World.* 5th ed. London: Oxford University Press.

Dodge, W.R. 1992. "Strategic Intercommunity Governance Networks (Signets of Economic Competitiveness in the 1990s)." *National Civic Review* (Fall/Winter): 403–17.

Downs, A. 1994. *New Visions for Metropolitan America.* Washington, DC: Brookings Institution.

Ehrenhalt, A. 1991. *The United States of Ambition.* New York: Times Books, Random House.

Florestano, P.S., and L. Wilson-Gentry. 1994. "The Acceptability of Regionalism in Solving State and Local Problems." *Spectrum* 67, no. 3: 26–33.

Frug, Gerald E. 2002. "Beyond Regional Government." *Harvard Law Review* 115, no. 7 (May): 1766–830.

Gardner, J.W. 1990. *On Leadership.* New York: Free Press.

Garreau, J. 1991. *Edge Cities: Life on the New Frontier.* New York: Doubleday.

Goldsmith, W.W., and E.J. Blakely. 1992. *Separate Societies: Poverty and Inequality in U.S. Cities.* Philadelphia, PA: Temple University Press.

Gulick, L.H. 1962. *The Metropolitan Problem and American Ideas.* New York: Knopf.

Hall, J.S. 2004. "Who Will Govern American Metropolitan Regions?" In *Metropolitan Governance without Metropolitan Government?* ed. Donald Phares, 7–33. Aldershot, Hampshire: Ashgate.

———. 2008. "Who Will Govern U.S. Megapolitans and How? An Intergovernmental Analysis." Paper presented at the Fourth TransAtlantic Dialogue, Milan, June 12–14.

Helmke, P., and M.S. Rosentraub, with A. McFadden. 1994. "Cooperation and Development in the in the Urban Political Economy of a Small City." Paper presented at the North American Institute for Comparative Urban Research Conference, University of Missouri-St. Louis, June 16–18.

Henderson, L.J. 1990. "Metropolitan Governance: Citizen Participation in the Urban Federation." *National Civic Review* (March/April): 105–17.

Judd, D., and M. Parkinson, eds. 1990. *Leadership and Urban Regeneration: Cities in North America and Europe.* Newbury Park, CA: Sage.

Katz, Bruce. 2007. *A Blueprint for American Prosperity: Unleashing the Potential of a Metropolitan Nation.* Washington DC: Brookings Institution.

Kettering Foundation. 1989. *The Public's Role in the Policy Process: A View from State and Local Policymakers.* Dayton, OH.

———. 1990. *Citizens and Policymakers in Community Forums: Observations from the National Issues Forums.* Dayton, OH.

Lang, Robert E., and D. Dhavale. 2005. "Beyond Megalopolis: Exploring America's New 'Megapolitan' Geography." Metropolitan Institute Census Report Series, 05:01 (July).

Lang, Robert E., and Arthur C. Nelson. 2007. "The Rise of the Megapolitans." *Planning* (January): 7–12.

Ledebur, L.C., and W.R. Barnes. 1992. *Metropolitan Disparities and Economic Growth.* Washington, DC: National League of Cities.

Leland, S., and K. Thurmaier. 2005. "When Efficiency is Unbelievable: Normative Lessons from 30 Years of City-County Consolidations." *Public Administration Review* 65, no. 4: 475–89.

Lineberry, R.L., and E.P. Fowler. 1967. "Reformism and Public Policies in American Cities." *American Political Science Review* 61: 701–16.

Nelkin, D. 1974. *Jetport: The Boston Airport Controversy.* New Brunswick, NJ: Transaction.

Odum, H.W., and H.E. Moore. 1938. *American Regionalism.* New York: Henry Holt.

Ostrom, V.; R. Bish; and E. Ostrom. 1988. *Local Government in the United States.* San Francisco: Institute for Contemporary Studies Press.

Peirce, N. 1996. "America in Civic Decline? Don't Believe It?" *Baltimore Sun,* February 6, 7A.

Peirce, N., with C. Johnson and J.S. Hall. 1993. *Citistates: How Urban America Can Prosper in a Competitive World.* Washington, DC: Seven Locks Press.

Peterson, P.E. 1981. *City Limits.* Chicago: University of Chicago Press.

Putnam, R.D. 2000. *Bowling Alone: The Collapse and Revival of American Community.* New York: Simon and Schuster.

Rusk, D. 1993. *Cities Without Suburbs.* Washington, DC: Johns Hopkins University Press.

Salamon, L.M. 1987. "Partners in Public Service: The Scope and Theory of Government Nonprofit Relations." In *The Nonprofit Sector: A Research Handbook,* ed. W. Powell. New Haven, CT: Yale University Press.

———. 2003. *The Resilient Sector: The State of Nonprofit America.* Washington, DC: Brookings Institution Press.

Salins, P.D. 1993. "Metropolitan Areas: Cities, Suburbs, and the Ties that Bind." In *Interwoven Destinies: Cities and the Nation,* ed. H.G. Cisneros, 147–66. New York: Norton.

Savitch, H.V., and R. Vogel. 1994. "Regional Patterns in a Post City Age, draft." Paper presented at the North American Institute for Comparative Urban Research Conference, University of Missouri-St. Louis, June.

Savitch, H.V. et al. 1992. "Central Cities, Suburbs, and the New Metropolitan Region." Paper prepared for the annual meeting of the American Political Science Association, Chicago.

Stein, R.M. 1990. *Urban Alternatives: Public and Private Markets in the Provision of Local Services*. Pittsburgh, PA: University of Pittsburgh Press.

Svara, J.H. 1990. *Official Leadership in the City: Patterns of Conflict and Cooperation*. New York: Oxford University Press.

Vale, L.J., and T.J. Campanella. 2005. *The Resilient City: How Modern Cities Recover From Disaster*. New York: Oxford University Press.

Walker, D.B. 1987. "Snow White and the 17 Dwarfs: From Metro Cooperation to Governance." *National Civic Review* 76 (January/February): 14–28.

Wallis, A.D. 1994. "Inventing Regionalism—draft." A study by the National Civic League, sponsored by the Carl & Lily Pforzheimer Foundation, September.

Warren, R.; M.S. Rosentraub; and L.F. Weschler. 1992. "Building Urban Governance: An Agenda for the 1990s." *Journal of Urban Affairs* 14, no. 3/4: 399–422.

Yankelovich, D. 1991. *Coming to Public Judgment*. Syracuse, NY: Syracuse University Press.

Yates, D. 1978. *The Ungovernable City: The Politics of Urban Problems and Policy Making*. Cambridge, MA: MIT Press.

5

Moving Toward Regional Governance Incrementally

The St. Louis Case

E. Terrence Jones and Don Phares

The political and fiscal organization of local governments in American metropolitan areas has long been a topic of scrutiny, academic and otherwise. The focus of this chapter is the St. Louis area, which has a long tradition of regional governance reform efforts dating back to the separation of St. Louis City from St. Louis County in 1876.

Reform Using the State Constitution

Provisions in the Missouri Constitution have provided a significant option for regional reform. There have been seven reform attempts, beginning with the separation of the city and county in 1876 and ending with the 1990 Board of Electors. The other significant attempts at reform have used a constitutional amendment route. Two other cases discussed below, the 1930 Metropolitan Federation and the 1962 Borough Plan, involved constitutional amendments to attempt reform in St. Louis.

Regional governance planning in St. Louis has proceeded along two distinct but intertwined paths. The first utilized provisions in the Missouri Constitution that provide the opportunity for more formal and comprehensive reform. This story starts in 1876 and has episodes in the 1920s, 1950s, and 1960s; its latest chapters are in the late 1980s and early 1990s. The second incremental path has had many templates, covered multiple policy areas, and assumed many forms (see Chapter 3). Its tale begins in the 1950s and continues to the present day.

Separation of the City from the County: The "Great Divorce"

By 1876 St. Louis City was a large city in a rural county that had very sparse population and limited commercial business activity and tax base. This produced pressure for the city to separate itself from the county and avoid the financial burden of supporting the county. The relationship between these governments had been characterized by "uninterrupted controversy" since the early 1860s (Cassella, 1959, p. 87). Separation was increasingly advanced as a better solution than consolidation or reorganization (ibid., p. 91).

With the constitutional convention in 1875 the city-county relationship was at the forefront. The convention adopted a provision that authorized separation. The new constitution was approved in late 1875. Using the new constitution, a Board of Freeholders was elected in early 1876 with a specific mandate to prepare a plan for the separation for voter approval. It was passed, after considerable controversy, on October 22, 1876. The city was "emancipated," and its size was increased from about eighteen to sixty-one square miles, an area deemed to be more than adequate for future growth.

One of the problems with the new constitution was that it contained no provision for any subsequent adjustment of city-county borders; they were fixed. By the early 1900s it was obvious that the city and county were becoming a unified urban area, with interrelated problems, but there was no way to deal with the regional issues due to the formal separation.

It is from this historical setting that the following Board of Freeholders proposals emerged to deal with the shortsightedness of the "great divorce." Ironically, this later planning for regional governance emerged out of the 1876 plan that was its antithesis.

Consolidation Under City Government: 1926

Following the city-county separation, it became more obvious that this might well have been a mistake and some type of merger might be appropriate. The city approached the change arrogantly. To correct this deficiency, deliberations began in 1922 to change the constitution. An amendment passed easily in November 1924 in the city, county, and statewide. It had three options:

1. The city would extend its limits to include the entire county,
2. The county would extend its limits to include the city, which could then extend its limits under existing law, and
3. The city could annex part of the county under the exclusive jurisdiction of the city.

On June 25, 1925, a Board of Freeholders was convened and held its first meeting. In March 1926, a plan was introduced (Board of Freeholders, 1926; Jones, 2000) that:

*   made the city charter the governing document for the new area,
*   eliminated all county offices and placed them under city control,
*   transferred all county property to the city,
*   eliminated all municipalities in the county,

- put the city police department in control of the entire new area, and
- abolished all county school districts, putting them under city school board control.

De facto it was a reentry or annexation but dominated and controlled by the city. County representatives on the board were outraged and presented counterproposals. However, through political machinations, the plan was accepted and placed on the ballot for October 26, 1926. It passed overwhelmingly in the city (by 87 percent) but failed in the county (by 67 percent).

A Metropolitan Federation: 1930

After a period to let things calm down after the turmoil surrounding the 1926 plan, interest was reignited in a cooperative endeavor between the chambers of commerce in the city and county. It was proposed to amend the Missouri Constitution to form an overarching metropolitan government to be called "Greater St. Louis." Trying to avoid the flawed equal membership requirement of the Board of Freeholders process, a statewide vote for a constitutional amendment was proposed and placed on the ballot for November 1930. However, the concerns from the 1926 proposal remained and it was defeated statewide. While it did pass narrowly in the city, it lost in the county (Jones, 2000, pp. 69–70).

The Metropolitan Sewer District: 1954

The fact that water naturally seeks a lower level, flowing from the county to the city, resulted in another Board of Freeholders in 1953. Beginning in the mid-1800s with a serious cholera epidemic, it became obvious by the early 1950s that treatment of sewage in the county was having a serious impact on the city. The county had a myriad of treatment facilities including fifteen municipal systems, twenty-four sewer districts, seventy-five subdivision systems, and thousands of septic tanks (Jones, 2000, p. 105).

In this context the Bi-State Development Agency conducted an engineering study of sewer needs in the county. The findings indicated the following (Metropolitan St. Louis Survey, 1957a, p. 68):

- there was a serious sewer problem in both the city and county,
- the health hazards were area-wide,
- the sewer problems could not be handled separately since the urbanized area of the county drained through into the city, and
- piecemeal efforts failed because they covered less than an entire watershed and had inadequate resources to address the issue.

The solution was to establish a special purpose district, the Metropolitan St. Louis Sewer District (MSD), which would include the city and the urbanized portion of the county. Reception at the polls was strongly positive (Jones, 2000, p. 107). The MSD was established in 1954. Later, in 1977, most of the remaining parts of the county were added to the MSD by an overwhelming positive vote.

A Metropolitan Transit District: 1955

In 1949, the Bi-State Development Agency was established to deal with transportation issues in the bi-state region. Bi-State was, as Jones (2000, p. 97) put it, a "governmental wimp." It had empowerment to deal with area transportation issues but no authority to tax or to do much else except "make plans." It could not set or implement policies.

In 1952, the question of who should own and operate public transit became an issue for the region. More than fifteen companies provided transit services. Out of this chaotic environment came a proposal for another Board of Freeholders (Metropolitan St. Louis Transit District, 1955) to deal with current and emerging transportation problems. A board was appointed in the spring of 1953 but was plagued by a lack of interest and attention, both pro and con.

This board decided to delay the issue of ownership of transit facilities and focus on control over the power to set fares being shifted from the state Public Service Commission to the new "Metropolitan St. Louis Transit District." This fledgling measure avoided the crucial issue of public ownership and satisfied virtually no one. Voter turnout was extremely light, 10 percent of city voters and 8 percent county. It was defeated by only 3,099 votes in the city and 2,110 in the county (*St. Louis Globe Democrat,* January 26, 1955, p. 1; Jones, 2000, pp. 96–99).

A Metropolitan St. Louis District: 1959

Over the more than three decades since the previous comprehensive look at the St. Louis area's governmental structure in 1926, the nation had gone through the Great Depression and World War II. Attention now shifted back to the region and its existing and emerging problems. This began with a large-scale study that examined the needs and problems of the St. Louis region. The Metropolitan St. Louis Survey project issued two reports (1957a, 1957b), which discussed metropolitan issues in great depth.

Two conflicting proposals were considered. The first was a metropolitan district that would deal with seven major functional areas. The second was a merger of the city and county into an entity called the "municipal county." The vote from the board on the plan was highly disputed but finally emerged as ten for the district and nine for the municipal merger (later called the Borough Plan).

The plan proposed by the 1959 Board of Freeholders was called the "Greater St. Louis City-County District." Specified for this district was the following set of functions (Metropolitan Board of Freeholders, 1959, pp. i–ii):

- establish and maintain a system of arterial roads, expressways, and major streets;

- regulate mass transit including fares, routing and schedules, traffic lanes, and other means of encouraging use of such facilities;
- take over the Metropolitan Sewer District established in 1954;
- organize civil defense under one central administration;
- encourage establishment of industrial locations to attract new business;
- engage in comprehensive area-wide planning; and
- coordinate a centralized police communication and reporting system.

In addition the plan could be amended to include "additional services" (not defined in the plan) when approved by a majority of voters in both areas. The plan was put on the ballot on November 3, 1959, and lost by large margins. The closeness of the split on the board—ten in favor of the district and nine for merger—led quickly to another proposal.

The Borough Plan: 1962

Out of the consternation surrounding the 1959 District plan, movement began immediately to draft a constitutional amendment to consolidate the city and county. It was essentially the same proposal put forth by the minority in the 1959 District proposal. However, it was decided to use a constitutional amendment process, as was done in 1930, rather than a Board of Freeholders. It was feared that once put in place a board might decide to adopt a different plan than the borough plan that was defeated by just one vote in the 1959 District plan. It would require statewide voter approval.

The new governmental entity was to be known as the Municipal County of St. Louis and would consolidate all governmental entities in both the city and county fulfilling the dual role of city and county. It would include cities, towns, villages, fire protection districts, the Metropolitan Sewer District, all other sewer districts, public water supply districts, and all other municipal corporations. School districts, however, were excluded.

The Municipal County would consist of twenty-two boroughs. Eight would be within the city, seven within the county, and the remaining seven would straddle the city-county border. The purpose here was to give the assurance that the city was not just swallowing up the county.

This plan was to become even more heated than the District plan proposed in 1959. Opposition emerged from all sides, and the Borough Plan constitutional amendment was heavily defeated. The results were viewed as a strong statement that consolidation (read merger) was not "the way" to solve city-county problems (Sengstock et al., 1964).

The St. Louis County Story

When voters approved the separation of the city of St. Louis from St. Louis County in 1876, there were only five incorporated cities in the county. By 1955 the number had expanded to ninety-six.

In commenting on the situation that had evolved since 1876, the Metropolitan St. Louis Survey noted in 1957 the following continuing problems for the St. Louis area. Fifty years later the list reflects not only the past but an almost prescient account of the present (1957a, pp. 83–85):

- wide disparities in the number and extent of public services provided,
- substantial variation in tax base to finance essential services,
- some essential area-wide services are inadequate,
- some communities have failed to recognize a responsibility to the entire urban area,
- competition among municipalities to increase their potential tax resources impedes planning for the entire area,
- growth will occur in unincorporated county areas and ad hoc annexations and incorporations will not provide an adequate solution,
- the county will have to provide an increasing amount of municipal services to unincorporated county residents.

Reform and the Power of the Budget

Presently, ninety-one cities exist in the county (see Map 5.1). They provide municipal services to almost 700,000 county residents, more than two-thirds of the total county population. Unincorporated portions of the county receive municipal-type services from county government. Several issues emerge from this organization.

First, in addition to providing all county functions, the county is also the largest single provider of municipal services. This requires an appropriate resource base for this dual responsibility. With the increased pace of annexations and incorporations, the tax base available to the county deteriorated.

Second, population for the present ninety-one municipalities ranges from the Village of Champ with 12 residents to Florissant with 53,948; two have less than 100 people, twenty-two cities have fewer than 1,000, twenty-one have more than 10,000, and only ten have a population in excess of 20,000.

Third, the local resource base available to support municipal services is distributed very unevenly among the existing incorporated areas. The result is vast differences in both the quantity and quality of services and a necessity in many instances for compromise on basic services.

Fourth, resource base disparities have been worsened by "land grab" annexation and incorporation activity. The most financially well-endowed areas of unincorporated county were being absorbed whenever possible. This leaves those areas (predominantly residential, often poorer) with fewer resources for the county to provide services, as diminishing resources allow, or for the residents to fend for themselves.

Map 5.1 **St. Louis County Municipalities**

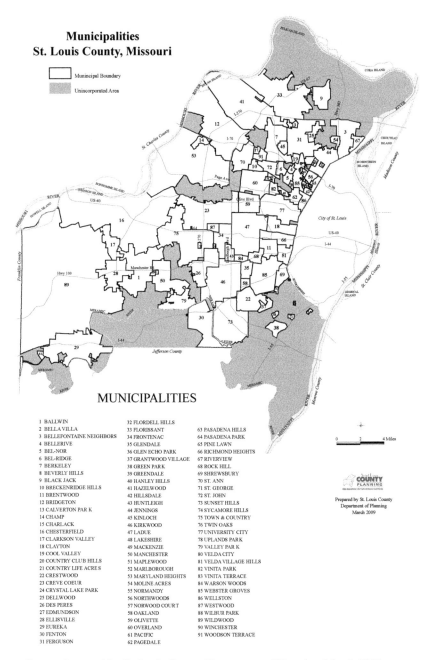

Municipalities
St. Louis County, Missouri

MUNICIPALITIES

1 BALLWIN	32 FLORDELL HILLS
2 BELLA VILLA	33 FLORISSANT
3 BELLEFONTAINE NEIGHBORS	34 FRONTENAC
4 BELLERIVE	35 GLENDALE
5 BEL-NOR	36 GLEN ECHO PARK
6 BEL-RIDGE	37 GRANTWOOD VILLAGE
7 BERKELEY	38 GREEN PARK
8 BEVERLY HILLS	39 GREENDALE
9 BLACK JACK	40 HANLEY HILLS
10 BRECKENRIDGE HILLS	41 HAZELWOOD
11 BRENTWOOD	42 HILLSDALE
12 BRIDGETON	43 HUNTLEIGH
13 CALVERTON PAR K	44 JENNINGS
14 CHAMP	45 KINLOCH
15 CHARLACK	46 KIRKWOOD
16 CHESTERFIELD	47 LADUE
17 CLARKSON VALLEY	48 LAKESHIRE
18 CLAYTON	49 MACKENZIE
19 COOL VALLEY	50 MANCHESTER
20 COUNTRY CLUB HILLS	51 MAPLEWOOD
21 COUNTRY LIFE ACRE S	52 MARLBOROUGH
22 CRESTWOOD	53 MARYLAND HEIGHTS
23 CREVE COEUR	54 MOLINE ACRES
24 CRYSTAL LAKE PARK	55 NORMANDY
25 DELLWOOD	56 NORTHWOODS
26 DES PERES	57 NORWOOD COURT
27 EDMUNDSON	58 OAKLAND
28 ELLISVILLE	59 OLIVETTE
29 EUREKA	60 OVERLAND
30 FENTON	61 PACIFIC
31 FERGUSON	62 PAGEDALE

63 PASADENA HILLS
64 PASADENA PARK
65 PINE LAWN
66 RICHMOND HEIGHTS
67 RIVERVIEW
68 ROCK HILL
69 SHREWSBURY
70 ST. ANN
71 ST. GEORGE
72 ST. JOHN
73 SUNSET HILLS
74 SYCAMORE HILLS
75 TOWN & COUNTRY
76 TWIN OAKS
77 UNIVERSITY CITY
78 UPLANDS PARK
79 VALLEY PAR K
80 VELDA CITY
81 VELDA VILLAGE HILLS
82 VINITA PARK
83 VINITA TERRACE
84 WARSON WOODS
85 WEBSTER GROVES
86 WELLSTON
87 WESTWOOD
88 WILBUR PARK
89 WILDWOOD
90 WINCHESTER
91 WOODSON TERRACE

Prepared by St. Louis County
Department of Planning
March 2009

Source: Prepared by St. Louis County, Department of Planning, March 2009.

What Scope for Metropolitan Government?

Release of an Advisory Commission on Intergovernmental Relations report (ACIR, 1988) brought again into focus the question of government organization in metropolitan areas. This report documented in great detail the innovative arrangements undertaken in St. Louis to respond to service needs.

Working within a public choice framework, the ACIR reports praised the creativity of public entrepreneurs and part-time officials in small cities. A myriad of service contracts, cooperative arrangements, informal agreements, shared systems, local associations, and volunteer officials provided the glue that binds together this complexity of local jurisdictions (see Chapter 3 for other examples).

In a planning context, one completes a reading of the ACIR report with the overpowering sense that:

- this is the way local government should operate;
- smaller, and implicitly more, is better; and
- the free market in governmental organization should be allowed to operate absent concern for the overall area-wide implications.

Release of the ACIR report on St. Louis coincided to the month (September) with the formal submission of a plan for a comprehensive governmental and fiscal reorganization within the county. There is stark contrast between the findings of this ACIR report (1988) and the provisions in the *Plan for Governmental Reorganization in St. Louis & St. Louis County* (Board of Freeholders, 1988a). The ACIR report praised the existing governmental arrangement, noting in conclusion: "The experience of the St. Louis area in metropolitan organization *has much* to teach the rest of metropolitan America" (ACIR, 1988, p. 168; emphasis added). In stark contrast, the Board of Freeholders (1988a), proposed a plan for a major restructuring for all county, municipal, and fire and emergency medical services (EMS) in St. Louis County. For reasons why metropolitan government probably will not emerge, see Chapter 2 in this volume.

Major Countywide Reform: 1987

Section 30(a) of the state constitution designates five types of reform that could be considered. The first three relate to reentry or merger between St. Louis City and St. Louis County. The fourth addresses the formation of an area-wide district(s) and was put in place in 1945. The fifth option was added to the constitution by a statewide referendum in 1966. It is very broad in scope and allows the board "to formulate and adopt *any other* plan for the partial or complete government of all or any part of the city and the county" (emphasis added).

Under the purview of the fifth option, a new Board of Freeholders was set up to delve into the myriad issues pertaining to local government organization within

St. Louis County. While this option provides constitutional authority to propose the restructuring of any and all local governments, including school districts and special districts, the board made a conscious decision to focus only on county and municipal issues. Such a focus also mandated an examination of fire-EMS services because twenty of the forty-three county providers of fire protection and EMS were municipal departments.

The board's focus on municipal and county government organization and finance derived directly from the adverse fiscal environment that had been evolving for decades. A context for its work was provided by several studies, one of which posed an intriguing question for the title of its final report, *Too Many Governments?* (Confluence St. Louis, 1987). After long and careful deliberation, this board developed several premises that guided its deliberations and the formulation of its plan.

First, the nearly 400,000 residents of unincorporated portions of the county generally were being inadequately served by the county's provision of municipal services. The complete incorporation of the county was proposed as a solution to this problem.

Second and related, it was proposed that county government no longer provide any municipal services; this responsibility would vest with newly created cities. This removed a situation where the county was responsible for providing both municipal and county services to the same area but where varying provision levels of the municipal-type services were often the case. As a guiding premise for this proposal a clear delineation of functional service responsibility between city and county was developed (Board of Freeholders, 1988b, pp. A1–A2).

Third, a structure was proposed within which all residents of the county would have access to adequate, basic municipal and fire-EMS services. During its lengthy deliberations, the board determined that the highly fragmented local government structure and associated large revenue base disparities produced an environment in which adequate public services were not available to all county residents.

Fourth, it was obvious that adequate financial resources must be made available to support municipal, county, and fire-EMS services. Documented vast differences in available public resources and service levels mandated a plan that would realign existing resources and also allow for the provision of additional resources as necessary. The prevailing concern was the need to guarantee basic service provision to all residents of the county, no matter where they lived, and to provide sufficient financing to accomplish this objective.

Fifth, an "end state" plan with clearly defined municipal and fire-EMS boundaries was specified rather than adopting a "process" or more step-by-step, incremental approach. The board's standing was to provide as much certainty as possible that the new governmental structure would incorporate the entire county and provide adequate resources to finance the reformulated county government, the proposed new cities, and the new fire-EMS districts.[1] The outcome was thirty-seven new municipalities, as shown in Map 5.2, and four fire-EMS districts covering the entire county. A detailed fiscal profile for each new city and the reconfigured county

Map 5.2 **Final Freeholders Thirty-Seven-City Proposal**

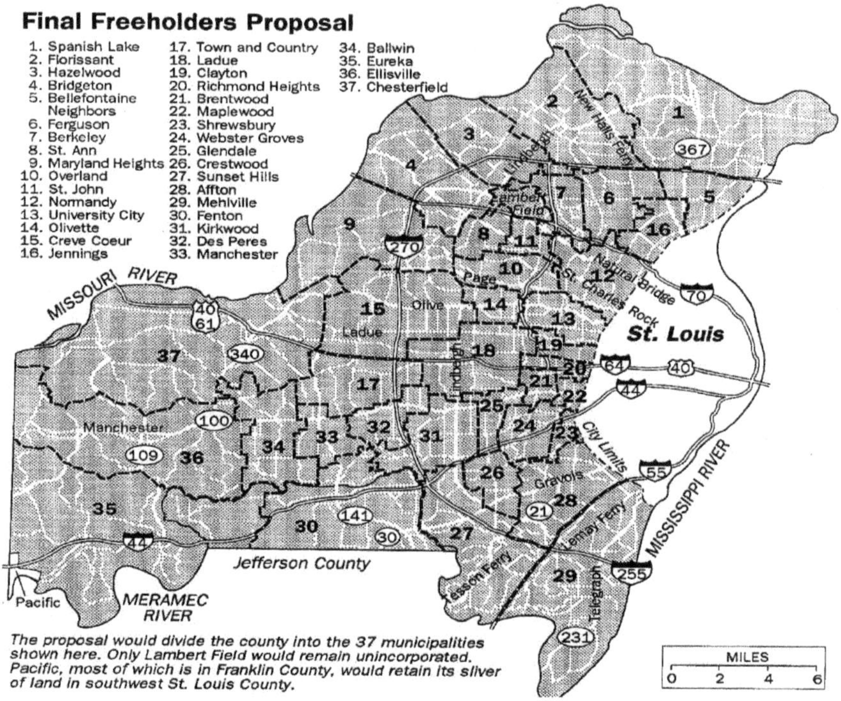
Final Freeholders Proposal
1. Spanish Lake
2. Florissant
3. Hazelwood
4. Bridgeton
5. Bellefontaine Neighbors
6. Ferguson
7. Berkeley
8. St. Ann
9. Maryland Heights
10. Overland
11. St. John
12. Normandy
13. University City
14. Olivette
15. Creve Coeur
16. Jennings
17. Town and Country
18. Ladue
19. Clayton
20. Richmond Heights
21. Brentwood
22. Maplewood
23. Shrewsbury
24. Webster Groves
25. Glendale
26. Crestwood
27. Sunset Hills
28. Affton
29. Mehlville
30. Fenton
31. Kirkwood
32. Des Peres
33. Manchester
34. Ballwin
35. Eureka
36. Ellisville
37. Chesterfield
MISSOURI RIVER
St. Louis
MISSISSIPPI RIVER
MERAMEC RIVER
Jefferson County
Pacific
City Limits
MILES
0 2 4 6

The proposal would divide the county into the 37 municipalities shown here. Only Lambert Field would remain unincorporated. Pacific, most of which is in Franklin County, would retain its sliver of land in southwest St. Louis County.

Source: St. Louis County Planning Department, 1987.

government was prepared to document an adequate balance between revenue and expenditure needs (Board of Freeholders, 1988b).The proposed new cities ranged in population from 6,400 to 78,200 with only five having less than 10,000 residents; the average population was about 27,000.

The board's plan was to incorporate the entire county into the new cities (Map 5.2) Most of the proposed new cities were derived using an existing city (or cities) as a core; six new cities, however, were formed primarily from then large unincorporated portions of the county.

As a pivotal component, the fiscal plan realigned municipal finances so that each of the new cities would have a revenue base that would allow it to provide adequate public services. The same procedure was followed for the reformulated county government that would now have the responsibility for providing only county-type service following the clear division of functional service responsibility discussed above (Board of Freeholders, 1988b, pp. A1–A2).

The fiscal component of the reorganization plan contained four major elements. First, a newly implemented 1 percent countywide earnings tax on wages, salaries, and business profits, fashioned after that already long in existence in St. Louis City (and Kansas City), would fund county government and the majority of fire-EMS services. It would also provide funding for a new revenue-sharing pool to be used for municipal resource equalization and infrastructure needs.

Second, a new 6 percent gross receipts tax on nonresidential utilities (gas, electric, water, and telephone) would provide additional revenue to each of the new cities. Third, all general sales tax collections in the county would be distributed on a 25 percent point-of-sale and 75 percent per capita (pool) basis. No longer would any city retain all sales taxes generated within its boundaries. Finally, reliance on the property tax would be substantially reduced. For the entire current operations portion of county government it would be eliminated.

Several objectives were accomplished by this plan. All municipal services would be provided by a city not by the county. The fiscal portion of the plan would balance resources with needs, and provisions for future revenue growth potential would be enhanced through reliance on a sales and income tax base rather than on property. Each city government and the county government would be fiscally enabled to deliver adequate basic services to its residents. In addition, adequate fire-EMS protection would now be available throughout the county.

Legal Challenges

During the process of its work, the legal status of the Board of Freeholders, and eventually of its plan, was considered by a variety of courts. These included the Federal District Court, the State Circuit Trial Court, the United States Court of Appeals for the Eighth Circuit, and the Missouri Supreme Court. Each court considered the interpretation of "freeholder" as requiring property ownership status as a prerequisite for board appointment. This had been questioned and challenged by a variety of groups as denial of equal protection under the U.S. Constitution because it excluded those who did not own property. After a long series of legal machinations, the board's constitutional status was upheld by the Missouri Supreme Court upon referral from the U.S. Court of Appeals.

The legal battle, however, did not stop there. On February 21, 1989, in a one-line order, the U.S. Supreme Court agreed to review the Missouri Supreme Court's decision in its fall session that was to begin *after* the already scheduled vote on the Board of Freeholders' plan. The final outcome of these myriad legal deliberations remained for the highest court of the land to determine.

The board had completed its work, all nineteen members signed the plan, and it was filed formally with the city and county Boards of Election Commissioners for submission to the voters in each area. The Board of Freeholders went out of existence on September 16, 1988. The voters would have exercised their prerogative on June 20, 1989, with a simple "yes" or "no" on the entire 155-page plan. The U.S. Supreme Court action delayed any vote pending its decision.

After a lengthy process of legal proceedings, as outlined above, the question of the constitutionality of the Board of Freeholders was granted *certiorari* by the U.S.

Supreme Court, on appeal from the Supreme Court of Missouri. The U.S. Supreme Court reversed the Missouri Supreme Court in a unanimous vote. It argued that the land ownership requirement for selection to the Board of Freeholders violated the equal protection clause of the U.S. Constitution (*Quinn v. Millsap,* 491 U.S. 95 [1989]).

This decision invalidated the Board of Freeholders, so no vote was held. Given the U.S. Supreme Court decision, the option of dealing with these issues through Article VI, Section 30 of the Missouri Constitution was now in question. The U.S. Supreme Court did not indicate any changes, remediation, or removal in its decision. The Missouri Supreme Court heard arguments on January 3, 1990, as to whether this section of the Missouri Constitution should remain intact, with "freeholder" clearly interpreted to be qualified elector not property owner, or whether it should be deleted from the constitution as a result of the U.S. Supreme Court decision.

The Missouri Court decided to leave this section of the Missouri Constitution in tact and to interpret "freeholder" to mean qualified elector. As a part of its decision it also required immediate appointment of a new board, a "Board of Electors," to prepare a new plan. With the legal status of the Missouri constitutional provision now settled by the U.S. and Missouri Supreme Courts, a new board could now revisit the plethora of problems and issues that had been discussed over the past 100-plus years.

The Board of Electors Plan: 1990

A Board of Electors began its work in July 1990. During its yearlong deliberations it considered a wide range of plans and ideas emanating from past proposals, including " . . . the formation of a single county government structure for the city and county" (Board of Electors, 1991, p. 2). However, it came up with two rather weak and narrow proposals: (1) establish a Metropolitan Economic Development Commission and (2) create a Metropolitan Park Commission. The Metropolitan Economic Development Commission would " . . . finance programs which will create, attract, retain, expand, develop, improve and enhance employment opportunities within the city and county" (ibid., pp. 5–6).

The Metropolitan Park Commission would " . . . govern, administer, repair, maintain, conserve, sustain, protect and improve any and all Commission Parks" (ibid., p. 24). De facto, only the 1,300-acre Forest Park in the city would be under its purview unless expanded authority and funding were approved by voters.

The final Board of Electors plan was placed on the ballot on April 7, 1992, and was defeated by voters.

Planning for Regionalism: An Incremental Perspective

If one examines the St. Louis area's attempts to govern more regionally primarily using comprehensive planning proposals such as governmental consolidation or multifunctional districts, the results show only failure (see some of the general reasons in Chapter 2). The 1954 Board of Freeholders has been the only such post-1876 group to secure approval, and it dealt with a single service: sanitary and storm water sewers.

Because St. Louis has high local governmental multiplicity, much of it rooted in self-interest and parochialism, because so many consolidation attempts have been proposed, only to fail at the ballot box or in the courts, and because the conventional wisdom among most civic leaders and the local media has been to decry localism and promote consolidation, St. Louis itself and the metropolitan planning reform community more generally have made the area the poster region for fragmentation.

The preoccupation with failed major reform plans has obscured the slow, in-cremental movement toward regionalism in the St. Louis area over the past half century. Starting with the establishment of the Metropolitan Sewer District in 1954 there has been increasing intercounty cooperation. Until recently, almost all of it occurred between the area's two largest jurisdictions—St. Louis County and the city of St. Louis. Over the past decade, however, efforts have encompassed a broader geographical area.

Cooperation has involved many service areas and taken on many forms. The services include sanitary and solid waste, education, cultural institutions and the arts, transportation, public safety, tourism, parks and open space, sports venues, economic development, and health care for the indigent. The forms include various types of public authorities, special purpose districts, intergovernmental agreements, cooperative arrangements, and umbrella organizations.

Governmental Cooperation: 1954–2006

Table 5.1 lists most of the major intercounty governance arrangements developed over the past fifty years. (See Map 5.3 on page 94 for location in the sixteen-county metropolitan area.) One could add more items to this list, mutual aid agreements between fire departments would be one example, but the point is clear: there has been an average of one intercounty institutional agreement every two years. The table does not list some attempts that have failed, such as unsuccessful efforts to add the St. Louis Symphony to the Zoo-Museum District (1989) and establishing a multi-county amateur sports district (1992).

What are some of the themes underlying these collaborations? Most obvious and least surprising is that a vast majority are distributive rather than redistribu-tive (Lowi, 1972). In Williams and Adrian's analogous but somewhat distinct taxonomy (1963), they are system maintenance items. The economic enterprise centers, more commonly called incubators, the sewer district, and the joint justice information system are key examples. All these constitute the "low-hanging fruit" for regional cooperation.

But what initially appears devoid of redistribution is not always so. For example,

92

Table 5.1

Multi-County Governance in the St. Louis Area, 1954–Present

Sanitary waste/storm water/solid waste		
Metropolitan Sewer District	City of St. Louis and St. Louis County	1954
St. Louis-Jefferson Solid Waste Management District	City of St. Louis, St. Louis County, Jefferson County, St. Charles County	1991
Education		
St. Louis Community College District	City of St. Louis and St. Louis County	1961
Southwestern Illinois College	Madison County and St. Clair County	1985
Cooperating School Districts	Most counties	1964
Cultural institutions and the arts		
Zoo-Museum District: Zoo, Art Museum, Science Center	City of St. Louis and St. Louis County	1971
Zoo-Museum District: Missouri Botanical Garden	City of St. Louis and St. Louis County	1983
Zoo-Museum District: Missouri History Museum	City of St. Louis and St. Louis County	1987
Regional Arts Commission	City of St. Louis and St. Louis County	1984
Public safety		
Major Case Squad	Ten counties	1965
Regional Justice Information System	Eight counties	1975

Transportation		
Bi-State Development Agency/Metro	City of St. Louis, St. Louis County, St. Clair County	1950, then expanded in the 1960s
Lambert International Airport	City of St. Louis, St. Louis County, St. Charles County	Originally City of St. Louis, then representation expanded in the 1980s and 1990s
East West Gateway Council of Governments	Eight counties	1965
Metropolitan Taxi Commission	City of St. Louis and St. Louis County	2003
Tourism and sports venues		
Convention and Visitors Commission	City of St. Louis and St. Louis County	1984
Edward D. Jones Dome	City of St. Louis and St. Louis County	1990
Busch Stadium III	City of St. Louis and St. Louis County	2006
Parks and open space		
Great Rivers Greenway	City of St. Louis, St. Louis County, St. Charles County	2000
Metro East Park and Recreation District	Madison County and St. Clair County	2000
Health care for the indigent		
Regional Medical Center	City of St. Louis and St. Louis County	1985–1997
St. Louis ConnectCare	City of St. Louis and St. Louis County	1997
Regional Health Commission	City of St. Louis and St. Louis County	2001
Economic Development		
St. Louis enterprise centers	City of St. Louis and St. Louis County	1991
Greater St. Louis Economic Development Council	Five counties	1994
Greater St. Louis Regional Empowerment Zone	City of St. Louis, St. Louis County, St. Clair County	1998

Map 5.3   **St. Louis Metropolitan Statistical Area (MSA)**

16 County MSA Region

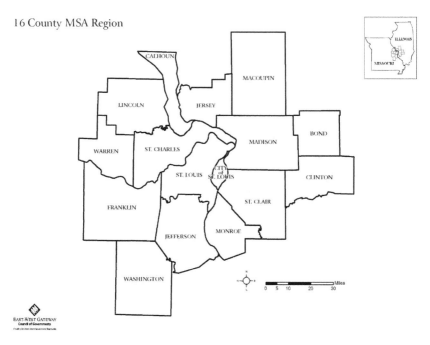

Source: East-West Gateway Council of Governments.

the two major original entities within the Zoo-Museum District (ZMD), the St. Louis Zoo and the Saint Louis Art Museum, were city of St. Louis agencies prior to the 1971 establishment of the ZMD and the adoption of a common property tax levy in the city of St. Louis and St. Louis County. In 1971, each jurisdiction's assessed valuation was about the same. In 2007, the county's valuation is about 80 percent of the total, meaning that two entities physically located in the poorer city of St. Louis receive about four-fifths of their tax support from the wealthier county.

Second, learning occurs. Regional creep happens. For example, Lambert International Airport is located in St. Louis County but is owned by the city of St. Louis. In the 1980s, the city acknowledged the county's stake by giving it representation on the airport's board. In the 1990s, recognizing that landing patterns affect St. Charles County to the west, it gave that jurisdiction board representation.

Next, political third rails are avoided. Race is a major fault line in St. Louis-area politics and, with the partial exception of health care for the indigent, has not been an issue in any of the successful ventures. One of the reasons an 1992 attempt to shift Forest Park, then (and now) the city of St. Louis's major gathering place, from being owned and operated by the city to a joint city-county district was the fear among many city African-Americans that the move would constitute a white takeover of "their park."

Fourth, devising intercounty arrangements over time lessens the transaction costs for any single deal. Feiock (2004, 2007) points out that the benefits of any collective action should exceed the costs of putting it together. In a midsized region like St. Louis (during this fifty-year period it went from just under 2 million to about 2.8 million) with a relatively low turnover rate in civic leadership, it does get easier (but not absolutely easy) over time. The Missouri Botanical Garden and the Missouri History Museum joining the ZMD are two examples. Over this period, the region has developed a cadre of regional brokers, lawyers, academics, public relationists, political aides, and civic do-gooders who have been there, done that, and are keen to try again.

Fifth, contrary to Feiock's (2007, p. 55) assertion that "in theory suburbs should be willing to join collective action that assists the central city out of a desire to protect their own financial well-being (but) nevertheless each has a self-interested incentive to withhold contributions and free ride on those of others, with the results that no one engages in the conduct from which all would benefit," for the past twenty-five years the more affluent and larger St. Louis County has repeatedly joined with the poorer and smaller city on several fronts. Why? Partially because of enlightened self-interest explicitly acknowledged in statements by several St. Louis county executives. Partially because of civic leadership pressure for the county to do its "fair share" for the region. Partially—and perhaps more subtly—because of the county's desire to be seen as the prevailing regional player, not second banana to the city's elected leadership who still garner much more media attention.

Sixth, crises, real or manufactured, help. Lose a National Football League franchise to Phoenix (the Cardinals)—build a venue to attract another one (the Rams). Defense cuts generate massive layoffs (McDonnell Douglas, now Boeing)—develop a coordinated economic development strategy (Greater St. Louis Economic Development Council). Falling behind in the race for conventioneers—combine and increase marketing funding (Convention and Visitors Commission).

Incremental Regionalism: Sanitation and Solid Waste

Sanitary and Storm Water Sewers

The formation of the Metropolitan Sewer District was described earlier. The district's original boundaries contained the entire city of St. Louis but less than half the acreage in St. Louis County. As the county more than doubled in population over the next two decades, causing a similar increase in the amount of urbanized land, most of the remaining portions of the county voted to join the MSD in 1977.

The city of St. Louis mayor and the St. Louis county executive each appoint three trustees who serve four-year terms. Reinforcing cooperation is a charter requirement that any action receive concurrent majorities from each jurisdiction's trustees.

The MSD's redistributive potential was severely limited during its first forty-six years by a charter provision that all capital improvements must be paid exclusively by "those lots or parcels of ground . . . as are benefited by said construction, improvement, or extension." Originally included in 1954 largely to protect city taxpayers from footing the bill to modernize the expanding county's sewers, it later became a broader ban on using more affluent property taxing potential to pick up the tab for impoverished areas. In November 2000, however, city and county voters amended the MSD charter to allow district-wide bonds, thereby removing the redistributive barrier.

Solid Waste

Following authorizing legislation passed by the Missouri General Assembly in 1989, the city of St. Louis, St. Louis County, and Jefferson County passed joint ordinances in 1991 establishing the St. Louis-Jefferson Solid Waste Management District. In 2002, St. Charles County joined, so that presently the district's population approaches 2 million. Each member jurisdiction's governing body appoints members of the district's advisory board. The district receives a tipping fee from waste taken to landfills. It then distributes these funds (about $1.5 million to $2.0 million annually) through a competitive grant program to local governments, nonprofits, and private businesses for projects that reduce waste and promote recycling.

Incremental Regionalism: Education

Community College Education

With a strong tradition of private higher education, St. Louis was a late entrant in the metropolitan move toward public commuter universities and colleges. As a result, the metropolitan area ranked near the bottom in proportion of college graduates.

When the state of Missouri in 1961 authorized the formation of community college districts and provided state aid on a per student basis, the civic leadership in the city of St. Louis and St. Louis County determined that a single city-county district with multiple campuses would be financially and educationally preferable to separate districts within each jurisdiction.

In April 1962, voters approved forming the St. Louis Junior College District including a property tax levy to operate it in temporary leased space. After two unsuccessful attempts in 1963 and 1964, the district received voter approval for an additional levy to construct three permanent campuses. Governed by a six-member board elected by subdistrict, it now provides credit and noncredit instruction to over 60,000 individuals annually. It opened a fourth campus in west St. Louis County in 2007.

On the Illinois side, the original Belleville Junior College, founded in 1946 and located in St. Clair County, expanded to the adjoining Madison County in 1985 with a separate campus in Granite City. Reflecting its broader regional role serving the area's two largest Illinois counties, having a combined population of about half a million, it changed its name to Southwestern Illinois College in 2000. It is governed by an eight-member board, seven elected by subdistrict and one chosen by the student body.

K–12 Education

The Cooperating School Districts (CSD) had been engaging in some joint activities since 1928, but became an official state-chartered entity in 1964. The CSD now includes sixty-three public school districts from Missouri and Illinois, the great majority of which are within the metropolitan area. It is a voluntary membership organization and its board consists of superintendents chosen by the districts.

Its original raison d'être was efficiency through making joint purchases, operating a collective film library, and assisting with information processing. In the ensuing years, its mission has expanded to professional teacher development and promotion of a single-state legislative agenda for its Missouri member districts, an agenda that CSD then lobbies for in Jefferson City. In 1994, it merged with two other regional educational operations—the International Education Consortium and the Regional Center for Education and Technology.

Incremental Regionalism: Cultural Institutions and the Arts

Cultural Institutions

Until 1971, the St. Louis Zoo and the St. Louis Art Museum were owned and operated by the city of St. Louis. As the city's tax base deteriorated, revenues for the two declined even as needs, especially for maintenance, accelerated. The zoo, which even then tended to use "the world famous" as a frequent descriptor, feared for its future as one of the nation's leading zoos, and the art museum also had its own aspirations. Neither would be possible on a declining revenue base.

Sparked by an energetic civic leader, Howard Baer, and supported amply by the business community, the Missouri General Assembly passed legislation in 1970 authorizing a Zoo-Museum District in the city of St. Louis and St. Louis County. As structured by the law, the ZMD was a coalition rather than a combination. Each entity would have its own distinct earmarked tax and each proposal for an institution to become a ZMD member would require a separate vote with concurrent majorities in the city and county.

The zoo and the art museum sought voter approval in 1971 and, to help the politics along, included a fledgling nonprofit Museum of Science and Natural History, then located in St. Louis County, as part of the package. The voters approved and the ZMD became reality. Its board has eight members, four each appointed by the city's and county's elected executives, and their separate subcommissioners for each institution. These individuals exercise little power since the legislation and the ballot language mandate the amount of tax revenues that pass through the ZMD on their way to the individual institutions.

In 2005, the ZMD collected and passed through over $67 million in property tax revenues to its five member institutions. When it was established in 1971, the assessed valuation in the city and county were close to equal. Now about four-fifths comes from the wealthier and larger county, even though all five member institutions have their major presence (the Botanical Garden operates a nature reserve and a butterfly house in the county) in the city.

In 1983, voters doubled the tax rate for the zoo and the art museum, quadrupled it for a new Science Center, and added the Missouri Botanical Garden to the ZMD. The garden had successfully had itself included on the eligible membership list earlier in the 1980s. In 1985, the Missouri Historical Society had the state statute amended to include it as a potential ZMD institution and, in 1987, the voters approved its joining the group.

Regional Arts Commission

In 1984, the Missouri General Assembly passed legislation authorizing the city of St. Louis and St. Louis County to increase their hotel-motel tax and use a portion (four-fifteenths) of the total tax revenues on grants for the arts. Later that year, the voters in each jurisdiction approved the tax and establishing the Regional Arts Commission (RAC) to administer a grant program for the arts.

Signaling that St. Louis County had become the bigger dog on the regional porch, its county executive appoints eight of the fifteen commissioners with the remainder named by the city of St. Louis mayor. RAC now awards over $3.5 million annually to more than 200 area arts organizations ranging from the very large (e.g., the St. Louis Symphony) to the quite small (e.g., the Compton Heights Concert Band).

Incremental Regionalism: Public Safety

Major Case Squad

Founded in 1965, the Major Case Squad (MCS) draws upon the law enforcement agencies in six Missouri counties (city of St. Louis, St. Louis County, Franklin County, Jefferson County, St. Charles County, Warren County) and four Illinois counties (Bond, Madison, Monroe, St. Clair) to tackle the more complex criminal cases that require extensive manpower (refer to Map 5.3). The participating jurisdictions collectively assign more than 400 personnel to be available when needed, and the MCS is able to mobilize a team within three hours of being notified. It handles about fifteen cases a year and is governed by a board of law enforcement leaders from the member police departments as well as private sector leaders.

Regional Justice Information System

Recognizing the need for a common information base, the city of St. Louis and St. Louis County entered into a joint agreement in 1975 to form the Regional Justice Information System (REJIS), governed by a seven-member commission, three each from the city and the county and the seventh appointed jointly by the two chief elected executives. In the ensuing years, REJIS has expanded its geographic reach to jurisdictions containing almost 90 percent of the area's population. Although still controlled by just the city and county, it provides its services, including its extensive database, to three additional Missouri counties (Franklin, Jefferson, St. Charles) and three Illinois counties (Madison, Monroe, St. Clair).

Incremental Regionalism: Transportation

Mass Transit

Until the early 1960s, buses and streetcars in the St. Louis metropolitan area were owned and operated by one of fifteen private firms. The Board of Freeholders convened in 1955 to consider a possible "Metropolitan St. Louis Transit District" had punted on the issue, and, as automobile trips increased and mass transit journeys declined, the firms started looking for a way out.

The Bi-State Development Agency, an Illinois-Missouri compact ratified by the national government in 1950, provided the mechanism to bring mass transit into the public arena. As originally designed, Bi-State was a public authority with limited powers. Although it was empowered to "maintain, own, and operate" selected transportation infrastructure ("bridges, tunnels, airports, and terminal facilities"), its primary initial role was permission to plan, not operate. Its management, however, was entrepreneurial, and, anticipating that the option to get into public transit might arise, Bi-State in 1959 had the respective state legislatures expand its potential portfolio to include "passenger transportation facilities."

In the early 1960s, Bi-State used revenue bonds to buy out all the private entities, transforming itself from a small and largely ignored planning agency into a substantial transportation public authority serving the city of St. Louis, St. Louis County, and St. Clair County. It originally anticipated that fare box revenues would cover both operating costs and debt retirement. Even though passenger levels had been slipping, as a public enterprise Bi-State was tax exempt and it expected that those savings would transform a red-ink private balance sheet into a break-even public one.

This scenario was short-lived. Despite federal assistance under the Urban Mass Transportation Act of 1964, by the early 1970s Bi-State needed additional public subsidy. The Missouri General Assembly then authorized the city of St. Louis and St. Louis County to institute a one-half-cent sales tax for "transportation purposes." Both did in 1973. Although neither jurisdiction is obligated to spend the proceeds on mass transit through allocating them to Bi-State, the city has traditionally given all of them to the agency while the county typically appropriates about one-half. Illinois funds come both directly from the state and through the St. Clair County Transit District, which passed a one-half-cent sales tax in 1993 for that purpose.

In 1994, after St. Louis traded some otherwise useless railroad right-of-way and a few other tokens to the national government in return for the feds' footing of the bill for a light rail line ("Metrolink") that now extends from Lambert Airport in northwest St. Louis County through the city of St. Louis and over the Mississippi River to Scott Air Force Base in eastern St. Clair County, Bi-State realized it did not have sufficient funds to operate it. The Missouri General Assembly authorized the city of St. Louis and St. Louis County to pass a one-half-cent sales tax, which, this time, could be used only for "public transportation purposes." In August 1994, a measure for half this amount (one-quarter cent) was on the ballot and passed easily in both jurisdictions.

Bi-State (now called Metro) is governed by ten commissioners, five from each state, all of whom must reside within the agency's territory. As Bi-State's importance grew, the city of St. Louis and St. Louis County began to squabble over the Missouri commissioner appointments. A truce was reached in 1980 and now Missouri law specifies, first, that the fifth or odd appointment rotates between the city and county and, second, that the appointments (two city, two county, one rotating) are made by the Missouri governor from a panel of three nominees submitted by either the city of St. Louis mayor or the St. Louis county executive, depending on whose turn it is.

Lambert Airport

Lambert International Airport is owned by the city of St. Louis but is physically located in St. Louis County. It is governed by the St. Louis Airport Authority, a creature of city government. Originally all the authority slots were held by city officials and residents. Given the airport's location and its regional role, other jurisdictions began seeking representation and, as a threat, even suggested that the airport should become a regionally governed entity. The city has resisted relinquishing ownership, both for financial (the airport often generates a surplus) and political (jobs and contracts) reasons. But it has responded to the pressure for places at the table and, presently, in addition to the ten city members, the St. Louis County executive appoints five members and the St. Charles County and St. Clair County governments appoint one each.

Metropolitan Taxi Commission

Responding to concerns that subpar taxi service with unkempt drivers and dirty vehicles generates a poor image, the city and county successfully sought the authorization of state legislation in 2002 to establish a joint city-county regulatory commission. The Metropolitan Taxi Commission formed in 2003. Its thirty-page code ranges from driver requirements ("speak . . . the English language") and driver behavior ("black slacks, no jeans) to license fees and fare structures. The nine-member commission has four members each appointed by the city of St. Louis mayor and the St. Louis county executive with the committee chair appointment alternating on a two-year rotation between the city and county. All appointments are confirmed by the respective legislative bodies.

Transportation Planning

Like all metropolitan areas, St. Louis has a metropolitan planning organization (MPO), and, like many other regions, it is housed in what began and still remains a council of governments. The East West Gateway Council of Governments (EWGCG) was formed in 1965 and included the chief elected officials from the city of St. Louis, East St. Louis, St. Louis County, Franklin County, Jefferson County, Madison County, Monroe County, St. Charles County, St. Clair County, and a mayor from one of the St. Louis County municipalities.

The present council retains these posts plus added representation from Illinois municipalities (two mayors), St. Charles County (one councilperson), St. Clair County (one county board member), and Franklin and Jefferson counties (one elected official rotating between these two jurisdictions).

In addition to exercising the authority granted by the 1991 Intermodal Surface Transportation Efficiency Act and its successors, EWGCG has also used the transportation lever to expand it regional policy agenda to air quality, open space, regional indicators, and workforce mobility. Its monthly board meetings have become the primary gathering place for the region's chief elected officials and the venue for a greater array of topics.

Incremental Regionalism: Tourism and Sports Venues

Tourism

Until the early 1980s, the city of St. Louis and St. Louis County went their separate ways in seeking a piece of the growing convention and tourism trade. The city had its Convention and Tourism Bureau while the county had a Committee on Tourism. In 1983, the city and county merged the operations into the newly titled Convention and Visitors Commission (CVC) and, a year later, the Missouri General Assembly passed legislation blessing the union.

This entity shares the hotel-motel tax (eleven-fifteenths goes to the CVC) with the Regional Arts Commission. It is governed by an eleven-member commission, five each appointed by the city of St. Louis mayor and the St. Louis county executive with the eleventh member and chair named by the governor of Missouri. Since 1991, the CVC has also managed the region's largest convention facility, America's Center, which previously had been a city of St. Louis operation.

Edward D. Jones Dome

In 1987, the National Football League Cardinals moved to Phoenix, sending St. Louis on a nine-year odyssey to find another NFL franchise, a journey that ended when the Los Angeles Rams came in 1996. To secure a franchise, a consensus quickly developed in the late 1980s that a new stadium—preferably domed, seating

60,000 or more, replete with luxury boxes, and located in downtown St. Louis—was a necessary condition for obtaining another team.

This was a $300 million project, requiring $24 million annually for thirty years to cover construction costs, interest payments, and operating expenses. The city of St. Louis concluded that its maximum contribution would be $6 million a year. St. Louis County elected officials proposed and, in 1990, the voters approved an increase in the county's hotel-motel tax from 3.75 percent (the amount supporting RAC and CVC) to 7.25 percent, enough for the county to match the city's $6 million, with a little left for the general fund. Then, using the combined forces of the city and county state legislative delegations (then controlled by democrats) as well as the business community's access to Republican Governor John Ashcroft, the region was able to get the state to contribute the remaining annual $12 million.

Busch Stadium III

Since 1966, the St. Louis Baseball Cardinals had occupied Busch Stadium II, one of several concrete doughnut joint baseball–football stadiums built in the 1960s. Despite retrofitting Busch Stadium II to have a more traditional baseball look in the 1990s, Cardinal ownership determined they needed a built-from-scratch retro ballpark, such as Camden Yards or Jacobs Field or Coors Field, to remain competitive.

The projected price tag was almost $400 million. Noting that public subsidies had become the norm elsewhere, the Cardinals went looking for governments to pick up a healthy share, a third or so, of the costs. All agreed that the most desirable location would be to stay in downtown St. Louis, immediately south of Busch Stadium II.

After years of negotiation and politicking, the same three governments that had supported the football venue agreed to be part of the financing for Busch Stadium III although the details were more complex. The city's share came from eliminating its 5 percent amusement tax, the county used some of the excess revenues from the hotel-motel tax increase passed originally for the Edward D. Jones Dome to underwrite a $45 million bond issue, and the state of Missouri provided $42.7 million in state tax credits and transportation improvements.

Incremental Regionalism: Parks and Open Space

Great Rivers Greenway

St. Louis 2004, a visioning initiative that dominated much of the civic dialogue in 1996 and 1997, produced a series of proposals. Probably the most successful was a call for the region to rediscover its rivers, which are so much a part of its heritage and its topography. St. Louis leadership persuaded the Missouri General Assembly to pass authorizing legislation for a multi-county special parks and open space district in 1999 and, in 2000, voters in the city of St. Louis, St. Charles County, and St. Louis County approved a one-tenth-cent sales tax. One-half of the tax remains within the originating county but the other half goes to the special district, now called Great Rivers Greenway (GRG).

GRG labels its grand plan "The River Ring," an interconnected set of trails and greenways that will include the area's major rivers (Meramec, Mississippi, Missouri) as well as other streams. Its ten-member board is appointed by the three jurisdictions' chief elected executives: five from St. Louis County, three from the city of St. Louis, and two from St. Charles County.

Metro East Park and Recreation District

This initiative worked both sides of the river, foregoing an interstate compact, which most thought would take too long, for parallel state action. In 1999, the Illinois legislature also enacted a statute authorizing the same structure on the region's eastern side. The two largest counties, Madison and St. Clair, also approved the one-tenth-cent sales tax in 2000, establishing the Metro East Park and Recreation District (MEPRD). Like its Missouri counterpart, it receives one-half of the proceeds with the other half remaining in the originating county.

MEPRD coordinates its planning with GRG and, to date, the cooperation between the two entities is extensive, creating a de facto five-county regional plan. MEPRD has a six-member board with three each appointed by the Madison County and St. Clair County boards.

Incremental Regionalism: Health Care for the Indigent

Regional Medical Center

For most of the twentieth century, the city of St. Louis owned and operated two public hospitals and St. Louis County had a single facility. As expenses rose and revenues declined, the city closed one major hospital in 1979, a controversial move, since it had been an anchor within the African-American community.

In 1985, after discussions between the city and county, the two governments simultaneously ceased operations at the remaining two facilities. To replace them, they engineered the establishment of a nonprofit hospital (St. Louis Regional Medical Center) located in the city but within one mile of the border with St. Louis County and signed a ten-year contract for it to provide tertiary services as well as some primary care. As health care costs continued to escalate, both the city and county decided to exit the arena in 1995, leaving Regional to survive largely on Medicaid reimbursements. That failed and, in 1997, Regional shut down.

St. Louis ConnectCare

Replacing Regional was a new public-private partnership, St. Louis Con-nectCare, which operates at the same site but now provides only primary and specialty care. Its fourteen-member board is a mix of hospital representatives (the two largest local hospital systems), medical school administrators (St. Louis University and Washington University), elected officials (two city of St. Louis aldermen), the directors of the city and county departments of health, and citizens. Its $40 million annual budget is an amalgam of state of Missouri funds (the largest single source), city and county contributions, insurance billings, and charitable donations.

Regional Health Commission

Recognizing that St. Louis ConnectCare was at best a partial solution to health care for the indigent, in 2001 the city of St. Louis, St. Louis County, and the state of Missouri formed the Regional Health Commission. To date, most of its work has been data collection and planning coupled with some awareness-building about the scale of the problem. The commission's nineteen-member board has three appointments each from the city of St. Louis mayor and the St. Louis county executive; two each by the governor of Missouri, St. Louis area health systems, and St. Louis area primary care clinics; one each from St. Louis ConnectCare and the local medical schools; and five at-large community members.

Incremental Regionalism: Economic Development

Greater St. Louis Economic Development Council

The city of St. Louis and St. Louis County chambers of commerce merged into a single metropolitan area unit in 1963. Ten years later, it realized that the two-county umbrella failed to cover all of the region's economy. It decided both to broaden its geography to embrace all the region's counties and to include labor, government, and nonprofit organizations within its membership, naming itself the Regional Commerce and Growth Association (RCGA). In 1999, it substituted "Chamber" for "Commerce" in its title.

As metropolitan economic competition intensified during the 1980s and early 1990s, business leaders, most notably then Monsanto CEO Richard Mahoney, determined that RCGA had to be redesigned and revitalized. To signal that regional economic development was being taken to a higher level, the Greater St. Louis Economic Development Council was formed in 1994. Its eleven-person board includes, ex officio, the city of St. Louis mayor and St. Louis county executive as well as top officials from St. Charles County, southwestern Illinois, labor, and business groups.

The council is grafted onto the RCGA, which provides the operational leadership for metropolitan-wide economic development. Although there is still some occasional tension between individual county economic development units, the overall approach for the most part is to shift economic development efforts from poaching from one another within the region to building enterprises across the metropolitan area.

Greater St. Louis Regional Empowerment Zone

When the federal government issued requests for proposals for empowerment zones in 1994, the city of St. Louis and East St. Louis submitted separate applications. Neither won the major empowerment zone designation and each only qualified for the consolation prize—enterprise community designation. By having its two most impoverished jurisdictions each go it alone, the region came up with a few crumbs rather than a whole cake.

When a second round opened in 1998, the St. Louis region prepared a single application that covered large segments of East St. Louis within St. Clair County and the city of St. Louis as well as a small portion (Wellston) of St. Louis County. Regional cooperation paid off and the proposal was fully funded, providing well over $10 million dollars for business development and underwriting $95 million in tax-exempt bonds for a major convention hotel in downtown St. Louis. The city of St. Louis mayor, the St. Louis county executive, the East St. Louis mayor, and the Wellston mayor are each ex officio board members along with public and institutional representatives.

What's Next for Reform in St. Louis?

Given the more than 130-year history of planning attempts to restructure governmental and fiscal arrangements in the St. Louis metropolitan area, one can legitimately pose the question, "what is next?" Clearly, the situation outlined above shows some progress incrementally toward dealing with specific issues. Problems remain, however, and may well worsen. In addition to the intra-St. Louis County issues that have been discussed, there remain concerns over effectively dealing with area-wide problems such as environmental quality, transportation, economic development, solid waste disposal, and sewage and wastewater treatment. Many attempts to date have focused on the city-county area but not the entire metropolitan area, which now includes sixteen counties (see Map 5.3) in the two-state St. Louis MSA (see Chapter 2 for a discussion of why this is not likely to occur). Also, one can make an argument that there is too little coordination among these incremental steps. Are they moving toward regional governance or just piecemeal responses to regional issues? Also are they reactive or proactive to area-wide problems and issues?

The more comprehensive attempts using the Board of Freeholders (now Electors) approach has failed in every attempt except two. The first, which separated the city from the county, was in 1876. In many respects this set the stage for many of the problems that continue to play out more than 130 years later. The second was the establishment of the Metropolitan Sewer District, which emerged from a major actual, and potentially even worse, health context. All five comprehensive proposals have failed at the ballot box, usually overwhelmingly.

St. Louis's leadership—both governmental and business—generally agree that the St. Louis area still requires more regionalism. The disagreements center around "what does more entail?" and in "what form will it be implemented?" Some within both sectors continue to argue for merging the city of St. Louis and St. Louis County, with the most frequent option being to have the city reenter the county as its ninety-second municipality (preserving city identity and political control) and cease performing its county functions. Others propose adding to the now quite long list of cooperative ventures (e.g., a regional airport authority) or expanding existing districts (e.g., the Zoo-Museum District) to include additional counties (especially St. Charles County).

In this sense, regionalism has perhaps won the rhetorical war. Even elected officials who are reluctant participants in the move toward metropolitan-wide efforts are sensitive about sounding too parochial. The debate is now much more about how rather than whether.

Over the years, much planning has been proposed and discussed, and many attempts have proved successful, but there is still weight to what remains. St. Louis has long been a textbook example of governmental structure problems. Might it become a textbook example of what can be done to correct them, more narrowly and incrementally rather than globally and all at once, given the *long-standing and very strong resistance* to regional government that prevails not only in St. Louis but across the United States?

Note

1. The Freeholders' plan also provided for two entities that formally link the city and county. This was required in the constitutional mandate under which the board was created. One is an Economic Development District that deals with the promotion of area-wide economic development; the second is a Metropolitan Commission that could be called into existence on an "as needed" basis to deal with area-wide problems as they arise in the future. Refer to Articles 3 and 4 of the board plan (1988a) for full detail.

References

Advisory Commission on Intergovernmental Relations (ACIR). 1987. *The Organization of Local Public Economies.* Washington, DC, December, A-109.
———. 1988. *Metropolitan Organization: The St. Louis Case.* Washington, DC, September, M-158.
———. 1992. *Metropolitan Organization: The Allegheny County Case.* Washington, DC, February, M-181.
Barclay, Thomas. 1962. *The St. Louis Home Rule Charter of 1876: Its Framing and Adoption.* Columbia: University of Missouri Press.
Board of Electors (St. Louis City-St. Louis County). 1991. *Plan for Metropolitan Economic Development Commission and Metropolitan Park Commission of the City of St. Louis and St. Louis County.* St. Louis, MO: St. Louis City-St. Louis County Board of Electors, July.

Board of Freeholders. 1926. *Board of Freeholders Proposal No. 8:* "Proposal for the consolidation of the territories and governments of the City of St. Louis and the County of St. Louis into one legal subdivision under the municipal government of the City of St. Louis."

———.1954. *Proposed Plan of the Metropolitan Sewer District.* St. Louis, MO: St. Louis City and St. Louis County Board of Freeholders to be submitted at a special election on Tuesday, February 9.

———.1988a. *Plan for Governmental Reorganization in St. Louis & St. Louis County.* St. Louis, MO: St. Louis City-County Board of Freeholders, September.

———. 1988b. *Supplement to the Plan for Governmental Reorganization in St. Louis & St. Louis County.* St. Louis, MO: Board of Freeholders, September.

Cassella, William. 1959. "City-County Separation: The 'Great Divorce' of 1876." *Missouri Historical Society Bulletin* 15 (January): 85–104.

Confluence St. Louis. 1987. *Too Many Governments?* St. Louis, MO: Confluence.

Feiock, Richard C., ed. 2004. *Metropolitan Governance: Conflict, Competition, and Cooperation.* Washington, DC: Georgetown University Press.

———. 2007. "Rational Choice and Regional Governance." *Journal of Urban Affairs* 29, no. 1: 47–63.

Jones, E. Terrence. 2000. *Fragmented by Design: Why St. Louis Has So Many Governments.* St. Louis, MO: Palmerston & Reed.

Lowi, Theodore J. 1972. "Four Systems of Policy, Politics, and Choice." *Public Administration Review* 32 (July–August): 298–310.

Metropolitan Board of Freeholders. 1959. "Proposed Plan of the Greater St. Louis City-County District." St. Louis, MO: prepared by the Metropolitan Board of Freeholders, for a special election to be held on Tuesday, November 3.

Metropolitan St. Louis Survey. 1957a. *Background for Action.* St. Louis, MO, February.

———. 1957b. *Path of Progress for Metropolitan St. Louis.* St. Louis, MO, August.

Metropolitan St. Louis Transit District. 1955. *Proposed Plan of the Metropolitan St. Louis Transit District.* St. Louis, MO: The St. Louis and St. Louis County Transit Board of Freeholders.

Sengstock, Frank; P. Fellin; L. Nicholson; and C. Mundale. 1964. *Consolidation: Building a Bridge Between City and Suburb.* St. Louis, MO: Heffernan Press, St. Louis University School of Law.

St. Louis County (Missouri). 2007. *2007–2012 Fact Book.* St. Louis, MO: St. Louis County Department of Planning.

Williams, Oliver P., and Charles R. Adrian. 1963. *Four Cities: A Study in Comparative Policy Making.* Philadelphia: University of Pennsylvania Press.

6

Governance and the Struggle for the Downtown

St. Louis, 1952–2005

Dennis R. Judd and David Laslo

The official story St. Louisians tell about their city is that the leadership that is needed to solve its problems has mostly been missing in action because the municipal government is hopelessly disorganized, fragmented, and dysfunctional. What this frequently repeated narrative about the city overlooks is that the political and civic elites of St. Louis have been able to sustain a decades-long downtown revitalization effort that rivals cities of much larger size and more resources. If they had been unable to overcome the obstacles posed by a famously fragmented political system, the downtown and its economy might have slipped past the point of no return. In this chapter, we endeavor to explain how St. Louis was able to build a system of governance sufficient to sustain the long, frustrating, but perhaps ultimately successful struggle to regenerate the downtown.

St. Louis began its long slide in the 1930s and even earlier, prompting *Forum* magazine to publish an article in 1939 commenting on "the desolation and desertion characterizing scores of blocks in the business district" (Teaford, 1993, p. 213). By the 1950s, the wasting disease that infected the downtown seemed to be spreading inexorably into the neighborhoods: "No new office building had been erected downtown in two decades, traffic in the central business district was a nerve-shattering mess, and half the city was blighted" (Primm, 1981, p. 493). The same rot could be found in all the cities of the industrial belt, but St. Louis seemed to be among the worst off. Throughout the postwar era it seemed almost as if St. Louis was locked into a dismal competition with its peers to see which of the old industrial cities could sustain the largest population losses, and by this measure it won the race for the bottom by shedding 61 percent of its residents in the half-century from 1950 to 2000. In 1950 it was the nation's eighth largest city, with 857,000 residents, but by century's end, with only 335,000 people left, its status as a big city had all but evaporated (U.S. Bureau of the Census, 1951). It had become less important in its own region, too. By the census of 2000 only 13 percent of the metropolitan area's residents still resided in the city, a free-fall from sixty years earlier when, with 57 percent of the population, it plainly was the center of population and economic activity (*Statistical Abstract of the United States,* 1987).

The effects of this demographic disaster were amplified by a process of economic restructuring that began to empty the city of its most vital business sectors. Like everywhere else in the industrial heartland, the region's economy revolved around goods-producing activities. In 1950 manufacturing accounted for 51 percent of the workforce in St. Louis, a figure that precisely matched the national ratio. But a historic deindustrialization process had already set in, and it accelerated decade by decade. By 1980 manufacturing provided just 16 percent of the region's jobs, and by then all but a few of the large manufacturing firms had left the city or had fled the metropolitan area entirely. The same trend unfolded in retailing, wholesaling, and other sectors (U.S. Department of Commerce, 1999). These developments devastated the downtown, where historically significant but obsolete office, warehouse, and commercial buildings presided over streets that were thinly populated in the daytime and empty at night.

All through this period, civic leaders expressed anxiety about the state of the downtown and the city, and they were determined that market forces would not dictate St. Louis's fate. In 1952 St. Louis received enormous national publicity for being the first city in the nation to receive federal urban renewal funds, and over the next few years, civic leaders raised more than $2 million in public and private funds for slum clearance and related projects. When urban renewal began to lose its luster, the tourism sector carried a large part of the burden of downtown redevelopment. Between 1965 and 2006 almost $1.5 billion of public and private capital was devoted to the task of building an infrastructure to support tourism and entertainment (Laslo, Louishomme, and Judd, 2003).

This infrastructure has changed the built environment in and near downtown, see Map 6.1. The Cervantes Convention Center, the attached Edward Jones Dome stadium (where the football Rams play), and a convention hotel built with public money anchor the northern end of the downtown. The latest Cardinals baseball stadium opened in 2006 and continues to define the southern perimeter. The Scottrade Center, built to house the St. Louis Blues hockey team, is located four blocks to the west, and in two more blocks one comes to a Rouse mall nestled in the bowels of the redeveloped Union Station. A mall opened in 1985, the St. Louis Centre, is now being redeveloped into the largest condominium project in the heart of the downtown. Laclede's Landing, an entertainment district close to the Mississippi River, is the site of a half-billion-dollar gaming complex, Lumiere Place, that opened in 2007. Looming over all of the downtown is the signature symbol of St. Louis, the Gateway Arch, which was opened in 1967 after thirty years of political maneuvering for federal funds.

This cluster of projects helped secure the downtown, though tenuously, until a critical mass of privately financed development began to appear in the late 1990s. By mid-2007 most of the historic warehouses and garment and shoe factories along Washington Avenue on the north edge of the downtown, where the convention

Map 6.1   **Downtown St. Louis**

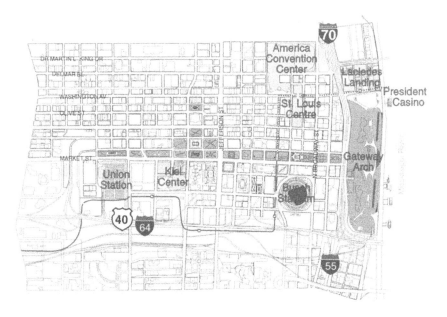

Source: Map courtesy of Planning and Urban Design Agency, City of St. Louis.

center, convention hotel, and domed stadium are located, have been in the process of being converted into housing, retail, and office space. With the opening of a handful of nightclubs and restaurants, on weekends it began to show fitful signs of a street life. If Washington Avenue succeeds, it may usher in the next phase in St. Louis's quest to become a center for tourism and entertainment—a shift from investment in big projects and sports to an emphasis upon street life and urban culture. Indeed, the Cardinals' management seems to have recognized these possibilities when they promised to build an "urban village" close by the stadium the Cardinals opened in 2006. Population growth in and near the central business district is an important component of what appears to be a historic turning point; for the first time in decades, the city gained population, from 348,189 people in 2000 to 350,759 by 2007 (U.S. Bureau of the Census, 2007).

St. Louis's renaissance, however slow, halting, and uneven, has required collaboration among civic elites to build the capacity to respond to the city's manifold problems. As we demonstrate in this chapter, the mix of participants and the terms guiding their cooperation has changed over time. Sometimes they pursued a clearly defined agenda, but not always. A powerful motive brought them together again and again: the knowledge that the city's continued decline would impose unacceptable costs on each of them unless they found a way to cooperate to produce the resources necessary for shaping St. Louis's destiny. But assembling the capacity to act was a daunting task in a city where the governmental structure and political culture seemed to make coherent leadership almost impossible.

Archaic Institutions and Weak Public Authority

For much of the twentieth century the fractured nature of St. Louis's politics has been regarded as a disease that constantly threatens to kill the city and the region's health and vitality. Accordingly, reformers in St. Louis have engaged in a long string of quixotic endeavors aimed at changing the relationship between the city and its region, as so thoroughly documented by Jones and Phares in Chapter 5 of this volume. The municipal charter adopted in 1876 separated the city from its surrounding county, fixing its boundaries forever at sixty-one square miles. The city's officials and voters favored this unusual arrangement because it allowed them to stop paying taxes to support services delivered to people living in the rural hinterlands of the county. The new boundaries seemed ample enough; after all, in addition to city streets, they enclosed stretches of woods and farmlands. But in the twentieth century the problems with this rash bargain became painfully obvious. Unable to annex land beyond its borders, the city inherited most of the problems but few of the benefits of metropolitan growth of this century. This recognition, as Jones and Phares point out in Chapter 5 on St. Louis governmental reform, led to a series of often troubled and always controversial attempts at reversing the separation of city and county.

Five major campaigns were launched to correct this defect; all came to grief. In 1926 voters in St. Louis County defeated a proposal to consolidate the city of St. Louis with the county. Four years later, the county's voters vetoed a somewhat less ambitious proposal that would have placed the city and county under a regional government, except for a few services and public functions (Teaford, 1997, p. 110). In 1959 the reformers gave it another try. This time they proposed a Greater St. Louis City-County District that would have assumed responsibility for forging a regional plan for promoting economic development; managing regional mass transit and traffic control on major streets and highways; administering all sewage facilities; and supervising all police training, communications, and civil defense. Municipalities would have been left with the responsibility of regulating local street traffic and providing police and fire protection and garbage pickup. Local officials in the county reacted by mounting a furious campaign in opposition, and voters soundly defeated the plan (Teaford, 1997, pp. 110–12). But even before tempers cooled from this attempt, reformers were at it again. In 1962 they proposed the "borough plan," which would have placed the city and county under a single government and divided the county into twenty-two boroughs, each exercising some limited powers. Municipalities would have been eliminated altogether. The plan was defeated by a four-to-one landslide, an even more lopsided margin than in 1959. The last major campaign, launched in 1987, did not try to change the city's status within the region, but it, too, floundered. Voters certainly would have defeated the proposal to reduce the number of municipalities in St. Louis County, but before they had the opportunity, it was thrown out by the U.S. Supreme Court (see Chapter 5).

There have been at least as many attempts to reform the institutional structure of the city's municipal government. The 1876 municipal charter not only land-locked the city by separating it from the county; it also left it with an exceptionally fragmented—in fact, weird—system of government. When the state legislature granted the St. Louis city-county divorce, it required that the circuit courts and additional services ordinarily provided through county government be administered within the city. The legislature made most of these offices elective, and scheduled the elections to coincide with state, not city, election cycles. The result is a political and governmental structure of mind-boggling confusion that defeats any attempt, however skillfully executed, to bring clarity to the situation.

In her book on St. Louis politics, Lana Stein (2002) has done as well as anyone can to negotiate the labyrinth: "The city had to elect magistrates and constables in district elections and also fill a large number—eleven at the time—of the so-called 'county offices.' The heads of each of these offices would be elected at large on a partisan ballot at the time of the state primary in August and in the general election in November" (Stein, 2002, p. 4).[1] A court reorganization approved by the legislature took effect in 1979; it helped to make structure less a spoils system than in the past by eliminating the eight elected constables, changing the eight elected magistrates into associate circuit judges appointed by the governor, and consolidating some overlapping jobs in the judicial system (ibid., p. 171).

By St. Louis's standards these changes seemed almost like earth-shaking reforms, but they still left a fractured system intact: eleven major officeholders (several elected) and their administrative staffs, including, among others, a sheriff, collec-tor of revenue, license collector, and treasurer, all more or less mirror images of similar city offices. Since these "county" offices are defined, by law, as state agen-cies, incumbents do not answer in any way to the mayor or the board of aldermen. The legislature fixes their salaries; the governor fills between-election vacancies. Though the law forbids the city's aldermen from serving as committeemen for the party organizations, the same restriction does not apply to county officials; thus, the sheriff, recorder of deeds, and state representatives and senators normally control these committees (ibid., p. 250). And although officials performing the equivalent of county duties are officially independent of the municipality, both governments share the same revenue base.

The story of governmental disarray becomes even more complex when the next layer of the onion is peeled. The municipal government is fractured into an even larger number of independent fiefdoms that operate alongside the "county posi-tions." The last time the city's charter was revised, in 1914, the state legislature created twenty-eight wards and a system in which a board of estimate composed of three independent officials—the mayor, the comptroller, and the president of the board of aldermen—share responsibility for overseeing the city budget. Additionally, a relic piece of legislation left over from the Civil War era gives control over the police department's budget to a committee of the state legislature, despite the fact that the city is required to pick up the costs.

When considered in its entirety, the structure of municipal government has served as a perfect recipe for a ward-based spoils politics and an emasculated mayor. This institutional legacy led Lana Stein to regard the city's unreformed government as the defining characteristic and main problem of the city: "Barriers in the political system destroy valuable political capital," leaving personality as "the only tool a St. Louis mayor can use to achieve more centralized authority" (2002, pp. xi, 224–25).

An Executive-Centered Regime

Considering the obstacles placed in the way of effective and coherent leadership, what made an ambitious program of downtown renewal possible in St. Louis? The answer to this question does not remain the same over time. For a brief period in the 1950s and 1960s, two mayors were able to forge a close and mutually beneficial relationship with corporate elites. The coalition thus formed was similar to one built in postwar Atlanta, which became the subject of one of the leading books in political science. In his pathbreaking book, *Regime Politics,* Clarence Stone (1989) traces the history of Atlanta's governance over a forty-two-year period stretching from 1946 to 1988. In his account, an alliance between City Hall and the corporate elite led a sustained effort to make Atlanta into the leading regional city of the South. It did so by transforming the physical environment of the downtown, providing support for the construction of an airport and a modern rapid transit system, engineering an ambitious urban renewal and housing program, and desegregating the city's police departments and schools.

Stone labeled the coalition that guided such a sweeping program of action an urban "regime" because the term suggested an enduring, stable, and cohesive structure of power. He noted that informal alliances like the one that anchored Atlanta's regime "facilitate cooperation to a degree that formally defined relationships do not. People who know one another, who have worked together in the past, who have shared in the achievement of a task, and who perhaps have experienced the same crisis are especially likely to develop tacit understandings" (Stone, 1989, p. 4). When such partnerships endure over time, participants accumulate the resources to "make and carry out governing decisions . . ." (ibid., p. 7). In Atlanta, a stable governing coalition was held together by the Central Atlanta Improvement Association (later renamed Central Atlanta Progress), which included among its members the mayor and major corporations and downtown property owners. This institutional structure facilitated the level of cooperation necessary for business to speak with a singular voice and to coordinate its efforts with City Hall.

The concept of urban regimes helps to provide a language and logic for explaining the coordination of downtown revitalization efforts in St. Louis for a brief period of time. A few years after the end of World War II, an informal but powerful partnership between St. Louis's mayor and civic leaders was forged. In 1950, when St. Louis was selected as the first city in the nation to receive urban renewal funds, Mayor Joseph M. Darst began assembling a coalition to carry the program forward. As recalled by his successor, Raymond Tucker, "About a year ago, a group of distinguished citizens of our community were called into the Mayor's office and there charged by Mayor Darst with the responsibility of giving leadership to a program to take advantage of the Housing Act of 1949 . . . many fine business institutions, sixty-nine in number, subscribed to a total in excess of $2,000,000 toward the capital structure of the [redevelopment] corporation" (Institute of Housing, 1952, p. 18). Soon thereafter, the Missouri state legislature created the Land Clearance for Redevelopment Authority of St. Louis, the agency charged with administering the urban renewal program.

The massive amount of funds that flowed through the agency altered politics-as-usual by centralizing resources and political authority in the mayor's office and in the broad civic alliance he enlisted to support urban renewal. Its five-member board was appointed by the mayor, and it presided over a program audacious in scope. With $28 million and more to come, it began to clear a 454-acre tract of land just to the west of downtown. Meanwhile, the city government continued to operate in its usual fashion, with the aldermen dividing the jobs and the funds made available from the city's own resources, but urban renewal had become the biggest game in town.

Mayor Darst had in mind an even more ambitious remaking of the local power structure when he called together eight of the most powerful businessmen in the city and asked them to form a civic organization to provide more effective leadership in St. Louis. Within a few months the eight civic notables chartered Civic Progress, Inc. Initially, Darst wanted the group to help campaign for a bond issue to finance public improvements and the city's share of urban renewal; he also hoped business leaders would help the city out of its chronic budget woes by supporting a city earnings tax. Over the years, Civic Progress worked with Mayor Tucker, who replaced Darst in 1953, by helping to campaign for a $110 million bond issue, a city earnings tax, a gas tax increase, public school reform, a locally financed downtown redevelopment project, a new downtown sports stadium, and other initiatives. Throughout this period, the relationship between City Hall and Civic Progress remained close. Soon after assuming office, when Mayor Tucker asked the members of Civic Progress to expand the group by ten members, they agreed to do so. By combining the urban renewal alliance and his close relationship with Civic Progress, Tucker was able to create, in effect, a "mayor's party" that allowed him to bypass the patronage politics that had long defined power in the city (Stein, 2002, p. 141).

In the urban renewal era in St. Louis, a time when two mayors exerted forceful leadership, the collaboration needed to produce civic capacity took the form of a stable and ongoing coalition between two partners, city hall and the corporate elite.

Opportunity in the form of federal dollars, and crisis, as expressed in the dire state of the downtown, brought them together. A symmetrical relationship formed around mutual interests made it possible for the partners to define, in common, an agenda of action much more sweeping than the particular undertakings that engaged them. The participants were able to build an impressive capacity to realize their goals because they were able to skillfully use federal urban renewal funds, increase the fiscal resources of city government, and mobilize private contributions on behalf of downtown renewal. St. Louis's regime proved to be a remarkably powerful mechanism for overcoming the limitations of St. Louis's peculiar governmental structure.

Even when racial turmoil and civil rights protests became the dominant issues in the 1960s, the alliance held. In 1964, Civic Progress provided financing for an inner-city program called Youth Opportunities Unlimited, to motivate high school dropouts to continue with their education and learn work skills (City of St. Louis, 1964). A year later, Tucker worked with corporate leaders to establish a race relations committee called the Dialogue Committee, which was composed of some Civic Progress members and members of the African-American business community (City of St. Louis, 1965). But St. Louis's version of an urban regime turned out to have a fatal weakness because there was no institutional mechanism for keeping the city hall–business coalition intact through subsequent mayoral elections and public controversies. Civic Progress could not act as such an institution because it closely guarded its independence. Mayors did not necessarily have a place at the table. Tucker's personality and his long-standing relationship with the members of Civic Progress were the only reasons the alliance held together as long as it did. In 1965, when he left office, St. Louis's version of a regime fell apart.

The Era of Corporate-Centered Governance

No St. Louis mayor would be able to put the pieces together again. By the mid-1960s the city's politics became focused on racial issues, which were generally expressed in a contentious tug of war between white politicians from south-side wards and black politicians from the northern half of the city. Tucker had been a professor at Washington University, but henceforth most mayors would come into office by the route of ward-based politics, a fact that "removed the notion of a separate 'mayor's party' from St. Louis's political lexicon" (Stein, 2002, p. 141).[2]

Despite the abrupt decline in the mayor's power, the effort to revitalize the downtown was never abandoned. In what may be called the Civic Progress era, the center of gravity moved decisively to the corporate elite, in large part because the centrifugal forces of St. Louis's political system exerted a pull too powerful to resist. St. Louis's mayors could not and did not want to head a "mayor's party" they could use as a counterbalance to the fragmented politics of the municipal government. In this circumstance, the mayor and Civic Progress still needed each other in significant ways, but the terms of cooperation changed fundamentally.

Henceforth, Civic Progress would pursue its aims on a project-by-project basis; the mayor's support would be recruited as needed. On the other hand, mayors who wished to push their own programs were obliged to enlist Civic Progress's participation, but the relationship was hardly symmetrical. The episodic method of cooperation produced resources for downtown renewal, but on a much-diminished scale compared with the urban renewal period.

A.J. Cervantes, who took office in April 1965, had good connections to ward politicians from both sides of the city. He owned an insurance agency and taxicab company, and was perceived by corporate leaders to be "in a very different league" (Stein, 2002, p. 144). Though he considered neighborhood preservation his highest priority, he undertook a couple of high-profile projects in the downtown. The abject and much-publicized failure of both of them loomed all the larger because they appeared to be pet projects he dreamed up without first securing political support. With the help of a handful of wealthy investors he bought the Spanish Pavilion, an especially impressive building left over from the 1965 World's Fair, and had it installed downtown. He thought it was an effective way to celebrate the Spanish heritage of the city, "but once it was in place, no one knew what to do with it" (Primm, 1981, p. 500). It closed within a year. His other venture came to a much more sudden and spectacular end, a few days after his latest purchase, a replica of Columbus's ship the *Santa Maria* arrived at the riverfront and within days sank during a violent storm. Many people in St. Louis interpreted this accident as a tragicomic comment on the state of the downtown and the leadership at the helm of the local state.

In 1973 Cervantes was defeated in his run for a third term by John Poelker, who had served four terms as the city comptroller and was not much connected to ward politics. Some members of Civic Progress gave contributions so that he could unseat Cervantes, but this support did not necessarily signal that they would close ranks with City Hall once a new incumbent was installed. Poelker attended the meetings of Civic Progress regularly and asked for the organization's support on a variety of civic matters, but he was clearly dependent upon their good graces (City of St. Louis, 1977). His successor, James Conway, who came into office in 1977, appeared to be even less bonded with Civic Progress, in his run for office in 1977 stating that these guys were not exactly in his crowd (Spitzer and Malone, 1979).

When Vincent Schoemehl replaced Conway in 1983, he formed a closer relationship with Civic Progress than had any mayor since Tucker. Just thirty-four years old when inaugurated, he aggressively pushed new programs for the downtown and for the neighborhoods. Even so, he was able to forge a less than symmetrical relationship with Civic Progress. Schoemehl was aware that Civic Progress commanded the resources he needed to pursue his most ambitious plans. However, he sought the support of corporate leaders one project at a time, and they preferred initiatives that entailed a "relatively brief commitment" (Stein, 2002, p. 198). This type of relationship caused dismay among some of the aldermen and other public officials, including Comptroller Virvus Jones, who complained that they could not do anything without their approval (Hernon, 1991a).

The impression that Civic Progress controlled the municipal agenda was given some credence when Schoemehl's economic development director, Christopher Grace, observed that Civic Progress "performs essentially a government function" (Hernon, 1991b). According to evidence gathered by the *St. Louis Post Dispatch*, there had been instances when the Board of Aldermen received an issue to discuss, only to learn it had already been decided by Civic Progress (Hernon, 1991a). The power that the members of Civic Progress wielded—or was perceived to wield—is evident in statements made by business owners who were not part of the corporate elite. Typical was a comment by a young civic activist, who stated that there is no real power for those who are trying to move up (ibid.).

The era of corporate governance began coming to a slow and uncertain end in 1992, when a few Civic Progress members became embroiled in a bitter public controversy over a deal they had struck with the city for public subsidies to help support the construction of a sports facility, the Kiel Auditorium, which houses the St. Louis hockey Blues. Much of the passion driving the dispute was energized by widespread resentments directed at the mysterious secret society that seemed to run St. Louis. Stung by criticisms that they were profiting at the public's expense, the corporate executives of Civic Progress withdrew from their high-profile status as the city's powerbrokers, although they have continued to play a pivotal but less public role in St. Louis politics.

The Kiel controversy hurried along a process that was beginning to unfold anyway. In 1997, the roster of Civic Progress members changed substantially due to retirements and corporate mergers and acquisitions that impacted many long-time members of the group (Civic Progress, 1997, p. 5). In fact, the group had already been changing; even in the early 1990s over half its members were not native St. Louisians (Civic Progress, 1995, p. 5). Reflecting the complexion of its new membership, Civic Progress took steps to overcome the impression that it was a secret society. In 1995 it issued its first annual public report. Admitting, in effect, that it had been playing a dominant role in determining the local agenda, it issued a statement that "Civic Progress cannot single-handedly solve the challenges the St. Louis region is facing" (Civic Progress, 1998). Two years later, Civic Progress commissioned a study to gauge the perceptions of the group among community leaders, and it asked forty-five prominent leaders to write white papers offering suggestions for Civic Progress's agenda. As a symbolic step, it no longer held its breakfast meetings at the exclusive Bogey Club. In 1998 Civic Progress decided to hire a staff so that it could work more effectively with the Regional Commerce and Growth Association, the intergovernmental organization representing local government and business, and two years later a new organization, the Regional Business Council (RBC), emerged to represent the heads of medium-sized companies that were not members of Civic Progress (Nicklaus, 2003). Civic Progress is now a formal partner with the RBC, with whom it has agreed to work on regional issues.

Until the 1990s it is doubtful that Civic Progress could have redefined its role in community affairs without creating a serious power vacuum. The disorganization of city government would have decisively gridlocked most initiatives. By then, however, other players had come onto the stage, thereby ushering in a new governance arrangement sufficient for overcoming the city's institutional fragmentation. Mid-level and small business owners began to assert themselves. Perhaps of more consequence, independent quasi-public authorities took on an increasing share of responsibility for the financing and administration of downtown projects. In 1984 the Convention and Visitors Commission assumed the task of running the Cervantes Convention Center; in 1989 it handed off administrative tasks to the St. Louis Convention and Sports Authority and shifted its focus primarily to city marketing. The St. Louis Development Corporation was brought into being under state legislation to coordinate the activities of eight authorities involved in economic development-related activities. The authority strategy had significant advantages because these institutions were able to generate their own resources, develop leadership and professional capabilities, and act with a speed and agility not available to general-purpose governments.

Much of the reason for this new capability can be traced to the fact that the mix of participants and the relationships among them became much more complex than they were in the past. Depending upon the issue at hand, leadership might come from the mayor, a diverse array of business leaders, or from professional policy entrepreneurs. Very significant resources could be mobilized for particular projects—in fact, on a scale probably larger than in the Civic Progress period. Political support and financing for the domed stadium, for example, pooled the resources of many players including, notably, participants from outside the city. The rise of special authorities in St. Louis and elsewhere virtually guarantees that nonlocal actors will play a pivotal role in producing the capacity to mobilize resources for civic purposes.

These developments have led to the emergence of a tripartite governance structure involving the mayor, the business leadership, and a cadre of professional policy entrepreneurs. Mayoral leadership, or at least acquiescence, continued to be essential for major public initiatives. Although it now operated behind the scenes more than in the past, Civic Progress offered financial support for particular projects. Quasi-purpose authorities constitute the third leg of the triangle. Major projects can be undertaken without such mechanisms (for example, the new stadium to house the Cardinals baseball team, which opened in 2006, was built by the Cardinals' owners, with indirect financial help from the city and also the state). But it is likely that most major undertakings will, as time goes by, be financed and administered through specialized institutional mechanisms established specifically for the purpose.

The complicated politics involved in the construction of a $300 million, multipurpose domed stadium connected to the Cervantes Convention Center (the combined complex is now known as America's Center) illustrates how the tripartite governance arrangement works. The mayor and corporate leaders assumed a lead role in this initiative; in fact, they lobbied for creation of the Convention and Sports Complex Authority as a means of coordinating their efforts. The city of St. Louis approved increases in restaurant and hotel taxes to support their share of a common pool of revenue needed to subsidize the stadium's annual operation, and St. Louis County approved an increase in hotel taxes that doubled the rate to 7.25 percent. The authority issued $259 million in bonds in 1991 and earned an additional $40 million by investing the proceeds. Local institutions such as the St. Louis Convention and Visitors Bureau provided marketing expertise, and individual members of its board lent their voices to the arguments for the expansion. Civic Progress supplied funds, but its members did not take the lead and they remained out of the public eye.

What allows institutions like the Convention and Sports Authority to become partners in governance is that once created they are able to generate ideas, resources, and political presence. The managers of the convention center, for example, work with an array of consultants and industry associations in the meetings industry who supply specialized development, financial, public relations, marketing, and information expertise. Engineering and architectural services are often provided by a handful of national firms. National public relations firms are also often hired to manage promotional campaigns, often from concept to tax approval campaign to construction. Likewise, national public accounting and public finance consulting firms with specialties in project finance and cost-benefit analysis provide the principal justifications for individual projects, and they justify public subsidies through feasibility and impact analyses. Included in these reports are data and information that are gathered and compiled by industry associations. In turn, accounting and bond-rating firms rely on industry-generated data and reports from consultants. Political support for new initiatives is sought from the mayor and other constituencies on an as-needed basis.

By establishing a presence in these ways, special authorities have become essential components of a complex ecology of local governance that involves city hall, business, and policy entrepreneurs in a bargaining relationship. The center of gravity in this system is in constant flux, depending upon the particular issue at hand and the relative strength of the participants at any given time. If the issue involves a plan to expand the convention center, the authority generates most of the information and attempts to enlist others in the cause. If city hall floats an idea dear to the mayor, the center of gravity may shift, on that issue, toward city government. And, finally, if the initiative comes from business, as it did in the case of the Cardinals stadium, some or all of the other players may need to come on board, and they may hold a veto power, but nothing more.

Is St. Louis an Exception?

It is tempting to conclude that the strategies for building the capacity to govern in St. Louis have been shaped primarily by a uniquely fragmented governmental structure and divided political culture; if this is so, they may not have necessarily evolved in any other city. As we have noted, St. Louisians have tended to link the chronic problems of urban decay to an institutional legacy peculiar to their city. This view is entirely logical; every city has a history of its own that reflects the composition of its economy, its political structures, its political traditions and cultures. From this "local autonomy" perspective, the political leaders and civic elites in a city may chart a path shaped mainly by the contours of local politics.

However, the literature on urban governance offers a wealth of evidence suggesting that the paths taken in St. Louis may not be as different from those of other cities as one might think. Let us take, in the first instance, St. Louis's urban renewal regime. The passage of the 1949 Housing Act, which funded the urban renewal program, catalyzed the formation of executive-centered coalitions in cities all across the country (Salisbury, 1964). The character of these coalitions was remarkably the same from city to city, seeming to indicate that federal resources and policy intentions had wiped out the nuances of politics that differentiated one city from another. In perhaps the most famous case, Richard Lee in New Haven, Connecticut, won the 1952 mayoral election and several terms thereafter by putting together a broad alliance in favor of urban renewal (Dahl, 1961). Federal resources provided him with the opportunity, and he seized it; however, it is important to note that the structure of the urban renewal program in effect required strong leadership. As was the case with other mayors, Lee was required to appoint an advisory board to oversee the local urban renewal authority. In addition, though the application for funding had to be submitted by the local authority, in practice it could not be done without assistance from city hall, which supplied planning and administrative support; indeed, federal funds were made available for this purpose. Lee proved to be adept at forging a coalition of government officials, civic notables, and labor leaders, but if he had not done so, it is likely that he would have been replaced by a mayor who would. The same might be said about St. Louis and, in fact, every city that received federal funds for urban renewal.

The second governance arrangement prevailed in St. Louis from the mid-1960s into the 1990s. By all appearances, this era of governance appeared to be the product of a local political culture presided over by a social and economic upper crust that still came together "in the exclusive insiders' clubs created by the turn-of-the-century elite, the small, exclusively male and predominantly Anglo-Saxon domains such as the Bogey and the Log Cabin clubs" (Primm, 1981, p. 495). In St. Louis, a consensus seemed to clearly emerge around the idea that Civic Progress was an anachronism, a throwback to an era that had passed long ago in most cities.

Such an impression may have been misleading. The corporate-centered politics that revolved around Civic Progress may have persisted longer in St. Louis than elsewhere, but, in fact, it seems to have been a ubiquitous feature of Sunbelt cities for a long period of time. According to Stephen Elkin, business leaders gained control over mayoral nominations in Dallas in the late 1930s, and they maintained their iron grip for more than thirty years. The system worked so efficiently that business elites could trust that "those who held elected and appointed office did not have to be told what to do" (Elkin, 1987, p. 68). Unlike Atlanta's regime, where power became centered in an institutionalized city hall–business alliance, in Dallas the political process was tightly managed by a business establishment. The powers of government could be put to good use, but public officeholders did not enjoy any meaningful independence.

Similar methods of governance emerged in cities all across the broad swath of territory that later came to be called the Sunbelt. In his landmark study, Carl

Abbott indicates that a wave of reform gripped Sunbelt cities after World War II, set in motion by business leaders anxious to use the levers of government to promote local economic prosperity. The reform programs they championed were designed to improve the administrative competence and efficiency of city governments and, at the same time, to reduce electoral participation. Large infrastructure and development projects were taken out of the political realm entirely and moved into independent agencies (Abbott, 1981). By changing the rules of game, business elites were able to preserve their hold on local politics for decades without much opposition. In Abbott's account, a politics of this stripe became the norm throughout the South and Southwest, and it persisted until an extraordinary mobilization of dynamic young challengers swept the region in the 1970s.

A tightly knit corporate leadership structure emerged in northern cities, too. The Allegheny Conference on Community Development, formed in 1943 under the leadership of R.K. Mellon, promoted the revitalization of Pittsburgh's Golden Triangle. It became the template for the New Boston Committee, founded in 1951; the Greater Baltimore Committee, 1955; Civic Progress, 1953; Central Atlanta Progress, 1961; and numerous similar organizations. They continued to emerge even as late as 1982, when some "leading business titans" organized Cleveland Tomorrow because they "preferred gatherings among peers in a boardroom, receiving a quick briefing by a colleague or a senior staff officer, and reaching a quick consensus on what to do" (Hanson et al., 2006, p. 11). The size of these groups varied from fewer than fifty members to as many as two hundred, but even in the larger and more inclusive of them, an executive committee made up of the CEOs of large corporations made the important decisions and operated behind closed doors (ibid., p. 12). As we have noted, in the urban renewal era mayors forged a partnership with corporate leaders, thus giving birth to urban regimes. Some of these alliances may have remained intact for long periods, as in Atlanta, but the evidence on this point is scant.[3]

Whether this style of leadership produced regimes or corporate-centered arrangements wherein mayors were held at arm's length, sometime in the 1970s or 1980s the globalization of local economies began to reduce the civic engagement of large corporations. As summarized by Royce Hanson and his collaborators,

> . . . waves of mergers and acquisitions transformed local corporate headquarters, converting icons of local industry into mere branches of distant firms. Executive suites were populated with a new generation of managers, many of whom had no local roots and were on career trajectories that involved frequent transfers to branches in other cities. All these institutional changes were accompanied by relocation of many headquarters offices to the suburbs. The combination of these forces led to changes in the nature of civic engagement by business leaders, their commitment to city and region, and the membership and structure of many of their organizations. (Hanson et al., 2006, p. 12)

The civic commitment of corporate elites was undermined by these developments. In the past, hometown bankers had played pivotal roles in committing funds and mobilizing addition financial commitment from other executives, but the deregulation and reorganization of banking that began in the 1980s meant that these hometown boosters "were often replaced by managers for whom success was measured by promotion to run a bank in a more important market, and eventually to the bank's central headquarters" (Hanson et al., 2006, p. 13). In other industries, too, interest in local community began to wane as the incentives to become involved in community issues gave way to priorities dictated by corporate politics. A CEO interviewed for a study in Baltimore told the researcher, "These guys are just passing through. Baltimore is a stopover. All they want is not to make a mistake" (Hanson and Norris, 2006).

Governance arrangements requiring a high level of interest in local affairs on the part of corporate CEOs have been (or are being) replaced by a new strategy for mobilizing the capacity to govern. The first element in this strategy is a broader, but less focused, civic leadership. The fastest-growth sectors of the global economy often are dominated by smaller businesses and high-tech enterprises that work closely with universities, hospitals, and nonprofit organizations. New organizations have come into being to represent these sectors, and the CEO-led organizations inherited from the past have expanded their membership. Increasingly, civic agendas focus on the region rather than the downtown or the central city because civic leadership itself has become so dispersed. St. Louis fits within this profile.

The second important element in the strategy involves the creation of new institutions to finance and administer projects requiring significant volumes of capital and coordination among governments and private-sector institutions. Globalization has wrought a revolution in local political institutions that is as far-reaching as it is underappreciated. In recent decades, independent, quasi-public authorities have assumed most of the responsibility for urban development projects, and in the process they have become components of an increasingly complex local state (Erie, Altshuler, and Luberoff, 2003; Flyvbjerg, Bruzelius, and Rothengatter, 2003; Sellers, 2002). Within all large urban regions, authorities have taken responsibility for transportation infrastructure such as highways, roads, bridges, tunnels, mass transit, airports, seaports, and harbors. In addition to such regional activities, special authorities by the dozen finance and manage tourism and entertainment facilities such as convention centers, sports stadiums, museums, and urban entertainment districts.

The rules under which special authorities operate help to make them effective instruments of urban development because they can escape the political gridlock that often characterizes urban politics in the post–urban-renewal era. Confronted by the fact that city government was too bureaucratic and fiscally limited to undertake expensive new projects, in the 1980s, energetic mayors and other civic leaders pioneered the development of institutions that could accomplish public purposes while not being bound by the rules that frustrated general-purpose governments. The special authorities thus created were able to operate much like private corporations, thereby avoiding public scrutiny of their operations (Perry, 2003). Special authorities are generally empowered to borrow money, issue bonds, and exercise critical powers such as eminent domain. These arrangements are the key to understanding how fiscally strapped cities were able to build the facilities and undertake the ambitious projects necessary to support a local economy of tourism and entertainment.

The new institutions have become embedded within an increasingly complex mode of local governance. Previously, ambitious mayors reached out to corporate leaders to assemble the resources necessary for urban revitalization. The relationship was not symmetrical even in the best of cases—the business coalition could make or break a mayor, but the opposite was not true. It was up to mayors to make a partnership work, and when they were not up to task or the conditions were unfavorable, corporate leaders stood ready to assume the main leadership role. With the decline of corporate commitment in the global era, mayors have been forced to seek new allies, and these come from two sources—business leadership more inclusive but less focused than before, and full-time policy entrepreneurs who represent quasi-public authorities.

Baltimore shows how a skillful mayor, William Donald Schaefer, managed to circumvent the slow-moving bureaucratic and democratic processes of city government. Schaefer relied on a network of quasi-public development corporations (which grew to more than thirty by 2002) to direct and implement the ambitious Harbor Place redevelopment effort. Proponents viewed these agencies as an "apolitical means for improving the city's development potential by infusing speed, flexibility, and technical expertise into the policy-making process" (Stoker, 1987, p. 248). In actuality they were not only embedded within the political process; they became the means of establishing a new process altogether—one that put Schaefer at the center.

The strategy for building the capacity to govern in the global era does not revolve around a fixed center of gravity. Much depends upon the leadership skills and powers available to a mayor, the degree to which business is represented by a tightly knit organizational structure or a loose and inclusive collection of institutions, the degree to which nonbusiness interests may assert a voice, and, finally, the independent political muscle exercised by professional policy entrepreneurs. No doubt the locus of power differs substantially from city to city.

Conclusion

Our study of St. Louis's postwar governance cannot lay to rest the issue of whether the city's unique brand of governmental fragmentation accounts for many of its problems. Despite the ability to achieve the capacity to govern in the postwar era, it is certainly plausible that the city's political and civic elites could have been more effective if they had not been forced to constantly confront the formidable obstacles presented by the extreme disorganization of the local state. The ability to govern was achieved, but it might not have been able to deliver more benefits in a different institutional setting.

In St. Louis, the extreme fragmentation of the city's governmental structure and its separation from St. Louis County kept the center of gravity situated firmly within ward politics, a pattern broken, in the urban renewal period, by the formation of a downtown-oriented regime. When urban renewal no longer exerted its centralizing force, Civic Progress provided the counterweight necessary for mobilizing resources on behalf of downtown projects, though its ability to do so was diminished. In the global era, a new ecology of governance has emerged wherein the mayor, a business leadership, and an emerging cadre of full-time policy entrepreneurs interact. The relationships they negotiate produce policies aimed at downtown renewal; otherwise, the centrifugal forces of St. Louis's politics would make it nearly impossible to focus on the downtown and its problems.

Despite St. Louis's peculiar system of government, the governance strategies fashioned by its political and civic elites have been quite similar to those that have emerged elsewhere, probably because, as Clarence Stone (1989, p. 1) has observed, the dispersal of power in local politics is the norm, not the exception. In all cities, governance is based upon informal understandings, negotiations, and agreements. From this perspective, St. Louis's governance experience in the postwar period is not as unusual as the standard narrative might suppose.

Notes

1. This account of St. Louis's fragmented politics is based upon Lana Stein's excellent book, which is the definitive work on St. Louis politics.
2. Stein employs the phrase, "the mayor's party," in her book (see p. 141).
3. Any judgment about this matter depends upon whether Stone's original conception of a regime is applied. If the definition of a regime is relaxed to include, for example, a coalition broader than the city hall-business alliance, then it is probably safe to conclude that many cities were governed by regimes even after urban renewal, and that many still are. However, we reject the concept-stretching necessary to reach such a conclusion.

References

Abbott, Carl. 1981. *The New Urban America.* Chapel Hill: University of North Carolina Press.
City of St. Louis. 1964. Office of the Mayor, files of Raymond R. Tucker, Series 4–14, University Archives, Department of Special Collections. St. Louis, MO: Washington University Libraries. Meeting notes, October 19, 1964.
———. 1965. Office of the Mayor, files of Raymond R. Tucker, Series 4–14, University Archives, Department of Special Collections. St. Louis, MO: Washington University Libraries. Meeting notes, June 9, 1965.
———. 1977. Office of the Mayor, Files of John H. Poelker, Box 7, University Archives, Department of Special Collections. St. Louis, MO: Washington University Libraries.
"Civic Progress and the Rest of Us." 1998. *St. Louis Business Journal,* November 20, Opinion. Available at www.bizjournals.com/stlouis/search.html (accessed July 23, 2005).
Civic Progress Annual Report. 1995. St. Louis, MO: Author.
———. 1997. St. Louis, MO: Author.
Dahl, Robert A. 1961. *Who Governs? Democracy and Power in an American City.* New Haven, CT: Yale University Press.
Elkin, Stephen L. 1987. *City and Regime in the American Republic.* Chicago: University of Chicago Press.
Erie, Steven; Alan Altshuler; and David Luberoff. 2003. *Mega-Projects: The Changing Politics of Urban Public Investments.* Washington, DC: Brookings Institution Press.
Flyvbjerg, Bent; Nils Bruzelius; and Werner Rothengatter. 2003. *Megaprojects and Risk: An Anatomy of Ambition.* Cambridge: Cambridge University Press.

Hanson, Royce, and Donald F. Norris. 2006. "Corporate Citizenship and Urban Governance in Baltimore: Implications of Restructuring and Globalization of the Economy" (unpublished draft).

Hanson, Royce, Hal Wolman, David Connolly, and Katherine Person. 2006. "Corporate Citizenship and Urban Problem Solving: The Changing Civic Role of Business Leaders in American Cities." A report to the Brookings Institution, June (unpublished).

Hernon, Peter. 1991a. "Crossroads: Group's Role Under Scrutiny." *St. Louis Post-Dispatch,* August 4. Western Manuscript Collection Archives, Vertical File s1694, Box 3, folder 76, University Archives. St. Louis, MO: University of Missouri-St. Louis, Thomas Jefferson Library, pp. 1A–5A.

———. 1991b. "Crossroads: Group's Role Under Scrutiny." *St. Louis Post-Dispatch,* August 5. Western Manuscript Collection Archives, Vertical File s1694, Box 3, folder 76, University Archives. St. Louis: University of Missouri-St. Louis, Thomas Jefferson Library, pp. 1A–5A.

Institute of Housing. 1952. "Proceedings." Mimeograph, University College, Washington University, St. Louis, Missouri, March 21–22.

Laslo, David; Claude Louishomme; and Dennis Judd. 2003. "Building the Infrastructure of Urban Tourism: The St. Louis Case." In *The Infrastructure of Play: Building the Tourism City,* ed. Dennis R. Judd, 77–103. Armonk, NY: M.E. Sharpe.

Nicklaus, David. 2003. "St Louis Equity Fund Passes an Important Milestone at 15 Years." *St. Louis Post-Dispatch Knight Ridder/Tribune Business News,* July 3.

Perry, David C. 2003. "Urban Tourism and the Privatizing Discourses of Public Infrastructure." In *The Infrastructure of Play,* ed. Dennis R. Judd, 19–49. Armonk, NY: M.E. Sharpe.

Primm, James Neil. 1981. *Lion of the Valley: St. Louis, Missouri.* Boulder, CO: Pruett.

Salisbury, Robert H. 1964. "The New Convergence of Power in Urban Politics." *Journal of Politics* 26 (November): 775–97.

Sellers, Jeffery. 2002. *Governing from Below: Urban Regions and the Global Economy.* Cambridge: Cambridge University Press.

Spitzer, D.L., and R. Malone. 1979. "Who Runs St. Louis?" *St Louis Magazine* (March) (Missouri Historical Society Library), 72–122.

Statistical Abstract of the United States. 1987. Table 27, p. 32; Table 34, pp. 29–31. Washington, DC: Government Printing Office.

———. 1993. Table 42, pp. 37–39. Washington, DC: Government Printing Office.

Stein, Lana. 2002. *St. Louis Politics: The Triumph of Tradition.* St. Louis: Missouri Historical Society Press.

Stoker, Robert P. 1987. *"Baltimore: The Self-Evaluating City?"* In *The Politics of Urban Development,* ed. Clarence N. Stone and Heywood T. Sanders, 244–66. Lawrence: University Press of Kansas.

Stone, Clarence. 1989. *Regime Politics: Governing Atlanta 1946–1988.* Lawrence: University Press of Kansas.

Teaford, Jon C. 1993. *Cities of the Heartland: The Rise and Fall of the Industrial Midwest.* Bloomington: Indiana University Press.

———. 1997. *Post-Suburbia: Government and Politics in the Edge Cities.* Baltimore: Johns Hopkins University Press.

U.S. Bureau of the Census. 1951. *Census of Population, 1950.* Vol. 1, Number of Inhabitants, Part 1. Washington, DC: Government Printing Office.

———. 2007. *Population Estimate Program, Table 1 Annual Estimates of the Population for Incorporated Places over 100,000: April 1, 2000 to July 1, 2007.* Washington, DC: Government Printing Office.

U.S. Department of Commerce. 1999. *County Business Patterns, 1951–1997.* Washington, DC: Government Printing Office.

7

Governmental Fragmentation and Metropolitan Governance: Does Less Mean More?

The Case of the Baltimore Region

Donald F. Norris, Carl W. Stenberg, and Tonya Zimmerman

In this chapter, we address whether governmental fragmentation in a metropolitan area is related to the governance that occurs there. (See also Chapter 8 for a look at this issue in four quite different metro areas.) Hence, our title: does less (fragmentation) mean more (metropolitan governance)? The test case for examining this question is the Baltimore, Maryland, metropolitan area (population of 2.3 million)—one of the least fragmented metropolitan areas in the United States. As we will explain later, it takes the agreement of only six local governments to make anything significant happen in the Baltimore metropolitan area—six governments, compared with a national average of over a hundred governments per metropolitan area. Therefore, the Baltimore metropolitan area ought to be an excellent location to learn whether less (fragmentation) does mean more (governance).

Fragmentation as a Rationale for Metropolitan Government

For more than fifty years, proponents of metropolitan reform in the United States have contended that the fragmentation of governments within metropolitan areas is an important reason to consider structural reform in these areas. The metropolitan reformers have argued that the effects of fragmentation are harmful both to central cities and suburbs alike and that governmental reorganization would improve the functioning of the overall metropolitan area. Here, we briefly summarize the arguments for why governmental fragmentation in metropolitan areas is thought to be undesirable and why a metropolitan government is thought to be a solution to fragmentation.

To metropolitan reformers, governmental fragmentation causes several serious problems for metropolitan areas, including disparities between fiscal resources

126

and source needs, spillovers or negative externalities, lost economies of scale, and reduced citizen voice in government (CED, 1970; Warren, 1978; Wood, 1958). We discuss each of these problem areas below.

With respect to disparities between tax resources and service needs, the reformers claimed that areas with the greatest needs have the least ability to pay for them. As early as 1930, Paul Studenski (1974) described the possibility of separation of wealth, and thus tax resources, from the service requirements of an area. Forty years later, the Committee for Economic Development (CED) argued that the educational system is worsened by fragmentation because, "[i]t directs resources in a way that makes them least adequate in those school jurisdictions which need them most" (p. 26).

The metropolitan reformers also claimed that spillovers or negative externalities occur because of decisions that individual local governments in metropolitan areas make to support their particular interests. This hurts not only that particular jurisdiction, but the entire region. Studenski argued that "[i]t is important to the well-being of the entire metropolitan region that these problems be properly solved" (1974, p. 30). However, he also observed that for various reasons, including lack of both resources and leadership, not all jurisdictions work together to address issues of water supply, sewerage, ports, transportation, parks, police and fire protection, and public health concerns.

The metropolitan reformers further argued that the needs of the overall metropolitan area were not adequately addressed under fragmentation. As Long (1958) noted, there is no organization that looks out for the interests of the metropolitan area as a whole. The CED (1970) asserted that separate operation of services such as policing, housing, employment training, and transportation prevented localities from coordinating actions.

Another problem produced by the fragmented metropolitan governmental system, said the reformers, was a loss of political voice and regional identity. The CED referred to the organization of metropolitan areas with terms such as, "confusing maze," "bureaucratic labyrinth," "baffling array," "crazy quilt" (1970, pp. 10–11). These terms implied that the system was difficult for citizens to understand and that citizens lost access to, and a voice in, government as a result of this confusion. More than a decade earlier, Robert Wood (1958) observed that, as a result of fragmentation and work-related commuting between cities and suburbs, citizens had become disenfranchised. Wood argued that, without geographically larger governmental bodies, people may lose the type of consciousness that would allow regional problems to be recognized and solved.

The reformers did not necessarily support the same approaches to metropolitan government reform. However, they all believed that metropolitan structural reorganization was necessary to deal with problems caused by fragmentation. Their solutions ranged from a single metropolitan government, to two- and three-tiered government, to councils of governments and regional authorities, to voluntary cooperative mechanisms (Walker, 1987). Regardless of their particular solution, the reformers claimed that the fragmented metropolitan system created or exacerbated numerous problems and that establishing regional governmental structures was the best solution to problems associated with fragmentation.

Despite these arguments, at the beginning of the twenty-first century, the vast majority of Americans live in fragmented metropolitan areas. Virtually none of these areas has structures of government to address the needs or protect the interests of the overall metropolitan territory. As noted in Chapter 2 of this book, Portland, Oregon, stands out as the only region (the only one among over 360 metropolitan areas) with something that looks and acts like a metropolitan government. And while not a government, the Twin Cities Metropolitan Council, created by the Minnesota legislature in 1969, is the only example of a nonelected authoritative multipurpose regional body for land use planning, sewer permitting, development control, and tax-base sharing.

If the reformers were right, it would follow that the least politically fragmented metropolitan areas would produce the greatest amount of regional governance. Even in the absence of region-wide government structures, as in Portland, regions with low levels of fragmentation should produce significant and observable forms of regional governance (e.g., consensus and action on the part of major regional actors to address pressing area-wide problems).

Our purpose in this chapter is to test the proposition that less governmental fragmentation produces more metropolitan governance. We do so with evidence from the Baltimore, Maryland, metropolitan area.

One of the striking characteristics of the Baltimore region is that in it only six governments really matter. They are Baltimore City and the five surrounding counties of Anne Arundel, Baltimore, Carroll, Harford, and Howard.[1] These six jurisdictions matter for at least two reasons. First, under Maryland law, county governments are the strongest local governments and, especially in "reformed" counties,[2] they exercise a wide range of municipal-type powers. Four of the five counties are also led by elected executives who have considerable power vis-à-vis their respective legislative bodies. Second, two of the counties (Baltimore and Howard) have no municipalities, and the remaining three counties have only a few small municipalities covering only a fraction of their respective territories and populations.

Following the logic of the metropolitan reformers' arguments, because of this relatively streamlined governmental structure, one would expect to find that the policy results produced in the Baltimore area as regards difficult regional problems and issues will be substantially different from those produced in more fragmented metropolitan areas. To put it differently, the prospects for regional governance should be enhanced by the structural simplicity of government.

Since the Baltimore region has no overarching structure of metropolitan government, any enhanced regional governance would be expected to manifest itself via mechanisms of intergovernmental cooperation and joint problem solving. To meet our test for regional governance, cooperation or other forms of joint action must occur around tough and controversial issues affecting the region as a whole or substantial portions of the region, issues such as land use planning, zoning, K–12 education, and law enforcement, among others. Oliver Williams (1971) called these "lifestyle" issues. Cooperation around "systems maintenance" issues (e.g., infrastructure construction and maintenance) is relatively easy, and therefore is insufficient to define or describe regional governance.

The Baltimore Region

In addition to streamlined structure, the Baltimore region is unique compared with most other metropolitan areas around the country. Some of this uniqueness is attributable to provisions in the Maryland constitution and statutes relating to local powers and structure. Other unique elements are due to the political, social, and economic characteristics of the region.

The Importance of County Government

The Maryland state constitution and subsequently enacted statutes have established counties as the preeminent local governments in the state. For example, since 1954, municipalities have not been able to be incorporated without permission of their counties. This has meant that only three municipalities have incorporated statewide since then, all in Montgomery County and all with the support of the county government (Norris, 1991).[3] Counties have considerable power over land use and development in their unincorporated territory through extensive planning and zoning powers. Charter (but not commissioner) counties have the power to adopt local ordinances in most areas of local government. Hence, they are not dependent on the General Assembly (Maryland's state legislature) for legislation when they decide to act on matters of local concern.[4] Counties in Maryland also are empowered to provide a wide range of public services (e.g., police, fire, sanitation, water and wastewater, health, parks and recreation, libraries, community colleges, streets and roads, etc.) that typically are reserved for municipal governments.[5] All of the school systems in Maryland are dependent (not independent) districts; have boundaries that are coterminous with their counties; do not have independent taxing authority; and must submit their budgets to their respective counties for approval.

Governmental Structure and Politics in the Region

Baltimore City is governed by a mayor-council form of government.[6] The council consists of thirteen members each elected from single-member districts, plus a council president elected citywide. The real power in city government resides with the mayor, who has strong executive budget authority and control over the appointment and removal of department heads. The mayoralty in Baltimore is one of the strongest such offices in the United States, and is the central focus of politics and administration in the city.

The mayor, who runs citywide, and all council members are elected every fourth odd numbered year (2011 is the next city election year) in partisan elections.[7] There are no term limits for any of the offices in Baltimore City. In addition to the mayor, two other municipal officers are elected citywide—the city council president and the city comptroller. During the terms of the past three mayors, none of the incumbents to these two offices was able to establish him/herself as a significant alternative center of power in city government, nor was the city council able to offer any significant counterweight to the mayor. Baltimore City is a solidly Democratic jurisdiction. No Republicans have been elected in the city for many years and none probably will be for the foreseeable future.

Four of the region's five counties have governments with elected executives that parallel the strong-mayor form found in Baltimore City. These are the charter counties of Anne Arundel, Baltimore, Harford, and Howard, in which citizens have adopted locally written county charters specifying the structure, functions, offices, and powers of these governments. These counties have elected county executives (essentially county mayors) who are elected countywide and county council members elected from single-member districts.[8] The county executives have strong executive budget authority, and they control the appointment and removal of their department heads; furthermore, like the mayor in Baltimore City, they are clearly the central political and administrative foci of their respective governments.

All county elections in Maryland are held every fourth even-numbered year (2010 is the next county election year) at the same time as the gubernatorial and General Assembly election. County elections are partisan and, in recent years, have been trending increasingly Republican. Only two counties have Republican majorities of registered voters, and one has a modest plurality (see Table 7.1). With the exception of Baltimore County, these jurisdictions have all had at least one period since 1986 of a Republican county council majority. All of the charter counties have had at least one Republican county executive during this period, while Carroll County has had Republican majorities on its commission throughout the period.

Harford County has become a solidly Republican county within the past ten years. Anne Arundel County leans Republican, but the voters choose either major party with equanimity in local, statewide, and national races. Howard County leans Democratic but is also a swing jurisdiction. Baltimore County appears to be strongly Democratic in local elections but swings between the two parties in national and statewide elections.

Carroll County has the traditional commissioner form of county government in which executive and legislative powers are exercised by an elected board of county commissioners.[9] Carroll County has three commissioners, who are elected countywide, and for the past two election cycles, all three Carroll County commissioners have been Republicans. Carroll County is the most solidly Republican county in the region. In fact, there are no elected county officials or state legislators in Carroll County today who are Democrats.

Table 7.1

Political Division in Baltimore Metropolitan Jurisdictions Since 1986

Jurisdictions	Elected executives (since 1986)		Council majorities (since 1986)		Voter registration[7] (% in 2007)	
	Democrat	Republican	Democrat	Republican	Democrat	Republican
Baltimore City	3	0	6	0	79	10
Counties of:						
Anne Arundel	2	3[1]	4	2[4]	44	38
Baltimore	3	1	6	0	59	27
Carroll	n/a	n/a	0	5[5]	32	52
Harford	2	1[2]	1	5[6]	43	43
Howard	3	1[3]	5	1	57	34

[1]1990–1994.
[2]Republican since 1998.
[3]1990–1998.
[4]Republican since 2002.
[5]Commissioner form of government.
[6]Republican since 1990.
[7]County voter registration has been trending more Republican for the past twenty years.
Source: Unpublished data collected from various sources by chapter co-author Donald Norris.

Regional Actors

Another distinctive feature of the Baltimore region is that it features only two organizations that have the potential to produce elements of regional governance. These are the Baltimore Metropolitan Council (BMC) and the Economic Alliance of Greater Baltimore (the Alliance). The BMC is essentially a subsidiary of the six principal governments of the region, while the Alliance is a cooperative venture of government, higher education, and the private sector. The region also boasts a private sector organization, the Greater Baltimore Committee (GBC), which is the public policy representative of the largest businesses in the region, and, from time to time, has endeavored to play a role in regional governance.[10]

In the following paragraphs, we discuss the roles and activities of these three organizations and their impact on regional governance. We also discuss the role of the news media and recommendations of expert studies that have been conducted of the region. As we will show, although there is considerable interlocal cooperation in the Baltimore region, hardly any of the "tough" regional issues have been addressed either bilaterally or multilaterally by the region's local governments or by the BMC, the Alliance, or the GBC.

The Baltimore Metropolitan Council

The Baltimore Metropolitan Council was established in 1992 as the successor to the Baltimore Regional Council of Governments (BRCOG) (Norris, 1994). The BMC is a quasi-governmental organization, established by state law and wholly controlled by the local elected executives of the region who serve as its governing board. The BMC has a small full-time professional staff headed by an appointed executive director.

Initially, the BMC board met about every two months to discuss items on an agenda approved by the elected executives. Generally, all of the elected executives attended BMC meetings. Their interactions were cordial, even friendly, and it is clear that they enjoyed the opportunity to meet together and discuss common concerns. In recent years, the frequency of meetings and the direct, hands-on participation by the executives has decreased.

Probably the most significant activity that the BMC undertakes is transportation planning. It functions as the Metropolitan Planning Organization (MPO) that is required by the federal Safe, Accountable, Flexible, Efficient Transportation Act: A Legacy for Users, 2005 (formerly the Transportation Equity Act for the 21st Century, TEA-21) to develop regional transportation plans, which, in turn, are required for local governments in Metropolitan Statistical Areas to be eligible for federal transportation funding.[11] Transportation planning was one of the principal reasons for establishment of the BMC (Norris, 1994).[12] However, no real regional planning occurs for transportation purposes. Instead, local jurisdictions amalgamate their respective wish lists, engage in bargaining, and cobble together what is called a regional plan—all for the purpose of securing federal transportation dollars.

Beyond transportation, the BMC addresses a relatively narrow range of issues, which is intentional. According to one of the founders of the BMC, the executives decided when they created the organization to operate on the basis of consensus. If they feel that consensus cannot be achieved or that an issue will be divisive, they will not place it on the agenda. The point is to accomplish what is feasible in terms of concrete actions taken by all or a subset of all of the governments.

Given the BMC's modus operandi, one cannot say with certainty how the organization might fare or what results might obtain if its members agreed to address controversial or divisive issues. An issue that might have offered a clear answer to this question never arrived on the BMC agenda. This involved Baltimore City's 1995 negotiated, out-of-court settlement of a lawsuit concerning alleged discrimination in city public housing. The settlement resulted in HUD Section 8 vouchers and certificates being provided to public housing tenants in Baltimore City. The recipients of the vouchers and certificates could move anywhere in the region, thus raising the specter of hordes of the urban poor (mostly black), moving to suburban neighborhoods.[13]

When the settlement became public knowledge, many public officials in suburbs reacted quite negatively, some openly and vigorously. More than one of the executives told us that he felt blindsided by Baltimore City's leadership. The executives also noted that in the best of times they would face considerable opposition from residents in parts of their counties who feared an influx of poor persons into their neighborhoods. Moreover, they felt that because of the way that the leadership of Baltimore City chose to act, that is, outside of a regional framework, what would in any event have been a bad situation was made worse.

A more current regional issue also reveals the BMC's inability to tackle divisive matters. Maryland was a big "winner" in the most recent federal base relocation and closure (BRAC) decisions, which are estimated to bring up to 60,000 jobs and 28,000 households to the state.

Nearly all of these new jobs and residents will locate around the Aberdeen Proving Grounds in northern Harford County and Fort Meade in northern Anne Arundel County. However, the BMC is not the principal (or even a secondary) vehicle for intergovernmental cooperation and coordination on this issue. Instead, the governor has tasked his lieutenant governor with a role in coordinating among state agencies and local governments, and an entirely new organization (the Chesapeake Science and Security Corridor) has been formed to address BRAC-related issues in the region.

These were (and one still is) significant regional issues—controversial and highly divisive. They could have been brought to the BMC for discussion and potential resolution, but were not. These examples speak volumes about the capacity of the BMC to handle the really tough issues that confront the region.

The Economic Alliance of Greater Baltimore

The Alliance is a nonprofit corporation that focuses on regional economic development, particularly economic development marketing. The Alliance was established in 1993 by the Baltimore Metropolitan Council and the Greater Baltimore Committee (as the Baltimore Development Alliance). Its purpose is to undertake economic development marketing for the region, especially to build the image of the region, attract businesses from other states and countries to locate in the area, and provide seamless customer service to newly relocating employers. One of the Alliance's major contributions to regional cooperation has been its co-sponsorship, with the GBC, of a periodic "State of the Region Report." Its principal contribution, though, has been its economic development marketing efforts on behalf of the entire region. Here, both because of the way it defines its role (economic development marketing for the region) and because it has to work with elected officials as well as with the business community, the Alliance eschews anything related to politics and policy. Indeed, according to its president, the Alliance "stays out of politics."

Greater Baltimore Committee

The Greater Baltimore Committee consists of the largest 500 or so businesses in the region. Among other things, the GBC mission is to develop public policies and projects to address the region's problems and improve its economic competitiveness and visibility. The GBC has been an important source of policy advocacy on behalf of greater regional cooperation for many years. In 1997, the GBC released a report titled "One Region—One Future" in which it advocated various regional solutions. This was followed in 1998 by a "State of the Region Report," which was essentially a benchmarking study comparing Baltimore with selected other regions in the United States, along a number of social and economic dimensions. The GBC hosted regional forums to release and discuss both reports.

The GBC was a major proponent of the "Maryland Regional Economic Competitiveness Act" (HB 970), which was introduced in the 1999 session of the General Assembly. The act would have established a regional tax-base sharing plan under which a percentage of property tax revenue resulting from new development in Baltimore City and the five counties would be provided to the Baltimore Metropolitan Council for expenditure, on a regional basis, to address "problems of public safety, economic and workforce development, and conservation of older neighborhoods . . . in the region." The bill had virtually no political support in the state or region and died in committee.

News Media

Writing in 1958, political scientist Norton Long argued that the daily newspaper was perhaps the only organization that looked out for the interest of the metropolitan area as a whole. The only significant daily newspaper in the Baltimore region is the *Baltimore Sun*. The *Sun* does indeed weigh in periodically on issues of regional significance. In 1991, the *Sun* published a series of articles about regionalism by urban consultant Neal Peirce. In 1998, it presented a series of editorials about regionalism. And, throughout any given year, the *Sun*'s news stories, editorial page, and local columns will have some regional content. Indeed, the *Sun* may be the only regional organization that periodically (and more frequently than any others) addresses regional problems and calls for regional solutions.

Expert Studies

As noted earlier, for several years the Baltimore region has experienced a number of serious, overarching problems that are not addressed by any organization or mechanisms in the region, voluntary or otherwise. One might reasonably ask if it is possible that there has been no action on any of these problems because little is known about them or because the region lacks an intellectual consensus about them. Nothing could be further from the truth. Over the past two decades, seven major studies of the Baltimore area have been conducted (see Appendix 7.1). Each of the studies addressed significant regional issues and urged regional action. Moreover, while not identical, the studies have been highly consistent in their findings and recommendations.

First, the studies agreed broadly on the problems facing Baltimore City and the region. These problems tend largely to be those faced by Baltimore City, including loss of population, jobs, and tax base; concentration of poverty within the city; high incidence of social problems (especially drugs and crime) associated with concentrated poverty; an older housing stock; declining neighborhoods; and increasing disparities between the poor (mostly black) city and the more affluent (mostly white) suburbs. The studies were nearly uniform in their recognition that Baltimore City's public school system is in dreadful condition and that it is partly responsible for the continuing out-migration of residents from the city. To the extent that they considered race, the studies recognized it is a significant underlying issue that must be addressed. As an editorial series in the *Baltimore Sun* (1998) said, race "is the unspoken but first thought that comes across the minds of many when the conversation is [about] poverty, crime, education and wealth." The studies also largely agreed that the region experiences significant problems of inequitable housing opportunities and poor public transportation especially in the suburbs.

Second, the studies were mostly in accord about what should be done. For example, they generally concluded that the region's (and city's) most significant problems have regional causes, and can be "solved" only if they are addressed regionally. The argument, for the most part, is that factors such as the rigidity of political boundaries in the region, the city's inability to annex, suburban sprawl, the lack of regional control over land development, and insufficient low- and moderate-priced housing in the suburbs have doomed the city to become the repository of most of the region's poor. This, in turn, places a heavy burden on Baltimore City, first, by decreasing the city's fiscal ability to provide services, and second, by increasing the need for public safety, public education, and a range of social services. The high concentration of poor living in the city also contributes significantly to the range and extent of social problems it faces.

Third, some studies argued that as the city's problems spill over its borders into the suburbs, suburban governments will necessarily have to begin dealing with them. If, instead, the suburbs were to work together to address these problems (such as low-cost housing and tax-base sharing) now, this would reduce the extent and magnitude of spillover.

Fourth, a few studies contended that the economic health of the region is intimately bound up with the economic health of the city. This is, perhaps, the weakest argument found in these studies, and the one that is believed the least by suburban officials and residents (Vicino, 2006).

Fifth, the studies recognized that solutions based on greater regional cooperation or on regional governance will be difficult to achieve. Nevertheless, they recommended several common strategies or policy options, including:

- more funding for Baltimore City (possibly through regional tax-base sharing);
- regional land use planning and development management (e.g., to slow growth in the periphery and promote reinvestment in older areas);
- fair share housing legislation (e.g., to facilitate a dispersion of the poor); and
- improved public transportation (e.g., to permit lower income persons to reach jobs in the suburbs).

Finally, these studies share another important, if unenviable, characteristic. Virtually have of their significant recommendations have been adopted or implemented.[14] In addition, despite occasional efforts by various actors in the region to generate interest, the recommendations do not appear to be on the radar screens of most local elected officials or the BMC. This is because they threaten local autonomy and are often seen by suburban elected officials and their constituents as "bailouts" for Baltimore City. Thus, they are politically unpalatable to suburban residents and, by extension, to their local elected officials and their representatives to state government. Of equal importance, most local citizens and many local officials give no appearance of believing that the governmental units in the region are interdependent, and that the problems so manifest in Baltimore City could spread across its boundaries into the suburbs.

What the Region's Elected Leaders Say

Despite the relatively simple structure of government in the region, despite the existence of quasi-governmental and private-sector organizations that devote considerable energy to regional issues, despite an active major daily newspaper, and despite a series of studies of the region that all point in similar directions, there is very little that resembles regional governance in the Baltimore area. To try to better understand why this is the case, between 1999 and 2000 we interviewed each of the current and former top elected officials in the region.[15] Those interviewed included the then incumbent mayor of Baltimore (in the final year of his third four-year term), his immediate predecessor and the chief of staff of his successor, two of the three commissioners of Carroll County (both of whom had served in previous commissions), and the current and immediate past elected executives of the four charter counties in the region. We asked them a number of questions about the state of the region, intergovernmental cooperation in the region, the BMC, and related issues. In this section, we report the results of these interviews.

We asked the elected executives what they believed to be the most important issues facing the Baltimore region.[16] Their answers demonstrated that they clearly understood that the region faced problems or issues beyond the capacity of any single jurisdiction to address. Nearly all of the executives mentioned economic development as a key regional issue. Indeed, this was mentioned more frequently than any other issue. Next came transportation (i.e., surface transportation such as roads and highways was of chief concern) and crime. Additional issues included "the plight of Baltimore," education (particularly the disparity in educational outcomes between Baltimore City and the suburbs), race (especially the fact that the city is majority black and the suburbs are majority white), and air quality.

In addition, we wanted to know which issues had received the greatest degree of regional collaboration and which had seen the least. Three issues mentioned most frequently (in order of the frequency with which they were mentioned) as receiving high degrees of collaboration were economic development, transportation planning, and crime. When the executives mentioned efforts to attract new industry by "speaking with a unified voice" on economic development, quite frequently they noted the Greater Baltimore Alliance. When they mentioned transportation, they usually mentioned the Baltimore Metropolitan Council. When they mentioned crime, they usually mentioned the Robbery Task Force that was organized through the BMC between Baltimore City and County to catch a gang of bank robbers who were working across the borders of the two jurisdictions.[17]

Regardless of its limitations, the elected executives we interviewed for this study generally felt that the BMC was effective, especially in its transportation planning function.[18]

The elected executives also felt that it provided a useful forum for officials in the region to meet with one another, discuss issues of common concern, and learn from one another and from the experiences of other governments in the region. Finally, the executives said that the BMC enables them to craft approaches to issues that arise periodically, such as the response to the bank robberies in the region.

In our interviews, the region's elected executives generally agreed that issues that might cause disagreement and division did not appear on the agendas of these organizations, particularly BMC. As one of them said, "regionalism can only work when there are issues that we can all agree and work on." Another felt that the executives can only address things on which they believe they can achieve success. A third said, "You have to establish priorities where you can get agreement. In areas where there is no agreement, you can't build regional cooperation."

Regarding areas in which cooperation was difficult or did not occur, the executives mentioned the tougher issues, including housing, fiscal disparities between Baltimore City and the suburbs, public education, regional revenue sharing, and race. At least one of the executives opined that these areas were so fraught with contention that they could not even be brought to the agenda for discussion. He felt that it was easy for the executives to agree on cooperation on what were essentially systems maintenance but very difficult to cooperate in areas of lifestyle. For the most part, the other executives agreed with this sentiment.

We were interested in the executives' opinions about why greater levels of regional collaboration, especially around the tough issues, did not occur. The factor mentioned most frequently was the individual jurisdictions' parochial interests and autonomy. No single jurisdiction was willing to give up anything (especially money or power) to advance the interests of the overall region. Other factors mentioned included race relations, suburban residents (including black suburbanites who had recently left the city) being unwilling to have their tax dollars used to assist Baltimore City, and both city and suburban citizens being unwilling to support regionalism if it meant giving up autonomy.

Several of the elected executives felt that, for cooperation to occur on controversial issues, county residents must believe that their fate hinges on the condition of the city. However, the county executives whom we interviewed indicated that their residents did not agree this was the case. Even the county executives who felt that their jurisdictions were interdependent with Baltimore City said that their residents neither understood nor believed that such interdependence existed and that the fate of their jurisdictions depended on the fate of the city. Despite the fact that many county residents commute to jobs and attend cultural and athletic events in the city, there is no regional political identity, and it is doubtful there ever will be.

Finally, we inquired about whether the elected executives believed that the region's streamlined governmental structure aided or inhibited regional cooperation. All of the executives agreed that the relatively small number of local governments in the region combined with the legal powers of these governments made regional cooperation and action easier. Essentially, they said that if the elected executives of the six jurisdictions wanted something to happen, it would happen. However, the executives agreed that the same structure that makes regional collaboration and cooperation easier also makes it more difficult. If one or more of the jurisdictions decides not to participate in an effort or activity, that jurisdiction does not have to participate. Such nonparticipation can limit or even prevent regional cooperation. In fact the ability of member jurisdictions to "go their own way" and not participate, or to actually veto regional decisions was cited by the elected officials we interviewed as limiting the BMC's ability to address difficult or controversial issues.

Overall, the executives reinforced much of what the literature tells us about the difficulties of achieving regional governance. What is particularly revealing, however, is that these factors apparently have just as much power to limit or even prevent regional governance in a region that is not fragmented as in a region with high levels of fragmentation. (See, for example, Chapters 5 and 6 about the St. Louis region and Chapter 8 about four quite different regions along the fragmentation-consolidation continuum.)

Conclusion

We began this chapter by asking whether the extent of governmental fragmentation in a metropolitan area is related to the amount of governance that occurs in that area. Does less (fragmentation) mean more (governance)? We inferred from the writings of the metropolitan reformers that they felt this would be the case. They argued that fragmentation either caused or exacerbated numerous, serious problems for the overall metropolitan territory, and they called for various (mostly structural) resolutions to metropolitan fragmentation.

We used the Baltimore metropolitan area as the test case to examine this question because this area exhibits exceptionally little governmental fragmentation. If metropolitan governance does not occur in this area, then we can conclude that the absence of fragmentation is not a *necessary condition* for metropolitan governance. As a *necessary condition,* the absence of fragmentation would be *THE* factor without which metropolitan governance could not occur. If we do not find evidence of regional governance in the Baltimore metropolitan area, we can reasonably conclude that less fragmentation does not mean more governance. Quite possibly the metropolitan reformers had gotten it wrong. Factors other than fragmentation may be more important to metropolitan governance.

The Baltimore region is clearly blessed with structural simplicity. Only six local governments matter in the governance of the overall territory. If the six can agree on something, there is a high probability that it will happen. If the six or if one or a few of them disagree, then the probability is high that it will not happen.

As we learned, the structural simplicity of the Baltimore region is both a blessing and a bane. The same structure that makes regional collaboration and cooperation easy also makes it difficult. This is because there is nothing to compel jurisdictions to participate. There are no incentives to participate and significant disincentives exist (e.g., actual or perceived local citizen opposition, loss of funds, loss of power and autonomy).

County governments in the region are not only autonomous but also, under Maryland law, they are very powerful. Consequently, they can choose to cooperate with one another, or they can choose not to cooperate. For the most part, they do not cooperate to address significant, especially controversial, issues that affect the overall territory or benefit the city. The issues on which they do cooperate almost always involve systems maintenance versus lifestyle issues.

The findings of our study of the Baltimore region strongly suggest that although fragmentation may exacerbate the difficulty of achieving regional governance (no matter how the term is defined), the real culprit that significantly limits or prevents regional governance is local government autonomy. Our research supports the conclusion of previous literature (e.g., Danielson, 1976; Downs, 1994). And local government autonomy exists in regions across the nation regardless of the level of fragmentation that they exhibit. In the end, therefore, we are left to conclude that less local structural fragmentation does not mean more metropolitan governance.

Appendix 7.1. Expert Studies of the Baltimore Region

Baltimore Sun. 1998. "Regionalism that Works." Editorial series, January 4–10.
Greater Baltimore Committee. 1997. *One Region-One Future: A Report on Regionalism.* Baltimore, MD.
Greater Baltimore Committee and Greater Baltimore Alliance. 1998. *State of the Region Report.* Baltimore, MD: Commissioned by these organizations and prepared by Johns Hopkins University, Institute for Policy Studies.
Orfield, Myron. 1997. *Metropolitics: A Regional Agenda for Community and Stability.* Washington, DC: Brookings Institution Press/Lincoln Institute for Land Policy.
Peirce, Neal R. 1993. "Baltimore: Breaking the Boundaries." In *Citistates: How Urban America Can Prosper in a Competitive World,* 123–55. Washington, DC: Seven Locks Press. Originally published as a special section of the *Baltimore Sun* in 1991.
Rusk, David. 1996. *Baltimore Unbound.* Baltimore, MD: Abell Foundation.
Szanton, Peter L. 1986. *Baltimore 2000: A Choice of Futures.* Commissioned by the Morris Goldseker Foundation.

Notes

1. One of the peculiarities of Maryland law is that counties are the supreme local governments. Maryland has 23 counties (plus Baltimore City, which is accorded the status of a county) and 156 municipalities. However, for the most part, municipalities (except for Baltimore City) are subordinate to counties, and counties literally are the governments that matter most—politically, legally, and financially.

2. All but Carroll County in the Baltimore region are charter counties.

3. These municipalities, Chevy Chase Section 3 (1982), Chevy Chase Section 5 (1982) and Martin's Addition (1985), had been special taxing districts, and the county as well as the municipal residents felt that municipal status was more appropriate to the needs of the areas in question.

4. Their actions are, of course, limited by Dillon's rule, which holds that local governments have only those powers explicitly found in their charters, and the state legislatures retain legislative prerogatives in some areas. Nevertheless, charter counties have far more flexibility to act locally to meet real or perceived needs than commissioner counties.

5. This is somewhat less true of commissioner counties than charter counties.

6. In one of the peculiarities of Maryland local government structure, Baltimore City has the status of both a city and a county. This came about partly as a result of Baltimore City having been legally separated from Baltimore County in 1851. Note that this was also done in St. Louis (a highly fragmented metropolitan area) in 1876 (see Chapter 5).

7. Because of the overwhelming Democratic voter registration in Baltimore, the Democratic primary election in September is the de facto city election. The results of the primary are ratified in the general election in November. There are no Republican municipal officeholders in Baltimore, and the Republican Party rarely fields candidates for council or citywide offices.

8. The number of council members varies: Anne Arundel—seven; Baltimore—seven; Harford—six plus a council president elected at large; and Howard—five.

9. Efforts to adopt a charter form of government in Carroll County have been attempted twice in the past thirty years, but both were defeated at referendum. Most recently (2006), the county commissioners have been discussing the possibility of adopting what in Maryland is known as "Code" home rule that would require only the affirmative vote of the commissioners, not a vote by the citizens of the county. At this writing, the commissioners have not yet taken action to adopt Code home rule.

10. Myriad other organizations exist in the region that have attempted to influence regional cooperation and governance over the past few decades, but none have had any considerable or long-lasting influence. Some might argue that the Citizen's Planning and Housing Association (CPHA) is a notable regional organization. We would disagree. Most of its members and emphasis are within Baltimore City where, at best, it has had limited policy success. Outside of the city, CPHA has little recognition or influence. The state of Maryland is also a key player in regional affairs. The state has provided financial and administrative relief to Baltimore City by assuming responsibility for a number of services and functions, including the jail, community college, airport, port, and mass transit, as well as providing in one form or another about one-third of the city's budget.

11. The MPO is not exactly synonymous with the BMC, as it also includes the city of Annapolis, and the secretaries of the Maryland Department of Transportation and the Department of the Environment, and also the director of the Maryland Office of Planning.

12. This outcome is, apparently not uncommon across the country. See, for example, Meade (2001).

13. That is, to anywhere in the metropolitan area where landlords had voluntarily agreed or were required by law to accept Section 8 vouchers and certificates.

14. There have been two exceptions. The Maryland Stadium Authority built a stadium and lured a professional football team to Baltimore (a recommendation of one study), and the state legislature passed the governor's Smart Growth program into law (regional growth control was been recommended by several of the studies).

15. Although we conducted these interviews in 1999–2000, it is fair to say that there have been no substantial (and few, if any, minor) changes in the regional dynamics since. If anything, the BMC is less relevant today and the region's elected leaders are less committed to area-wide cooperation. See, for example, Green (2007).

16. We use the term "executives" to refer to the mayor of Baltimore, the elected executives of the charter counties, and the commissioners of Carroll County whom we interviewed for this chapter.

17. This was a narrowly focused, time-limited, bilateral (Baltimore City and Baltimore County) effort in cooperation. After the bank robbers were caught, the task force was disbanded.

18. Most of the BMC's strengths and limitations derive from its structure, a significant feature of which is that BMC is controlled by the elected executives. This structure provides a forum for the executives to meet and discuss issues of common concern upon which they

can achieve consensus. A different structure, especially one that would give the BMC or any regional organization for the area more autonomy, independence, or scope to address regional issues would not be politically acceptable to the elected executives. That type of structure was clearly one of the principal reasons for the demise of the BMC's predecessor organization, the BRCOG (Norris, 1994).

References

Baltimore Sun. 1998. "Regionalism that Works." Editorial series, January 4–10.

Committee for Economic Development. 1970. *Reshaping Government in Metropolitan Areas: A Statement on National Policy by the Research and Policy Committee of the Committee for Economic Development.* New York.

Danielson, Michael. 1976. *The Politics of Exclusion.* New York: Columbia University Press.

Downs, Anthony. 1994. *New Visions for Metropolitan America.* Washington, DC: Brookings Institution.

Greater Baltimore Committee. 1997. *One Region-One Future: A Report on Regionalism.* Baltimore, MD.

Greater Baltimore Committee and Greater Baltimore Alliance. 1998. *State of the Region Report.* Baltimore, MD: Commissioned by these organizations and prepared by Johns Hopkins University, Institute for Policy Studies.

Green, Andrew A. 2007. "United Front on BRAC Favored." *Baltimore Sun* (August 18), 1A. Available at www.baltimoresun.com/news/local/brac/bal-md.brac18aug18,0,6378909. story (accessed July 21, 2008).

Long, Norton. 1958. "The Local Community as an Ecology of Games." *Journal of American Sociology* 64, no. 3: 251–61.

Meade, Timothy D. 2001. "Governing Charlotte-Mecklenburg." *State and Local Government Review* 32, no. 3: 192–97.

Norris, Donald F. 1991. "Introduction to Local Government, and Municipal Powers and Limitations." In *Handbook for Maryland Municipal Officials,* ed. Brian M. Gardner, 15–30. College Park: University of Maryland System, Institute for Governmental Service.

———. 1994. "Killing a COG: The Death and Reincarnation of the Baltimore Regional Council of Governments." *Journal of Urban Affairs* 16, no. 2: 155–67.

Peirce, Neal R. 1993. "Baltimore: Breaking the Boundaries." In *Citistates: How Urban America Can Prosper in a Competitive World.* Washington, DC: Seven Locks Press. Originally published as a special section of the *Baltimore Sun* in 1991, pp. 123–55.

Studenski, Paul. 1974. *The Government of Metropolitan Areas in the United States.* New York: Arno Press. First published in 1930 by the National Municipal League Committee on Metropolitan Government.

Vicino, Thomas E. 2006. "Suburban Crossroads: An Analysis of Socioeconomic Change in Baltimore's First-Tier Suburbs, 1970 to 2000." Doctoral diss., University of Maryland Graduate School.

Walker, David B. 1987. "Snow White and the 17 Dwarfs: From Metro Cooperation to Governance." *National Civic Review* 76, no. 1: 14–29.

Warren, Charles R. 1978. "Regional Reform: Prospects and Alternatives." *Southern Review of Public Administration* 2, no. 1: 93–104.

Williams, Oliver P. 1971. *Metropolitan Political Analysis.* New York: Free Press.

Wood, Robert C. 1958. "Metropolitan Government, 1975: An Extrapolation of Trends the New Metropolis: Green Belts, Grass Roots or Gargantua?" *American Political Science Review* 52, no. 1: 108–22.

8

Consolidated and Fragmented Governments and Regional Cooperation

Surprising Lessons from Charlotte, Cleveland, Indianapolis, and Wyandotte County/Kansas City, Kansas

Suzanne M. Leland and Mark S. Rosentraub

Across the Midwest and Northeast there is renewed interest in regionalism and the consolidation of local government. This latest interest in reducing the number of governments is linked with the persistent economic stagnation that has plagued the region. Across America's manufacturing belt there is surprising consistency in the view that consolidated governments would be better able to coordinate the public sector's role in regional economic development initiatives to reverse the decades-long declines in population and economic importance. It is widely accepted that consolidated governments would be in a stronger position to lead plans for regional development while reducing taxes through the efficient production of services and the elimination of departments that duplicate services provided by and to many small jurisdictions. In part the rationale is based on the premise that collaboration across governments is needed to achieve sustainable regional economic development and deliver services more efficiently. However, little empirical evidence sustains this claim and the theory guiding scholars is divided into two camps—new regionalism versus fragmentation (public choice). While the regionalists' perspective advocates consolidation, public choice theorists argue this approach will fail to achieve any efficiency with regard to the use of scarce resources. Indeed, in their view, single-unit governments are more likely to behave as monopolists and reduce the quality of services while prices (taxes) rise.

Conversely, in the Sunbelt there is also renewed interest in regionalism and the consolidation of local governments to deal with the growing pains resulting from inadequate infrastructure, congestion, limited mass transit options, pollution, and the threat of annexation. Many of these challenges are linked to uncoordinated and decentralized patterns of residential, commercial, and retail development. Once again, little empirical evidence is available to sustain the perspective that consolidated local government systems would be or are more effective in dealing with these challenges (see Chapter 2 for reasons against).

The components of the arguments for consolidation used by well-intentioned individuals, whether the concerns are economic stagnation or growth management, are widely known. In stagnating areas, advocates point out that investment capital is highly mobile and firms see Cleveland, Indianapolis, Kansas City, Louisville, St. Louis, and others, as regions (somewhat interchangeable) that must compete to become desired locations. Cities within these regions—it follows—must concentrate on efforts to cooperate to minimize taxes and maximize efficiencies, even if that means consolidation and the merging of smaller cities to form larger governments. The consolidation of governments not only leads to unified plans for redevelopment but also to the elimination of duplicate service departments and to the increase of economies of scale needed to lower taxes, provide better services, and create a pro-business environment. In the case of growing areas, consolidation is touted as a route to rationalized planning that reduces the duplication of services and patterns of development described as undesirable and unnecessary "sprawl."

These emphases on government consolidation to advance economic development through the more efficient production of urban services and the production of unified plans for public-sector activities have been challenging for some members of the academic and policy communities. While there are many voices calling for consolidated governments to advance economic development, others equally passionate about developing their regions have argued that efficiencies in the provision and financing of public services is more likely to occur when numerous cities within a region compete to attract residents and businesses. Outlined by Tiebout (1956) and expanded by Ostrom, Tiebout, and Warren (1961), an alternative view of the organization of metropolitan areas has been sustained in numerous studies.

This anticonsolidation perspective suggests that regions with numerous governments are more likely to produce desired mixes of high quality public services at lower costs as a result of the pressure to attract businesses and residents and enhance local tax bases. In the view of these advocates and scholars, any system that relaxes the pressures for efficient behavior by local governments could result in more monopolistic or oligopolistic behavior by local governments. Such behaviors, these individuals fear, will lead to less desirable service levels and higher taxes.

A seemingly inherent assumption within the perspective put forward by advocates of consolidation is that the leaders of fragmented areas would be far less likely to respond to the same interregional competitive forces or forge a regional economic development strategy. It might follow that leaders of cities in areas with fragmented governance systems, while perceiving the need to compete with other regions, are unable or unwilling to set aside local issues, jealousies, or other factors to achieve a higher level of coordination.

Those who argue that fragmented regions are likely to be more efficient put for-

Table 8.1

Levels of Functional and Structural Consolidation of Example Cities

City and county	Functional consolidation: Major services (law enforcement, public works, fire)	Structural consolidation: Elected officials
Charlotte/Mecklenburg County, North Carolina	Yes	No
Cleveland/Cuyahoga County, Ohio	No	No
Indianapolis/Marion County, Indiana	No	Yes
Kansas City, Kansas/ Wyandotte County	Yes	Yes

ward a different implicit assumption. Their argumentation suggests it might be equally plausible to expect leaders of cities in areas with fractionated local governments to also seek cooperative ventures to become more competitive and ensure rational, efficient land use practices. They have the same incentive to attract investment and minimize the problems of congestion and sprawl as leaders of governments that are consolidated. However, in a fragmented system, cooperation would take the form of interlocal service agreements and cooperative or countywide financing and planning initiatives. Such outcomes if they did exist would run counter to the argument that only when governments consolidate do shorter-term goals related to individual political advantage get relegated behind economic advantages that contribute to sustainable growth.

To explore the issue of the role of form (consolidated governments versus fragmented governments) and substance (cooperative relationships), this chapter looks at four regions—Charlotte, Cleveland, Indianapolis, and Kansas City, Kansas—and their experiences with regional service delivery activities. Studying these areas allows a consideration of both structural and functional consolidation, to highlight whether either type of consolidation impacts the level of regional cooperation (King, Keohane, and Verba, 1994).

First, we look at Charlotte and Mecklenburg County. These governments functionally consolidated services while leaving the structures of individual cities intact. The second focus is on Greater Cleveland where there is neither a structural or functional consolidation. The third region analyzed, Indianapolis, is where the central city and surrounding county created a consolidated government, but for decades left most service delivery systems intact and therefore highly fragmented. The fourth region, Kansas City, Kansas, has a consolidated government (excluding three minor municipalities) and service delivery units. Does it follow that in the Greater Cleveland area there exist fewer regional or countywide cooperative programs, while far more are found in the Kansas City, Kansas, area? The chapter explores this issue against the backdrop of these four case studies (see Table 8.1).

When trying to understand why structural consolidation occurs, many previous scholars (Mead, 2000; Rosenbaum and Kammerer, 1974) have pointed to the development of a "crisis" that propelled city and county leaders to consider consolidation. "Finger pointing" when a crisis emerged (the act of shifting both blame and responsibility), scandal, corruption, patronage politics, and economic decline are often cited as the reasons consolidation is placed on the public's agenda and eventually the ballot. However, even with some or all of these factors present, consolidated governments are rarely created. If this perspective were valid then Charlotte-Mecklenburg would have little reason to consider political consolidation. The city and county governments have well-deserved reputations for being professionalized, and few if any publicized scandals have contradicted the image of professionalism or affected the public's confidence in their civic leadership. The city of Charlotte and Mecklenburg County both have structures that could be classified as variations on the council-manager form of government. The municipality is financially sound with an AAA bond rating. Over the past thirty years the Charlotte area has experienced tremendous growth and economic prosperity.

For the most part, efficiency (notably pertaining only to the city of Charlotte and Mecklenburg County) has been achieved through annexation and functional consolidation of an exhaustive list of services (see Table 8.2).

One could argue that the two governments' long-standing practice of cooperation explains why talk about city-county consolidation persists. Why should city and county political leaders not join forces and consolidate when almost all of the services are already functionally consolidated? However, proconsolidation forces such as the chamber of commerce have still not convinced citizens that this step would be beneficial or is necessary.

There is a long history of structural consolidation attempts between Charlotte and Mecklenburg County, but functional consolidation and annexation are what have succeeded. In addition, the proposed charters have allowed for six other towns to be excluded from consolidation because of their opposition to merging with Charlotte. These areas comprise but 10 percent of the population but are growing faster than the region. While early structural consolidation efforts followed the traditional path of reform, later efforts in the 1960s, 1970s, and 1990s have emphasized improved regional leadership and coordinated planning. It was only in the early 1970s that the Charlotte Chamber revived interest and placed political consolidation on the ballot, where it was met with resounding defeat (Mead, 2000). At this point in time the county was only one-fourth of its current size. Mecklenburg County now has 827,445 residents with a 60 percent growth rate from 1990–2000 (see Table 8.3).

Since 2000 Charlotte-Mecklenburg has experienced explosive growth driven by the banking industry. Through aggressive annexation (North Carolina has some of the nation's most liberal annexation laws), Charlotte has been able to expand and capitalize on suburban growth. Eventually, the boundaries between the city and the county will be coterminous.

The relationship between the city and county does not explain the political

Table 8.2

City of Charlotte and Mecklenburg County Fiscal Relationships

City provides:
- Planning
- Emergency management
- Animal control
- Community Relations Committee
- Zoning administration
- Risk management
- Procurement services
- First responder
- Police
- Wireless communications (radio, towers)
- 311 (Customer Service Center)
- Cultural facilities plan
- Light vehicle fleet maintenance garages (pending)
- Cable TV administration (recent state legislation may change relationships)
- RideShare (CATS)
- 911 services
- False Alarm Ordinance administration and enforcement
- Sexually Oriented Businesses Ordinance administration and enforcement

County provides:
- Board of Elections
- Veterans services
- Parks and recreation
- Building standards
- Tax Office (listing, collections, and assessments)
- Historic Landmarks Commission
- Storm Water Quality Management Program
- Uptown baseball

Jointly provided:
- Engineering Departments' reciprocal services
- Recyclable waste collection and sales

Source: Ron Kimble, assistant city manager of Charlotte.

currents that shape debates about consolidation. There are six independent towns in Mecklenburg County experiencing population growth at a rate that exceeds levels in Charlotte. This rapid growth places inordinate pressure on the delivery of educational and transportation (roads) services and on environmental protection. These challenges require regional collaboration, but there is little formal cooperation between Charlotte and the independent jurisdictions. Many believe this is a result of the reluctance of the smaller cities and surrounding counties to cooperate with Charlotte and Mecklenburg County. The city and county are derisively referred to as "The Great State of Mecklenburg." Only four intercounty or intracounty special purpose governments have been created: the Charlotte City Housing Authority, the Charlotte-Mecklenburg Hospital Authority, WVTI Public Service Authority, and

Table 8.3

Population Growth in Mecklenburg County, 1990–2006

County/city	2006	2000	1990	Percent growth		Percent of county, 2006
				2000–2006	1990–2006	
Mecklenburg County	827,445	695,454	511,433	19.0	61.9	
Charlotte	630,478	540,828	395,934	16.6	59.2	76.2
Davidson	8,760	7,139	4,046	22.7	116.5	1.1
Huntersville	38,796	24,960	3,014	55.4	1187.2	4.7
Cornelius	20,449	11,969	2,581	70.9	692.4	2.5
Mint Hill	18,663	14,922	11,567	25.1	61.4	2.3
Matthews	26,296	22,127	13,651	18.8	92.6	3.2
Pineville	3,784	3,449	2,970	9.7	27.4	0.5

Source: U.S. Census Bureau, Population Division; available at www.census.gov/popest/cities/.

the Mecklenburg Soil and Water Conservation District. The Charlotte City Housing Authority's board made up of seven political appointees (two appointed by the mayor and five appointed by the city council) is limited to people who live in the city. The U.S. Bureau of the Census (1990) does not classify the school system as a special purpose government because it is fiscally dependent on the county for its revenues and budget.

Growing Pains

Like most rapidly expanding cities in the Sunbelt, the metropolitan area of Charlotte must confront significant infrastructure issues. Faced with increasing commute times and traffic congestion, increasing demands for water, and increased pollution levels, city leaders have focused on a new mass transportation plan. The U.S. Environmental Protection Agency cited the Charlotte region—now ranked ninth worst in the nation—for nonattainment of air quality standards in 2007. The region will lose federal highway funds if air pollution levels are not reduced. Currently, Charlotte's transit system serves only 30 percent of the region's population. A city agency, Charlotte Area Transit (CAT), provides bus service inside the city limits as well as to several other cities in the county. Focused on building a new light rail system to reduce pollution and congestion levels, the challenge for Charlotte is to convince other communities to help finance construction of the system. Does a perceived need for light rail to address regional issues that have a more concentrated impact on Charlotte overcome the self-interest of voters in smaller communities to force Charlotte to assume responsibility for the local share of the system's costs? The Metropolitan Transit Commission rejected the idea of moving to a special purpose government to oversee regional transit solutions including the extension of the light rail system beyond Charlotte's borders. A citizen-led petition to repeal the countywide transit sales tax was placed on the November 2007 ballot; if enacted, it would have required the city of Charlotte to assume all responsibility for the cost of the system. While it failed to muster a majority, and the tax remained in place, it slowed down progress on any rail extensions, particularly in the northern corridor. Neighboring towns are wary of any new expansions when it is apparent such opposition exists. The transit system is one example of how a region with functionally consolidated city and county services can fail to establish a base for regional perspectives on transportation and a regional vision for the economic future of the community.

Cleveland and Cuyahoga County

Cleveland and Cuyahoga County have been the focus of conversations regarding government consolidation and reform for more than thirty years. More recently, however, the region has been engaged in a wide-ranging set of conversations involving "regionalism" and improved relationships between the public, private, and nonprofit sectors to advance economic development. The reasons for a focus on economic development are underscored by a decades-long decline on a number of important indicators. There is great hope that a coordinated and regional approach to economic development will reverse these trends. First, the city of Cleveland has suffered a massive decline in terms of the number of people residing in the city, and this exodus has continued for more than fifty years. At its apex, Cleveland's population was 914,000. A small loss of less than 40,000 in the 1950s was followed by steep declines, leaving the city with less than 425,000 residents by 2005. The loss of residents has not been limited to Cleveland. Cuyahoga County reached its zenith in 1970 with almost 1.5 million residents; recent (2006) estimates place the county's population at approximately 1.3 million. In 2008 the U.S. Bureau of the Census reported that no county in the country had lost more residents than Cuyahoga County since the 2000 Census.

Second, the loss of residents was not the only negative challenge for the city and county. The region's manufacturing sector—while reporting substantial gains in productivity with increases surpassing the national average—lost 23.2 percent of the jobs that existed as recently as 2000. More than 8,000 jobs were lost in the motor vehicle industry alone and more than 6,000 jobs in metal works were also lost. While other parts of the United States saw similar job losses, those declines were offset by gains in other parts of the local economies. Unfortunately the growth in other sectors of northeast Ohio's economy were not sufficient to offset the lost wages, and many manufacturing workers could not and did not find other positions. As a result, the demand for real estate declined, reducing property values.

When these factors were added to the problems associated with subprime mortgages there was little surprise when Cuyahoga County had one of the nation's leading home foreclosure rates. Several of the region's leading corporations also moved, with British Petroleum relocating to Chicago and TRW moving to the West Coast. With no shortage of declining indicators, the region's leading newspaper, the *Plain Dealer,* reflected on the "Quiet Crisis." Prominent attention was directed to the multiplicity of governments and the frustrations with leadership and consensus-building activities to forge new initiatives.

Across the past twenty-five years there have been at least two initiatives to consider reorganizing local government; both focused on restructuring the county to permit it to exercise more authority under a single executive. Three commissioners selected through countywide elections lead Cuyahoga County. Complaints about their leadership were the driving forces for reform movements in the 1980s and in 2004. The fractured nature of decision making with regard to economic development for the region was apparent and frustrating, but evidence linking the lethargic decision-making activity with economic decline does not exist. Indeed, Keating, Krumholz, and Metzger (1995) acknowledged the difficulties when many elected officials were involved with economic development decisions. But they also noted that when there was sufficient unity to permit the assembling of large tracts of land as requested by developers to permit larger-scale initiatives, the existing market (demand) was too weak and investors would not commit to building some of the anticipated new homes and commercial space for businesses. A more consolidated decision system could not have accomplished more relative to land assembly because market conditions prevented the hoped-for results in terms of jobs and private-sector investment.

Nevertheless, the government reform proposal put forward for Cleveland and Cuyahoga County would have created a county executive reporting to an elected county council. The preferred election method would have involved districts drawn to include areas throughout the county for a new council. No cities or the services they provide would be consolidated. As a result the new county executive would have considerable responsibility and authority for economic development, wielding the county's administrative prowess. However, the county executive would not have authority for the delivery of most urban services, as that would remain with individual cities. Service consolidation, if it was to occur, would need to be negotiated between cities or with the county executive once the program was established. This reform process failed to gain sufficient support and was not ratified. The Cuyahoga County Bar Association in partnership with a local university reintroduced the topic of government reform in 2004.

This effort involved a review of outcomes of consolidations and different approaches to county and city government with a series of public discussions involving leaders from communities across the nation that had consolidated—to some extent—local governments in their region. At the conclusion of these discussions no action emerged, as various petition efforts to place different consolidation models and reforms failed to secure the needed number of signatures. As expected, the county officials opposed any new structures or reforms and the active commitment of their political influence against change doomed the efforts. Not willing to create a conflict with the county, no mayor of any of the county's larger cities supported any changes.

This history combined with the existence of fifty-nine cities, towns, and townships, thirty-one independent school districts, fifty-eight municipal police departments, and thirteen public safety forces for hospitals, universities, and housing authorities in the county, suggests to some that unified service delivery activities by local governments is unlikely. That would be a premature and largely inaccurate conclusion.

First, there are no fewer than fourteen unified (countywide) service delivery systems in Cuyahoga County. These include a regional transportation district that delivers fixed-rail or bus transit options to every part of the county, a solid waste district, and a park district that operates one of the nation's largest set of outdoor recreational facilities, parks, golf courses, and nature reservations. There is also a water and sewer district authority that is part of Cleveland that on a contract basis provides water to numerous cities throughout the region. Second, Cleveland's three facilities for the region's professional sports teams are the result of a partnership between the center city and Cuyahoga County. County government has provided the majority of the funding for the ballpark (Cleveland Indians), the football stadium (Cleveland Browns), and arena (Cleveland Cavaliers) while allowing Cleveland to retain the tax revenues generated by the teams (amusement, income, parking, and property).

Third, there has also been countywide cooperation to ensure funding for the building and maintenance of the Rock and Roll Hall of Fame and Museum, the Science Center, and Playhouse Square (home to several theaters for the performing arts). These facilities attract more than 1.5 million visitors to downtown Cleveland, and again all of the tax revenue generated by spending at events or related to attendance accrues only to Cleveland. The three sports venues annually attract in excess of 3.5 million visitors to the downtown area, and the spending by fans generates substantial tax revenues. The amusement tax and the parking tax contribute important revenues to Cleveland and those revenues would be much less without the sports and entertainment facilities that are financed at the county level.

Fourth, it is also important to note that there is a planning commission for the county that works in partnership with Cleveland's Planning Commission. While these commissions can have their decisions overruled by the County Commissioners, there is still a high level of coordination with regard to planning and development. Fifth, the countywide Port Authority has taken a very aggressive role in financing economic development projects throughout the county and in several different cities. This is another joint city-county agency. There is also a countywide library system even though some cities maintain their own libraries, a regional planning agency, and a countywide health board.

Sixth, and probably of most importance, the local income tax in Cuyahoga County is an earnings tax with revenue accruing to the locality where an individual works. Cities are free to add a small addition to the tax, but the 2 percent tax rate applies only in the locality where a job is located. The earnings tax is now Cleveland's largest source of revenue and the principal reason it has avoided more severe fiscal problems even as the population has declined and the average income of residents (compared with that of residents of the county) has plummeted. The earnings tax is effectively a regional tax-base-sharing program. Indeed, compared with Minneapolis/St. Paul's property tax-base-sharing program, greater Cleveland's earnings tax-base-sharing program involves far more revenues and a much greater and more progressive redistribution of wealth as those individuals with the highest incomes who work in Cleveland live largely in the suburbs. Their earnings' taxes annually provide more than $200 million in revenues to the central city. Cleveland remains the location of the region's two largest employment centers, making it the largest recipient of local income tax dollars in the region. While Cleveland has lost jobs and important businesses, presently it is still home to the region's largest employers including the Cleveland Clinic, University Hospitals, Key Bank, National City Bank, AmTrust Bank, Eaton, Sherwin-Williams, Forest City Enterprises, and numerous other national real estate development firms. Because few of these firms' employees live in Cleveland, the earnings tax becomes one of the nation's largest regional tax-base-sharing programs.

Table 8.4

Municipal Service Collaborations in Cuyahoga County

Administrative area	Number of collaborations	Cities involved
General administration	8	40
Arts	1	2
Building inspections	3	7
Court/judicial process	3	10
Economic development	1	2
Environment	3	17
Finance	2	49
Health programs	1	4
Human resources	1	5
Purchasing	6	73
Recreation services	8	33
Safety services	31	184
Senior citizen activities	12	47
Service delivery (other)	16	75
Total	96	548

Source: Cuyahoga County Mayors and City Managers Association, 2008.

Note: Fifty-seven cities are members of the Cuyahoga County Mayors and City Managers Association. These organizations had developed and signed a total of ninety-six different agreements for service provision or to share the costs of delivering a service. Some of these agreements involved several cities at the same time. The number of collaborations reported in the table refers to the total if one adds all of the cities involved in each agreement. For example, there are thirty-one different agreements involving safety services. For some of these agreements only two cities are involved. In other contracts or agreements as many as thirty cities are involved in a single agreement or contract. The "Cities involved" column tabulates the number of cities involved in each agreement or contract.

Finally, these formal governance structures that span the county are not the only examples of joint service delivery programs. In 2004 the Cuyahoga County Mayors and City Managers Association—a voluntary association where the leaders of every city meet to discuss the county's future, development, and service issues—tabulated the number of interlocal service agreements each community had established. Omitted from this tabulation were any single-year or ad hoc relationships.

As shown in Table 8.4, there were a total of 96 different collaborations involving intergovernmental agreements and contracts for service delivery or service coordination. Some of these individual contracts or agreements involved more than one city. If the number of cities participating in the 96 agreements is tabulated—recognizing that individual cities participated in several agreements or contracts and that several cities were parties to numerous agreements, the total number of municipal interactions was 548. This means that 96 agreements produced cooperative relationships that involved the cities in extensive service delivery networks despite an absence of any form of consolidated government.

In May 2008 the Cuyahoga County Mayors and City Managers Association also announced a new program for sharing tax revenue produced by new development taking place anywhere in Cuyahoga County. A total of 40 percent of new property and earnings tax revenue occurring anywhere as a result of new construction or the new relocation of a business would be placed in a fund to be shared by all cities based on a formula tied to the number of households in the city and the age of its housing stock. This, combined with the earnings tax, would give the county the most extensive revenue-sharing program in any metropolitan area in the United States.

All of these forms of cooperation for revenue sharing, service delivery, and the building of large capital assets took place in the absence of a consolidated government. There is thus substantial evidence of a robust level of cooperation that has emerged in response to desires to minimize taxes, to lower the costs of government, and to build desired and valuable civic assets.

Indianapolis and Marion County

As one of the three largest city and county consolidations from the 1960s and 1970s, UniGov has been repeatedly studied and looked to as an example of how local governments can coordinate activities for unified economic development strategies. The redevelopment of downtown Indianapolis from a dilapidated and obsolete state to a site for national and international events has linked government consolidation to discussions of downtown revitalization and economic development. Indianapolis remains at the focal point of conversations as a result of the publicity it receives when it is a finalist to host events such as the National Football League's Super Bowl and several collegiate championships. Those premiere events are the envy of most cities, and the fact that Indianapolis is now in competition for them suggests to many that consolidated government is an important element in the establishment of unified economic development and downtown revitalization plans.

What makes Indianapolis an interesting case study as an example of consolidated government is that the original consolidation between Indianapolis and Marion County focused largely on economic development and not on the delivery of most urban services (Rosentraub, 2000). The consolidated government had responsibility for economic development, land use, public works, and transportation. The newly created Department of Metropolitan Development of the consolidated city-county government was where all planning, zoning, and land use decisions were to be made. This agency was even responsible for these functions for the cities of Beech Grove, Lawrence, Southport, and Speedway, which decided not to formally join the consolidated government. As a result, residents of these cities voted for the mayor of Indianapolis as the county administrator and for members of the city-county council while electing mayors and city council members for the independent cities (Blomquist and Parks, 1995). With no consolidation of other urban services, UniGov left the Indianapolis township structure intact, which meant that the city had nine other broad units of local government within its new boundaries. The townships that remained intact were the service delivery units for public safety and education. One of the excluded cities retained its parks department, and one had its own independent school district separate from the township.

In addition, the new governance plan did nothing to reduce the number of school districts (eleven), police departments (eleven), and fire departments (eight). The number of special district governments increased from sixteen to twenty. These overlapping layers of government within Indianapolis meant that the consolidated city-county actually had eighty-five different taxing jurisdictions produced by the overlapping service delivery boundaries. For example, some taxpayers received police, fire, and educational services from different governments even though their homes were less than one-half mile apart, but they received park, economic development, water and sewer, and sanitation services from the same unit of government. When all of the service boundaries were identified for property tax assessment and collection, there were eighty-five distinct taxing jurisdictions administered by the consolidated city and county of Indianapolis and Marion.

UniGov was designed to implement a unified economic development plan for downtown Indianapolis, and while the connection between the governance plan and the execution of the area's rebuilding is unclear, there is no debate that a great deal was achieved after consolidation. Consolidation afforded access to financial capital, as a city of 350,000 suddenly had almost a million residents and a far greater tax base to sustain bond payments. Money to rebuild downtown Indianapolis was easier to obtain at lower rates given the higher bond rating of a consolidated city compared with one that not only was far smaller but also was the location of far fewer expensive homes and properties.

The amount of building that then took place in downtown Indianapolis is the material of the hopes for many declining central cities. There were more than seventy major development projects in the last twenty-five years of the twentieth century and the initial decade of the twenty-first century at a cost of more than $8.3 billion (in 2006 dollars). That amount reflects the region's public sector investment and that of the Indianapolis Colts for a new stadium for the football team, and that precipitated another $250 million investment from a variety of sources for the Indiana Convention Center. The tax instrument used for the public sector's investment in the facility for the Indianapolis Colts was unique for Indiana. Marion County and each of its surrounding counties agreed to use a food and beverage tax to pay for the new stadium in downtown Indianapolis. This was the first time that the suburban counties had ever agreed to contribute taxes collected and paid within their jurisdiction to a development project in downtown Indianapolis. The irony of this interlocal agreement is that it occurred outside of the creation of a consolidated or larger-scale regional government.

This level of investment in rebuilding downtown Indianapolis in the years 1976 through 2007 was also unique in that it involved substantial commitments from the private and nonprofit sectors; two-thirds of the dollar investments were from private or nonprofit sources. Indianapolis's total investment was $2.52 billion (in 2006 dollars), giving it an impressive leveraging ratio of $3.29 for each dollar it spent. A public-private partnership with that level of return is the envy of most cities, with only San Diego's Stadium District and Columbus, Ohio's Arena District producing any similar level of private and nonprofit investment in exchange for the public sector's investment in facilities for either professional sports facilities or convention centers.

Three immediate questions emerge. First, did Indianapolis's complex consolidation plan actually mean that the costs for financing the redevelopment were sustained by the county? Reworded, in the context of investments in Cleveland, did the residents of the old city of Indianapolis fare better in terms of their responsibility for paying for the redevelopment of downtown Indianapolis because of consolidation? Remember, in Cleveland, without a consolidated government, Cleveland's sports and entertainment facilities that spurred downtown development were financed at the county level with the city retaining the tax revenue. Did Indianapolis's center city area gain anything in terms of the costs for economic development? Second, would the investments in downtown have been made without consolidation? Third, did the participation of the surrounding counties in a financing plan for the new stadium for the Colts initiate a new form of regional cooperation?

With regard to the first question concerning which jurisdiction paid the public's investment for the rebuilding of downtown Indianapolis—the answer's complexity matches the multiple layers in UniGov's governance structure. Leaving Indianapolis's township structure in place meant that the property tax system was not consolidated. There were not only eighty-five individual taxing districts created as a result of overlapping service boundaries, but separate taxing districts for each township (Center Township roughly approximates the boundaries of the old city of Indianapolis). Debt can be assumed against any combination of these taxing districts. In other words, if one of the townships borrows money, that debt is the responsibility of only the property owners in the township. But when Indianapolis borrows money for a project for the downtown area, that debt can be supported by the entire consolidated city and county. For some projects it is also possible for Indianapolis to borrow against the tax base of Center Township only, meaning that property owners in that area are responsible for the debt. For rebuilding downtown Indianapolis that is located within Center Township did the consolidated city-county government use its entire tax base or just that of Center Township?

If it used the entire county's tax base then the wealthier communities in the more suburban sections of the city assumed some of the burden. However, if the money were borrowed against the property in Center Township there would be a greater burden on inner-city neighborhoods. In contrast, all of the sports and entertainment facilities in Cleveland were financed by Cuyahoga County. As one would expect given the complexity of the UniGov system, the answer is complex, with residents of the old city of Indianapolis responsible for some development costs while all residents of consolidated Indianapolis were responsible for others.

The consolidated government of Marion County financed the initial redevelopment projects completed in the aftermath of the creation of UniGov. These projects included Market Square Arena—the original facility built for the Indiana Pacers to move them from midtown to the downtown area—and the new government services building for the unified government. When additional funds were required for a new arena for the Pacers (Conseco Fieldhouse was built in the late 1990s), taxes on food and beverages, hotel rooms, and rental cars were administered across the entire county. For a range of other projects involving the state of Indiana, land that previously generated property taxes was taken, and Center Township or the old city of Indianapolis lost those revenues. For a large number of other development projects, Indianapolis provided property tax abatements, and those forgone revenues had an immediate impact on Center Township (the old city of Indianapolis) but not on property owners in other townships.

A substantial portion of the more than $2.5 billion invested by the public sector in downtown redevelopment involved property tax abatements and the creation of a very large tax increment financing (TIF) district for the building of a new downtown shopping center. To the extent that forgone tax revenues were sacrificed by the consolidated city, the burden of this loss was entirely the responsibility of Center Township or the old city of Indianapolis. The burden imposed by the TIF and the property tax abatements is borne by property owners in Center Township. Those incentives constitute the vast majority of Indianapolis's public sector investment to rebuild the downtown area. The issue then is not whether or not the public's financial investment was sustained by the old city of Indianapolis as opposed to the consolidated government. Center Township's property owners sustained a large portion of the cost of rebuilding the downtown area. Debate remains concerning whether or not abated property taxes represent forgone revenues (Mikelbank et al., 2007) and whether the net cash flow from TIF districts are positive or negative (Man and Rosentraub, 1998).

Indianapolis's downtown area was deteriorating in the 1970s when the redevelopment program was initiated, and there was a large-scale relocation of businesses and residents to the eight other townships in the county. If some or all of the redevelopment that took place in the downtown area occurred only as a result of the abatements offered, then those property taxes would likely never have accrued to Center Township. There are of course alternate perspectives. Jacobs's (1961) theory of urban regeneration would suggest that: (1) some of the forgone property taxes might have been paid as lower value properties were developed on abandoned sites, or (2) the exact same level of development would have taken place at some point in time.

It is not possible to sustain the perspective that the forgone revenues resulting from the abatement were taxes Indianapolis would not have collected. Similarly, it cannot be determined whether some portion of the forgone taxes would have been paid by investors or renters attracted to land by lower prices. It is probably appropriate to conclude that the abatement guaranteed a future property tax stream (when the abatement period ended), and that some, perhaps a majority, of the forgone revenue would never have existed given market conditions.

However, it is clear that the existence of the redevelopment did generate service delivery costs (public safety, etc.) that were the responsibility of local governments in Center Township. Further, it is also possible that residents in other townships received benefits from the redevelopment of downtown (increased demand for housing in those townships, for example). Those benefits would have been received without any investment, as the costs of the investment were supported by Center Township.

A similar benefit imbalance may exist as a result of the creation of the TIF to build the large downtown mall. This TIF needed to be expanded several times to ensure that sufficient revenues were generated to pay for the public's investment in the mall. The final boundaries of the TIF were so large that the possibility of benefits for Center Township from accelerating property values in land adjacent to the TIF area was substantially reduced. This underscores the extent to which Center Township and the old city of Indianapolis were responsible for a substantial portion of the public sector's investment in the redevelopment of downtown Indianapolis. That observation does not reduce the importance of the very high level of private and nonprofit sector funds leveraged by that investment, but it does reduce the importance of the creation of the consolidated government in the finances for the rebuilding of downtown Indianapolis.

UniGov and consolidation did create a single entity for Marion County that was responsible for economic development. The Department of Metropolitan Development was able to develop and sustain a plan for downtown's redevelopment that might well have had far less unified support in the absence of a consolidated government. There was also a set of countywide taxes that were used for some of the development, but as evident in Cleveland's experiences, countywide financing mechanisms were also used in the absence of a consolidated government. Further, in Indianapolis, the first regional tax for development spanning all of the metropolitan counties involved areas that were not part of the consolidated government. Hence, while UniGov did create the agency that created and oversaw a successful economic development strategy, the consolidated government did not sustain a substantial portion of the public sector's investment.

The largest and most significant employer in central Indiana is the Eli Lilly and Company pharmaceutical corporation. The Lilly family has also created one of the nation's largest philanthropies, and the substantial commitments for redevelopment from the nonprofit sector involved the Lilly Endowment. With the corporation's headquarters in downtown Indianapolis, one is left to wonder whether the redevelopment effort would have occurred without consolidation simply to ensure the company's presence. This is another conundrum, in that large companies have dominated other cities that have not enjoyed the level of redevelopment sustained in downtown Indianapolis. This has led some to conclude that redevelopment of downtown was likely even without a consolidated government, as local governments and regional leaders would have been willing to work together to ensure the Lilly corporation's continued presence in downtown Indianapolis (Walcott, 1998).

In this regard it is interesting to contrast development patterns between Cleveland and Indianapolis. Downtown Cleveland has struggled to retain residents and businesses even though it is home to several large banks, the nation's largest real estate development firm, and several large manufacturing firms. The regional leadership in greater Cleveland has not been able to develop a plan for redevelopment of downtown Cleveland and sustain a focus on the downtown area. Hence, it may be too cavalier to dismiss the importance of the Indianapolis Department of Metropolitan Development in advancing the redevelopment agenda for that city. In the absence of UniGov, it is unlikely that the department would have existed. Yet the extent to which Greater Cleveland developed countywide tools to finance development and improve the central city's fiscal health in the absence of consolidation suggests that fragmented governments do unite for collective action and economic development initiatives.

Kansas City, Kansas/Wyandotte County

The history of consolidation attempts in Wyandotte County and Kansas City, Kansas, can be traced to the late 1960s, when the Kansas House of Representatives formed a commission to study the merits of consolidating the two governments. A series of community discussions and citizen interest in the 1980s and 1990s culminated in passage by the Kansas State Legislature of Bill 464, which created a five-member commission of Wyandotte County residents to determine whether merging the two governments was a viable solution to the continual decline of the quality of life. The commission recommended consolidation, and the voters approved it via referendum in 1997 (Leland, 2004; Leland and Thurmaier, 2000). At the time, the city and county were both suffering economically. The city and county had the highest property tax and rates in the state, and the city and county earned far less sales tax revenues per capita than did other governments in region. Kansas City, Kansas, itself was even included in David Rusk's list (1994) of "cities past the point of no return" alongside East St. Louis. Reformers, led by the chamber of commerce and real estate investors, advocated for consolidation because they hoped that it would lead to a more professionalized local government that would help curb urban decline and fiscal stress. The reformers wanted to change the negative image and reputation of local governments that they believed contributed to the county's economic decline. Wyandotte County was identified with high levels of political patronage through its Democratic Party machine. In recent years, a sheriff had been indicted amid several charges of favoritism in the awarding of lucrative contracts. The county also lacked a personnel classification system and had an antiquated line-item budget prepared by the auditor (Leland, 2004; Leland and Thurmaier, 2000). Most disturbing of all, the city had lost more than 30,000 of its 180,000 residents since the 1960s, despite annexation of 5,000 additional residents in the Piper Township in the early 1990s (Wood and Leland, 2007).

Finally, what was considered the biggest barrier to consolidation—the merging of law enforcement—had already taken place and there was very little overlap or duplication left between the city and county. The consolidation charter carefully retained the sheriff as an elected official, and he maintained his political power as overseer of the city and county corrections functions. The city police department maintained its role as the primary provider of road patrol for the city and county. This translated into little change for departments (with the exception of budget and personnel). However, it also meant that cost savings would have to occur via reform of patronage practices and cost-cutting measures as opposed to the elimination of duplicate departments. But in contrast to Unigov, it is important to note that all services were brought under one unified jurisdiction and separate service districts were not necessary.

The three remaining towns were excluded from consolidation and were assessed fees for county services on an activity basis.

It is interesting to note that while strongly opposed to the merger, these towns were allowed to have representation in the new government, and the mayor of Edwardsville, Tiny McTaggert, was able to secure a seat on the (newly) Unified Board of Commissioners. Prior to consolidation, no one from Edwardsville had ever held a seat on the county commission (Leland, 2004).Ten years after the consolidation, there has been a fiscal, demographic, and economic renaissance in Kansas City, Kansas-Wyandotte County, Kansas, and the promises made by consolidation supporters have been kept (see Table 8.5). "While the move [consolidation] helped the combined governments cut their workforce and trim property taxes four years running, it also had a less tangible but no less crucial impact; the periodic scandals that had beset both county and city governments came to an end, and the unified government's relationship with state government in Topeka has dramatically improved. That, in turn, helped the region secure the location of the Kansas Speedway, that now anchors a state "tourism district" and budding retail center" (Gurwitt, 2002, p. 2). The effort to "clean up" city and county government was provided a boost soon after the consolidation when the Unified Government created an ethics commission, hired an ethics administrator, and developed ethics policies and related employee ethics training programs (Wood and Leland, 2007).

The selection of Wyandotte County as the site for the new NASCAR track and the surrounding development of Village West, a 400-acre retail and entertainment destination district that includes leading retail outlets, a minor league baseball park, a destination hotel, and a family destination resort, have contributed to the revitalization of Kansas City, Kansas. The NASCAR race track and Village West development have led to rising home values and a housing boom, increased sales and property tax revenue, and attracted millions of tourists each year (Wood and Leland, 2007). According to Marinovich (2004), "In 2003, Kansas City, Kansas tallied its highest single-year total of housing starts in the past forty years with 433 new single-family housing permits issued." The Homebuilders Association of Greater Kansas City ranked Kansas City, Kansas, sixth out of sixty-eight metro communities in the number of new housing starts (ibid.).

Table 8.5

Functional Consolidation in Wyandotte County

Service function	1990	1996	2007
Fire protection	CI	CI	F
Social services	CU	CU	F
Law enforcement	S	F	F
Parks and recreation	S	S	F
Planning	S	S	F
Economic development	S	S	F
Utilities (water/sewer)	CI	CI	F
Public works	S	S	F
Public health	CU	CU	F

Source: Modified from Wood and Leland, 2007.
Key:
CI = City function only
CU = County function only
F = Functional consolidation (city and county operations combined into single department)
S = Separately provided by both city and county
Italic letters denote a change.

Despite this success, one interesting point must be made about the consolidation of Wyandotte County and Kansas City Kansas. New regionalists such as David Rusk who argue for consolidation believe that consolidation can help the inner city increase its tax base via annexation of suburban territory. This would allow the city to capture lost revenue from those who consume city services by day but go home to nearby suburbs to pay their property taxes (even though some might argue that the property taxes paid by business and related spending by commuters offset any created tax burdens). This simply did not occur in Wyandotte County because the city already comprised 97 percent of the county's population. The remaining 3 percent of the population resides in the smaller municipalities of Bonner Springs, Edwardsville, and part of Lake Quivira, areas excluded from consolidation. Essentially no new suburban territory was gained through the consolidation, and Wyandotte County still has 18 special-purpose governments and is 1 of 5 counties that make up the metropolitan area. While Wyandotte County still participates in the Mid-America Regional Council (an association consisting of the 9 counties and 120 cities in the Kansas City region that acts as the metropolitan planning organization for the bi-state region), the consolidation of Wyandotte County-Kansas City, Kansas, has left the level of fragmentation and cooperation in the region as a whole largely unchanged. While consolidation ended some of the patronage problems and assisted in the negotiations for the NASCAR track, consolidation itself did not exactly bring about increased regional cooperation on a larger scale.

Conclusion

Much of the debate over metropolitan organization has been focused in terms of extremes such as city-county consolidation, which are for the most part politically infeasible and therefore exotic (Parks and Oakerson, 2000). Despite a renewed interest in consolidation across the nation to solve the aforementioned problems plaguing local governments, the vast majority of modern consolidation efforts (approximately 80 percent since 1970) have failed to secure electoral support. It seems that while many reformers advocate consolidation, the American people have consistently rejected their advice (Leland and Thurmaier, 2005). Are these rejections a result of a fear of larger governments, concerns about a loss or change of political power, or an assessment that scale and scope of government may well be independent of the ability and success of the public sector to address regional issues such as sustainable economic development?

The four case-study areas presented in this chapter demonstrate that regional approaches to infrastructure, development, and environmental issues emerge under fractionated and consolidated schema, and also fail to emerge under both frameworks. Inferring patterns or their lack from four case studies is problematic, and a data set limited to selected outcomes in four areas fails to establish a definitive link between consolidation and regional collaboration.

In the future we plan to add additional data and cases. However, the lessons learned from these four areas illustrate far more regional activity in fractionated areas than one might anticipate and far less consistent support for expanded regional activities in areas with existing consolidated governments. There have been important regional successes from consolidation as well as important regional successes in areas with fragmented governments. These experiences suggest that when regionalism and consolidation are discussed, the scope of the debate must be broadened to recognize that in some instances, local government consolidation could assist in reaching regional goals, and in some circumstances, other, more feasible and pragmatic options for cooperation among local governments could lead to the accomplishment of important regional objectives.

In addition, as Unigov and Wyandotte County-Kansas City, Kansas, demonstrate, there is substantial variation in what is described as a consolidated government and there are different levels of regional cooperation and service arrangements. The structural arrangements created in those regions to address their specific needs might not meet the needs of other areas. The challenges and solutions required for the problems in any other region, whether economic or environmental, may not be found within the structures and configurations of any existing consolidated government but in the *governance* arrangements (both formal and informal) that can be created to respond to a particular problem.

References

Blomquist, William and Roger B. Parks. 1995. "Fiscal, Service, and Political Impacts of Indianapolis-Marion County's Unigov. *Journal of Federalism* 25:4: 37–54.

Gurwitt, R. 2002. "Public Officials of the Year: Carol S. Marinovich." *Governing Magazine* (November). Available at www.governing.com/archive/2002/nov/poy.txt.

Jacobs, Jane. 1961. *The Death and Live of Great American Cities.* New York: Modern Library.

Keating, Dennis W.; Norman Krumholz; and John Metzger. 1995. "Postpopulist Public-Private Partnerships." In *Cleveland: A Metropolitan Reader,* ed. Dennis W. Keating, Norman Krumholz, and David C. Perry, 332–51. Kent, OH: Kent State University Press.

King, Gary; Robert Keohane; and Sidney Verba. 1994. *Designing Social Inquiry. Scientific Inference in Qualitative Research.* Princeton, NJ: Princeton University Press.

Leland, Suzanne. 2004. "Reforming Politics through Reorganization: City-County Consolidation in Wyandotte County/Kansas City, Kansas." In *Reshaping the Local Government Landscape: Case Studies of Local Government Consolidation,* ed. Suzanne Leland and Kurt Thurmaier, 261–71. Armonk, NY: M.E. Sharpe.

Leland, Suzanne, and Kurt Thurmaier. 2000. "Metropolitan Consolidation Success: Returning to the Roots of Local Government Reform." *Public Administration Quarterly* 24, no. 2 (Summer): 202–21.

———. 2005. "When Efficiency Is Unbelievable: Normative Lessons from 30 Years of City-County Consolidations." *Public Administration Review* 65, no. 4 (July): 475–89.

Man, Joyce A., and Mark S. Rosentraub. 1998. "Tax Increment Financing: Municipal Adoption and Its Effects on Property Value Growth," *Public Finance Review* 26: 6 (November 1998): 523-547.

Marinovich, Carol. 2004. "State of the Government." Speech, January 27, Kansas City, Kansas.

Mead, Tim. 2000. "Governing Charlotte-Mecklenburg." *State and Local Government Review* 32, no. 3 (Fall): 192–97.

Mikelbank, Brian, and Mark S. Rosentraub, Charles Post, and Tom Bier. 2007. *Cleveland's Residential Tax Abatement Program: An Assessment of Its Impact, Effects, and Value.* Cleveland: Levin College of Urban Affairs, Cleveland State University.

Ostrom, Vincent; Charles Tiebout; and R. Warren. 1961. "The Organization of Government in Metropolitan Areas: A Theoretical Inquiry." *American Political Science Review* 55, no. 4 (December): 831–42.

Parks, Roger, and Ronald Oakerson. 2000. "Regionalism, Localism, and Metropolitan Governance: Suggestions from the Research Program on Local Public Economies." *State and Local Government Review* 32, no. 3 (Fall): 169–79.

Rosenbaum, W.A., and G.M. Kammerer, eds. 1974. *Against Long Odds: The Theory and Practice of Successful Governmental Consolidation.* Beverly Hills, CA: Sage.

Rosentraub, Mark S. 2000. "City-County Consolidation and the Rebuilding of Image: The Fiscal Lessons from Indianapolis's UniGov Program," *State and Local Government Review,* 32: 3 (Fall 2000): 180-191.

Rusk, David. 1994. "Bend or Die." *State Government News* (February), 6–10.

Tiebout, Charles. 1956. "A Pure Theory of Local Expenditures." *Journal of Political Economy* 64 (October): 416–424.

U.S. Census Bureau. 1990. Profile of Population Statistics: 1990–2006. Census 1990 Mecklenburg County. Available at www.census.gov/popest/cities/.

Walcott, Susan M. 1998. "Eli Lilly and Company: Medical Roots of Regional Renaissance," *Environment and Planning-A* , 30:10, 1723–1741.

Wood, Curtis, and Suzanne Leland. 2007. "Improving the Efficiency and Effectiveness of Service Delivery in Local Government: An Assessment of City-County Consolidation in Wyandotte County/Kansas City, Kansas." Paper presented at the Urban Affairs Association Annual Meeting, Seattle, Washington, April 25–28.

9

Louisville Transformed but Hardly Changed

A Survey of a City Before and After Merger

Hank V. Savitch, Ronald K. Vogel, and Lin Ye

Failure and Success in City-County Consolidation

City-county consolidation (merger) is one of the most radical reforms local governments can undertake. This is because it abolishes small jurisdictions, relocates power in central decision makers, and is rarely reversed. It is not surprising that consolidations have been relatively infrequent in the United States. Since the nineteenth century, less than 20 percent of referenda have been passed by local electorates and only thirty-four have come into effect (Leland and Thurmaier, 2000).

It is easy to carry through a merger, and multiple factors need to work in tandem for it to be successful. Rosenbaum and Kammerer (1974) suggest that consolidation can prevail only when it passes through three necessary stages, or as they put it, a C^3 model. This model consists of: (1) a *crisis climate* caused by inefficient services, financial deficit, or corruption; (2) an *inadequate response* by local authorities to the crisis; and (3) a *catalytic event that triggers* the public to vote for consolidation. Leland and Thurmaier (2004, 2005) revised and augmented Rosenbaum and Kammerer's consolidation (C^3) model. As they see it, the common element underlying successful consolidation is that "the civic elites develop a vision for the community's economic development—a vision that was larger than the city, encompassing the county as a whole" (2005, p. 487). Only after civic elites believe that existing fragmented institutions are inadequate and develop a suitable alternative will they organize and take their campaign to the voters. In this situation every possible resource will be mobilized to convince the electorate. Other factors such as efficiency, equity, and accountability may also play a role in supporting consolidation success.

Theoretical Issues of Consolidation

In the larger scheme of things, consolidation can be placed in the tradition of "progressive reform." The progressive tradition holds that institutional change of this sort can bring about greater efficiency and accountability. Some of its salutary effects are brought into being by consolidation's ability to expand and unify the parameters of local government. The rationale has historic validity. Historically, cities grew by annexing unincorporated territory or absorbing adjacent localities, and this process came to be seen as a form of local imperialism (Kotler, 1969). Within this expansion, unification is made possible by fixing power in the hands of an effective executive, whose decisions are ratified by a directly elected council. Consolidation is a nineteenth-century idea that stresses formal authority as well as older notions of *government* rather than a newer, more flexible emphasis on *governance*. Savitch and Vogel distinguish *governance* from *government* as follows.

> The classic idea of *government* entailed formal institutions and elections and established decision-making processes and administrative structures. . . . By contrast, *governance* conveys the notion that existing institutions can be harnessed in new ways, that cooperation can be carried out on a fluid and voluntary basis among localities, and that people can best regulate themselves through horizontally linked organizations. (2000a, p. 161)

We have in consolidation an institutional change that relies on centralized instruments of government (strong mayor, metro council, and effective bureaucracy) to carry out certain objectives. Because of its emphasis on single, large-scale authority, consolidation fits within a "monocentrist government" school of thought. There are arguments in favor of this approach. Some scholars believe consolidation can improve efficiency and accountability of public services (Norris, 2001; Stephens and Wikstrom, 2000). Others have investigated the issue, and in doing so point out that service efficiencies can be achieved through three factors: economies of scale, more professionally accountable structures, and elimination of duplicated service units (Leland and Thurmaier, 2004, p.19–20).

Another argument supporting consolidation lies in the hope that a consolidated regional government can rescue the declining inner city by drawing together metropolitan-wide taxation, policymaking, and land use planning. According to the theory, a single dominant, local government unit would have the capacity to harness resources, work at optimal levels, and control the movement of population and capital (Burns, 1994; Rusk, 1995).

On the other hand, there are critics who blame big box government for excessive bureaucracy, red tape, and political heavy-handedness. Some theorists value small jurisdictions and local democracy rather than larger centralized authority. This school of thought has been referred to as "polycentrist" because it supports the integrity of independent, local jurisdictions and their creative ability to construct cooperative agreements through "governance" (Parks and Oakerson, 1989). Polycentrist governance is by definition looser. It would not preclude regional cooperation, but seeks it through incremental, gradual adjustments between localities rather than abrupt, comprehensive actions.

Put another way, monocentrists rely on a presumed singular "voice" of citizens to exercise a collective, popular will. By contrast, polycentrists place their trust in the presumed ability of individuals and households to express their will through voluntary initiatives or by entering or exiting the many jurisdictions available to them.[1] The Louisville case affords us an opportunity to examine what happens when a jurisdiction shifts from what might broadly be called a polycentrist governance model to one that emphasizes monocentrist government. In taking up this case, we pay particular attention to issues of local democracy, budget, costs, and efficiency.

Merger in Louisville

Metropolitan consolidation had failed in Louisville no less than three times before citizens voted to consolidate in 2000. In 1956, the Mallon Plan was proposed to local voters in order to extend the city's boundaries. That plan was to cover all the urbanized areas of Jefferson County, a forty-six-square-mile area with 68,000 residents, intended to extend urban services to suburban residents. There were also significant hurdles for the Mallon Plan. Passage required a dual majority, and both city and county voters would have to approve. While a majority of city voters cast favorable ballots, suburbanites voted against Mallon by a two to one margin, bringing it down to defeat (Vogel, 1994).

Like many other American cities, Louisville underwent deindustrialization in the 1970s. It is also a city divided by class and race. The South End is typically white and working class, the West End is predominantly black and poor; whereas the East End is white and middle- and upper-income. The central city continued to lose population after the 1960s, and the surrounding suburbs absorbed much of the economic growth. While the central city population dropped from 390,000 in 1960 to 256,000 in 2000 (a decline of 34 percent), the county population jumped from 611,000 in 1960 to 694,000 in 2000, recording a gain of 13 percent.[2] Business and residential development also moved into suburban areas.

In 1982, local business elites pushed for city-county consolidation once again. The mayor, county executive, and an organization of business leaders lobbied the state to authorize the creation of a charter commission to study city-county consolidation. As eventually proposed, the consolidation plan exempted over more than eighty incorporated suburban cities from being merged. It also safeguarded existing fire and special districts.

The reaction to merger was strong. Within a short time a black-white working class from the South and West Ends stood in opposition. Merger was defeated, but by a very narrow margin, just 1,450 out of 182,000 votes, or a 50.4 percent to 49.6 percent defeat. Having come so close to success, merger's proponents enthusiastically tried again, just one year later. In 1983, a revised merger plan was placed before the public, and this time the electorate turned down merger by 5,600 votes.

As the suburbs grew and enriched its land with new development, the city began searching for ways to attach these new revenue sources. In 1985, the Louisville Board of Alderman sought to annex all of the unincorporated areas of Jefferson County. Fearing that it would lose revenue, the county took countermeasures. Thus began the "annexation wars" of the 1980s, and tensions mounted between the two jurisdictions. In order to reconcile these differences, both governments adopted the Louisville-Jefferson County Compact (the Compact).

The Compact turned out to be innovative as well as viable—a type of polycentrist governance based on voluntary, horizontal cooperation between two localities. Under its terms, the city and county agreed to share occupational (income) tax collection based on actual collections over the previous three years, with the city granted approximately 58.7 percent of the revenue and the county 41.3 percent. The Compact also established a comprehensive interlocal service agreement. The city and the county also agreed to divide up a number of previously independent joint city-county agencies. The city gained responsibility for the human relations commission, zoo, museum, and emergency services while the county was assigned air pollution, health, crime commission, and planning. Library, transit authority, sewer district, and parks remained as joint agencies. Economic development and attracting new business were also placed in a new joint Office of Economic Development.

Although the city and the county voiced periodic complaints, the Compact worked astonishingly well over the years. For one, it put an end to the "annexation wars" that had prevailed prior to its inception. Second, it produced more than a decade of relative stability and prosperity across the metropolitan area. Third, it induced cooperation between the mayor and county executive and was widely perceived as a success. In fact, the Compact achieved national recognition for showing how competing jurisdictions could work together toward common ends.

Initially set for twelve years, the Compact was renewed in 1998 for another ten years, with minor modifications. During this period, one of the most significant changes in the political profile of the city was the creation of Greater Louisville Inc. (GLI). As it stood, GLI was formed by combining the Greater Louisville Economic Development Partnership and the Louisville Area Chamber of Commerce into one common enterprise. GLI also proved to be the catalyst for revisiting merger. Despite improved fiscal conditions, elites felt the Compact was inherently incomplete—a "Band-Aid" measure, as it was called. By the 1990s consolidation returned to the local agenda (Savitch and Vogel, 2000b).

During this time, the Jefferson County Governance Project was established in 1994 to study local governance and a Citizen Task Force was appointed. Two years later, the Task Force found that the proposed reorganization would not ensure the city's viability and recommended rejecting the idea of consolidation (Savitch and Vogel, 1996). However, by September 1999, that recommendation was reversed. Louisville mayor David Armstrong and county executive Rebecca Jackson proposed consolidating the city and county governments. In January 2000, a state task force voted to endorse the proposal and the General Assembly passed a merger bill the following spring. Merger was once again on the ballot and scheduled for a vote in the general election of November 2000.

Claiming that overlapping city and county government had hindered the area's prosperity, a strong pro-merger network was established by local business and influential politicians. Merger proponents organized their campaigns under a bipartisan partnership called UNITY, which included former mayor Jerry Abramson as well as current mayor Dave Armstrong—both of whom were Democrats. These Democrats were joined by the Republican county executive Rebecca Jackson and the Republican minority leader of the U.S. Senate, Mitch McConnell. Also supporting the UNITY campaign were Louisville's powerful business organization (GLI), the city's only mainstream newspaper (the *Courier Journal*), a public utility (Louisville Gas and Electric), and lesser-known politicians.

Major opposition revolved around a group called Citizens Organized in Search of the Truth (COST). The opposition fought against merger on grounds that it would increase taxes, render services less stable, and compromise local democracy. Most of all, COST argued there was no evidence merger would create significant benefits and, in the absence of an evaluation, voters should turn it down. Led by a popular African-American county commissioner named Darryl Owens, COST was a grassroots organization that gathered under its tent labor unions, civil rights groups, much of the city's gay population, members of the Board of Aldermen, and neighborhood associations. While COST had popular appeal, it was no financial match for UNITY. Just one month before the voting, COST had raised only $41,000—about one-seventeenth of UNITY's initially reported $700,000.[3]

Despite its best efforts COST was not able to organize an effective campaign against consolidation. Unlike the previous campaigns of 1982 and 1983, it simply could not muster a high enough vote among its core constituencies. White and black working-class voters from the South End and West End did vote against merger, but not in the same numbers. Meanwhile, residents in other parts of the city as well as the East End suburbs voted for consolidation. In November 2000 merger passed by a 55 percent to a 45 percent margin. By January 2003 a new consolidated government began operations.

Returning to our discussion at the outset of this article, we note that merger's passage contained none of the Rosenbaum-Kammerer attributes for success. It was not preceded by crises, responses from local authorities were not inadequate, and there were no catalytic events to trigger to passage. What did enable merger's passage was closer to Leland and Thurmaier's formulation that local elites presented a vision for the future. That vision was couched in consolidation's promises to strengthen the local economy, accompanied by themes related to efficiency and a better-performing metropolitan government. There was also a prestige factor related to bigness. Consolidated Louisville and Jefferson County would draw a larger circle around a newly defined metropolitan city, thereby increasing its population to nearly 700,000 people.[4] All this was bolstered by a heavily financed campaign and carried through by unified elites.

Map 9.1   **Louisville, Jefferson County, and Suburban Cities**

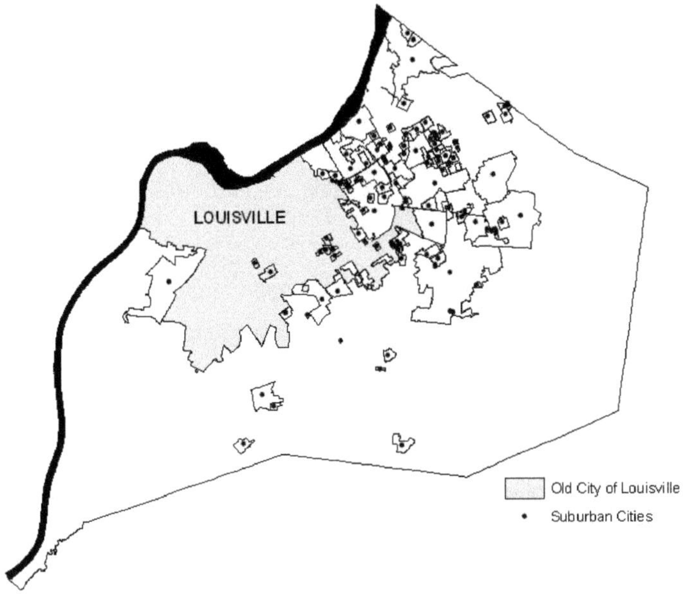

LOUISVILLE

☐ Old City of Louisville

• Suburban Cities

Source: Louisville/Jefferson County Information Consortium (LOJIC).

Political Parties, Campaigns, and Elections

In one sense, merger had a significant impact. It radically altered the landscape of the jurisdiction, from a medium-size Midwest town of sixty-two square miles to a merged metropolis of 385 square miles, larger than the five counties of New York City.

The distance between the eastern and western boundaries of consolidated Louisville is now more than thirty miles, roughly the same mileage as from Baltimore to Washington, DC. More important, territorial realignment altered the political and social profile of the city. Map 9.1 shows the basic geographic configuration of merged Louisville.

As shown in Map 9.1, merger left more than eighty independent suburban cities untouched. Leaving those cities out of merger had always been a crucial strategy in past efforts. This was because of strong opposition from the economically affluent and politically influential suburbs, who guarded their autonomy. Suburban residents were afraid that being included in the metro government would threaten their service capacity, increase their tax burdens, and possibly bring unwanted residents into their jurisdictions.

Table 9.1 shows some basic features of Louisville as they existed before and after

Table 9.1

Louisville Before and After Merger

	Before (city)	After (county)
Land area (sq. miles)	62	385
Total population	256,231	693,604
White	161,261 (62.9%)	536,721 (77.4%)
Black or African-American	84,586 (33.0%)	130,928 (18.9%)
Median household income	$28,843	$39,457
Unemployment rate	7.4%	5.0%
Homeownership rate	52.5%	64.9%
Median house price	$82,300	$103,000

Source: U.S. Census Bureau, Decennial Census 2000; city data are from http://censtats.census.gov/data/KY/1602148000.pdf and county data are from http://censtats.census.gov/data/KY/05021111.pdf (accessed June 1, 2007).

merger. One of the consolidation's most salient features is its emphasis on a "strong mayor," and Louisville typifies that quality. Mayors can be elected for three terms of office, they possess strong budget authority, they enjoy considerable leeway in selecting members to crucial boards (such as planning and zoning), and they nominate commissioners (subject to council approval). Nonetheless, the office is subject to significant political realities, and consolidation has brought the suburbs into the picture. Mayoral candidates have to win a majority of suburban constituencies and deal with a suburban-oriented metro council. Contrary to the expectations of some writers, instead of giving the pre-merged city a boost, the long-term consequence of the merger augured for diminished attention to neighborhoods in the urban core.

Campaigns and voting also hold implications for the city's minorities. Consolidated government left African-Americans with a decreasing proportion in the metro council. As indicated in Table 9.1, the African-American population declined from 33 percent in the pre-merged Louisville to below 20 percent under the metro government. A new twenty-six-member Louisville Metro Council replaced the previous Board of Aldermen and County Commission. Six out of the twenty-six metro council seats are held by African-American councilmen, accounting for 23 percent of the legislative votes. All six of those districts are from the West and South Ends of the city, containing lower-income communities.

While the number of seats held by blacks more than reflects the proportion of minority residents, there is some disgruntlement. Recently one of the metro council members asserted that residents from the West End and South End "have always felt like a stepchild . . . not a lot of attention has been given to them even since the merger" (Green, 2007, radio interview). With declining voting powers, it has become more difficult for these communities to compete with other parts of the county. Under consolidation, approximately two-thirds of the votes and an even higher number of council seats come from white, suburban districts, giving those constituencies significant political advantages.

There is a long-standing debate over whether consolidation enhances local democratic participation. Several empirical studies of consolidated jurisdictions identified declines in voting participation, particularly among minorities (Feiock, 2004; Oliver, 2001). In Louisville, merger proponents argued that merger would bring government closer to the electorate. Since every council member speaks for just 25,000 people, proponents argued that voting would be enhanced. To some extent this expectation has been borne out. While the effects could be temporary and part of a "first blush" effect, electoral turnouts show a moderate increase in voting participation. The average voter turnout in primary elections between 1999 and 2002 (prior to merger) was 15.4 percent, while the average figure from 2003 to 2006 (after merger) rose to 17.9 percent.[5]

Campaign spending is another important matter. Merger proponents also argued that, as opposed to former county commission districts (225,000 people), smaller metropolitan districts (25,000) would lower campaign costs. This turned out to be incorrect. In the 1998 and 2000 general elections, the average spending for each aldermanic candidate in the pre-merged city was only $3,800. The figure soared to $12,000 for each candidate in the 2004 and 2006 metro council elections, amounting to more than a 200 percent increase in average spending.[6] The mayoral campaign showed similar jumps in campaign costs. In 1998, the last mayoral campaign year before the merger, candidates spent $1.24 million (in 2006 constant dollars) in both primary and general elections. In 2006, the total campaign expenditures in both elections increased to $2.15 million, representing a 73 percent jump. At the same time, grassroots campaigning for the office has been overwhelmed by politicians who are able to raise money.

Theoretically, consolidation has made possible a more competitive two-party system, but it is not so much parties as different geographies that compete. Thus, we do not see closely matched Democratic and Republican candidates contesting a seat, as much as Democratic, urban districts versus Republican, suburban districts struggling against one another in the metro council. Party labels mask and separate geosocial affiliations. The general tenor of the metro council is manifested in the physical segregation of its members. One member asserted that metro government created "a massive bureaucracy centered around the Republican and Democratic offices." Representatives from urbanized Democratic districts one through thirteen are located on one floor of the metro building, while suburban Republican members are located on another floor (Owen, 2005).

Budget and Costs

As previously discussed, monocentric government theory argues that greater efficiencies can be obtained through budget and cost improvement. A pre- and post-assessment of Louisville's budget provides some useful illustrations about this assertion. Figure 9.1 displays some basic measures on this subject in a series

Figure 9.1   **Total Personnel and Budget Expenditure: Fiscal Years 2000–2009**

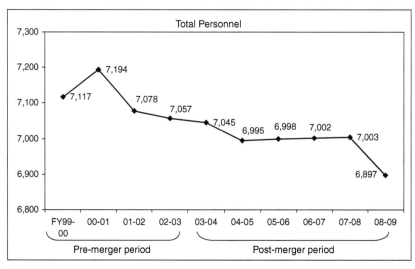

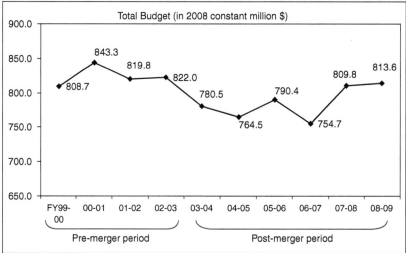

Source: Louisville and Jefferson County Executive Budget, 2000–2009. Several budget data categories, including total personnel and city total budget before FY 99–00 were not available.

of line graphs. Shown in the graphs are total government personnel, total budgets, and expenditures per capita as well as per employee. The time periods are divided into pre-merger years and post-merger years.

The immediate period after merger recorded some budget saving (mostly

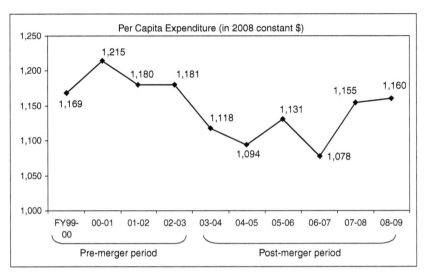

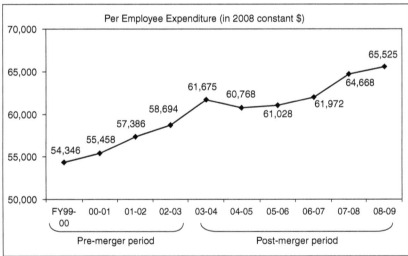

from 2003 through 2005). The total budget decreased by about 5 percent with about 1,000 positions eliminated. However, the savings have been short-lived and budget figures gradually climbed back after 2007, coming close to the level of pre-merger years. For the most recent budget, Louisville had a total budget of $813 million, with 6,897 employees. Before the merger (FY 2002–3), the combined budgets of the old city and county, amounted to $822 million with 7,057 permanent positions. After controlling for inflation, we calculate a saving of approximately 1 percent for these years (FY 2002–3 through FY

2008–9). The total reduction in workforce between these two periods came to 160 positions.

In examining Figure 9.1, we also see that expenditures per government employee have been rising steadily throughout the years, except for a slight drop from 2004 to 2005. This trend has continued through the merger years, with an over 11 percent increase from 2003 to 2009 (controlling for inflation). Expenditures per government employee reached a historic high of $65,525 in the recently approved budget of FY 2008–9. While metro government did eliminate some positions, total personnel costs continued to rise.

Per capita expenditure shows a slightly different pattern. Taking a gross view for the periods before and after merger, we see that per capita expenditures declined from $1,180 to $1,160. Accounting for inflation this represented a 1.7 percent decrease in expenditures during a seven year period. Again, we also see that per capita expenditure has begun to climb back toward previous levels.

In general, any reductions in budgets, personnel, or costs have been small.[7] The basic pattern has been for expenditures to modestly recede for a short period, only to climb back to previous levels. This has occurred with gross budget amounts, numbers of employees, expenditures per employee, and expenditures per capita.

We also note that the costs of transition have been substantial in other cities that merged, though these data are not available for Louisville. Some expenditures in Louisville's transition may be contained in the higher costs per employee, as noted above. Prior to merger, considerable salary differences existed between county and city employees. The merger agreement required the ratcheting up of salaries in one jurisdiction, so they were the same across the new metropolis. Faced with higher costs, metro officials could have decided to cut some jobs, leaving the new government with fewer but better-paid employees.

Exactly what accounts for other "cost rebounds" is also unclear. It might be that the newly merged government believed it could achieve savings and experimented in certain areas, only to have costs rebound in other areas or at a later date. It might also be that the newly merged government wanted to show gains during its initial years and squeezed minor savings out of the system, only to discover that this approach could not be sustained.

Most important, it is hardly plausible to talk about efficiency without examining service performance. Cost reductions can always be made through performance reduction. Merged or unmerged, it is certainly not difficult for a city to shave a budget while also deferring or squeezing services. In the next section we take up this issue by examining selected functions of police, roads, and the environment.

Service Delivery: Police, Roads, and the Environment

Crime and police performance have always been major issues for cities. While monocentrists would claim that consolidated police departments work better, that assertion is disputable. Indeed, some studies show that consolidated police forces are less responsive to the citizenry, less sensitive about particular situations, and less well-regarded by the communities they serve (Ostrom, 2000; Parks and Whitaker, 1973; Savitch, Vogel, and Seales, 1998). Part of the gap may be due to additional layers of bureaucracy and narrower spans of control, which call for more supervisors to manage a more complex police department. Also, consolidated police forces are spread over larger and more differentiated territories, making it harder to attain the knowledge and relationships necessary for successful policing.

Applied to the Louisville experience, monocentrist theory is questionable. Merger proponents promised to reduce crime (Abramson, 2004). Four years after the merger, the new metro mayor claimed to have built "a city that's safer" (Abramson, 2004, 2006). Official statistics show a different picture. According to the Federal Bureau of Investigation Uniform Crime Report, there were 625 reported violent crimes, including homicide, rape, robbery, and aggregated assault, in 2005, a 20 percent increase from 2003. A 2006 FBI report shows that while the national property crime rate went down, Louisville's number of reported cases kept rising and the locally increasing violent crime rate also far exceeded the national average (Zambroski, 2006).

More serious are accusations of reporting discrepancies between local and federal sources. The issue had taken on a political content. During one political campaign the Republican nominee for mayor and current councilman, Kelly Downard, pointed to discrepancies in reporting murder rates. As Downard put it:

> The FBI says 55, the police say 59, our records show 64. What do yours show? Mine said 66. . . . The discrepancy is almost scandalous—the numbers change everyday I see them. I mean, people are being murdered and the numbers just change. That's shameful." (Zambroski, 2006)

While cities may not be able to do much to reduce crime, they are accountable for police performance. One measure of that performance is the crime clearance rate.[8] The higher the clearance rate, the better for the city because more cases are disposed. Lower clearance can be an indication of failed performance. Figure 9.2 displays those clearance rates for both violent crimes (including murder and nonnegligent manslaughter, forcible rape, robbery, and aggravated assault) and property crimes (including burglary, larceny-theft, motor vehicle theft, and arson) in Louisville. The figure covers the periods three years before (2000–2002) and three years after (2003–5) the merger.

According to the official statistics released by the Louisville Police Department, clearance rates fell for both categories of crimes. Before the merger, Louisville cleared approximately 50 percent of violent crimes and about 23 percent of property crimes. During the three years after the merger, the clearance rates dropped to about 40 percent and 19 percent for violent crimes and property crimes, respectively. These statistics do raise questions about why the drop occurred and whether it was related to having consolidated an urban department with a very different suburban/rural one.

Environmental conditions are another factor to consider. Some scholars point out that single, big box governments do better at cleaning up the environment.

Figure 9.2   **Clearance Rates: Violent and Property Crime**

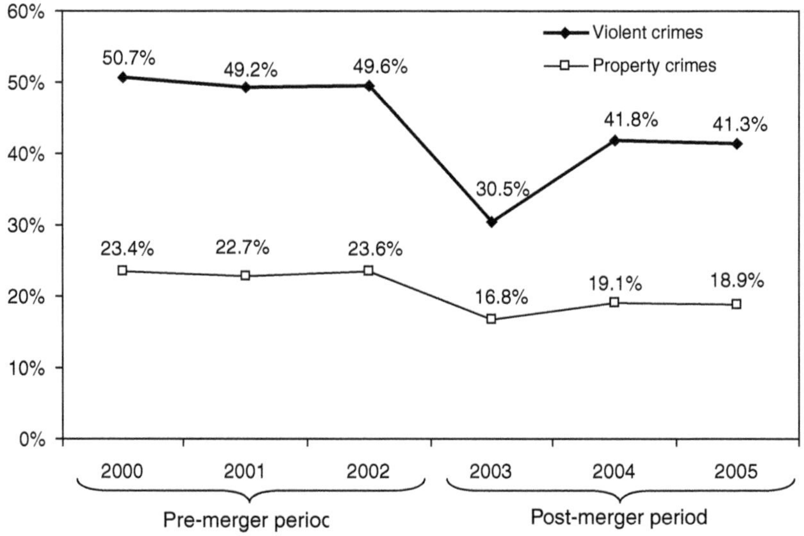

Source: Crime Analysis Unit, Louisville Metro Police Department, Louisville, Kentucky.

For example, both Matthew Crenson (1971) and Nancy Burns (1994) claim that consolidated localities are better at fending off pollution-prone businesses.

Environmental issues have also resonated in Louisville, and the new metro mayor has promised to reverse a rather dismal record. Greater Louisville continues to be among the most polluted localities in the country (American Lung Association, 2006). Table 9.2 displays a record of air quality in Louisville-Jefferson County between 1998 and 2007. The table breaks this record into numbers of days characterized as "good," "moderate," and "unhealthy."

Taking a gross view of air quality, we see that the record has improved. While averages can be deceptive, they are worth mentioning. Prior to merger Louisville-Jefferson County registered an average of 171.2 "good days," and after merger that average rose somewhat to 181 "good days." The real gain however, occurred after merger where the number of "unhealthy days" was reduced by more than half from 34.8 to 15.4. This was a significant reduction, though the record is very uneven and jumps around quite a bit. Thus, we see a particularly bad year (1999) in the pre-merger period where the number of "unhealthy days" days reached 53. We also see two bad years (2005 and 2007) in the post-merger period where the number of "unhealthy days" was 27. Of some concern is the most recent year of available data, 2007, where metro seems to have rebounded to a bad year. These bad years in the post-merger period were offset by two good years (2004 and 2006) where the number of "unhealthy days" dramatically fell.

Table 9.2

Air Quality in Louisville-Jefferson County, 1998–2007

	Year	Good	Moderate	Unhealthy
Pre-merger period	1998	254	74	37
	1999	148	164	53
	2000	147	197	22
	2001	142	199	24
	2002	165	162	38
Post-merger period	2003	182	170	13
	2004	195	169	2
	2005	157	181	27
	2006	191	166	8
	2007	181	157	27

Source: U.S. Environment Protection Agency, Air Quality Index Report (Washington, DC).
Note: Numbers indicate the number of days when air quality is good, moderate, or unhealthy (both for sensitive groups and general populations).

Table 9.3

Road Conditions in Louisville-Jefferson County, 2001–2005

	Year	Poor	Mediocre	Fair	Good
Pre-merger Period	2001	16	33	28	22
	2002	17	40	17	26
Post-merger Period	2003	12	41	23	24
	2004	12	41	25	22
	2005	11	40	21	28

Source: The Road Information Program (TRIP), Washington, DC.

Finally, we consider the condition of metro Louisville's roads. Transportation infrastructure is an important component of a city's viability. Road maintenance is conducted through a simple technology and under the direct and sole control of local government. One would expect any improvements in this area to be relatively rapid and effective.

Table 9.3 shows road conditions for metro Louisville for the years 2001 through 2005. As can be seen, road conditions are categorized on a continuum as "poor," "mediocre," "fair," and "good."

The results are checkered. While the number of roads in "poor condition" declined, those in the next worse category of "mediocre" grew. At the same time, while the number of roads in "good" condition saw a modest increase, those in the next best category of "fair" saw a modest drop. While it may be difficult to determine what lies behind this classification, it does seem reasonable to observe that Louisville's road infrastructure continues much as before, though with some shifting of places.

For our selected functions we can say that the performance record is mixed. The condition of the city's air did improve. However, clearance rates for the police have declined and too many roads are still in disrepair. Again, these findings are for selected functions and thus more illustrative than conclusive. In the absence of comprehensive analysis, we cannot know precisely how the costs and benefits will sort out, but our findings do suggest that the alleged advantages from merger should be viewed skeptically.

Other Considerations: Libraries as a Common Public Good

An assumption made by monocentrists is that big boxes create more enlightened societies. The traditional reformist approach is to enlarge the sphere and thereby attain heightened attention to the public good (Wilson and Banfield, 1971). Other consolidations in Indianapolis and Jacksonville were said to have brought in well-educated populations that appreciated public goods and were willing to invest in them. The question arises, what does the Louisville experience tell us?

Louisville's recent referendum on its library system exemplifies how the merged city treats a public good. Metro's library system has been woefully underfunded and among the least adequate in the nation (for comparable cities). Its hours of operation are short, its access to residents below par, and its technology is well behind that of other systems.

The city had been well aware of these inadequacies and tried twice before to pass a library tax. In 1986 and again in 1991 residents of pre-merged Louisville went to the polls. Despite strong campaigns by library supporters, the vote failed on both occasions—once with 57 percent of the vote cast in opposition and again by a closer margin of 52 percent of the vote cast in opposition.

Some people believed that a post-merged Louisville, holding better-educated and more affluent suburban residents, would respond differently. In 2007 the proposal was posed to voters again. It required raising the occupational tax by two-tenths of one percent, costing a worker who earns $38,000 a year about $76 or $2 for every $1,000 earned by workers and businesses in Jefferson County. Had the referendum passed, it would have brought in about $40 million in the first year for library expansion and operating costs. This time, the library referendum went down by an even larger margin, with 67 percent voting against and only 33 percent for the proposal.[9]

What is revealing about this event is not the defeat of a common and badly needed public good, but that library supporters were considerably more prominent in the pre-merged city than the suburbs. Map 9.2 shows the votes for the library as they are mapped across metropolitan Louisville. For the most part the numbered districts lie within the pre-merged city, while those not numbered are suburbs.

Note the higher percentages of favorable votes are closer to the center of the pre-merged city. The farther one moves from the center, the fewer favorable votes

Map 9.2   **Voting in the Library Referendum of 2007**

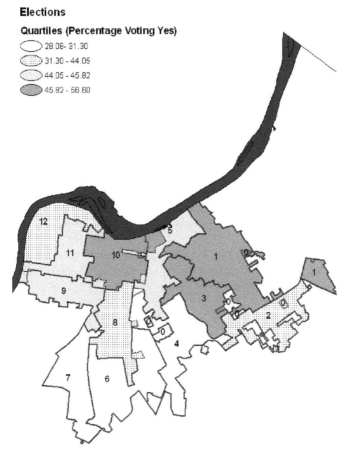

Elections

Quartiles (Percentage Voting Yes)
- 28.08 - 31.30
- 31.30 - 44.05
- 44.05 - 45.82
- 45.82 - 56.60

Source: Authors constructed map from data from Election 2007, Jefferson County Board of Elections, Louisville, Kentucky. Wards 1 to 12 are the former wards of pre-merged Louisville. The rest of Jefferson consists of the independent cities and unincorporated areas of pre-merged Louisville.

for the library. The strongest support for the library, whose collective votes would have passed the referendum, came from districts one, three, and ten—all of which are heavily urban and either at the center or close to it. Once we get to the suburbs and beyond the numbered districts, those voting "yes" fall to less than 31.3 percent.

The Louisville experience belies the contention that expanding city bounds is likely to increase public goods or make the city more "progressive." Affluence and higher education do not necessarily lead to an appreciation of the commonweal. Much depends on who benefits and loses as well as attitudes toward government.

Other Considerations: Outmigration and Porous Boundaries

One of the arguments made by proponents of consolidation is that it will strengthen regional cooperation by establishing definitive boundaries (Parr, Riehm, and Mc-Farland, 2006). By this reasoning a single government should be able to contain urban development and keep populations from beyond the boundaries of the new jurisdictions. Merger proponents in Louisville picked up this idea, pointing out that consolidation would not only contain the city's population but also draw out-migrants back to it.[10]

As mentioned at the outset of this chapter, merger is a nineteenth-century idea that is supposed to enhance the city with fixed boundaries. But is this a reasonable assumption for the twentieth and twenty-first centuries, with spreading urbanization and mobile populations? We can better examine this issue by bringing up data from the Louisville experience.

Figure 9.3 shows the net population migrations from Jefferson County to sur-rounding areas and the income level between the out- and in-migration from 1995 to 2004.

During this period of time, the only year that the county gained population was in 2002. Although the number of out-migrations was not extremely high (an annual average around 500), the data show net out-migration. The region did relatively well just before the merger (2002). However, residents started to move out of the county again during the first two years after the merger, 2003 and 2004.

The income level of out-migration residents is erratic, having peaked in 2001 and sharply slowed down in 2002, only to pick up again recently. Just as significant is the income disparity between residents who moved out from and moved into the county. Merged Louisville continued to lose its wealthier populations to the surrounding areas, and the net income level in 2004 was over $4,000 per household.

Louisville's experience teaches us that merger is hardly a solution to out-migration. Monocentrism may be too heavy-handed an approach to establishing regional cooperation because smaller localities outside the consolidated areas, can feel threatened by their much larger neighbor. It may be more feasible for smaller, equally sized jurisdictions to establish interlocal agreements that contain exurban sprawl.

Conclusions

Merger transformed Louisville by redefining its territory, population, and govern-ment. Merger gave monocentric government a place, enabling the mayor and the council to enlarge their domain nearly sevenfold and triple its population. Merger also stimulated voting turnout in the first few elections, but made it financially more difficult to run for at-large seats or even district constituencies.

Most other factors hardly changed. After a short period of minor savings, Louisville experienced sharp rebounds. Budgets, employees, and per capita costs

Figure 9.3 **Population Migration and Income Disparity for Jefferson County, 1995–2004**

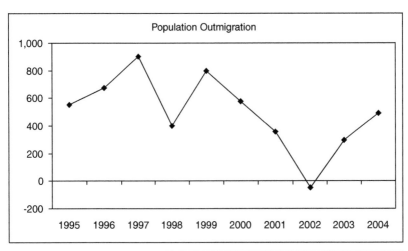

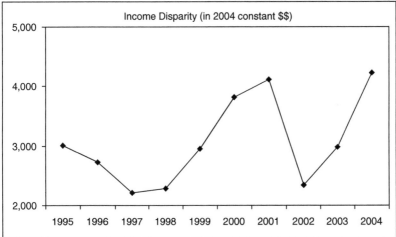

Source: Internal Revenue Services County-to-county Migration Flow Data, 1995–2004, Washington, DC. Year 2003 was the first year after the merger.

climbed back to previous or near-previous levels. While air pollution was reduced, performance in other categories such as police and roads was doubtful—either having remained the same or somewhat declined.

To what extent this experience is a comment on monocentric government theory remains to be seen. Karl Popper's (1968) insight about disclaiming a theory when it is falsified surely resonates in this case. Popper's law that a negative finding can be generalized is strengthened by the fact that Louisville typifies Middle America. It is neither flooded with riches like San Francisco nor in dire straits like Newark. Louisville has not been up against the wall, though it has wrestled with very important choices about strategies for the future (Savitch and Vogel, 2000b). All this makes its own experience relevant and the lessons derived from it quite valuable.

Notes

1. One variant of the polycentrist school, known as "public choice," emphasizes efficiencies that can be gained though a marketplace of many local jurisdictions, but it does not give priority to interlocal cooperation. Public choice also emphasizes a presumed freedom of citizens to move from one jurisdiction to another. As the theory goes, "voting with one's feet" will induce localities to attract residents by maximizing efficiencies and accountability (Bish, 1971; Tiebout, 1956).

2. The city population figure for 2000 is from the Decennial Census and the 1960 figure is from *Population of the 100 Largest Cities and Other Urban Places in the United States: 1790 to 1990,* available at www.census.gov/population/www/documentation/twps0027.html (accessed May 31, 2007). The county population figure for 2000 is from the Decennial Census and the 1960 figure is from County Population Census Counts 1900–90, available at www.census.gov/population/www/censusdata/cencounts.html (accessed May 31, 2007).

3. Later reports indicated that UNITY had raised more than $1 million. For a detailed account of the merger campaign, please see Savitch and Vogel (2004, pp. 766–68).

4. The nearby rival city of Lexington had consolidated in the 1970s, and its combined city-county population threatened to overtake unmerged Louisville. While comparing a county population to a city population is inappropriate, the idea of Lexington as Kentucky's largest city was an emotional factor that influenced voting.

5. The figures are from Kentucky Registry of Election Finance, available at www.kref.state.ky.us/krefsearch/.

6. The figures are from Kentucky Registry of Election Finance, available at www.kref.state.ky.us/krefsearch/, and have been adjusted for inflation to 2006 constant dollars.

7. While the scale of consolidations are vastly different and not a feasible comparison with Louisville, Selden and Campbell's (2000) study of Athens-Clark County, Georgia, did locate savings. The economies found by Selden and Campbell did not pertain to all departments.

8. The FBI reports that an offense is cleared by arrest when all of the following conditions have been met for at least one person: arrested, charged with the commission of the offense, or turned over to the court for prosecution. In certain situations, elements beyond law enforcement's control prevent the agency from arresting and formally charging the offender. These offenses can be cleared by "exceptional means" (Federal Bureau of Investigation, U.S. Department of Justice, 2006).

9. Some of those voting against the referendum would claim they were not so much against library expansion as against the way the plan had been constructed. In fact, a "no tax library plan" was proposed as an alternative. However, the feasibility of providing a public good without raising taxes is another matter, which we do not address here.

10. The merger campaign often pointed to the ability of consolidation to retain its youth within the new jurisdiction. Joan Riehm, the deputy mayor of metro Louisville, claimed that the new metro had a bright future to keep and attract new talent (Riehm 2005).

References

Abramson, J. 2004. *State of the City Address.* January 1. Louisville, Kentucky.
———. 2006. *State of the City Address.* January 19. Louisville, Kentucky.

American Lung Association. 2006. *State of the Air.* Available at http://lungaction.org/reports/ sota06_cities.html (accessed June 12, 2007).

Bish, R. 1971. *The Political Economy of Metropolitan Areas.* Chicago, IL: Markham.

Burns, Nancy. 1994. *The Formation of American Local Governments.* New York: Oxford University Press.

Campbell, R.W., and D. Durning. 2000. "Is City-County Consolidation Good Policy? A Symposium." *Public Administration Quarterly* 24, no. 2: 133–39.

Crenson, M.A. 1971. *The Un-Politics of Air Pollution: A Study of Non-Decision-Making in the Cities.* Baltimore, MD: Johns Hopkins University Press.

Federal Bureau of Investigation, U.S. Department of Justice. 2006. "Crime in the United States: Clearances." Available at www.fbi.gov/ucr/cius2006/offenses/clearances/index. html (accessed August 13, 2008).

Feiock, R.C. 2004. "Do Consolidation Entrepreneurs Make a Deal with the Devil?" In *Reshaping the Local Landscape: City-County Consolidation and Its Alternatives,* ed. J.B. Carr and R.C. Feiock, 39–52. Armonk, NY: M.E. Sharpe.

Green, J. 2007. Metro District 1 Councilman, interview. Louisville, Kentucky. No date.

Johnson, L.S., and R.C. Feiock. 1999. "Revolutionary Change in Local Governance: Revisiting the Rosenbaum and Kammerer Theory of Successful City-County Consolidation." *Journal of Political Science* 27: 1–29.

Kotler, M. 1969. *Neighborhood Government: The Local Foundations of Political Life.* New York: Bobbs-Merrill Company.

Leland, S.M., and K. Thurmaier. 2000. "Metropolitan Consolidation Success: Returning to the Roots of Local Government Reform." *Public Administration Quarterly* 24, no. 2: 202–13.

———, eds. 2004. *Reshaping the Local Landscape: Case Studies of City-County Consolidation.* Armonk, NY: M.E. Sharpe.

———. 2005. "When Efficiency is Unbelievable: Normative Lessons from 20 Years of City-County Consolidations." *Public Administration Review* 65, no. 4: 475–89.

Norris, D. 2001. "Whither Metropolitan Governance?" *Urban Affairs Review* 36, no. 4: 532–50.

Oliver, J.E. 2001. *Democracy in Suburbia.* Princeton, NJ: Princeton University Press.

Ostrom, E. 2000. "The Danger of Self–Evident Truths." *PS: Political Science & Politics* 33. no. 1:33–44.

Owen, Tom. 2005. "Metro Council Roundtable." Lessons from Merger Workshop, ARS National Forum on Regional Stewardship, Louisville, Kentucky, November 8–11.

Owens, D.T. 2000. "Eight Most Asked Questions about the Proposed Merger of Louisville and Jefferson County." Jefferson County, Kentucky.

Parks, Roger B., and Gordon P. Whitaker. 1973. "Suburban Police Departments: Too Many and Too Small?" In *The Urbanization of the Suburbs,* ed. Louis H. Masotti and Jeffrey K. Hadden, 367–402. Beverly Hills, CA: Sage.

Parks, Roger B., and Ronald J. Oakerson. 1989. "Metropolitan Organization and Governance: A Local Public Economy Approach." *Urban Affairs Quarterly* 25, no. 1 (September): 18–29.

Parr, John; Joan Riehm; and Christiana McFarland. 2006. *Guide to Successful Local Government Collaboration in America's Regions.* Washington, DC: National League of Cities.

Popper, K. 1968. *The Logic of Scientific Discovery.* New York: Harper and Row.

Riehm, Joan. 2005. Lessons from Merger Workshop, ARS National Forum on Regional Stewardship, Louisville, Kentucky, November 8–11.

Rosenbaum, W.A., and G.M. Kammerer. 1974. *Against Long Odds: The Theory and Practice of Successful Governmental Consolidation.* Beverly Hills, CA: Sage.

Rusk, D. 1995. *Cities Without Suburbs.* 2d ed. Washington, DC: Woodrow Wilson Center.

Savitch, H.V., and R.K. Vogel. 1996. "Report to the Jefferson County Fiscal Court on Final Recommendations of the Jefferson County Governance Project." Louisville, Kentucky, June 11.

————. 2000a. "Paths to New Regionalism." *State and Local Government Review* 32, no. 3: 158–68.

————. 2000b. "Metropolitan Consolidation versus Metropolitan Governance in Louisville." *State and Local Government Review* 32, no. 3: 198–212.

————. 2004. "Suburbs Without a City: Power and City-County Consolidation." *Urban Affairs Review* 39, no. 6: 758–90.

Savitch, H.V.; R.K. Vogel; and S.C. Seales. 1998. "Size, Deployment, and Performance: Considerations in Consolidating Police Services in Louisville and Jefferson County." Report, Fiscal County of Jefferson County, Kentucky, October 12.

Selden, S.C., and R.W. Campbell. 2000. "The Expenditure Impacts of Unification in a Small Georgia County: A Contingency Perspective of City-County Consolidation." *Public Administration Quarterly* 24, no. 2: 169–201.

Stephens, G. Ross, and Nelson Wikstrom. 2000. *Metropolitan Government and Governance: Theoretical Perspectives, Empirical Analysis, and the Future.* New York: Oxford University Press.

Tiebout, C.M. 1956. "A Pure Theory of Local Expenditures." *Journal of Political Economy* 44: 416–24.

Vogel, R.K. 1994. *Local Government Reorganization.* Louisville: League of Women Voters of Louisville and Jefferson County; Department of Political Science, University of Louisville.

Wilson, James Q., and Edward Banfield. 1971. "Political Ethos Revisited." *American Political Science Review* 46, no. 4: 1048–63.

Zambroski, J. 2006. *FBI Report: Louisville Crime Rate Outpacing National Average.* WAVE3 News, September 6. Available at www.wave3.com/Global/story.asp?S=5021890 (accessed June 12, 2007).

10

Regional Roles and Relationships

A Fifty-Year Evolution of Governance in Metropolitan Phoenix, 1960–2008

Rob Melnick and John Stuart Hall

Evolution of the Phoenix Urban Region

The Phoenix metropolitan area provides a particularly rich and challenging laboratory to examine the mix of public policy, governance, and economic development under conditions of rapid and extreme urban growth, sprawl, and low density. Earlier reports (e.g., Altheide and Hall, 1983; Gammage, 1999; Gober, 2006; Hall, 1986; Melnick, 1988) have described in some detail the factors that have led to the emergence of the Phoenix region as the prototype urban outcome of widespread American achievement of such personal goals as a home in the suburbs and responsive local government. According to Anthony Downs (1994), the American pursuit of these goals over the past fifty years has resulted in a dominant and common vision that has guided metropolitan growth best described as *unlimited low-density sprawl*.

The achievement of the goals Downs described has carried high costs in the form of growth-related problems such as traffic congestion, air pollution, rising taxes for infrastructure, loss of open space, and separation and segregation of the poverty stricken in inner-city neighborhoods. To some degree, most American metropolitan areas face increasingly tough choices because of these dynamics and the not coincidental stream of twenty-first-century challenges. The many diverse communities within the booming Phoenix region as well as the rapidly expanding region itself represent natural experiments for understanding public capacity to respond to such big-ticket forces as the impact of increased immigration and diversity, scarcity of resources, environmental erosion, and decreasing emphasis on community in exchange for sprawl and individuation.

Metro Phoenix Governance Facts and Fractions

"What is Phoenix?" is an easy question for lawyers and geographers to answer. The city of Phoenix is surrounded by twenty-three other cities and towns that make up metropolitan Phoenix. The city of Phoenix alone occupies 516 square miles, and the entire urban region covers a vast 9,226 square miles, which includes some unincorporated territory. Approximately 3.7 million people, more than half of Arizona's population, live in this metropolitan area. This accounts for the curious fact that despite low-density development and the rural character of much of the state, Arizona is officially classified by the Census Bureau as one of the nation's "most urban" states.

Because experts in U.S. government and urban affairs are accustomed to multiple counties converging in one metropolitan area, it surprises many of them when they discover that all of this space and population is encompassed by Maricopa County. Also, there are far fewer local governments in this region than in such well-known extremes as the Chicago, Pittsburgh, and St. Louis (see Chapter 5) regions and generally fewer than in many other similar regions.

The Paradox of a Community of Transients

For Sandra Day O'Connor, Alice Cooper, John McCain, Randy Johnson, and millions more, metro Phoenix is home, although these luminaries, like many other residents, spend much of their time elsewhere. Strength of subjective community identification is a major challenge for metro Phoenix, which is occupied by so many transients.

Metro Phoenix defines transience and vice versa. In addition to those who live in metro Phoenix part of the time (usually the winter) but return year after year, there are thousands who move there, stay a short time, and then move on. During the decade of the 1990s, approximately 100,000 people moved into metropolitan Phoenix each year, but nearly that many moved out, too. For example, in 1995, 123,000 moved in, and 82,000 moved out (Williams, 1996). This annual pattern of three in, two out endured for at least fifteen years, with the churn ratio declining only marginally in the late 1990s and early twenty-first century as out-of-state and global migration increased even more rapidly than in past periods (Gober, 2005). Between 1995 and 2000, Phoenix attracted 518,000 out-of-state migrants and lost 275,000, for a net gain of 243,000 (ibid.).

This churning has consequences. Many who move to metro Phoenix still think of someplace else as home and remain loyal to institutions, athletic teams, and even neighborhoods in their former place of residence. Likewise, many branch managers of local businesses with corporations headquartered elsewhere have been known to refer to their metro Phoenix duty as temporary. As one local reporter put it: "Phoenix is a place you move to; Pittsburgh is place you bring with you. It's easy to be a stranger in Phoenix because everyone is from somewhere else" (Montini, 1996).

With characteristically powerful logic, Norton Long (1991) described this "paradox of a community of transients" as a threshold issue for governance and economic development of most U.S. urban areas. Because of the rapid growth, change, and relative newness of metro Phoenix, implications of this paradox for this place are widespread and profound.

Metro Phoenix as a Product of Public Investment

Phoenix has a fascinating history, although a full-blown treatment of its transitions and characters would not be appropriate for this chapter (for the best such description, see Gammage, 1999; Gober, 2006; Luckingham, 1989; Sargent, 1976). However, what is useful to know is that the region has passed through distinctive eras since its settlement and, in each, its economy and society were profoundly affected by private management of public investment.

In the big picture, public investment in physical infrastructure has tended to come first. The National Reclamation Act of 1902 funded the delivery of water and, therefore, large-scale development of agriculture in this desert. That act also paved the way for one of the regions most influential "shadow governments," the Salt River Project (SRP), a special district that from its inception to this day has been controlled by landowners of the region who vote on the basis of one vote per acre. Although this voting method has from the beginning resulted in domination of agricultural interests, development and real estate interests are increasingly represented (Gammage, 1999). Presently, the SRP is seen by many as an effective "shadow government," the region's principal public voice in water allocation, flood control, and electricity for metro Phoenix.

Water allowed agriculture to thrive and helped Phoenix to develop into a major trade center for its progressively prosperous agriculture economy. It also made it possible for more than a million people to live in this desert community. Yet, important as the delivery of water was and still is to the growth of the region, this is but one example of a long list of big-ticket public investments that have shaped Phoenix. A partial inventory of such investments includes:

- federally funded agriculture experimentation programs and subsidies, which led to the development of Arizona's most lucrative crop—cotton;
- railroad and airport subsidies, farm-to-market road projects, and mail contracts in the 1920s;
- various public investments associated with the city's status as state capital and county seat;
- Great Depression–related public projects that played a major part in developing the region's physical infrastructure;
- World War II investments, particularly in U.S. Air Force bases, that created major direct economic effects and indirect spin-offs;
- high levels of federal revenue for virtually all local government functions during the late 1960s and 1970s;
- federal investment in completion of the U.S. interstate highway system through the metro area in the 1970s and 1980s, which stimulated the construction

industry and influenced the area's pattern of urban growth; and
* state and local investments in freeway systems begun in the late 1990s, continuing through 2010; Light Rail originated in 2005.

These public investments, and many others, had a profound effect on the region's capacity to grow and develop. Although private investment also stimulated growth, what is most important to consider, given the theme of this book, is that the dominant form of governance for the region has persistently facilitated strong private political influence in the development of metro Phoenix.

Although the region's phenomenal growth and general patterns of economic development were rooted in large-scale, long-term public investment and technological change during the first half of the twentieth century, subsequent growth and economic development after 1948 were managed more by the marketplace than by local government. Local public policy was developed from private–public governance partnerships, with a heavy emphasis on the private side.

Knowledge of this history helps in understanding the development of the Phoenix region and its place in the context of national urban trends. The pace of the region's growth, change, and economic development has been much more rapid than that of most other regions in the country for the past five decades. The role of privatization, or, some would say "strong private and public sector collaboration" (well before the increased popularity of the terms in public policy literature) in the development and delivery of many public services differentiates metro Phoenix from many other regions.

Yet, to some degree, all U.S. urban areas face similar issues and challenges. Problems stemming from social and structural disorder are profound in this region. Despite its high ranking on certain valued economic indicators such as employment and job creation, there remains an abundance of urban social problems as documented by crime rates, high school dropout rates, teen suicides, and behavioral health problems that exceed national norms.

Governance Phoenix Style Is Governance Light

The way that these and other human and social public problems and issues have been dealt with in the Phoenix region reflects a style of governance and view of local government functions that we call *governance light*. That is, compared with many other American metro regions, relatively low levels of public planning and funding have been available to cope with many of the issues that are normally considered a part of such functional categories of local public policy as health care, social services, employment and training, housing and community development, and arts and culture. In addition, in metro Phoenix there has been a tendency to rely on many agencies rather than on a single government to plan for and deliver such services.

According to the Urban Institute's large-scale study (Hall et al., 1985) of government and nonprofit-sector spending for social and human services in sixteen urban regions of the United States, the Phoenix region was far lower in total per capita spending—government and nonprofit—for most of the extensive list of social and human service areas examined (ibid.). Also, governments in Maricopa County made more extensive use of nonprofit organizations to deliver those services. Although this pattern of relatively low public funding and relatively high use of contracting with nonprofit agencies for delivery of services was demonstrated most thoroughly by the Urban Institute's 1985 study, more recent years of state and local budget cuts and tax limits and significant declines in federal and state intergovernmental revenues for many of these program areas have not led to radical changes in per capita spending or in organizational arrangements for service delivery. In addition, according to the executive director of the region's largest United Way organization, greater Phoenix continually ranks "toward the bottom of the list" among regions of comparable size in per capita giving (Williams, 1996, p. A-13). In one recent study of percentage of discretionary income given to charity by residents of the fifty largest metropolitan areas, Phoenix ranked forty-seventh (*Chronicle of Philanthropy,* 2003).

Governance light tends to be reactive governance. At times it is responsive and perhaps less fiscally fattening; at times it is less satisfying because of its ad hoc, episodic, and temporary solution nature. Dominant themes that have shaped the development of both the region and its governance processes have included belief in the values of maximum growth, minimum public control and direction, and high levels of private influence and management of public policy. Resulting metro Phoenix governance may be the quintessential example of Salamon's (1977) formal model of the "private city," where governmental power is put at the disposal of business elements in their private pursuit of wealth.

However, the private-city model is just that, a model. Neither Phoenix nor any other real city fits perfectly. Nevertheless, the recent history of Phoenix and its satellite cities is one of substantial public assistance to private development, strong council-manager forms of city government founded on the belief that they promote a businesslike approach to government, adherence to the principles of limited government, and fiscal restraint. When taken together, one can define the regional governance style as one of governance light.

Operationally, governance at the municipal level in this region has sometimes meant that important functions of local, general-purpose government elsewhere have been formally assigned to special districts, state agencies, and/or nonprofit organizations; examples include public education, public health, and welfare.[1]

Because of this tradition, the answer to Dahl's (1961) classic question "Who governs?" when applied to metro Phoenix is "Often many and sometimes no one." The power of government to deal with the region's specific problems and issues is often dispersed among special and general-purpose governments and private entities. This dispersal of power and authority may have many consequences, including limiting the size and activity of some governments, enhancing local control, and increasing "public choice." But local government fragmentation raises questions about the potential of effective regional governance for metro Phoenix; can these fractions of power and authority be added to derive coherent, efficient, and accountable regional policy and problem-solving unity? If so, how? Under what circumstances and arrangements can regional unity and policy be developed?

Evaluating Governance Light in Metro Phoenix

What are the results of this governance light approach? Is the form and function of governance of metro Phoenix responsible for some of its current problems? Have the region's popular themes of individualism and privatism added to the social isolation and separatism that seem to haunt most efforts to solve problems collectively? Or have experiments and experiences in metro Phoenix governance provided valuable preparation for an era in which genuine collaboration and the "strength of weak ties" (Granovetter, 1973) may prove necessary for survival?

There are clear and different perspectives concerning the capacity of the metro Phoenix governance approach to meet its urban challenges. On the one hand, those who subscribe to earlier public choice arguments see metro Phoenix as a virtual model for viable regional governance. Competing jurisdictions, offering different bundles of public goods and services at different tax prices to consumers/taxpayers, are seen by these theorists as the way governance *should* work in a democracy.

A similar admiration can be found in popular appraisals of the metro Phoenix experiment, including Garreau's (1991) well-known *Edge City*. In his Phoenix chapter (ch. 6, pp. 179–208), Garreau theorized that the region's strength lies in its many *shadow governments*—quasi-public and private entities. He contends that in the midst of chaotic growth and multiple political turmoils that caused damage to highly visible institutions, thousands of low-profile, small—and sometimes not so small—regimes filled the vacuum, taking on power and the responsibility for running daily life (p. 186).

It is also important to underscore that there is evidence of cooperation among the region's cities leading to significant regional consequences. Indeed, metro Phoenix has received national recognition for regional models of intergovernmental regional cooperation such as the 911 multijurisdictional emergency system, a multicity wastewater treatment collaboration, and an innovative, highly effective cooperative agreement among regional fire units responding to emergencies in the region. In fact, one study of the eastern part of metro Phoenix documented hundreds of examples of *joint utilization*, defined as "an inter-governmental relationship in which the cost of services, personnel, facilities, or equipment is shared by two or more governments" (Melnick et al., 1987, p. 2).

The many shadow governments and intergovernmental agreements including joint utilization remain strong tools of governance in the Phoenix region. Governance light in this form of issue-specific arrangements is the custom and culture of the place.

At the city manager and professional city staff level, the Phoenix area laboratory has yielded significant experimental evidence about regional cooperation. Also, the Maricopa Association of Governments (MAG) has initiated many important efforts, task forces, and studies aimed at understanding and resolving broad, regional issues. In view of significant organizational and fiscal constraints, these arrangements represent vital regional resources. It is in these ways that the formal fractions of public responsibility are at times added together to cope with regional issues and problems in metro Phoenix. Facilitated by formal and informal networks—perhaps, most important, by the Maricopa Association of Governments—formal interests of the region have at times been organized, compromised, and coordinated.

But the theoretical public choice justification for such metropolitan fragmentation has long been questioned, just as its application to the Phoenix metropolitan area has recently been criticized. Early theorists stated that central, formal regional government could deal more effectively and equitably with the growth and development of regions (Gulick, 1962; see also Chapter 2 of this book).

Citistates and Metro Phoenix Governance

An early critic of fragmented local government was Charles Merriman who, in the early 1930s, called for the transformation of large metropolitan areas into city-states. After looking carefully at metropolitan Phoenix and four other comparable U.S. urban regions, Peirce (1993) came to the same one-word conclusion in his book, *Citistates*. The spelling is different to reflect the full meaning and rationale for this development to contemporary urban America and to metro Phoenix. To facilitate understanding of this new word, after many sessions concerning the book and its implications, the authors caucused and nominated the following definition for some future edition of Webster's *New World Dictionary:*

> **ci– ti –state**, *n.*, a region consisting of one or more historic center cities surrounded by cities and towns that have a shared identification, function as a single zone for trade, commerce, and communication, and are characterized by social, economic, and environmental interdependence. [Hist., similar to city states of antiquity (e.g., Athens, Carthage) or medieval times (e.g., Italian states or the Hanseatic League)], except that modern citistates engage in instant electronic communication and capital transfer and are the chief recipients of world population growth.

Citistates may be the logical and natural, if not inevitable, entities of the future in the new world economy. Citistate logic requires development of a fuller and more lasting collaboration among regional stakeholders to solve regional problems. Regional collaboration and capacity to forge comprehensive and coherent regional strategies in a mature citistate will require more than occasional joint agreements and compromises among the many guardians of local government power. To move beyond episodic governmental cooperation to high-impact regional governance,

Phoenix and other metropolitan areas will need to attend more closely to three important issues. First, they will need to build civic infrastructure, which the late John Parr, former president of the National Civic League, defined as the formal and informal processes and networks that communities use to make decisions, solve problems, and cope with pressing issues. Second, they will need to develop social capital, that is, "features of social organization, such as networks, norms, and trust that facilitate coordination and cooperation for mutual benefit" (Putnam, 1993, pp. 35–36). Third and finally, metropolitan areas will need to stimulate regional civic identity and encourage full participation of regional stakeholders in public decisions.

Some regions have a head start on such an effort. But because all U.S. regions are different in critically important ways, there is no boilerplate blueprint to be prescribed and followed to citistate excellence. It is necessary, however, for each region to achieve a genuine understanding of cause-effect relationships within a region and of the needs, expectations, and resources of the region's mechanics of governance and economic development. In community life, as in mathematics, it is often easier to understand the value of a whole number after having studied the fractions from which it is composed.

After looking at the same Phoenix-area governance and economic landscape that was surveyed by Garreau (1991) and Peirce (1993, pp. 39–80) and examined over time in several of the other studies cited here, there is agreement about some fundamental and positive changes in the region's physical and civic development. In a 1994 article in which Peirce and Hall (1994) reexamined big-picture changes in metro Phoenix compared with an initial snapshot in 1988, they concurred with Garreau about certain bright spots, including a reinvigorated Phoenix downtown; the blossoming from a handful to several hundred neighborhood organizations; the emergence of inclusive citizen-infused strategic planning efforts such as the Phoenix Futures Forum; and various citizen involvement efforts in large bond campaigns, village planning committees, and block watches. Likewise, following the lead provided by the city of Phoenix, officials in other valley cities (cities of the Phoenix region are frequently referred to as "valley cities" to reflect location in what some have called the "Valley of the Sun") conducted their own look into their future and their interrelationships. These cities, including Mesa, Tempe, Scottsdale, Chandler, and Glendale, have also witnessed amazing growth in neighborhood organizations since 1988. Through such activities, it has become clearer that the area's future well-being is increasingly going to be a function of vertical and horizontal, grassroots, and intergovernmental relationships.

These positive efforts by committed individuals and groups may be necessary, but not sufficient, for bringing about the type of renaissance that *can* be accomplished in the Phoenix region. To understand their implications for qualitative regional change, these achievements should be viewed in context. Civic reform, the development of social capital, the citistate, and the notion of citistate mathematics are all concepts that promise more effective regional collaboration and governance.

They also are suggested as positive changes from the normal way of doing public business in the urban region. But these approaches raise questions of practicality and effectiveness. To understand how they might unfold in the metro area, in the next section, we present a close look at the relationship between governance and economic development in metro Phoenix.

Regional Economic Development: Governance Light Evolves

One way to view and evaluate the Phoenix-area experiment is to focus on economic development. But to understand how current economic development efforts are adjudicated in this complex, fast-growing metropolitan region, one first needs to examine the historical mindset of the region toward growth and economic opportunism.

A Short History of a Fast-Growth Economy

Metro Phoenix has enjoyed relatively steady and remarkable economic success. A well-known correlate to this success is the area's phenomenal growth over recent decades. From 1970 to 2008, the Phoenix metropolitan statistical area population increased from 971,000 to about 4,200,000 (U.S. Bureau of the Census). The population increased 55.4 percent between 1970 and 1980, 41.2 percent from 1980 to 1990, 40.4 percent from 1990 to 2000, and 26.8 percent from 2000 to 2006. Such rapid population growth, as well as similar increases in developed land area, increased land and home values, expanded business profits, and improved all manner of educational, economic, and leisure opportunities. Needless to say, this phenomenon also substantially increased public revenues. Thus both the public and private sectors substantially benefited from this steady, robust economic development.

In fact, the economic growth pattern that metro Phoenix has followed over the past fifty years is typical of patterns that occurred in many western U.S. cities after World War II. In short, rapid population growth and outward expansion of the metropolitan land area were simply operating assumptions for the area's planners, economic development professionals, and elected officials. Likewise, almost all metro residents embraced this trend and benefited from it. This pattern of very fast growth and obvious urban sprawl became so fundamental to the mindset of residents that they were shocked by what happened in the mid-1980s and in a subsequent economic downturn in the national and local economies in the early 1990s.

Even more recently, when the mortgage crisis hit the Phoenix area hard in 2008, leaders and residents alike still seemed largely unprepared to accept economic growth that was relatively slower than what they had taken for granted for so long. In short, the mindset was this: do nothing to create economic development opportunities and robust growth happens anyway, or do something and it just happens faster. Some would argue that such remarkable economic development in the metropolitan area—notwithstanding the downsides associated with such growth (e.g., traffic congestion and environmental degradation)—made many political and business leaders in this region complacent.

Thus, for many years, there did not seem to be much need for a strong or coordinated effort to encourage, let alone govern, economic development. This meant that economic development in metro Phoenix was left primarily to traditional, minimal, and rather basic efforts by local chambers of commerce, some cities, the state, and individual businesses.

This approach continued into the early 1980s when things began to change. A credit crunch pushed mortgage interest rates to unprecedented highs. These rates became a significant obstacle to home buying; thus the construction/real estate industry—so vital to the region's economy—was hit hard. However, this situation did not so much stop economic growth as serve as a warning that the area, despite its enormous past success, was, in fact, vulnerable to the powerful external economic and financial forces of the national economy. As mentioned earlier, this was again borne out during the national mortgage crisis that started to unfold in 2007. Economic development of the metropolitan area in the 1980s also started to be affected by concerns about the environment. As environmentalism gained widespread strength as a public policy issue, people began to seriously challenge the region's historical attitude that growth is automatically good. These forces, among others, planted the seeds of what was to become a significant and continuing policy debate later in the decade over *how* the region should grow and what organization(s) should orchestrate regional economic development.

Recognizing the need to think "metro area" as well as "city"—an economic development precursor to citistate logic—the Phoenix Chamber of Commerce created the Phoenix Metro Group in the early 1980s. This organization soon changed its name to the Phoenix Metropolitan Chamber of Commerce in recognition of the interplay of economic opportunities among the many, rapidly growing cities in this region. However, partially in response to this regional initiative, the city of Phoenix, by far the largest city in the metro, moved in the other direction by creating a more parochial approach to economic development.

In 1985, the city established the Phoenix Economic Growth Corporation, a public–private venture, to focus economic development opportunities on the city. Soon thereafter, other cities in the region followed suit. Mesa (the second-largest city in the area) formed the Mesa Economic Growth Association in 1986; other cities (e.g., Scottsdale, Tempe, Glendale, Peoria, and Chandler) expanded their economic development organizations as well. This escalation can only be described as a zero-sum mentality among leaders—if one city won an economic prize, such as the relocation of a major business from out-of-state, other local cities lost the jobs and all-important sales tax revenue that could result from such a relocation. Eventually, the many and various economic development organizations in the region were frequently in hot pursuit of the same potential clients. This, of course, did a disservice to the region by balkanizing local governments, giving potential new business "locates" a great opportunity to play one city's offer (e.g., tax abatements, city-provided infrastructure) against another's, and, ultimately, creating formidable obstacles to regional cooperation.

Although metro Phoenix remained a desirable region in which to live and work through this time of intense internal competition among cities, it was also developing a national reputation as a place that did not have its act together. To some businesses considering relocation to the area and to indigenous ones considering expansion, the competition among cities for economic spoils was perceived negatively. To others, it was the aforementioned opportunity to play one city off against another in an effort to get the best deal. It was not long before this frenzy became recognized for just what it was—a boon to certain businesses, a headache to local governments, and an entanglement for those who believed in, or who were responsible for, regional planning such as Maricopa County government—which overlays the entire Phoenix metro region—and the Maricopa Association of Governments, the regional council of government.

Fortunately, smarter thinking began to prevail, and in 1987, the Phoenix Metropolitan Chamber of Commerce had enough volunteers to form the short-lived, but nevertheless significant, Greater Phoenix Partnership, Inc. This group's primary purpose was to urge a consolidation of the many fragmented and often counterproductive approaches the valley had taken on economic development. But an even more significant event—called a "kick in the pants" by the mayor of a prominent city in the valley—came in the form of articles that were highly critical of the area's approach to economic development and its trajectory.

The first salvo was fired by the *Peirce Report,* published in both the morning and evening Phoenix newspapers in February 1987. This report challenged leadership's overriding belief in growth as an economic cure-all and pointed to many economic threats on the horizon. Most notable was an absence of an economic "plan B," which could focus on such vital issues to economic well-being as diversification, more compact growth, and shared assets such as infrastructure, neighborhoods, and radically improved education and career training (Peirce 1993, p. 78).

A second article significantly affected the reformulation of an economic development strategy into a more region-wide approach. It appeared in *Barron's* in December 1988. If the *Peirce Report* stimulated debate, the *Barron's* profile of metropolitan Phoenix was devastatingly bad national publicity.

Not coincidentally, the article came at a time when the national savings and loan crisis was unfolding and shaking confidence in the area's historical engine of growth. *Barron's* pointed out a number of rather uncomplimentary facts about the area— political scandals, overbuilding, challenging demographic trends, fragmentation, and duplication of efforts. Local leaders, particularly mayors, went through the usual phases associated with such civic trauma: denial, then indignation, and finally action.

Action, in this case, took the form of the creation of the Greater Phoenix Economic Council (GPEC) in August 1989. It received funding from valley cities, Maricopa County, and the private sector. Its mission was to develop a consolidated, strategic, regional approach to economic development. In other words, GPEC was to be the clearinghouse and prevailing organization for business recruitment for metro Phoenix. This, it was hoped, would reduce the chaos of competition among cities and, instead, create the proverbial rising tide that would lift *all* cities' fortunes.

Unlike many of its predecessors, GPEC has clearly succeeded in creating coherence where little formerly existed. It remains a very strong and visible organization today and is widely regarded as a successful leader of *regional* economic development efforts (although valley cities and some businesses still maintain economic development organizations that have a local focus). For example, GPEC helped rally numerous cities in the region in 2007 in support of one of their own when a local city was trying to attract a noteworthy but controversial life science business that would create a very significant number of high-paying jobs. Likewise, GPEC played a critical role in 2006 in sorting out which of several valley cities had the greatest potential for attracting a major new facility of a world leading computer manufacturer. A private, not-for-profit organization without the formal, legal powers of government, GPEC's political and business supporters have steadily grown throughout the years, making it the "go to" place for economic development strategy and business attraction services for the region. This has helped give GPEC the aura of such powers and made it an example of governance light consistent with Max Weber's classic distinction between power and authority.

This short history is offered as background for understanding how organized regional economic development has occurred in metro Phoenix beyond, or perhaps in spite of, the work of governmental entities traditionally responsible for this public function. It is an example of how this metropolitan area has matured and benefited from nongovernmental governance.

Regional Opportunities for Economic Development

The weather and allure of a southwestern lifestyle will continue to be natural stimulants to this region's economy. But it is clear that they will no longer be sufficient to ensure economic prosperity, especially in the context of a globally competitive economy. In spite of the coherence that GPEC added to regional economic development efforts, local leaders have come to realize that economic opportunities and ways of doing business are rapidly changing, thus demanding constant reconsideration and new strategies.

The Phoenix metro area, like its peers, is still wrestling with which economic opportunities should take priority, what its most significant competitive advantages are, what its image should be, which niches among business sectors best suit the place, and how organizations can best work together. The state, Maricopa County, cities and towns, nonprofits, local institutions of higher education, and the private sector are all providing input on these issues. But one result of the region's maturation is that the private sector no longer singularly dominates these discussions as it so clearly had done in the especially formative years of the region's economic trajectory back in the 1960s and 1970s.

The region's proximity and cultural ties to Mexico give rise to much thinking about the opportunities associated with international trade with and foreign direct investment from this country and others, particularly the Asian Rim and Canada. Likewise, the area is reasonably well grounded in so-called fourth-wave industries (aerospace, information technology, life sciences, etc.). Tourism, recreation, and construction continue to be drivers of economic growth, as does the success of professional athletics that spread from downtown Phoenix to adjacent cities. Indeed, significant redevelopment of downtown Phoenix has clearly created a rebirth of the core of the region. In fact, downtown Phoenix is developing into a highly diverse economic and social community, different in character and demographics than what preceded it. Within a decade, it is likely to become the type of true regional center that local leaders have long described as an important, missing element in the region. Recent regional actions have also revitalized past attempts to create long-sought-after superindustrial projects such as development of a dry riverbed into a commercial area and cultural amenity; building of a mass transit system that will link the central city with outlying cities and towns starting in early 2009; and establishment of a major downtown Phoenix campus of Arizona State University. And, of course, there is always population growth as an economic engine with its powerful downstream effect on suppliers of materials and services needed by new residents.

So, no matter which opportunities prevail in the metro, even in times of relative economic stress, there seems to be no shortage of them. In reality, no one in this metro area *really* believed that prosperity had come to an end when the economy "hit the wall" in the mid-to-late 1980s and they did not believe that to be the case in 2008 during the mortgage crisis either. Rather, just below the surface, a lot of people who had been made anxious by various economic downturns just *knew* things would get back to the good old days.

But that one first, truly scary economic experience almost two decades past *did* leave some lasting impressions. The most sophisticated local leaders had already been talking about the need to invigorate new regional approaches to economic development *before* the bust in the 1980s. They had warned others of overdependence on population growth, lack of economic diversification, the potentially disastrous consequences of not creating sound infrastructure for the long term, failure to comply with federal air and water mandates, continuation of the "metropolitan pluralism prevailing in metro Phoenix" (Luckingham, 1989, p. 207), and the need to engage more residents in civic and public policy decisions.

These warnings and the obvious dynamics of the dawning of a new age of economic development at that time were instructive to those people who are concerned with, or are responsible for, economic development in the region and its geopolitical subsets. They had come to realize that metro Phoenix is, as Carl Abbott has described many urban areas in the American West, a quintessential multicentered area, a group of networked cities for which future economic success will depend on relatively long-distance relationships, the adequacy of transportation systems, and the quality of intergovernmental relations. These characteristics differentiate the region—and for that matter, many western metro regions—from peers in the Midwest, East, or South.

Thus began the maturing of economic development in the Phoenix region and the quasi governance thereof. Its leaders came to realize that the dynamics of economic growth in the twenty-first century are considerably different from those of the past. Nevertheless, the region still does not have an entity that formally *governs* economic development decision making.

Regional Strategic Planning for Economic Growth: 1990–2008

For Arizona, 1990 was a year of serious introspection about economic strategies. Led by local entrepreneurs who were big-picture thinkers, a movement started that was to have profound effects on how economic development strategy would be both developed and carried out in the state and region and who the players would be.

Most fundamentally and compared with earlier approaches, this movement was extraordinarily inclusive. Titled the Arizona Strategic Plan for Economic Development (ASPED) project, this multiyear effort engaged all manner of businesses, citizens, and government officials—not just a few key business leaders and economic development experts as previous strategy sessions had done—in the development of a new approach to enhancing the state's and the metro's economic strength.

ASPED did much to change thinking about economic development in both the state and the region. For one, its cutting-edge blueprint deemphasized recruitment of new businesses in favor of strategies that focused on policies and investments that give the region a competitive advantage. By strengthening its foundations and quality of life, this new approach declared, the state, the region and the metro's cities will make themselves naturally attractive to businesses considering relocation and will also help retain and expand existing businesses.

The foundations that were identified during the ASPED project include skilled human resources, accessible technology, available capital, advanced physical infrastructure, and a competitive tax and regulatory climate. In addition, ASPED required participants (literally thousands) to look at the businesses that existed in Arizona at that time and to identify business "clusters." The notion of business clusters—"geographic concentrations of interdependent, competitive firms in related industries" (GPEC Annual Report, 1992–93)—captured people's imagination and has now become a fundamental concept in economic development circles. Even more interesting is the fact that when the regional economy is considered in the context of this new paradigm, surprising things emerge. Suddenly, buyers and suppliers *within* the area who had not previously known each other were talking and doing business, and concentrations of businesses (i.e., economic strengths) became obvious.

The clusters concept is the basis for economic development policymaking that enables regions to take advantage of "what is" and to craft that into a competitive advantage. Indeed, GPEC was an early adopter of clusters and other strategies that came about as a result of the ASPED project as a "conceptual framework for its marketing efforts" in the early 1990s (GPEC Annual Report, 1992–93).

A prominent local economic development policy analyst extracted some basic new rules for economic development from this experience. Although there are eight such rules, three of them have had the most impact on regional economic development and politics in the Phoenix metro. These rules helped give coherence to regional economic strategies. First, the economic development community should "think building blocks, not gimmicks." Second, they should "think clusters of firms, not individual firms." Finally, they should "think economic region, not political boundaries" (Waits, Kahalley, and Heffernon, 1992).

As valuable as these prescriptions were more than a decade ago, an even more significant value was added to regional economic development efforts as a result of the ASPED experience. That is, it made people more aware of the need to co-operate in view of increasing economic competition from other metro regions in the nation and around the world.

A Conceptual Framework in Hand, but a Learning Curve Ahead

The ASPED project was a great boost to metro Phoenix. It injected much-needed creativity into the region's economic development processes and made them less of a default to the vaunted population growth engine. Nevertheless, many policy debates about economic strategy continued. There is still considerable tension among leaders of the region on a number of critical policy questions such as the appropriate amount of resources that should be devoted to recruitment of new businesses versus strengthening existing ones; the incentives, if any, that should be utilized by cities and the state in business recruitment; the value in creating new jobs if they are low-paying, yet plentiful; and which policies will best promote "quality" growth.

Getting good answers for these questions is always made difficult by Arizona's political climate and its historic arguments about economic theory between tradi-tional Democrats and Republicans, supply-siders and Keynesians. For example, many politicians who embraced and helped institutionalize ASPED also favored significant personal and corporate tax breaks, which in tough economic times have proved to result in insufficient revenue being available for public investment in the very foundations that ASPED identified as so important (e.g., human resource development, public education, public infrastructure).

The political debate over how to stimulate Arizona's economy most effectively gives rise to the notion that in spite of the ASPED experience, the region still does not have a fully acknowledged definition of economic development. Furthermore, there is considerable disagreement as to what constitutes quality growth.

Although such discourse is healthy to a degree, common definitions and shared goals would help the region gain economic stability over the long term. Partly in recognition of this, a task force organized by the Maricopa Association of Governments, established some regional values in 1994. This group included representatives from throughout the region who identified economic development values. Albeit rather broad, their description was a valuable point of departure for coming to agreement on definitions and goals:

> An active, diversified economy which maintains the region's character and contributes to its natural environment and offers balanced wage scales and provides a variety of employment opportunities and potential to the residents of the MAG region. (Maricopa Association of Governments, 1994, p. 2)

The dynamics of seeking common ground are essential to the development of social capital and the formulation of regional economic policies. This process helped the region to evolve by adding new players and new rules and by recognizing changing conditions in the world external to metro Phoenix. In an article written (before ASPED) for a state-level town hall discussion of economic development in Arizona, Worden accurately characterized the elusiveness of finding solutions to this problem when he wrote that "most communities and their political leaders have not systematically examined their definitions or objectives for economic development . . . [and are] content to believe that they will know it when they see it" (1990, pp. 10–11). Although Worden believed a clear definition and objectives are required before an effective regional economic development policy can be developed, he recognized that it is unrealistic to expect that such a definition will be agreed upon by all.

The Maturing of Economic Development in Greater Phoenix: Governance Light at Work

As the metro Phoenix area nears the end of the first decade of the twenty-first century, territorialism, history, and political philosophy continue to make it inconceivable that the region will create an entity to govern economic development with legal authority. Nor would such action, even if it were politically possible, be desirable. For the foreseeable future, GPEC will continue to act on behalf of the region as a quasi-governance, but certainly not a government, mechanism and the de facto policy leader for economic development. However, even with its considerable assets and opportunities, the region could still "blow it" by not figuring out ways to deal with critical issues and real liabilities.

In the liabilities column, the region continues to be a branch town with a dearth of national headquarters operations when compared with other regions of its size. Mass transit, in the form of light rail and bus service, is far behind what competitor regions such as San Diego, Los Angeles, Portland, and Salt Lake City already have in place. The highway system and other major economic infrastructure (e.g., energy and water delivery systems) are highly challenged to keep pace with growth throughout the so-called Sun Corridor area, which encompasses the Phoenix and Tucson area economies. Outstanding issues also include how to deal with demographics that clearly foretell a future of an increasingly older and more culturally diversified workforce, continued competition among cities, questionable air quality, water supply and, perhaps most important, political wrangling about whether to make major public investments in strengthening the state's economic assets and policy tools or letting market forces alone determine the region's economic trajectory.

Discussion over this last issue has gone on forever in the region, perhaps the legacy of Barry Goldwater's imprimatur on the state's philosophy of government. But the evidence is clear for the region—economic development that would put the current Greater Phoenix region and the larger, rapidly developing Sun Corridor mega region ahead of the pack in the twenty-first century will certainly require more than just a "let the good times roll" mentality. For all its success, Arizona ranked fortieth among the fifty states in per capita income in 2007 (Bureau of Economic Analysis, U.S. Department of Commerce, March 2008) and its average wages were approximately 95 percent of the national average toward the end of that same year (Bureau of Labor Statistics, U.S. Department of Labor, April 2008).

The good news for the greater Phoenix area is that GPEC matured and became sophisticated as the region's primary economic development organization in its capacity as a quasi-governance mechanism. In the mid- to late 1990s it developed a strategy that added "product improvement" to its tactics and continues to refine that strategy. Product improvement meant that GPEC and its member governments and businesses formally recognized the importance of improving state and regional policies and the quality of life, in general, to make the region more attractive for purposes of business attraction and retention. These became key companions to the organization's traditional recruiting activities. It devoted considerable attention to building, in essence, the "foundations" called for in the ASPED strategy. In addition, GPEC embraced a significant public–private–nonprofit program to make greater Phoenix a player in bioscience industries ("Arizona's Bioscience Roadmap," Battelle, 2002; sponsored by the Flinn Foundation) and began to focus on international opportunities for the first time in 2006, especially on the foreign direct investment aspect. Heretofore, the organization had been almost exclusively devoted to attracting domestic businesses. As another illustration of "governance light," GPEC played a leading role in development of an important statewide policy and program called the Arizona Global Network. In the absence of adequate leadership for effective international economic development by other economic development agencies, GPEC took the leadership role. GPEC also embraced and promoted several other new strategies for economic development, including ones that focused business attraction activities on "emerging technologies" and an intense partnership with the major university in the metropolitan area, Arizona State University, which had become an increasingly recognized force in economic development policies since 2001. These strategies are articulated in GPEC's 2008 Action Plan, "Implementing GPEC Next" (GPEC, May 2007).

There are plenty of capable, well-intentioned organizations, institutions, and individuals ready to contribute to (but not govern) economic development efforts in the region. As greater Phoenix matures and becomes part of a megapolitan Sun Corridor economy of more than 8 million residents in the next twenty-five years, it is even more likely to accept governance light, not government, as the appropriate mechanism for guiding public policies and strategies for economic development.

Building the Phoenix Citistate

Our portrait of recent dynamics of regional economic development in Phoenix, combined with examples of governmental cooperation to solve regional prob-lems, is an illustration of significant change. It was not many years ago that more significant public issues in the region were settled within jurisdictions by a small, powerful group of businessmen and legislators who called the shots for the state and the region. In contrast, we now find a new and broader leadership that is able, at least part of the time, to retreat from the parochial city competition games and collaborate on issues.

New leaders, processes, and old and new networks are fusing with global eco-nomic trends and declining economic importance of the nation-state to change the Phoenix region fundamentally. But what form will change take? How rapidly will the change occur? Passive evolution will not be fast enough in these times. The principle to begin with is that locally based and coordinated *actions* consistent with these larger trends are needed to surmount the major barriers to development of U.S. urban regions. For Phoenix, as well as other metropolitan areas, this includes overcoming three great disabilities that are described in *Citistates* (Peirce, 1993) and enumerated in Chapter 2 of this book.

For regions to overcome these hurdles, to be competitive economies, and to become healthy social entities, *Citistates* urges actions that are termed guideposts (see Chapter 2). Downs (1994, ch. 10) also called for regional action. He contended that each metropolitan region needs to follow a series of steps toward new visions of growth and new regional decision-making processes that closely resemble *Citistate* guideposts.

This calls for action within a general framework that redefines—beyond existing political-legal boundaries—the scope and locus of decision making. It also broad-ens participation in the process so that it can be called a paradigm shift. But the action called for under these general guidelines does not seem as radical in today's Phoenix as it would have a short time ago. As we have seen, new cooperative and cross-sectoral community-building efforts and important changes in regional eco-nomic development and strategies are under way, which if refined and sustained, are headed in the direction of more coherent regional action.

Many challenges remain, and old habits of behavior and politics are hard to break. There is, however, little doubt that the Phoenix region, its problems, leaders, institutions, needs, resources, and capacities are changing rapidly. Old models and formulas may not accurately capture this change and the state of the region.

People acting on regional futures need to have better feedback about the regional economy and society and the effects of change as measured by the new mathematics of the citistate and the megapolitan area. Increasingly, people will require, and benefit from, the long-term economic progress of the entire region, not just from the short-term formal jurisdiction budget fractions. A process of continuous objective learning, which some have called "learning governance," could nurture better public decisions for the region's long-term development (Rosell, 1999). Steps in this direction include determining the contributions and resources of the region's various institutions and leaders, and quantifying the goals, benchmarks, costs and benefits, and indicators of regional success that must become a way of thinking, a way of doing business, a way of making public policy. Is there a citistate in metro Phoenix, or is there one in the making? Can a common unified regional vision and identity be crafted from fractions? Only time, and the ability to calculate progress based on citistate mathematics, will tell.

Note

1. The state passed legislation in 1993 enabling the county to seek charter powers by a vote of the people. A charter proposal was defeated by voters in November 1996.

References

Altheide, D.L., and J.S. Hall. 1983. "Phoenix: Crime and Politics in the New Federal City." In *Crime in City Politics*, ed. A. Heinz et al., 193–234. New York: Longman.
Battelle. 2002. "Arizona's Bioscience Roadmap." Power Point presentation in Phoenix on December 3. Available at www.flinn.org/bio/roadmap.cms.
Chronicle of Philanthropy. 2003. "Charitable Giving in America's Biggest Urban Areas." May 1.
Dahl, R. 1961. *Who Governs? Democracy and Power in an American City*. New Haven, CT: Yale University Press.
Downs, A. 1994. *New Visions for Metropolitan America*. Washington, DC: Brookings Institution.
Gammage, Grady Jr. 1999. *Phoenix in Perspective: Reflections on Developing the Desert*. Tempe: Arizona State University.
Garreau, J. 1991. *Edge City: Life on the New Frontier*. New York: Doubleday.
Gober, P. 2005. "Thinking Small But Living Big: Demographic Challenges of Modern Phoenix." Paper presented at the Arizona State University faculty seminar on the "Changing Character of Metropolitan Phoenix," January 26. Available at http://changingphoenix.asu.edu/.
———. 2006. *Metropolitan Phoenix: Place Making and Community Building in the Desert*. Philadelphia: University of Pennsylvania Press.
Granovetter, M. 1973. "The Strength of Weak Ties." *American Journal of Sociology* 78, no. 6: 1360–80.
Greater Phoenix Economic Council. 1993, 2007 (GPEC). *Annual Report*. Phoenix.
Gulick, L.H. 1962. *The Metropolitan Problem and American Ideas*. New York: Knopf.
Hall, J.S. 1986. "Retrenchment in Phoenix, Arizona." In *Reagan and the Cities*, ed. G.E. Peterson and C.W. Lewis, 185–207. Washington, DC: Urban Institute.
Hall, J.S. et al. 1985. *Government Spending and the Nonprofit Sector in Two Arizona Communities: Phoenix/Maricopa County and Pinal County*. Washington DC: Urban Institute.

Long, N.E. 1991. "The Paradox of a Community of Transients." *Urban Affairs Quarterly* 27: 3–12.

Luckingham, B. 1989. *Phoenix: The History of a Southwestern Metropolis.* Tucson: University of Arizona Press.

Maricopa Association of Governments. 1994. *Statement of Regional Values.* February.

Melnick, R. et al. 1987. *Inter-Governmental Cooperation in the East Valley: Pooling Resources to Benefit Citizens.* Tempe: Arizona State University, Morrison Institute for Public Policy.

Melnick, R., ed. 1988. *Urban Growth in Arizona: A Policy Analysis.* Tempe: Arizona State University, Morrison Institute for Public Policy.

Montini, E.J. 1996. "Pittsburgh Colors Views of Phoenix." *Arizona Republic.* Phoenix.

Peirce, N. 1993. *Citistates: How Urban America Can Prosper in a Competitive World.* Washington, DC: Seven Locks Press.

Peirce, N., and J.S. Hall. 1994. "Phoenix, Quite a Change in Seven Years." *Arizona Republic,* January 30, D-1, D-3.

Putnam, R.D. 1993. *Making Democracy Work.* Princeton, NJ: Princeton University Press.

Rosell, S.A. 1999. *Renewing Governance: Governing by Learning in the Information Age.* Oxford: Oxford University Press.

Salamon, L.M. 1977. "Urban Politics, Urban Policy, Case Studies and Political Theory." *Public Administration Review* 37: 422–24.

Sargent, C.S. 1976. *The Conflict Between Frontier Values and Land-Use Control in Greater Phoenix.* Tempe: Center for Public Affairs, Arizona State University.

Waits, M.J.; K. Kahalley; and R. Heffernon. 1992. "Organizing for Economic Development: New Realities Call for New Rules." *Public Administration Review* 52: 612–16.

Williams, C. 1996. "Population Churning in Valley." *Arizona Republic,* April 14, A-13.

Worden, M. 1990. "What Is Economic Development? In *The Many Faces of Economic Development in Arizona—57th Arizona Town Hall.* University of Arizona, October, 9–42.

11

New Orleans, Land of Dreams

Metropolitan Governance After Hurricane Katrina

Robert K. Whelan

Several years after Hurricane Katrina, many pose the same question: Why is the New Orleans recovery effort proceeding so slowly? In the *Washington Post,* historian Douglas Brinkley notes that "the Big Easy is barely limping along, unable to make truly meaningful reconstruction progress" (2007). New Orleans *Times-Picayune* reporter Coleman Warner calls the metro area "a confounding mix of progress and despair," and notes signs of recovery along with "glacial speed and frustration" (2007).

The same, of course, can be said about metropolitan governance in New Orleans. As will be seen below, any changes to the metropolitan governance system since Hurricane Katrina have been slow to occur and incremental in nature. First the argument will state that the lack of change, in large part, stems from long-standing political characteristics of the New Orleans political system.

The chapter begins with a discussion of New Orleans metropolitan governance before Hurricane Katrina. This will be followed by a discussion of changes since Hurricane Katrina, focusing on levee boards and the assessor system. Then the analysis will turn to the general fragmentation in the New Orleans metropolitan area, and the particular political characteristics that constrain changes in the metropolitan governance system.

Metropolitan Governance in New Orleans: Pre-Katrina

Metropolitan "government" was nonexistent in New Orleans before Hurricane Katrina. Metropolitan "governance" was limited and highly problematic. In an assessment some years ago, Brandt and Whelan concluded:

> There is almost a total lack of cooperation among parishes for any common purpose. Inter-parish relations are characterized by mistrust. There is political warfare among the region's parishes. Generally, the political warfare pits the city (New Orleans) versus the suburban parishes. The continued exodus of the middle class from the city and the increased separation in the region along racial and economic lines exacerbate the problem and present a serious obstacle to achieving any type of regional cooperation within the foreseeable future. (Brandt and Whelan, 2004, p. 151)

Many metropolitan regions were discussed in *Metropolitan Governance without Metropolitan Government?* (Phares, 2004). Of the numerous North American and West European areas in this collection, New Orleans was one of the most fragmented—possibly the most fragmented. (For a close parallel, see Chapter 5 on St. Louis, in this volume.) It was highly polarized between African-Americans and whites, and between the affluent and the poor. The original research by Brandt and Whelan cited above was undertaken in 1994. What has happened since that time?

In 1999, David Rusk was hired to do a study of the New Orleans metropolitan region. Rusk, the former mayor of Albuquerque, New Mexico, and the author of several books on urban problems, has done similar reports in a number of large metropolitan areas. Rusk's sponsors were Pres Kabacoff, a civic-minded developer, and the Greater New Orleans Foundation, the most significant nonprofit agency in the area.

Rusk's report (1999) is titled "The New Regionalism: Planning Together to Reshape New Orleans' Future." His report headlines "Race and Sprawl Shape Greater New Orleans." He notes the gap between blacks and whites, the rise of urban sprawl, and the necessity for comprehensive planning in land use and in economic development. In Rusk's view, Jefferson Parish (the suburban parish just west of New Orleans) was "teetering on the brink of decline," that is, showing the signs of declining suburbs in the Northeast and Midwest. St. Tammany Parish was seen as the major area for growth and sprawl. In Rusk's view, St. Tammany could look to such areas as Montgomery County, Maryland, for guidance in dealing with its problems. He characterized pre-Katrina New Orleans as having "concentrated poverty causing social meltdown" (Rusk, 1999).

Among other policy suggestions, Rusk mentioned the need for: (1) a statewide "smart growth" strategy, (2) regional planning, (3) improvements in voluntary land use planning, and (4) a state-level land use law for the Greater New Orleans area. Very little has been done in this regard since the Rusk report, although the state has shown some interest in "smart growth" strategies since Hurricane Katrina, as will be discussed below.

On a number of occasions in the past decade, New Orleans's political leaders have made efforts on behalf of regional cooperation. New Orleans mayor C. Ray Nagin, Jefferson Parish president Aaron Broussard, and St. Tammany Parish president Kevin Davis have all spoken and voted on behalf of regional cooperation. While some very modest steps were taken, there was never any sustained effort on behalf of regional planning or governance. In part, this can be attributed to lack of interest and leadership at the state level.

Metropolitan Governance in New Orleans: Post-Katrina

Of course, the biggest event in New Orleans since 1994 was Hurricane Katrina. Indeed, Katrina is among the greatest disasters in U.S. history. Why would Hurricane Katrina bring about a change in metropolitan governance? There are at least four reasons why this might be so: a theoretical reason, a historical reason, a policy-governance reason, and human reasons.

The theoretical reason comes from the metropolitan-governance literature. The idea is that it takes some sort of dramatic event, that is, an "accelerator" to bring about significant change in metropolitan government. For example, a major scandal in a local government may make voters more amenable to governmental changes. This line of reasoning stems from the work of Chalmers Johnson (1966) on revolutionary change. Johnson's model was applied to governmental consolidation by Rosenbaum and Kammerer (1974) in a study of several Florida cities. Recently, their framework has been used by Linda Johnson (2004) and Feiock et al. (2006). The important point here is that some urban scholars would expect change after a major disaster like Katrina.

The historical reason is easier to see. Students of urban history and politics know that the Galveston hurricane of 1900 (Larson, 2000) brought about the creation of the commission form of local government. While we now view the commission as an old-fashioned governmental form, it was a progressive and innovative response to a major disaster a century ago (Rice, 1977). Thus, past disaster forced an innovative approach. Hurricane Katrina might do the same.

The policy-governance reason comes from the extent of the disaster. Danger and destruction in the New Orleans metropolitan area were such that it exceeded the capacity of local government to respond. Higher-level governments might force a change. Local governments are the legal creatures of state governments. While state governments in the United States have generally been reluctant to force metropolitan-governance changes, Canadian provincial governments have often affected major changes (see Chapter 12), without an "accelerator." Similarly, if the federal government spends billions of dollars in the area, it is not unreasonable to expect a federal demand for regional cooperation. Extant cooperation before Hurricane Katrina, as in the Regional Planning Commission's distribution of federal transportation monies, was often forced by the federal government.

Finally, there are human reasons to expect more cooperation. Hurricane Katrina devastated the entire metropolitan region. Almost all housing in St. Bernard and Plaquemines parishes was flooded, as were 80 percent of residences in New Orleans. There was also a substantial amount of home flooding in Jefferson and St. Tammany parishes. It is reasonable to think that there might be some sense of shared disaster and loss, and a feeling that cooperative efforts would help the overall recovery. Such a view depends on an optimistic view of human nature, as opposed to a darker "Hobbesian" view.

Further, we know that cities are durable and resilient. As Vale and Campanella note: "Whether they are reconstructed to accommodate and restore ongoing urban life or rebuilt to serve as sites for periodic visitation and commemoration, it has become exceedingly rare for a major city to be totally or permanently lost" (2005, p. 5).

The Louisiana state government has imposed some governmental reform on the New Orleans metropolitan area. There has been some consolidation of levee boards in the region, with the aim of curtailing the wide-ranging activities of the Orleans Levee Board. New Orleans has also had an almost unique system of multiple assessors, elected on a district basis. State legislation will bring a single assessor to New Orleans, eventually. There have been incremental improvements in criminal justice system cooperation. All the living former mayors of New Orleans and the suburban parish presidents went to New Orleans City Hall in early 2006 to tell the federal government that rebuilding of the levees was the highest priority. In 2008, the Louisiana state legislature was considering a bill that would create a Southeast Regional Airport Authority, which would eventually transfer control of Louis Armstrong Airport from New Orleans to the state of Louisiana.

Andrew Jackson is New Orleans's greatest hero, and deservedly so. In many ways, New Orleans local government represents the vast excesses of Jacksonian democracy run amok (Kaufman, 1963; Tregle, 1999).

Levee Boards

The stated purpose of levee boards is "constructing and maintaining levees, levee drainage, flood protection, and hurricane flood protection." Levee boards have been criticized for being patronage-ridden and for having scandals. This is especially true of the Orleans Levee Board, whose members are appointed by the governor. Levee boards have also been criticized for their involvement in diverse activity that may not fit the above mission. These include running airports, operating casinos, maintaining police forces, and developing a university research park. And, of course, the biggest problem of all is that the levees were breached during Hurricane Katrina. They were overtopped somewhat, but mostly they were breached. Along with the U.S. Army Corps of Engineers, the Levee Board became the subject of criticism (see especially van Heerden and Bryan, 2006).

The Louisiana legislature met in a special post-Katrina session in the fall of 2005. State Senator Walter Boasso proposed consolidating the levee boards for Orleans, St. Bernard, St. Tammany, and East Bank Jefferson into one regional board. This proposal was defeated in the state house of representatives. Business leaders supported the Boasso bill and were unhappy with the result. A state coastal protection and restoration authority was established in the special session.

Shortly thereafter, a grassroots group, called Citizens for 1 Greater New Orleans, was formed. Women dominated the efforts. The group's founder and chair was Ruthie Frierson, an uptown realtor (for those who believe in an older sociological form of analysis, it is parenthetically noted that Frierson's husband is a former Rex, King of Carnival). In three weeks' time, Citizens for 1 Greater New Orleans got 46,000 signatures on petitions that called for a unified, professional levee board. Governor Kathleen B. Blanco supported Boasso's bill, after seeing this effort.

The new coastal restoration and protection authority addressed levee boards in its first meetings in February 2006. Their work provided the basis for the reform bill. An East Bank Authority was created, which involves seven parishes: Orleans,

Jefferson, and the Lake Borgne Levee District parishes (St. Bernard, St. Tammany, Tangipahoa). In addition, the east banks of St. Charles and St. John the Baptist parishes will be involved in regional projects. A West Bank Authority will oversee the West Jefferson Levee District and the West Bank of Orleans Parish. Indeed, another regional fragmentation is East Bank versus West Bank.

Several new levee authorities will be created. These include a Southeast Louisiana Flood Protection Authority, and the East and West Bank Authorities mentioned above. These bodies were approved in a statewide vote. Members of the authorities are chosen by the governor, from a list drawn up by university, professional, and civic groups. When all is said and done, do we need levee boards at all? A task force appointed by former governor Buddy Roemer recommended abolition of levee boards in 1988. Why do you need them? Could these functions be handled by existing city and/or parish agencies? Such a "radical" solution was not considered.

Assessors

Assessors in New Orleans and in southeast Louisiana are elected officials. To compound this, in New Orleans the seven assessors are elected by district. The Bureau of Governmental Research (BGR), a New Orleans watchdog group, studied the different assessors and their appraisal of property after Hurricane Katrina, in unflooded areas only. Properties were appraised in wildly different ways. In some areas, there were dramatic reductions. The BGR condemned the system for wasting money and being prone to corruption and inefficiency. A proposed state constitutional change will reduce the number of assessors from seven to one. This change will occur in 2010, allowing 2006 electees to complete their terms. Ultimately, this must pass both statewide and New Orleans votes. A case might be made for an elected assessor, but a case for district election of multiple assessors for a city is not sustainable. In many places, professional and technical values would dominate.

Courts

There is a plethora of courts—civil and criminal district courts, most notably. There are a number of related offices such as recorders of mortgages, custodian of the national archives, and the registrar of conveyances. All of them are elected. The deficiencies have been noted by the BGR, among others. A 2006 state law called for the merger of New Orleans criminal and civil courts, as of January 1, 2009. As of May 2008, a state judge has halted the merger, because there had been no referendum on it in Orleans Parish.

Policing

Orleans, Jefferson, St. Bernard, and Plaquemines parishes are working together on a joint crime and DNA lab, a joint police training academy, metro-wide criminal intelligence system, and an interoperable communication system. These cooperative efforts are a positive development, as police forces struggle with crime problems after the storm. One negative is the existence of a multiplicity of police forces, especially in New Orleans, as many boards and authorities maintain their own forces.

Bring Back New Orleans Commission-Governmental Effectiveness Committee

The Bring Back New Orleans Commission was established by Mayor Nagin shortly after the storm. Committees were established on land use, infrastructure, culture, education, health and social services, economic development, and governmental effectiveness. The last is our concern here. This was the only committee of the commission *not* to have a report. The Land-Use Planning Committee, in contrast, had a lengthy, detailed report and a formal PowerPoint presentation.

Its recommendation included: (1) one assessor for New Orleans; (2) overhaul of the permitting process; (3) elimination of the city council's power to override the City Planning Commission, the Historical District Landmark Commission, and the Board of Zoning Adjustments; (4) consolidation of court systems and reduction in the number of judgeships; and (5) the consolidation of police forces.

These recommendations, while admirable, are hardly comprehensive and far-reaching. In neighboring Mississippi, two cities, Bay St. Louis and Waveland, are talking about a merger. While these are smaller communities, this is the kind of significant governmental change we might expect after a major disaster.

To sum up, there has been some progress in governmental consolidation. Some of the above developments are encouraging. Still, reforms have been very limited and grudgingly made; some await voter approval. Certainly, some resentment was stirred in legislative debate, as some New Orleans representatives felt (with some justification) that suburban jurisdictions had no right to force reforms on New Orleans without considering changes in their own governmental structures.

Still, a great opportunity for reform was missed. The governmental effectiveness committee of Mayor Nagin's Bring Back New Orleans Commission was the only committee that did not submit a written report. Although the present New Orleans charter dates from the 1950s, no major charter changes were proposed by the Bring Back New Orleans Commission. The city's reduced size makes it a much better candidate for a city manager system of government. Changing demography might make regional cooperation more feasible than it was before Katrina.

Overall, post-Katrina changes in metropolitan governance are very limited. Why is this the case? We think that fragmentation in the metropolitan area is one major reason for the lack of change in metropolitan governance. Another major reason is the political system characteristics of New Orleans itself. We will discuss each of these in detail.

Fragmentation in New Orleans

One of the key problems as the New Orleans metropolitan area rebuilds is fragmentation. This fragmentation is governmental, political, racial, and economic. Governmental fragmentation is a more serious problem than many think. In the New Orleans metro area, there are at least five parishes that suffered major storm damage. In several cases, there are city and parish governments sharing space and jurisdiction. The greater the governmental complexity, the greater the potential problems in rebuilding. In addition to horizontal governmental fragmentation, there is vertical complexity. What, exactly, is the federal government's role in relation to rebuilding? More important, there is no history of a regional body working together with the federal government to solve problems for the collective good.

In fact, the reverse is true, with highly dysfunctional bodies. For example, the Aviation Board was known over the years for fights over patronage, airport noise, the location of the runways, policing responsibilities, and representation.

Political fragmentation has a long and interesting history. The New Orleans City Council is usually at odds with the mayor, and often thwarts mayoral policy initiatives. The separately elected school board was responsible for a total financial disaster in the schools before the storm. Again, aside from reasonably conflicted local politics, there is no history of political cooperation with other parishes. City-suburb relations have often been antagonistic. This was especially so when Mayor Ernest Morial proposed a commuter tax in the 1980s. Historically, things may have been different. Mayor DeLesseps Morrison thought it was a great achievement of his administration to bring a Kaiser aluminum plant to Chalmette (in outlying St. Bernard Parish) in the 1950s.

Racial and Economic Fragmentation

In the 2000 U.S. Census, the eight parishes (counties) comprising the New Orleans metropolitan region had 1.3 million residents. The population of the city of New Orleans was 485,000. Jefferson Parish, directly neighboring the central city, had 455,000 residents, and was beginning to exhibit the characteristics of older, declining suburbs around the country. St. Tammany Parish, north of Lake Pontchartrain had close to 200,000 residents, and was the major growth center. As of July 2007, the U.S. Census Bureau reported a population of 239,124 in New Orleans (Liu and Plyer, 2008). The Jefferson Parish population was estimated at 423,520, almost a return to its pre-Katrina level. St. Tammany Parish gained population, especially from devastated St. Bernard Parish, and its population was estimated at 226,625 people in the summer of 2007 (U.S. Census Bureau, 2007).

The racial composition of New Orleans contrasts sharply with that of its suburban neighborhoods. In the 2000 Census, two-thirds of the city's population was

African-American, while almost 75 percent of the suburban population in the Metropolitan Statistical Area was white. The most recent population estimates show a greatly changed picture for New Orleans, with 59 percent black and 37 percent white. Jefferson Parish population estimates are 65.7 percent white, 26.4 percent black, and 8.3 percent Latino (Louisiana Department of Health and Hospitals, and Louisiana Recovery Authority, 2006). At present, it is clear that New Orleans has a population that is more white than before the storm. Meanwhile, the African-American population declined—both absolutely and relatively.

The racial polarization is compounded by class polarization. In the 2000 Census, 28 percent of the city's residents lived in poverty, with a high percentage of African-Americans in this category. At the same time, an average household income of more than $43,000 in the city indicated that quite a number of people were doing very well. Jefferson Parish and St. Tammany Parish had higher levels of household income and lower levels of poverty, as one would expect. The city has affluence, along with a large poverty population historically. The suburbs are generally more middle income in character.

Before Hurricane Katrina, New Orleans was 70 percent African-American. The other parishes were at least 70 percent white. Population estimates by the Census Bureau in June 2007 show the metro region to be more white and less black than previously. In theory, more homogeneity should affect more cooperation. In practice, there is good reason to doubt the census estimates (and many of the other population estimates emanating from the city and other sources). For example, St. Tammany Parish has seen an influx of people from New Orleans and St. Bernard Parish. Yet, this population growth does not show up in school enrollment.

Political System Characteristics of New Orleans That Promote Fragmentation

Ambivalence: Lack of a Unified Vision

Fragmentation, of course, is found to a greater or lesser degree in all metropolitan areas. Our question is: How does the governing coalition (if one exists) overcome fragmentation? One thing that might help in getting things done is some sense of a unified vision, some agreement on where the city and region are heading.

There has never been a unified vision among New Orleans's political and governmental elites. While cities like Atlanta, Dallas, and Houston moved ahead with business-oriented planning, New Orleans floundered in the past half century. Many in New Orleans were modernizers, who believed in undertaking major projects that moved the city forward. The port, the zoo, the aquarium, and the development of the downtown area are testimony to their efforts. Even in elite sectors, those with vision often clashed with other views: the Mardi Gras mentality ("Let's have fun and let's not worry about community projects") and the historic preservation-in-all-circumstances mentality. The latter has often conflicted with economic development efforts in recent decades.

The ambivalence and lack of a unified vision have been evident post-Katrina. What is the vision for a future New Orleans? What will it look like? What will its functions be? Is the vision that of city reconstruction "czar" Ed Blakely's focus on seventeen commercial centers? Is the vision that of the Louisiana Reconstruction Authority's emphasis on a "New Urbanism" approach? Is the vision that of the Unified New Orleans Plan's focus on individual neighborhoods? The city says that it wants former residents to return. Several years later, have its policies promoted that return—in housing, in jobs, and so on?

The state-local disconnection contributes to the problem. Historically, the state government has often conflicted with the city. Many in northern Louisiana are at odds with the city's "sin" and corruption. It is unclear exactly how the state sees the city as fitting into the state's economic plans, regardless of the personal conflicts in the mayor's and the governor's offices.

Similarly, even before Hurricane Katrina, there was a massive federal-local disconnection. What does the federal government see for the region—given its policies on such diverse matters as levee protection, coastal deterioration, defense facility location, and public housing?

Veto Groups Rule

Power, in cities, is often expressed negatively, that is, power is reflected in the ability to keep something from happening. Certainly, it is normal for upper-income elite political actors to keep uninvited land uses away from their homes or pet development projects. In New Orleans, negativism goes much further than that. The city council has seven members—five selected from districts and two at large. By informal agreement, the district members have veto power over planning and zoning changes in their districts. Veto power is not limited to the elite. In the 1950s, the Comiskeys (white machine politicians) and their working-class constituents kept New Orleans from entering the federal urban renewal program. More recently, preservationists have fought all sorts of commercial uses, including coffee shops, supermarkets, and drugstores (in one case of the latter, the vacant property turned into a market for drug dealers). African-Americans have allied with white preservationists to stop some projects and to win concessions on others. In some cases, African-Americans have successfully fought against proposed land uses viewed as harmful for their neighborhoods. Again, this long-term pattern creates difficulties for the rebuilding effort.

Since Hurricane Katrina, New Orleans has persisted in allowing veto groups to rule. The best evidence was in the Bring Back New Orleans Commission's suggestion to redevelop the city at differing paces, and to keep some areas from rebuilding (at least in the short run). Rather than fight angry homeowners, the city has gone for the "jack-o-lantern" approach (where only one person might return on a block, creating a jack-o-lantern look).

Lack of Dynamism in the New Orleans Elite

New Orleans has steadily fallen in the hierarchy of American cities. Some of this resulted from national and global economic forces. But, some of it resulted from the "Mardi Gras" mentality of many in the New Orleans elite. In any review of recent history, it seems that New Orleans missed out between 1950 and 1970 in a number of areas. Some of these, such as urban renewal and the port, were physical development issues. Some failures were even more fundamental. Here is one example.

Robert Crain's classic book, *The Politics of School Desegregation* (1969), devotes an entire section (100 pages of 400) to the integration of New Orleans's public schools in 1961. One of the chapters is titled "The Failure of an Elite." In 1961, most observers thought that New Orleans would be more sympathetic to integration than many other southern cities because it was Roman Catholic, it was cosmopolitan, and it had a tradition of integration. Among other things, the schools chosen for the initial integration effort were in the then white working-class Ninth Ward. This was probably the part of town where racism was strongest. It was also closest physically to St. Bernard Parish, then part of the domain of segregationist Leander Perez. Given this proximity, it was easy for Perez to organize protests, including picketing of the schools.

Crain notes the general withdrawal of the New Orleans elite from politics. He found the elite to have only a mild interest in such issues as economic development. The elite were dominated by old wealth, and it was difficult for outsiders to break into this group. Crain saw a resistance to new ideas and new values. The school board, elected officials, and the civic elite did nothing to prevent violence in 1961. The public school situation became a long-term disaster.

Again, this pattern is evident since Katrina. There are exceptions, of course: the work of King Milling in coastal restoration, the work of Ruthie Frierson, Anne Milling, and others in anti-storm groups, the work of many with the Greater New Orleans Foundation—all should be credited. However, at present there is only one Fortune 500 company in New Orleans (Entergy), and it is in trouble.

Corruption

Louisiana is known for its corruption at the state and local levels. If you have to pay off at a number of different places, it makes it difficult to get things done. Perhaps the best recent example is the introduction of casino gambling in the 1990s. Tyler Bridges's excellent book, *Bad Bet on the Bayou* (2001), provides the best account of this twisted situation. Louisiana's "regulation" of casinos restricted licenses and ensured payoffs. In contrast, Mississippi opened casino gambling to the marketplace. The Mississippi Gulf Coast became the center for the gaming industry. Mississippi received the benefits that everyone thought would come to Louisiana.

At the city level, Marc Morial and Congressman William Jefferson were the most powerful politicians a few years ago. Morial, a two-term mayor, is now head of the National Urban League. An ongoing investigation by the U.S. Attorney's office has not touched Morial directly. However, his uncle's wife, Lillian Smith Haydel, pleaded guilty in October 2004 to federal charges of paying kickbacks to an Orleans Parish school official. Morial's uncle, Glenn Haydel, admitted to stealing $540,000 from the Regional Transportation Authority. Haydel is making restitution as part of a cooperation agreement with federal prosecutors. Jefferson has been indicted by the federal government for taking money illegally from an investor. Most recently, Councilman Oliver Thomas pleaded guilty to accepting a bribe in relation to the Morial-Haydel investigation. Aside from the aura of corruption around major political figures, there is a steady pattern of lower-level corruption: fixing parking tickets, demanding money for permits, and so forth. All of this makes the federal government and foundations hesitant to pour large sums of money into New Orleans.

Aversion to Planning

The traditions of privatizing and individualism are strong in the historical development of American cities. New Orleans perhaps carries these traditions to extremes. City planning has been shunted aside by New Orleans city government and elites.

The City Planning Commission appoints the planning director. In general, city planning has not been viewed as a core city function. At present, New Orleans does not have a city plan with the force of law.

In the early 1990s, Baton Rouge embarked upon a major city planning effort, with substantial expenditure for outside consulting help. In the same era, New Orleans chose to develop a new city plan on the cheap. The city's effort was innovative, and it involved a substantial number of citizens as well as neighborhood participation. The resulting plan has never attained statutory force.

Strong Antigovernment Bias

This combination of factors—especially the corruption and the aversion to planning—contribute to a strong antigovernment bias. Many New Orleans (and Louisiana) voters routinely vote "No" on any proposed governmental expenditure because of their belief that the money will inevitably further corruption. However, it is generally accepted that the private sector is superior to the public sector—whether in education or in any potential government activity. After Hurricane Katrina, many still prefer the marketplace to governmental intervention.

These characteristics—fragmentation, lack of unified vision, the rise of veto groups, lack of dynamism, corruption, aversion to planning, and antigovernment bias—all fit well with city governance that is, in many ways, traditionalistic. By and large, they are characteristic of the caretaker regime that ruled New Orleans for many years. The questions are: If city governance is dominated by the above characteristics, how does it deal with a crisis of the magnitude of Hurricane Katrina? Is change in the governance system inevitable and, if so, what direction will it take? Is a disaster such as Katrina simply overwhelming for New Orleans's governance capacity?

Before addressing these questions, we should note the one conspicuous exception to the stories mentioned above. This is strong commitment to the promoting of development in the Central Business District (CBD), the Warehouse District, and the riverfront areas therein since the early 1970s. Smith and Keller (1986) discuss the development of the Superdome, the Poydras Street CBD corridor, and Canal Place (a mixed-use development project) as part of a strategy of "managed growth." The development was effected by a business–government coalition. Later efforts were stimulated by the 1984 World's Fair. Major residual benefits of the fair included a new convention center (subsequently enlarged in three later phases), the Riverwalk shopping center, and a revived Warehouse District, including arts, entertainment, and residential development. Along the riverfront, Woldenberg Park was created, an aquarium was opened in 1990, and a casino was built after the old Rivergate Convention Center was razed.

The pace of this development slowed in the later 1990s and early 2000s. One major effort since 2000 centered around the New Orleans Saints football stadium situation. The state government operates the Superdome Stadium. A committee appointed by former Louisiana governor Mike Foster, considered three options: building a new stadium, "reengineering" the Superdome (i.e., by imploding it and building an outdoor stadium on the site), and substantially renovating the Superdome. While there was some debate, it is important to note the widespread consensus on the need for a major effort to keep the Saints franchise in New Orleans. Ultimately, the state decided on major renovation of the Superdome as the course of action.

Hurricane Katrina changed this situation, as it did every other situation. The dome roof suffered significant damage, and major repairs were necessary after its service as an emergency shelter. Major expenditures were necessary to bring the dome back quickly as a football stadium. There are many areas of need, and many things that New Orleans must have—housing, jobs, education, transportation, economic development, and so on—to rebuild. The point is that no one questioned the major expenditures on dome repair even though it was paid for, in large part, by the federal government. Of course, the dome needed to be repaired, but why was the relative priority so high?

The Current State of Fragmentation

Mayor Ray Nagin was reelected in a close race against Lieutenant Governor Mitch Landrieu in 2006. In the same election, New Orleans voters rejected three city council incumbents running for reelection. The council now has four new members out of seven as the city rebuilds, and it has a white majority for the first time in more than two decades. Council politics seemed to be less contentious, post-Katrina, for a time. At Nagin's mid-term in May 2008, mayor–council relations had deteriorated again. In 2007, council member Stacy Head had issued a subpoena to a member of the Nagin administration to appear before the council committee. This was the first time since the 1980s that a city hall executive had been subpoenaed by the council. In 2008, council members again threatened use of the subpoena power before the city's chief technology officer handed over records on the city's crime camera and customer service program.

The school board was contentious shortly after the storm. Not much has been heard from this highly conflicted body lately, but it must be remembered that the state board of education took over the operation of the overwhelming majority of the schools after the storm. Few schools reopened in 2005–6, and many have not reopened in the succeeding two years. Not every school will reopen in a smaller New Orleans, but the convenience of public schools might well be part of a family's decision to return. The schools were in disastrous financial shape before the storm.

Racial and Class Fragmentation

Population estimates by the U.S. Census Bureau in June 2007 show the metro region to be more white and less black than it was previously. In theory, more homogeneity should influence more cooperation. In practice, there is good reason to doubt the census estimates (and many of the other population estimates emanating from the city and other sources).

In addition, the storm introduced some new elements. New Orleans has always had a substantial Hispanic population. In recent decades, that population has been augmented by refugees from Central America and Cuba. The Hispanics, by and large, have flown under the political radar. They do not live in the same neighborhoods in large enough numbers to influence elections.

Since the storm, many migrants are working in cleanup and construction in the metro area. Many are from Mexico. There has been much negative comment about Mexican workers taking jobs away from African-Americans who are displaced and would like to return. Crime brings out prejudice and fears, as indicated by the arrest of a Mexican suspect after the brutal murder of a woman on a jogging path at La Freniere Park in suburban Kenner in early 2006.

Vietnamese have lived in New Orleans for at least thirty years. Before Hurricane Katrina, they were never heard from as a political force. Since the storm they have become newly assertive about their right to rebuild in their flooded neighborhood in New Orleans East, and also in their opposition to the reopening of a landfill in their neighborhood (seemingly, they have won this fight).

Mayor Nagin's "chocolate city" speech on Martin Luther King Day 2006 may have been an inspired stroke, as far as his reelection was concerned. No major

African-American politician chose to run against him. His three major opponents were all white. However, that bit of rhetoric hurt Nagin in terms of city and metropolitan governance. On the other hand, it must be noted that both candidates in the mayoral runoff drew a substantial "crossover" vote.

Since the storm, we have heard often of the Federal Emergency Management Agency's failures. The trailers sitting in Arkansas have been cited again and again as evidence of failures. Not all the blame belongs on the federal level. Trailers are in evidence in New Orleans neighborhoods next to homes, but not in large trailer parks. One reason for the absence of trailer parks is social. The New Orleanians who escaped the storm relatively unscathed and the early returnees do not want trailer parks. After several battles with the council, the Nagin administration gave up on this issue.

Conclusion

The past and current history of political, governmental, racial, class, and economic fragmentation does not bode well for the rebuilding of New Orleans.

First and foremost, the diaspora, the forced evacuation of New Orleans citizens throughout the United States, looms over other issues. Precise estimates are impossible to find, but it is clear that many New Orleans residents have not returned. Do they want to return? The city has responded with characteristic ambivalence. Evacuees are told they are welcomed home. However, their homes may lack basic services. Rebuilding programs focus on homeowners; a large proportion of pre-Katrina New Orleans residents were renters (53.5 percent in New Orleans in the 2000 Census, as opposed to 33.8 percent nationwide). Displaced residents, at the minimum, need housing, jobs, education, health care, transportation, and daycare. There are few clear signals for individuals making decisions that these services will be available, that housing will be affordable, and that jobs will be available.

The diaspora has created a new regional dynamic. Before the storm, Baton Rouge was poised to become the largest city in Louisiana by the 2010 Census. Much of the post-Katrina population movement occurred between New Orleans and Baton Rouge, on both sides of Lake Pontchartrain. Effective governance must take into account the whole region. There is little indication that anyone, at any level, is thinking *regionally.* Past and present fragmentation does not make this easier.

It is not easy to achieve cooperation, even within jurisdictions. The Policy Consensus Initiative (PCI) is a national public interest group, which seeks to develop a collaborative system of governance at the state level. The PCI sent board members and staff to New Orleans in February 2006 to see if they could do any useful work. After meeting with leaders and viewing storm devastation, the PCI concluded that this is an example of a situation where collaboration is not yet possible. Using collaborative governance to address a problem of this nature requires all affected governments and partners to be ready to find mutual agreement on purpose and objective. The necessary partners for recovery and restoration in Louisiana first need to agree upon a framework for combining their efforts. Given the fragmentation, some possible donors and grantors will not even enter New Orleans. Many who give aid will do so with great trepidation.

It would be nice to close on an optimistic note. The present and past realities of New Orleans politics do not allow us to be optimistic. In relative comparison with the nongovernmental sector, the private sector, and the efforts of individual citizens and even foreign governments, the governments have failed badly in the wake of Hurricane Katrina. Despite the infusion of massive amounts of aid, the federal government's failure in the aftermath of Katrina is etched in the hearts and minds of all New Orleanians. The state government's immediate response was inadequate. The state's main program (The Road Home) was forced on the state when the Bush administration declined to support a federal program sponsored by former Representative Richard Baker (R-Baton Rouge). The Road Home program has been a bureaucratic nightmare.

Under the new administration of Governor Bobby Jindal, elected in 2007, the state has passed significant ethics legislation. At the local level, the Nagin administration lacks vision and seems overwhelmed by the tasks at hand. As we have seen above, the three levels of government (federal, state, and local) have not worked well together in facing the difficult problems of the post-Katrina era.

References

Brandt, James, and Robert K. Whelan. 2004. "New Orleans: Metropolis Against Itself." In *Metropolitan Governance without Metropolitan Government?* ed. Donald Phares, 135–53. Burlington, VT: Ashgate.

Bridges, Tyler. 2001. *Bad Bet on the Bayou: The Rise of Gambling in Louisiana and the Fall of Governor Edwin Edwards.* New York: Farrar, Straus, and Giroux.

Brinkley, Douglas. 2007. "Reckless Abandonment." *Washington Post,* August 26, p. B1.

Crain, Robert L. 1969. *The Politics of School Desegregation.* Garden City, NY: Anchor Books.

Feiock, Richard C. et al. 2006. "Structuring the Debate on Consolidation: A Response to Leland and Thurmaier." *Public Administration Review* 66, no. 2 (March): 274–78.

Johnson, Chalmers. 1966. *Revolutionary Change.* Boston: Little, Brown.

Johnson, Linda S. 2004. "Revolutionary Local Constitutional Change: A Theory of the Consolidation Process." In *City-County Consolidation and Its Alternatives: Reshaping the Local Government Landscape,* ed. Jared B. Carr and Richard C. Feiock, 155–82. Armonk, NY: M.E. Sharpe.

Kaufman, Herbert. 1963. *Politics and Policies in State and Local Governments.* Englewood Cliffs, NJ: Prentice Hall.

Larson, Erik. 2000. *Isaac's Storm: A Man, a Time, and the Deadliest Hurricane in History.* New York: Vintage.

Leland, Suzanne M., and Kurt Thurmaier. 2006. "Lessons From 35 Years of City-County Consolidation Attempts." *Municipal Yearbook 2006.* Washington, DC: ICMA, 3–10.

Liu, Amy, and Allison Plyer. 2008. "State of Policy and Progress." Washington, DC: Brookings Institution.

Phares, Donald, ed. 2004. *Metropolitan Governance without Metropolitan Government?* Burlington, VT: Ashgate.

Rice, Bradley R. 1977. *Progressive Cities: The Commission Government Movement in America, 1901–1920.* Austin: University of Texas Press.

Rosenbaum, Walter, and Gladys Kammerer. 1974. *Against Long Odds: The Theory and Practice of Governmental Consolidation*, Beverly Hills, CA: Sage.

Rusk, David. 1999. "The New Regionalism: Planning Together to Reshape New Orleans' Future." *New Orleans Times-Picayune,* September 8, advertising supplement.

Smith, Michael Peter, and Marlene Keller. 1986. "Managed Growth and the Politics of Uneven Development in New Orleans." In *Restructuring the City: The Political Economy of Urban Development.* Rev. ed., ed. Susan S. Fainstein et al., 126–66. New York: Longman.

Tregle, Joseph G. Jr. 1999. *Louisiana in the Age of Jackson: A Clash of Cultures and Personalities.* Baton Rouge: Louisiana State University Press.

U.S. Census Bureau. 2007. "American Community Survey." Available at www.uscensus.gov.

Vale, Lawrence J., and Thomas J. Campanella, eds. 2005. *The Resilient City: How Modern Cities Recover from Disaster.* New York: Oxford University Press.

van Heerden, Ivor, and Mike Bryan. 2006. *The Storm.* New York: Viking.

Warner, Coleman. 2007. "Progress and Pain." *New Orleans Times-Picayune,* August 27.

12

A Review of Canadian Metropolitan Regions

Governance and Government

Andrew Sancton

Canadian Metropolitan Regions: Governance and Government

Despite the country's vast territory, Canada's population is concentrated in a relatively small number of urban areas not far from the border with the United States. The border is important because the Canadian approach to governing urban areas is quite different from the American one. Growth in Canada's population is occurring almost exclusively in urban areas and in nearby towns and villages, and the challenges to the institutions of urban governments are therefore great. Like the United States, Canada is a federation. Each of its ten provinces has constitutional jurisdiction over "institutions of municipal government" and each makes use of such jurisdiction in different ways, making it almost impossible to generalize about the Canadian approach to city governance, other than that it is different from the American approach. The chief difference is that Canadian provinces are much more interventionist than American states; they are much more likely to adopt laws relating to local municipal structures that might not have the explicit approval of local councils and voters (Sancton, 2002).

The aim of this chapter is to describe and analyze the various approaches adopted within Canada to the problems of metropolitan governance over the past fifty years. This has been a period of exceptionally rapid urban growth, especially in areas immediately outside the boundaries of central-city municipalities. Such growth has caused the various provinces constantly to seek changes in local governmental institutions so as to adapt to this growth and to attempt to shape it efficiently and effectively.

Importance of Metropolitan Areas

In the 2001 census Statistics Canada for the first time provided data for a new kind of urban entity, "major urban regions." Only four regions in the country qualified: the

Table 12.1

Canada's Four "Major Urban Regions," 2001

Urban Region	Population in millions	Increase from 1996 (%)	Share of relevant provincial population (%)	Share of Canadian population (%)
Extended Golden Horseshoe	6.7	9.2	59	22
Montreal and its Adjacent Region	3.7	2.8	52	12
Lower Mainland and Southern Vancouver Island	2.7	7.3	69	9
Calgary-Edmonton Corridor	2.15	12.3	72	7

Source: Statistics Canada, "Growth Concentrated in Four Large Urban Areas," July 23, 2003; available at http://geodepot.statcan.ca/Diss/Highlights/Page9/Page9_e.cfm/.

Extended Golden Horseshoe (Toronto); Montreal and its Adjacent Region; the Lower Mainland and Southern Vancouver Island; and the Calgary-Edmonton Corridor. In 2001, these major urban regions had a combined population of 15.3 million or 51 percent of the entire Canadian population, up from 49 percent in 1996 and approximately 41 percent in 1971. Between 1996 and 2001, the four major urban regions grew by 7.6 percent, compared with a 0.5 percent increase in the rest of the country (Statistics Canada, 2003). For more information on these major urban regions, see Table 12.1.

Unfortunately, because the category of "major urban regions" is new and still not permanently established or defined, Statistics Canada does not present detailed demographic data based on their boundaries. We must rely instead on the much more firmly established census metropolitan areas (CMAs). Statistics Canada states that:

> A census metropolitan area (CMA) is formed by one or more adjacent municipalities centred on a large urban area (known as the urban core). The census population count of the urban core is at least 100,000 to form a census metropolitan area. To be included in the CMA or CA, other adjacent municipalities must have a high degree of integration with the central urban area, as measured by commuting flows derived from census place of work data. (Statistics Canada, 2006).

In this chapter, we focus on Canada's ten largest CMAs, as listed in Table 12.2. The main difficulty in using this list of CMAs relates to Toronto. The five CMAs of Toronto, Oshawa, Hamilton, Kitchener, and St. Catharines-Niagara are contiguous, forming a continuous built-up urban area often known as the Golden Horseshoe, because of the horseshoe shape it forms as it wraps around the western tip of Lake Ontario. The "Extended Golden Horseshoe" used by Statistics Canada to describe Toronto's "major urban region" is, of course, based on this name. Only two of the

Table 12.2

Canada's Ten Most Populous Census Metropolitan Areas (CMAs), 2006

CMA	2006 population (no.)	Increase since 2001 (%)	Population in central city (%)	Visible minority (%)	Foreign born (%)
Toronto	5,113,149	9.2	49.0	42.9	45.7
Montreal	3,635,571	5.3	44.6	16.5	20.6
Vancouver	2,116,581	6.5	27.3	39.6	41.7
Ottawa-Gatineau	1,130,761	5.9	71.8	16.0	18.1
Calgary	1,079,310	13.4	91.4	22.2	23.6
Edmonton	1,034,945	10.4	70.6	17.1	18.5
Quebec	715,515	4.2	68.6	2.3	3.7
Winnipeg	694,668	2.7	91.1	15.0	17.8
Hamilton	692,991	4.6	72.8	12.3	24.3
London	457,720	5.1	77.0	11.1	19.3
Canada, total	31,612,897	5.4	n.a.	13.4	18.4

Source: Statistics Canada, "2006 Census release topics"; available at www12.statcan. ca/english/census06/release/index.cfm/.

CMAs in the Extended Golden Horseshoe—Toronto and Hamilton—are in the top ten. For the purposes of this chapter, each will be treated separately.

Table 12.2 shows that there is considerable variation in the demographic characteristics of Canadian metropolitan areas. Between 2001 and 2006, five of the ten most populous metropolitan areas grew faster than the national average of 5.4 percent, with Calgary growing at a rate of 13.4 percent. At the opposite end of the scale was Winnipeg at only 2.7 percent. Probably the most significant demographic differences among these CMAs relate to the diversity of their respective populations as measured by the percentages of both visible minorities and the foreign-born. Here both Toronto and Vancouver rank extremely high, attracting immigrants of all racial backgrounds from all over the world. The equivalent numbers for Quebec City are very low, confirming the city's image as a governmental center populated by provincial civil servants and as a regional center for Canadians whose French origins go back many centuries.

Toronto and Vancouver are both globalizing metropolitan areas with significant population growth fed by very high immigration levels. Montreal, once Canada's largest urban area, continues its secular decline in relation to Toronto but continues to function as the metropolis of the increasingly dynamic and self-confident French-language community based in Quebec. Although not as attractive to immigrants as Toronto and Vancouver, Montreal has increasingly become a magnet for French-speaking immigrants from places such as Haiti, Vietnam, Lebanon, and North Africa, and for immigrants who are willing to learn French as a second or third language. The result is that Montreal has become the main physical location for the transformation of French Canada from an ethnically and racially homogeneous community to a much more diverse one, the members of which continue to share a common language (Germain and Rose, 2000).

Calgary and Edmonton are both riding a resource boom led by rising oil prices. As the corporate and financial center of the Canadian oil industry, Calgary has been especially prosperous in recent years, but neither place is a significant global city. Even less so are the remaining metropolitan areas listed in Table 12.2.

Public Framework for Addressing Policy Issues

Canada is a highly urbanized and highly decentralized federation. Under the Canadian Constitution, provinces have direct responsibility not only for municipal institutions but also for education and health care facilities. This means that many of the most important decisions about public sector institutions within Canada's metropolitan areas are under provincial jurisdiction. In theory at least, the federal government can spend money on such provincial matters as education and health, but it cannot attempt to regulate them by enacting legislation. There is no constitutional obligation for provinces even to establish municipalities and local special-purpose bodies such as school boards, let alone to devolve authority to them.

Most provinces have articulated strategic land use policies, which municipalities are expected to follow. Most provinces have also been highly interventionist with respect to municipal structures, such that Canadian metropolitan areas over time and in different provinces have experienced almost every kind of institutional arrangement imaginable. The fact that provinces have been heavily involved has meant that nongovernmental actors have been less important in metropolitan governance, certainly in comparison with metropolitan areas in the United States where involvement of private sector and voluntary agencies has been a hallmark of what has often been labeled the "new regionalism" (Sancton, 2001; see also Chapter 2 in this volume).

Among the ten largest CMAs in Canada, there are effectively four different types of institutional arrangements for metropolitan governance:

- No metropolitan level of government; various single-purpose authorities; and strong provincial involvement in metropolitan issues. This is the institutional arrangement for Toronto.
- A multifunctional metropolitan-level institution covering all or most of the CMA, as found in Montreal, Vancouver, and Quebec City.
- A federal government institution (the National Capital Commission) with multifunctional capability in the National Capital Region, which straddles the provinces of Ontario and Quebec.
- A single municipality that covers all or most of a CMA, making another level of metropolitan government unnecessary.

This is the arrangement for each of the remaining top-ten CMAs, including Ottawa in Ontario and Gatineau in Quebec, which are the dominant municipalities within the National Capital Region. Ironically, it is also the situation in Quebec City, where the central city comprises more than 70 percent of the population of the CMA and there is a form of metropolitan government.

Each arrangement will be described in turn.

Toronto

The Municipality of Metropolitan Toronto (1954–97) was probably Canada's best-known municipal institutional innovation. "Metro" and its constituent municipalities became the textbook example of a successful two-tier system. The upper-tier Metro council was created by the province of Ontario in 1953, primarily to solve a service crisis in the rural and suburban municipalities surrounding the city of Toronto. These municipalities had been unable to cope with the infrastructure demands in the Toronto region caused by the explosive growth of the postwar economy. With its functional responsibility for water supply and sewage treatment systems, arterial roads, and regional planning, Metro facilitated, in a relatively orderly way, the continued growth of the Toronto CMA in the late 1950s and 1960s (Frisken, 2008). By the 1970s, however, the Metro system in Toronto was facing at least three major problems:

- Suburban municipalities within Metro had collectively surpassed the population of the central city, largely because of the infrastructure paid for through taxes collected within the central city. Once in the majority, suburbs seemed unwilling to use Metro to help rebuild deteriorating infrastructure within the central city and political tensions between the two sides mounted.
- Most of the new urban growth within the Toronto CMA was taking place outside the boundaries of Metro, but the provincial government did not extend its boundaries, thereby ensuring that Metro's regional planning functions became increasingly irrelevant.
- Because the upper-tier authority was spending an increasing share of total municipal revenues, there was increasing pressure to have members of the upper-tier council directly elected to serve only at that level, rather than to have Metro councilors chosen by the lower-tier councils from among their own members. After the new arrangements for direct election were implemented in 1988, jurisdictional battles and disputes between elected politicians at the two levels became more common and the two-tier system was increasingly seen as politically dysfunctional.

In late 1996 the government of Ontario announced that the Municipality of Metropolitan Toronto and its constituent parts would be merged into one new City of Toronto. The primary stated purpose of this policy was to save money.

The policy caused a huge political battle that has been well documented elsewhere (Boudreau, 2000; Horak, 1998; Sancton, 2000). The key point for this chapter is that the controversial amalgamation had nothing to do with metropolitan governance. In 2001, the population of the new city was 2.48 million, while that of the Toronto CMA was 4.68 million. In fact, as already noted, the real population of Toronto's metropolitan area is closer to 6.70 million within the Extended Golden Horseshoe. In short, all the difficult issues associated with metropolitan growth were taking place *outside* the new city's borders.

From 1998 until 2001, there was the Greater Toronto Services Board with a territory and mandate similar to what has just been proposed. It was replaced by a Central Ontario Smart Growth Panel with a territory closer to that of the Extended Golden Horseshoe, but its only mandate was to produce a report about how to manage future growth, a mission it accomplished in 2003. Since then, the government of Ontario has effectively become the metropolitan planning agency for an area it calls the Greater Golden Horseshoe (Sancton, 2008).

Multifunctional Metropolitan Institution: Vancouver, Montreal, Quebec City

In the late 1960s the legislature in British Columbia established a network of "regional districts" throughout the entire province that remains in place today. Metro Vancouver (or GVRD as the regional district is now called) provides a mechanism for metropolitan government in British Columbia's most populous CMA (see Chapter 13).

The provincial government in British Columbia was anxious to emphasize that a new level of government was not being created. The regional districts were to include many existing intermunicipal special-purpose bodies and to act as an institution through which increased intermunicipal cooperation could be encouraged. Regional districts are governed by a "board of directors," not a council; directors themselves are all elected members of municipal councils, and they have multiple votes depending on the size of the population they represent; municipalities can opt out of many regional services or, if they are near the outer boundaries, opt in to the services being provided by a neighboring district; the districts were created without changing any existing municipal boundaries. Although there have been some calls for direct election to the boards of directors of regional districts (Smith and Stewart, 1998), no government has moved toward implementing such a change, presumably because of a concern about the jurisdictional conflicts that would likely ensue.

Metro Vancouver has twenty-one member municipalities with a population in 2006 of 2.12 million. Its territory corresponds exactly to that of the Vancouver CMA. The population of the city of Vancouver was 578,041.The suburban city of Surrey is not far behind, with a population of 394,976 (Statistics Canada, 2006). In short, by Canadian standards, the municipal system of the Vancouver CMA is quite highly fragmented, but the GVRD acts to provide regional services such as public transit, water and sewage services, garbage disposal, and regional parks.

Although it is impossible to determine objectively an ideal institutional model for metropolitan governance, it is hard to imagine a mechanism that could better combine local self-government through established municipalities with the existence of an institution at the metropolitan level that can provide a degree of consensual metropolitan leadership (the strategic plan) as well as a framework within which municipalities can voluntarily cooperate with each other. Those who must live with the system find it hard to believe that the system they often find frustrating can be judged so positively. What they need to do, however, is to compare Vancouver with other places, something this volume makes possible.

In 2000, the Quebec legislature established somewhat similar institutions, called metropolitan communities, for Montreal and Quebec City. The territory of the Montreal Metropolitan Community (MMC) corresponds very closely to that of the Montreal CMA. It comprises the territories of the urban agglomeration councils of Montreal and Longueuil and of sixty-one other municipalities. The MMC has potential responsibilities relating to regional planning, waste disposal, regional parks, coordination of public transport, economic development, regional infrastructure, and cost sharing for public housing. It is governed by a twenty-eight-person council, of which thirteen come from the Montreal urban agglomeration council. The council's chair is the mayor of Montreal, who is the MMC's main political spokesperson (Communauté métropolitaine de Montréal, 2005). Similar structures are in place for the Quebec (City) Metropolitan Community, which comprises twenty-seven municipalities on both sides of the St. Lawrence River and on the historic Ile d'Orleans. It is still far too early to assess the impact of the new metropolitan communities on Quebec's two major CMAs.

The National Capital Commission: Ottawa and Gatineau

Canada's fourth most populous CMA is Ottawa-Gatineau, with a 2006 population of 1,130,761. Of this number, 846,802 lived on the Ontario side of the Ottawa River in the city of Ottawa. The remainder lived on the Quebec side in what, since 2002, has been the amalgamated city of Gatineau. The territory of the CMA is roughly coterminous with the territory of the National Capital Commission (NCC), an agency of the federal government that has existed in its current form since 1959. The commission comprises fifteen members appointed by the federal government. In its earlier institutional manifestations it played a major role in drawing up and implementing a regional plan for the entire area, the most notable feature of which is a Greenbelt around the original city of Ottawa. The NCC is also responsible for significant green spaces and recreational areas on the Quebec side of the river. An important constitutional ruling of the Supreme Court of Canada in 1966 held that "the federal government had the power to plan for the National Capital Region, and to expropriate land for its purposes, including land for the Greenbelt" (Fullerton, 1974, pp. 1-14). Such a power related exclusively to the fact that the area in question was the federal capital. Similar federal powers do not exist in other Canadian CMAs.

In the past few decades the NCC has built parkways, removed railway tracks from Ottawa's downtown, renovated historical buildings, provided sites for national museums, and created a winter skateway on the frozen Rideau canal. In short, it has done many of the things that are often expected of metropolitan governments. The difference, of course, is that metropolitan governments are generally accountable in one way or another to metropolitan residents. In the case of the NCC, board members are accountable only to the federal government that appointed them. Although there have been many examples of localized objections to NCC actions, most residents of Ottawa-Gatineau are highly appreciative. They should be; the NCC spends money from all Canadians to provide urban amenities for the approximately 3 percent of Canadians who live in the National Capital Region.

A Single Municipality that Covers All or Most of a CMA

Calgary is Canada's fifth most populous CMA, with a 2006 population of 1,079,310. The 2006 population of the city of Calgary was 988,193, meaning that there was no possible reason for a distinct metropolitan level of government. The city's territory has increased incrementally over many decades as a result of a continuing series of annexations. Some have been controversial and have generated intense opposition. Decisions on annexation applications from cities in Alberta are made by a quasi-judicial body, the Local Authorities Board (LAB). The usual pattern in the past has been for Calgary to ask for very large annexations and for the LAB to grant less than what it asked for (Masson and LeSage, 1994, pp. 164–66).

The creation of a single-tier metropolitan authority without there having been a strong two-tier system is likely to be possible only within metropolitan areas that do not have large populations. Calgary is perhaps the exception that proves the rule. Its municipal evolution has been made possible by a continuing process of annexation combined with the absence of longstanding urban municipalities nearby. Simple as single-tier structures are, they are not without their problems. Annexation battles— even in Calgary—are often slow, messy, unpopular, and expensive; occasionally the provincial government has to step in directly to sort out intractable disputes. If long-standing, distinct urban, suburban, and rural communities are brought together by legislative fiat, there will be continuing pressures for decentralized decision making and/or secession.

The territory of the city of Edmonton has also increased dramatically over the years using the same Alberta laws and practices that were in force in Calgary. The difference in Edmonton is that incorporated suburban municipalities are nearby and they have generally fought hard against forced annexation. As a result, while the 2006 population of the Edmonton CMA was 1,034,945, the population of the city was only 730,372 or 70.6 percent of the total CMA population. Although this percentage is small compared with Calgary, it is high compared with most North American central cities. There is no pressure from anyone for a distinct level of metropolitan government. However, the city of Edmonton has often called for municipal amalgamations over the years while the suburban municipalities have claimed that voluntary intermunicipal cooperation is quite sufficient. The latest institutional vessel for such cooperation is the premier's Capital Region Integrated Growth Management Plan.

Like Edmonton, Canada's tenth most populous CMA, London, Ontario (halfway between Toronto and Detroit, Michigan) has also grown incrementally through annexation and amalgamation, but other significant incorporated municipalities are still within the CMA. The city of London comprises 77 percent of the 2006 CMA population of 457,720. It clearly dominates the area and has ample developable land for future growth.

Winnipeg is Canada's eighth most populous CMA. In 1970 the social-democratic party that at the time controlled the Manitoba provincial legislature (the New Democratic Party—NDP) decided to create a single City of Winnipeg—a "unicity"—to replace a two-tier system of municipal government comprising the Corporation of Greater Winnipeg and its twelve constituent municipalities. The main declared objective of the provincial government was to equalize taxes and service levels within the territory of the new unicity (Brownstone and Plunkett, 1983).

The Manitoba NDP believed at the time that it could create a single, amalgamated city and simultaneously create innovative mechanisms for decentralization and citizen participation. Indeed, there was great initial optimism that a new era in municipal government was being launched. The first unicity council had fifty members, each of whom sat on one of thirteen community committees that would advise the main council on matters of more local concern. These committees were in turn advised by resident advisory groups whose members were chosen at open community meetings. Over time, enthusiasm for consultation and advice waned, especially as it became evident that the unicity council could not possibly do what every councilor and local group wanted. By 1992, the council had been reduced to fifteen members and much of the special machinery for citizen participation had eroded or been abolished. Since then, the provincial government has seemed more concerned with managing growth outside the unicity's borders than managing the institutions within (Manitoba, 2003). In 1991, unicity comprised 94.5 percent of the population of the Winnipeg CMA. In 2006, the equivalent figure was 91.1 percent, meaning that the CMA area beyond the unicity's boundaries is growing faster than unicity itself.

The remaining CMA among the ten most populous is Hamilton, which is immediately west of Toronto and now considered by Statistics Canada to be part of the Extended Golden Horseshoe. As in Winnipeg in 1970 and Toronto in 1998, Hamilton's two-tier system of metropolitan government was completely amalgamated in 2001.

Agenda Setting, Political Representation, and the Exercise of Power

Not surprisingly, the politics of metropolitan areas varies quite dramatically, depending on the institutional settings that are involved. Nevertheless, some significant generalizations apply more or less to all major Canadian metropolitan areas. First, no metropolitan governments are themselves the subject of great political loyalty, conflict, or functional importance. As we have seen, the city governments of Calgary, Winnipeg, Hamilton, and London can be viewed as metropolitan governments because of their wide territorial scope and because they include such a high proportion of the population of their respective metropolitan areas. These governments are seen as important, but not because they are metropolitan. They are important because they do the normal things that city governments do. The Montreal and Quebec metropolitan communities are so new, so functionally weak, and so overshadowed by recent debates about municipal de-amalgamation that only a tiny proportion of the metropolitan population would know that they even exist.

Because provincial governments play such important roles with respect to policymaking for health, income security, education, and social services, none of these policy areas are thought of by Canadians as having a particularly metropolitan focus. Social housing is often considered to be more a municipal function in Canada, but metropolitan institutions, to the extent that they exist at all, have no direct operational role with respect to housing. At best, notably in the province of Quebec, they have a potential role as planners for the territorial distribution of social housing.

Above all, the "metropolitan agenda" in Canada is about urban infrastructure (roads, rapid transit systems, sewers, water supply systems) and the regional planning that is required to build such infrastructure in a reasonably effective manner such that the inefficiencies resulting from uncontrolled urban sprawl are at least minimized, if not prevented. To the extent that there is popular interest in such issues, it comes from commuters caught in traffic jams, truckers who cannot move their cargoes, developers concerned about servicing capacities, and environmentalists of many different stripes, whose concerns in most cases are antithetical to the other groups. But such conflicts are not manifested in a metropolitan political arena. They sometimes play themselves out in local municipal politics, but more often in provincial politics.

Outward and explicit evidence of conflict in metropolitan policymaking is not often found in election platforms, political advertising, or in the other kinds of political activity that usually attract the attention of the media. Instead, the conflicts are often buried in municipal official plans, consultants' reports, and in the assumptions made by developers as they compete with each other in a complex marketplace. At various times and in various provinces, there have been requirements that some kind of metropolitan institution come up with a *regional plan*.

The making of such plans sometimes reveals the real stakes in metropolitan politics but, just as often, unfortunately, the plans simply paper over political conflicts so as to meet the technical requirements of the plan-making exercise. Worse still, regional plans sometimes get formally adopted, but are then ignored as circumstances change, new governments come to power, and items that were once political priorities (e.g., homelessness) seem to fall off the political agenda.

Because metropolitan issues are often seen as technical and specialized, they rarely provoke significant political mobilization. Perhaps because provincial governments are usually seen as having the capacity—and sometimes even the political will—to tackle metropolitan infrastructure problems, it is relatively rare for urban business interests to attempt to build community coalitions designed to act as substitutes for governments. Such coalitions are famously prevalent in American cities, precisely because governments appear so often to be unwilling or incapable of addressing metropolitan issues.

In recent years Toronto has perhaps become the Canadian exception to the rule. In the absence of any metropolitan governmental structure for this area, a business-led group called the Toronto City Summit Alliance has emerged to attempt to provide some leadership with respect to city-region issues. Like its counterparts in many American city-regions that also lack formal mechanisms for city-region governance, the Alliance brings together representatives from many of Toronto's various communities and attempts to arrive at some consensus as to how public and private resources can be used to confront the area's many problems and to enhance its global competitiveness (Toronto City Summit Alliance, 2003).

With respect to managing growth, it now appears to be the provincial government itself that is taking the initiative. A common argument advanced in Canada in general and in Toronto in particular in recent years is that, in this age of global city-regions, the ten provinces that comprise the Canadian federation have no long-term future as viable units of government. Instead, they will somehow give way to institutions of government that are based on the most important of the city-regions, Toronto being a prime example. But new initiatives from the government of Ontario to shape the nature of Toronto's long-term growth and to provide for greenbelts and other conventional mechanisms of regional planning suggest that the role of the provincial government with respect to urban affairs might well be increasing, rather than decreasing (Ontario, 2005). Indeed, it is likely that provincial governments, instead of simply fading away, will consolidate their roles as the real strategic authorities for Canada's city-regions.

Metropolitan Policy

In addition to the formal metropolitan structures described previously, almost every other conceivable mechanism for addressing metropolitan issues can be found in one Canadian city or another. For example, intermunicipal agreements are a mechanism through which the city of Toronto provides water for two of its northern suburban neighbors (White, 2003). Similarly in Toronto, a special-purpose authority provides fixed-rail transit for the larger Toronto metropolitan area, although there is continuing controversy as to exactly who should be subsidizing what. Because, as we have seen, regional planning has largely been taken over by the province, there are no longer any metropolitan institutions concerned with crucial government function.

In British Columbia, on the other hand, there has been much controversy about the extent to which regional land use plans formulated by the regional districts should have precedence over the local plans of their constituent municipalities. Regardless of the legal technicalities, regional districts have played a major role in managing growth, aided by the provincial Land Reserve Commission, which is charged with protecting agricultural and forest land from undue urban development (Bish and Clemens, 1999, p. 127). Metro Vancouver's Livable Region Strategic Plan appears to be playing a significant role in maintaining and enhancing the remarkable quality of life for which Vancouver is so well known. If winning international awards is a measure of success in such things, then Metro Vancouver has done very well (Greater Vancouver Regional District, 2005).

Unlike Vancouver, in Calgary almost all of the metropolitan area is governed by one municipality, the city of Calgary. The city's official objective is to maintain at least a thirty-year supply of developable land within its boundaries. Having this land supply allows for the long-term planning necessary to accommodate Calgary's high rate of growth and to facilitate the planning and budgeting of infrastructure (sewers, roads). Periodic annexations are proposed to maintain a long-term land supply. The city claims that its annexation policy is a key part of Calgary's "growth management strategy." It helps ensure that sprawl does not occur, that is, haphazard development, often at very low density. Calgary's planned suburban communities now achieve densities of six to eight dwelling units per acre. This is almost 40 percent denser than communities built in the 1970s and 1980s, and some twelve to sixteen times more land efficient than existing rural residential development outside Calgary's borders (City of Calgary, 2005). The city's strategy has been greatly aided by the absence of any significant nearby urban municipalities that have been in the path of its outward expansion.

In Winnipeg's metropolitan area there is similarly only one significant municipal government. The expectation of the creation of the "unicity" in 1971 was that the growing tax base of suburban areas could be used to support the deteriorating position of the central city. But, as suburban political strength grew over time within the unicity council, it became increasingly obvious that such an outcome was far from automatic. Tax levels might be equal, but decisions about infrastructure investment were always the result of a political process that depended largely on where the votes were. Parts of the central city of Winnipeg remain among the most troubled in any city in Canada. To the extent that they have been assisted by new infrastructure investment, the source of the funds has been the federal government rather than suburban Winnipeg taxpayers.

Although Winnipeg has long been a grateful recipient of federal bounty, other cities are now beginning to benefit from a deliberate attempt by the federal government to enhance its role in urban policymaking. Whether the federal government attempts to use its powerful fiscal resources and newly found interest in urban affairs to actually get directly involved in strategic decisions about urban development in particular city-regions is now one of the great unanswered questions about the future of Canadian federalism. Although the mayors of major Canadian cities— and especially the mayor of Toronto—will no doubt be thoroughly involved in developing the answers to this question, the fact remains that mayors of central cities in the four most populous Canadian metropolitan areas can never claim to speak on behalf of the whole area.

Urban municipalities in Canada are overwhelmingly dependent on the property tax for their revenues. This is one of the major reasons why they have recently been so aggressive in seeking new federal financial aid. In only a few cases do they have direct access to taxes collected by the provinces. For example, the city of Montreal receives from the Quebec government 1.5 cents per liter of the provincial gasoline tax collected within its boundaries. Metro Vancouver receives 11.5 cents per liter, and it is turned over to the Greater Vancouver Transportation Authority, which manages public transit and planning for major traffic arteries throughout the region. The federal and Ontario governments are phasing in the sharing of gasoline tax revenues as well, but such sharing applies to all municipalities with public transit systems. It is not targeted at the largest CMAs. There are no municipal income or sales taxes in Canada.

The term "metropolitan governance" now has virtually no political salience in Canada. As we have seen, in seven of Canada's ten largest CMAs the municipality of the central city is sufficiently significant in its territorial scope to itself act as the government of the metropolitan area. Metro Vancouver is clearly a form of metropolitan government, even if officially it is primarily a mechanism to facilitate intermunicipal cooperation. The Montreal Metropolitan Community is so functionally weak and so recent in its creation that it has not entered the public consciousness. Only in Toronto is there any serious concern about how metropolitan issues can be confronted. But, even here, it is becoming increasingly obvious that an institutional solution is in sight—the provincial government of Ontario is taking direct control itself.

Possible Future Shapes of Metropolitan Governance

Of the major CMAs being analyzed here, only Vancouver has a distinct metropolitan-level institution of government with any real functional capabilities (see Chapter 13). But even here, Metro Vancouver acts as a kind of umbrella institution for various special operating authorities for water, sewerage, and transportation. Metro Vancouver is obligated to adopt a regional planning document, but it must mobilize significant local municipal consent before its own plan is legally enforceable.

It is impossible to imagine, even in the Canadian context, that there will ever be a single municipality encompassing more than 70 percent of the population of the country's three most populous CMAs (Toronto, Montreal, and Vancouver). But what of the remaining seven? Is the large central city or single-tier model worthy of emulation? The first point is that, by international standards, these CMAs are relatively small, with populations ranging from 1 million in Calgary to 450,000 in London, Ontario. In all of these places, boundary extensions or outright municipal amalgamations have been extremely controversial and have been accomplished without the approval of the people who were forced to join the central city. There are many countries, certainly including the United States, where such a mechanism for extending municipal boundaries is simply out of the question.

But, if such changes were politically possible elsewhere, are they desirable? The Canadian experience is ambiguous at best. In Winnipeg, where a social-democratic provincial government legislated complete municipal amalgamation largely in order to equalize tax rates, suburban politicians quickly dominated the new council and were reluctant to invest in heavily deprived areas of the central city. Meanwhile, secession movements sprung up (one of which, in Headingley, was successful) and urban growth took place at a faster rate outside the city's boundaries than within them, causing policymakers to fret about the need for planning arrangements covering both the (relatively) populous city and the mainly rural municipalities that surround it. In Edmonton, annexation battles have been extremely controversial; the central city has not attained the complete consolidation it has been seeking for many years and there is still therefore a perceived need for a voluntary metropolitan coordinating mechanism.

Hamilton and London—both in Ontario—have large rural areas within the city boundaries, yet the boundaries are still not so perfect that they eliminate the need for difficult negotiations with their municipal neighbors, especially around transportation issues. In both places there are concerns about the representation of rural areas in city decision making, and in Hamilton there is a rural secessionist movement, the strength of which is difficult to gauge.

Calgary would appear to be the single-tier system that has worked most smoothly, but questions remain about how long it can continue its apparently ceaseless expansion across the prairie and toward the Rocky Mountains. Eventually, it will come up against significant towns in its hinterland and the traditional intermunicipal metropolitan conflicts will inevitably break out.

Governance arrangements for the CMAs of Vancouver and Calgary appear to have been sufficiently successful so as to offer potential Canadian models for other countries. The new metropolitan communities in Montreal and Quebec City might one day—after they have become better established—offer yet another model. But it is Toronto that appears to be the model of how not to govern a metropolitan area. In the early 1990s it looked as though the provincial government was moving toward establishing a form of metropolitan government for much of the Toronto CMA and beyond. But this plan was rejected by a provincial government of a different political stripe and with much strength in the outer suburbs. This government chose to ignore the larger issues of metropolitan governance and invest its political capital in sponsoring a forced merger of the component parts of the Municipality of Metropolitan Toronto into one City of Toronto. The result was a municipal behemoth having a population of more than 2 million, but with no capability to influence growth patterns in the suburbs beyond its borders. The next provincial government to face the problem has effectively chosen to itself become the metropolitan government. This model might well turn out to be functionally effective, especially in the eyes of those who favor greenbelts and limits on urban sprawl. But it will confound those who believe that city-regions should govern themselves and that Canada's provinces are outmoded relics of the days when Canada was a rural nation, rather than an urban one.

Except in Ottawa-Gatineau, Canadian provincial boundaries do not bisect metropolitan areas, and in Ottawa-Gatineau, the federal government's National Capital Commission pulls them together. This means that Canadian provinces are much better suited than American states are to act as overarching governments for entire city-regions. The absence of provincial constitutions that limit provincial involvement in otherwise local issues reinforces the capacity of Canadian provinces to be strong institutions for metropolitan planning and governance.

References

Bish, Robert L., and Eric G. Clemens. 1999. *Local Government in British Columbia.* 3d ed. Richmond, BC: Union of British Columbia Municipalities.

Boudreau, Julie-Anne. 2000. *Megacity Saga: Democracy and Citizenship in this Global Age.* Montreal: Black Rose Books.

Brownstone, Meyer, and T.J. Plunkett. 1983. *Metropolitan Winnipeg: Politics and Reform of Local Government.* Berkeley: University of California Press.

Calgary, City of. 2005. "Annexation: Frequently Asked Questions." Available at http://content.calgary.ca/CCA/City+Hall/Business+Units/Development+and+Building+Approvals+and+Land+Use+Planning+and+Policy/Land+Use+Planning/Current+Studies+and+Ongoing+Activities/Annexation+Information/Annexation+FAQ.htm (accessed October 5, 2005).

Communauté métropolitaine de Montréal. 2005. "Council." Available at www.cmm.qc.ca/index.php?id=332 (accessed October 5, 2005).

Frisken, Frances. 2008. *The Public Metropolis: The Political Dynamics of Urban Expansion in the Toronto Region, 1924–2003.* Toronto: Canadian Scholars' Press.

Fullerton, Douglas H. 1974. *The Capital of Canada: How Should It Be Governed.* Ottawa: Queen's Printer.

Germain, Annick, and Damaris Rose. 2000. *Montreal: Quest for a Metropolis.* New York: Wiley.

Greater Vancouver Regional District. 2005. "2005 Annual Report—Livable Region Strategic Plan." Available at www.metrovancouver.org/planning/development/strategy/Pages/LivableRegionStrategicPlan.aspx (accessed October 5, 2005).

Horak, Martin. 1998. "The Power of Local Identity: C4LD and the Anti-Amalgamation Mobilization in Toronto." Research Paper 195, Center for Urban and Community Studies, University of Toronto.

Manitoba, Province of. 2003. "A Partnership for the Future, Putting the Pieces Together in the Manitoba Capital Region." Report. October. Available at www.gov.mb.ca/ia/capreg/reports_docs/reports/recent/2003finalrpt/ (accessed October 5, 2005).

Masson, Jack, and Edd LeSage. 1994. *Alberta's Local Governments: Politics and Democracy.* Edmonton: University of Alberta Press.

Ontario, Province of. 2005. "Greenbelt Protection." Ministry of Municipal Affairs and Housing. Available at www.mah.gov.on.ca/Page187.aspx (accessed October 5, 2005).

Sancton, Andrew. 2000. *Merger Mania: The Assault on Local Government.* Montreal and Kingston: McGill-Queen's University Press.

————. 2001. "Canadian Cities and the New Regionalism." *Journal of Urban Affairs* 22: 543–55.

————. 2002. "Local Government in North America: Localism and Community Governance." In *Local Government at the Millennium,* ed. Janice Caulfield and Helge O. Larsen, 185–201. Opladen: Leske & Budrich.

————. 2008. *The Limits of Boundaries: Why City-regions Cannot Be Self-governing.* Montreal and Kingston: McGill-Queen's University Press.

Smith, Patrick J., and Kennedy Stewart. 1998. "Making Local Accountability Work in British Columbia." Report. Ministry of Municipal Affairs and Housing Government of British Columbia, June. Available at www.sfu.ca/igs/report/assets/intro.pdf (accessed October 5, 2005).

Statistics Canada. 2003. "Growth Concentrated in Four Large Urban Areas." July 23. Available at http://geodepot.statcan.ca/Diss/Highlights/Page9/Page9_e.cfm (accessed October 5, 2005).

————. 2006. "2006 Census release topics." Available at www12.statcan.ca/english/census06/release/index.cfm (accessed June 11, 2008).

Toronto City Summit Alliance. 2003. "Enough Talk: An Action Plan for the Toronto Region." April. Available at www.torontoalliance.ca/docs/TCSA_report.pdf (accessed October 5, 2005).

White, Richard. 2003. *Urban Infrastructure and Urban Growth in the Toronto Region, 1950s to the 1990s.* Toronto: Neptis Foundation.

13

Even Greater Vancouver

Metropolitan Morphing in Canada's Third-Largest City Region

Patrick J. Smith

The history of regional/metropolitan governance in British Columbia (BC) is both long and short. Short because its recent past dates only from the mid-1960s when BC established a province-wide system of Regional Districts—a template for mostly voluntary, largely indirectly elected, service delivery institutions to provide a range of intermunicipal/jurisdictional functions.[1] One of these—the Greater Vancouver Regional District (GVRD)—was established in 1967, just forty years ago (Oberlander and Smith, 1993). The history is long because despite this rather recent experience in metropolitan governing, Greater Vancouver, and its adjacent metropolitan neighbors, have a much longer history of city-regional cooperation (Oberlander and Smith, 1998; Smith, 1994). What has been distinctive about the Vancouver metropolitan region is that much of this experience of determining regional solutions to local challenges has been the result of local recognition of need and intermunicipal initiatives rather than provincial action. Where provincial action has occurred, it has often been described as "gentle imposition."[2] Examples of this interlocal cooperation include creation of a regional sewerage and drainage district before World War I, a new regional water board in 1926, health boards in the 1930s and 1940s, and the establishment of the Lower Mainland Regional Planning Board (LMRPB) in 1948 (Oberlander and Smith, 1993). In this local inclination to regional collective action, the Vancouver city-region stands out as something of a metropolitan exception in Canada.

The norm for provincial action on matters municipal and metropolitan in British Columbia has been, as noted above, one of "gentle imposition." It has been—with a few notable exceptions—the standard for the past several decades in British Columbia (Smith and Stewart, 2005, pp. 25–26). The exceptions have not been without impact. These include the province's temporary suspension of the GVRD's capacity to manage its watershed supply, the suspension of local school boards, and the setting aside of local bylaws that crossed with provincial interests, such as "right to farm" legislation. Most recently, in April 2007, the British Columbia provincial government introduced legislation to significantly redefine what "metropolitan Vancouver" is. For those unfamiliar, a few bits of nomenclature are useful to understand:

• *Greater Vancouver* (GVRD) is an amalgam of twenty-one municipalities and one unincorporated area—ranging in population from 1,000 to 600,000 plus, including the city of Vancouver. In August 2007, the Greater Vancouver Regional District (GVRD) voted to change its name to *Metro Vancouver*.[3]

• BC's *Lower Mainland* is currently made up of the GVRD and the Fraser Valley Regional District (FVRD)—the latter consisting of six municipalities and eight unincorporated areas.[4] This has essentially represented what Jane Jacobs (1984) calls the "city-region"—though as subsequent definitions of metropolitan Vancouver attest, this is changing. It runs for approximately ninety miles along the Fraser River from the city of Vancouver until it meets the Coastal Mountains at Hope and contains a little over half of BC's population.

• BC's *South Coast* has mostly been a term for local weather forecasters. It includes the Lower Mainland and part of the adjacent Regional District to the north—the Squamish-Lillooet Regional District's municipalities of Squamish to Pemberton, including the Resort Municipality of Whistler. Collectively, this South Coast has had no political status. That appears to be changing in one of the notable exceptions to gentle imposition by the province with the creation of a South Coast BC Transportation Authority (SCBCTA) to replace the GVRD's Greater Vancouver Transportation Authority (Translink). In its current form, the SCBCTA corresponds to Metro Vancouver; the legislation allows for incremental expansion to this larger South Coast region. If completed, it will represent the most significant recent redefinition of the Vancouver metropolitan region.

• The *Pacific Fraser Region*—so called in a book on an emerging Vancouver-centered region, *From Desolation to Hope*, the title of which reflects the geographic ends of this unofficial region. It includes, BC's Fraser Valley Regional District in the east, the GVRD, the lower half of the Squamish-Lillooet Regional District *and* the Sunshine Coast Regional District to Desolation Sound (Artibise and Seelig, 1991). The latter includes numerous ferry commuters to metro Vancouver for work. This also lacks any official status.

• The *Georgia Basin* does have official status—a creature of the province during the first half of the 1990s. This "provincial region" combines the South Coast/Pacific-Fraser definitions with the south- to mid-eastern parts of Vancouver Island, including BC's provincial capital, Victoria. This entity has had little ongoing impact on more traditional metropolitan Vancouver.[5] It does, however, form the Canadian portion of a bioregion called Georgia Basin-Puget Sound, running south to Washington's capital, Olympia, and includes nearly two-thirds of BC's total population. The Georgia Basin Initiative/Puget Sound entity provides for BC–Washington State cooperation on matters that are mostly coastal water environmental.

• *Mainstreet Cascadia* is the U.S. I5/BC Highway 99 megalopolis corridor from Eugene, Oregon, through Portland to Olympia/Tacoma/Seattle, Washington, and on to Metro Vancouver and Whistler/Pemberton (see, for example, Smith 2008a). It has a variety of iterations, some governmental and some nongovernmental (Smith, 2008a). The governmental forms include a Cascadia Mayor's Council and a Cascadia Metropolitan Forum, where the councils for the GVRD, Puget Sound Regional Council, and Portland Metro meet at least annually to discuss matters of mutual interest. A much bigger definition of Cascadia is included in the governmental Pacific NorthWest Economic Region (PNWER), which includes working groups and annual meetings of state and provincial officials (Smith, 2008b). The nongovernmental forms include entities such as Seattle's Discovery Institute, whose work includes Fast-Train proposals for a Mainstreet Cascadia high-speed rail link from Eugene, Oregon, to Whistler.

In sum, "metropolitan Vancouver" has been the GVRD—now renamed "Metro Vancouver." The metropolitan region now includes most of its eastern neighbors in the Fraser Valley Regional District—collectively, the "Lower Mainland" harkening back to 1948–66 when there was a Lower Mainland Regional Planning Board (LMRPB) and covering the same geographic area; and with provincial legislation for a new/larger metropolitan transportation authority for the metropolitan Vancouver region, it seems to be becoming "the South Coast."

BC's newest definition of its main metro region—covered by the South Coast British Columbia Transportation Authority Act (Bill 36)—was introduced in the provincial legislature on April 26, 2007. It came about due to a political dispute between the Greater Vancouver Transportation Authority (Translink, which was established in 1998) and the BC minister of transportation (a suburban Vancouver-area politician). The dispute, played out over a couple of years, also involved the Greater Vancouver Regional District, whose clear policy preference was for more transit-friendly development as the way to a more "sustainable region"; the province's priorities—contained within its Gateway Project—seem now to be more clearly highway and freeway focused.[6] In terms of debates about governance versus government, this Vancouver transportation case, discussed in more detail below, contains many of the elements needed to detect trend lines on who has and who will govern this expanding Vancouver metropolitan region in the twenty-first century.

The first comparative thing to say about Vancouver in terms of the theme of twenty-first-century metropolitan governance is that British Columbia's major metropolitan region is unlike Canada's other city-regions. Other Canadian metropolitan centers such as Halifax, Toronto, Ottawa, Hamilton, or Winnipeg, and even perhaps Montreal, have mirrored a more common recent experience toward an amalgamated or megacity model (see Smith and Stewart, 2006b). On this, despite being Canada's third largest city-region, metropolitan Vancouver to date remains the "odd one out" of this Canadian trend line toward bigger is better.

The other noteworthy point for comparative purposes is that the constitutional order Canadians and their local governments work under is a product of the 1860s—when three-quarters of the country lived in rural/agricultural settings and "local" really was local. Today, as noted in our most recent 2006 national census,

80 percent of Canadians live in urban centers of 10,000 people or more, and rural population has continued to decline. More important, in terms of this volume on twenty-first-century metropolitan governing, approximately two-thirds of Canada's population, or more than 20 million people, live in thirty census metropolitan areas (CMAs) (see Map 13.1) and over half in the four largest metropolitan regions. Despite this, a constitutional order leaving "municipal institutions" as "creatures of each province" remains at a time when major urban issues confronting Canadian city-regions require more full government horizontal or multilevel approaches to governance, with all levels of government working cooperatively on particular issues (Smith and Stewart, 2006a).

The Setting

British Columbia and the Vancouver Metropolitan Region

Municipalities and Regional Districts in British Columbia operated under three important principles up to 2000: (1) they had to follow rules set out by the province, (2) they were mandated by the provincial government to perform certain administrative activities, and (3) any actions undertaken by municipalities or regional districts had to be authorized by provincial legislation (Bish, 1990, p. 9). Although the newer Local Government Act (2000) and the subsequent Community Charter (2004) increased the power held by municipalities (though not yet regional districts), these three basic tenets of municipal government remain important, as municipal powers are legislatively, not constitutionally, entrenched in each province of Canada. This is a point noted by Sancton as well (see Chapter 12).

Other recent BC legislation, such as the Significant Projects Streamlining Act (2004), serves as a continuing reminder of a more traditional provincial-municipal relationship—the "imposition" side of the gentle leniency noted earlier. This act grants ministers the authority to override local governments on specific projects about which the province and any local government cannot reach agreement. Although the province has as yet not used these new powers, its use of related jurisdictional superiority, when it feels thwarted by local actions, continues as a reminder of the constitutional order.

British Columbia

British Columbia is Canada's third most populous province—with its 4.3 million residents representing approximately 13 percent of the total Canadian population. Eighty-three percent of the provincial population (or just under 3.5 million of BC's residents) resides in 157 municipalities covering just a little over 1 percent of the overall provincial territory. The province is also divided into twenty-eight Regional Districts. Over half (54.4 percent) live in the Vancouver-centered "Lower Mainland," which is described as the economic engine of the province (Bond, 1996; Davis and Hutton,

Map 13.1 Canada's Metropolitan City Regions

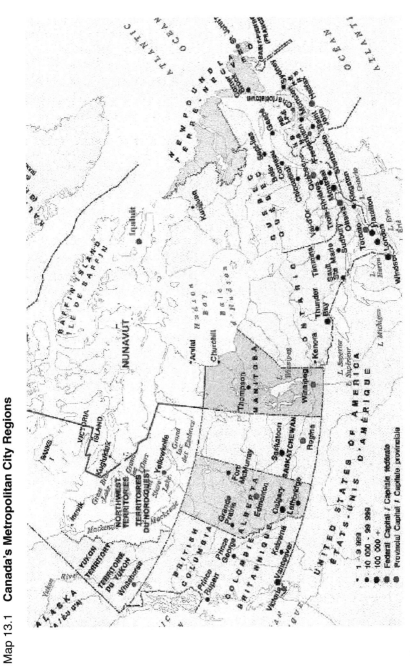

Source: www.canadainfolink.ca/canadiancities.htm (September 3, 2007).

1989). The Lower Mainland is composed of the two regional districts along the Fraser River Valley adjacent to Vancouver. This Lower Mainland (bounded on the south by the U.S. border, on the north by mountains that extend virtually without interruption to Alaska, and on the east—at Hope, approximately ninety miles away—by similar mountain ranges, with its western extremity, including the city of Vancouver, the gulf waters of the Pacific Ocean) represents the economic center of the province.[7]

Politically, the region elects just over half (50.7 percent) of the members of the legislative assembly of the province. In Jacobs's terms, this Vancouver-centered Lower Mainland forms the central components of one coherent metropolitan "city region" (Jacobs, 1984).

Metropolitan Vancouver

Greater Vancouver (however defined) is Canada's third largest metropolis. It is one of the fastest-growing urban areas in North America; it is Canada's fastest. The Greater Vancouver region has grown to over 2 million (2.127 million as of 2007)[8]; it is the core of British Columbia's Lower Mainland. The official Vancouver CMA now essentially corresponds to a redefined Greater Vancouver Regional District.[9]

Established in 1967, the GVRD is currently an amalgam of twenty-one municipalities and one unincorporated electoral area, covering 3,250 square kilometers (see Map 13.2).

The Greater Vancouver region contains a little over half (51.3 percent or 2.127 million people) of the provincial population and a majority (six of nine) of the largest (over 100,000 population) and eleven of nineteen (over 50,000 population) local authorities in the province.[10] For the May 2005 BC General Election, this Lower Mainland had forty-seven provincial legislative seats (59.5 percent) and the Vancouver metropolitan region had thirty-nine of the seventy-nine legislative seats, 49.4 percent of the provincial total.

One product of the rapid growth of the Vancouver metropolitan area is that the ethnic makeup of the region's population has become increasingly multicultural; half of the public school population of Vancouver has English as a second language, for example, and other municipalities are not far behind. This translates, increasingly, into politics around who will represent these communities. In metropolitan Vancouver, that has produced new representatives for the Indo-Canadian communities and the first provincial representative from the Chinese community (in the May 1996 BC General Election); others were elected in the subsequent 2001 and 2005 BC general elections. The 2006 Canadian general election also included an increased number of ethnic/visible minority community candidates.

In terms of where metropolitan Vancouver fits in BC, there has also been a growing dichotomy between the Lower Mainland and the rest of the province: much of the history of the BC economy has been resource extractive, with heavy reliance on logging, mining, and fishing, and a limited manufacturing component. The economic base of the Lower Mainland, however, is increasingly service-

243

Map 13.2   **Greater Vancouver/Metro Vancouver Regional District**

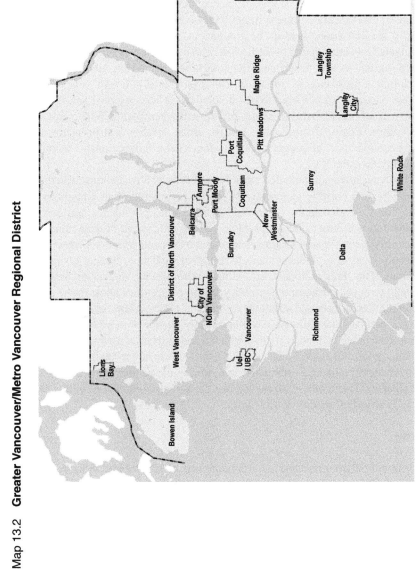

Source: Prepared for the author by the Greater Vancouver Regional District.

oriented, with a strong reliance on personal and corporate services, including tourism and province-wide distribution of goods and services.[11] Combined with its significant international population, a more interdependent—and internationally oriented—regional economy, and its Pacific port location (the port of Vancouver is the second busiest in North America, and the busiest in Canada),[12] metropolitan Vancouver has become an international city and has helped make the provincial economy more global.

The last factor of note that impacts on economic development decision making and intergovernmental relations in the Vancouver-centered region is the fact that most of the best arable land in the province is found in this metropolitan Lower Mainland. Only one-quarter of the land in British Columbia is suitable for any form of farming, and most of the prime agricultural land is in the Vancouver region, where development pressures are strongest. This has created potential policy conflicts and the necessity of devising regional solutions. These regional solutions even involve cross border issues, like air quality with neighboring Whatcom County, Washington. Regional solutions to resolve urban development problems as part of any economic development strategy—domestic or international—become immediately apparent.[13]

The increasing nature of such transregional activity also demonstrates the need to look beyond existing territorial boundaries for metropolitan Vancouver solutions. The Cascadia option—variously defined—has provided a new territorial and institutional dimension for problem solving on a range of economic, social, and environmental issues. Examples such as the Cascadia Mayors' Council, which meets on issues of regional concern from the regional environment to crime, and meetings of the three regional/metropolitan authorities for Vancouver, Seattle, and Portland to develop metropolitan policy learning capacities attest to the growing interest in Cascadia-based solutions to regional policy dilemmas. As such, these also represent an inclination to develop capacity outside of more traditional local-senior (provincial and federal) governmental and individual metropolitan settings. As Rosentraub and al-Habib noted in Chapter 3, the need for flexibility and adaptability in metropolitan governing may be a twenty-first-century imperative. Sancton (see Chapter12) and others would add that the British Columbia Regional District model is already Canada's most "elastic."

Themes

In terms of brief comments on *levels of management in metropolitan Vancouver*, the regional district model, in place since the mid-1960s, has offered a fairly flexible, elastic, and efficient form of management for the Greater Vancouver region. The combination of limited *mandated* functions and a long list of *voluntary* functions has left much to be decided locally/regionally; the approach has, until recently at least, worked fairly well for Vancouver.

On *developing and implementing metropolitan reforms*, two factors stand out in metropolitan Vancouver. First, the development of regional institutions has mostly been locally inspired. Second, the provincial governmental role—until recent interventions (such as the forced reorganization of Metro Vancouver's Translink governance)—largely has been what commentators have described as gentle imposition.

And on *coordinating actors at the metropolitan level*, what has been a generally successful model of consensus decision making, through the regional district's two-tiered indirect election form, has begun to show signs of reaching its "accountability outer limits." Tensions within and critiques from outside the GVRD/ Metro Vancouver suggest a need to rethink the current form of coordination and governance—or government—for metropolitan Vancouver. The central issue here, as noted by Norris, Phares, and Zimmerman (see Chapter 2) is whether pressure for change and restructuring will produce more elastic forms of governance or more centralized metropolitan governing. The U.S. trend, identified by Norris and colleagues (in Chapter 2) and Metro Vancouver's already highly flexible governance form would suggest the BC trend will not be toward more government.

Finally, on *linking central government policies and metropolitan initiatives*, an ability to adjust metropolitan boundaries to generally reflect population growth patterns on the ground has helped in metropolitan Vancouver and reflected provincial governmental support for regional capacity. As noted below, there has been a range of shifts in the Vancouver region's capacity to act independently. Sometimes these have reflected an increase in metropolitan ability; in other, more recent, instances, it has been reflected in a reassertion of senior (provincial) ascendancy.

This suggests a series of related questions.

- What are the comparative governance lessons for the twenty-first century across metropolitan city regional settings?
- What comparative lessons can be learned from the changes in metropolitan governance over the past five postwar decades of the twentieth century?
- How have these changes occurred?
- What forms and outcomes have resulted?
- What have we learned about attendant local/regional-senior (provincial and federal) intergovernmental relations?
- Where are our "best metropolitan practices?"
- Are there identifiable city-regional experiences and global threads on which to base a new metropolitan—and intergovernmental—reconceptualization for the twenty-first century?
- What has the metropolitan Vancouver experience contributed to this debate?

The notion that "one size does not fit all" increasingly has become part of the discourse on metropolitan reform. Comparative studies of the metropolitan experiences in Canada over the last half of the twentieth century offer the best possibility of identifying needed governance options for this still new century.

This chapter on Metropolitan Vancouver poses the above questions for this city-region. Here, one conclusion is that despite a history of some considerable success—and indeed a perception that to date this has offered one best-practice model—there are limits to the regional district system found in British Columbia. Metropolitan Vancouver may now be past those limits.

As one of those who has argued for much of the past quarter century that regional districts and regional planning in British Columbia are among the most success-ful policy initiatives and governance forms, this conclusion may seem somewhat heretical. And the critique of Greater Vancouver's current governance model does not extend to all of the other twenty-plus regional districts in the province; it is largely Vancouver specific.

The intention here is to make four simple points.

- Governance matters—and its adaptability (or what Rosentraub and al-Habib in Chapter 3 would call elasticity) in the Vancouver city-region has been one of its strengths.
- Regional districts in British Columbia—and earlier regional organizational forms in the province—have worked well over virtually all of the past almost ninety years, and in all but the largest metropolitan region, regional districts continue to provide an efficient, flexible, and effective form of regional governance.
- In Vancouver, BC's largest metropolitan region, an accountability crunch has come to challenge regional district efficiency arguments and claims. This might result in the conclusion that for metropolitan versus regional governance in British Columbia, "one size does not fit all."
- What happens next, in metropolitan Vancouver would at least appear to require legislative reform toward a new, more politically accountable Metro Vancouver Authority (MVA). That has implications for how senior, especially provincial, governments and metropolitan initiatives might be linked. That future is also affected by new public management perspectives as well as new regional-ism experiences elsewhere. The push for more accountability in regional governance—as noted by Norris, Phares, and Zimmerman (Chapter 2)—is not uniform, however. Among the political considerations noted in Chapter 2, it might be mentioned that Canadian provinces have been much more prepared to intervene in such matters than their U.S. state counterparts.

Retrospective

As noted above, the history of regional planning in metropolitan Vancouver is both long (1) and short (2).

(1) There have been a variety of regional authorities created, dating from nearly the beginning of the twentieth century. Initially, these represented ad hoc (and often single-purpose) responses to a number of local/regional service dilemmas. Almost without exception, the early regionalization experiences were premised on locally

perceived necessity. These "regional" beginnings date from 1911, just twenty-five years after Vancouver's founding, when the city of Vancouver with its Point Grey, South Vancouver, and Burnaby municipal neighbors formed the Burrard Peninsula Joint Sewerage Committee. The committee funded a study that recommended "an ongoing co-operative response," and by 1914 had convinced the provincial government to pass legislation to create a Joint Sewerage and Drainage Board. Subsequent local action resulted in the creation of a regional Water District in 1926. This was followed by the establishment of four area health/hospital boards between 1936 and 1948 (Oberlander and Smith, 1993).

(2) Modern regional structures are best dated to post–World War II: in 1948—a year of significant flooding in the Vancouver-centered Lower Mainland/Fraser River Valley—amendments to the Municipal Act were passed allowing contiguous local authorities in a metropolitan region to develop a joint planning capacity. As a result, the Lower Mainland Regional Planning Board was formed the following year. It covered the whole physical region—from Vancouver, up the Fraser Valley to the mountains and Hope. In some ways this was recognition, and extension, of a voluntary planning association (of Vancouver, Burnaby, Port Moody, Coquitlam, and North and West Vancouver) created in 1937.[14]

Despite these various local initiatives, provincial action on regional government was slow. Tennant and Zirnhelt (1973) have persuasively argued that the proliferation and success of these early joint boards and authorities did lead the way to provincial consideration of more broadly based regional solutions to urban development problems, particularly with regard to their application in metropolitan Vancouver. They called the process of reform "gentle imposition by the province."

The thinking of W.A.C. Bennett's Social Credit provincial government (going from 1952 until 1972) was obviously affected by the early experience, and publicity, of metropolitan government reform in Toronto in 1954. As a result, community and regional planning provisions were added to the Municipal Act in 1957, which empowered the minister to direct adjacent municipalities in "metropolitan areas" to establish a joint committee "to study and report on such matters of an inter-municipal nature as shall be set out by the Minister." The already established LMRPB was able to undertake such a process, leading to an official regional plan for the whole of BC's Lower Mainland by the mid-1960s. *Chance and Challenge*—the "official regional plan"—was approved in August 1966. But as the LMRPB was moving toward this success, the provincial government, perhaps feeling threatened by a jurisdiction representing half the province's population—and by some local ambivalence (a consideration noted by Norris, Phares, and Zimmerman in Chapter 2)—determined that administrative and political diffusion was a more appropriate response (Oberlander and Smith, 1993).

Accordingly, a regional district system for the entire province was created between 1965 and 1967. As stated by then Municipal Affairs Minister Dan Campbell, the BC government's intention was clear: "regional districts are not conceived of as a fourth level of government, but as a functional rather than a political amalgamation."

As a result, the Lower Mainland was divided into four separate regions. Within the Greater Vancouver Regional District (originally incorporated as the Regional District of Fraser Burrard on June 29, 1967), as elsewhere in the system, functions were of two types.

1. To carry out *mandated functions* from the province to the new regional districts. These mandated functions included general planning for the region as well as responsibility for governing of the hospital district. In Greater Vancouver, mandated functions also included the Water Board and Sewage and Drainage District responsibilities.
2. *Voluntary functions* were the second category of responsibilities for the new districts. These voluntary functions were established by Letters Patent (essentially, provincial "Cabinet Orders"). They included seventy-eight functions from A to W (ambulance and animal control to unsightly premises and weed control), and each district could choose the function it was to perform; then individual municipalities could "sign on."[15]

In the 1970s, the new Greater Vancouver Regional District successfully completed a Livable Region Plan. It set out growth planning ideas such as regional town centers and preservation of agricultural and green space, which guided regional development into the 1980s. This continued despite the loss of formal planning authority in 1983—through a direct provincial legislative intervention removing regional planning authority from regional districts due to a land use dispute between the GVRD and the province (Oberlander and Smith, 1993; Smith and Oberlander, 1998). But by the 1990s, significant growth pressures confronted the region.

In metropolitan Vancouver and British Columbia, the response to regional growth management problems and issues of metropolitan democracy was to seek to build on the successes of prior regional agreements and form. In 1995, under a new left/New Democratic Party (NDP) administration, new provincial planning legislation—a Growth Strategies Act—was passed for British Columbia. This legislation required municipalities to plan regionally and allowed the province to establish mediative forms when local-regional agreement was not forthcoming. This new provincial legislation was the result of an extensive provincial-municipal consultative process that included consideration of other regional planning and governance models comparatively.

In 1995, the Greater Vancouver Regional District (with recently enlarged boundaries equivalent to the Vancouver CMA) arrived at the end point of a five-year-long local-regional process of consultation and discussion to establish a new Livable Region Strategic Plan (LRSP). This "Creating Our Future" process produced broad agreement, one initial major suburban dissent (Richmond), and the possibility of the first use of the province's "mediation to closure" procedures under the Growth Strategies Act. In early 1996, local-regional resolution of this dissent—and minor ones with Surrey and Langley Township—was arrived at without such provincial mediation. Greater Vancouver's Livable Region Strategic Plan was approved by the provincial government in the spring of 1996. Translating that into practice involved a reciprocal commitment by each municipality—through what are called "regional context statements"—to have local official community plans conform to the overall regional plan. The process was restated on a five-year basis by a subsequent Sustainable Region Initiative (SRI) to update the regional plan.

Both the new BC provincial planning legislation and metro Vancouver's planning process/resolution spoke directly to arguments about metropolitan governance, local/regional-provincial intergovernmental relations and growth management reform, and about the extent of "senior governmental interest or capacity" to address major urban issues, and suggestions that a "consensual model," as exemplified by metro Vancouver, was inherently weak and suffered from a lack of mandate, lack of representation, and an inability to achieve consensus on matters of specific policy. The Greater Vancouver and British Columbia experience of the early/mid-1990s suggested an alternative to metropolitan restructuring that was being pursued in other jurisdictions such as Ontario, Metropolitan Toronto Megacity and the Greater Toronto Area, Ottawa-Carleton in Nova Scotia with a new metropolitan Halifax, and elsewhere. The British Columbia experience also supported a notion of metropolitan governance as a clear alternative to metropolitan government, and to ideas such as bigger is better—a point reiterated by Sancton in Chapter 12.[16]

That was then, and this is now. We now move to an exploration of the more recent experience of British Columbia and metropolitan Vancouver and comments on the relationship between end of/turn-of-century restructuring forms such as the creation of a Greater Vancouver Transportation Authority (Translink) and its 2007–8 re-creation as SCBCTA, the creation of new provincial legislation, the Community Charter, and the arguments put forward in rethinking metropolitan government and governance for Greater Vancouver in the early twenty-first century.

Contemporary Greater Vancouver: Challenges Not Yet Met

Simply put, the first contention here is that much of the success of regional planning and governing in British Columbia has been tied to reform of local governing structures: whether in the 1940s with the provision that adjacent municipalities might begin to plan together establishing regional planning, through establishment of a first Municipal Act—and provisions for official regional plans in the 1950s—or the creation of regional districts themselves in the 1960s. The first three decades of regional planning in BC were closely tied to structural-governance reforms.

And it worked! It worked so well that regional planning either commenced or continued in the 1960s and 1970s, and perhaps more important, often continued (certainly in Greater Vancouver), albeit under a different guise, even when legally abolished in a provincial pique in the 1980s. It did so largely because of a number of governance factors. As Richard and Susan Tindal (2000, pp. 123–24) have noted, "municipal government reform in British Columbia . . . resulted in one of the most imaginative and flexible governing arrangements found anywhere in Canada. The regional structure allow[ed] existing municipalities to continue, with whatever communities of interest they represent[ed], provide[d] for the delivery of a variety of services by the regional authority, and avoid[ed] the bureaucratic build-up and duplication often associated with full-blown two-tier regional governments."

Former BC Municipal Affairs minister Dan Campbell, the BC spokesperson on regional districts in the 1960s, 1970s, and 1980s, argued consistently that regional districts were *not* regional governments, preferring a regional service delivery definition. Not all agreed. Donald Higgins, following the "if it walks and quacks like a duck test," concluded that regional districts had indeed become regional governments (Higgins, 1977, 1986). Bob Bish came to the same conclusion more recently but noted that the regional system in BC has allowed "the division of responsibility . . . 'who does what.' . . between municipalities and the regional government (to be) made by the municipalities themselves" (Bish, 2000, pp. 73–74). That seems closer to a range of the U.S. cases discussed elsewhere in this volume.

That aspect, both local recognition of the value of, and often local initiation of, particular regional solutions and resultant local buy-in produced a positive regional experience of success often following success. It is a view largely shared by Andrew Sancton, even in the context of major urban regions:

> Can a large city-region contain a number of municipalities, establish a regional-local government institution and avoid the pitfalls of two-tier municipal government? This is the biggest structural question facing urban government today. . . . All . . . Canadian city-regions require an institution similar to the GVRD (Greater Vancouver Regional District): one that is comprehensive in territory and flexible in function. Such institutions do not require large bureaucracies. In fact, they will probably work best if they have no operational responsibilities at all. Their aim should be to provide a forum where regional issues can be discussed, to act as a catalyst for the creation of inter-municipal agreements and special purpose bodies and to enact planning documents with sufficient legal status to coerce municipalities into adhering to broad strategic objectives for the use of land. (Sancton, 1995, pp. 98, 100)

What Next?

The questioning here is not about where we have been—which has been largely a positive policy, governance, and intergovernmental experience—but where we are going, a much less certain future as BC's largest regional structures take on more and more responsibilities. It is not a rejection of the success represented by the past fifty years of regional planning and governance in Metro Vancouver and British Columbia more generally. Rather, it is a query about whether that achievement of the past half-century can endure into the twenty-first millennium.

Current assessment is that increasingly citizens in BC's largest city-region, Greater Vancouver, have come to resemble Butch Cassidy and the Sundance Kid looking back at their pursuers and asking "who are those guys?" Citizens in metro Vancouver increasingly are wondering who is responsible for making more and more important and expensive decisions—on transportation, infrastructure, maybe policing and beyond.

The Metro Vancouver Translink Case

Perhaps this accountability dilemma is illustrated nowhere more obviously than in the case of Greater Vancouver's Transportation Authority—Translink. In June 1998, the second leftist NDP (Clark) government initiated the Greater Vancouver Transportation Authority. Under this act responsibility for transportation, transit, and related services in metropolitan Vancouver was passed from the provincially appointed British Columbia Transit to the Greater Vancouver Transportation Authority (commonly known as "Translink"). The act mandated that Translink and the GVRD "work together to establish a mutually agreeable strategic transportation plan and growth management strategy." But while the provincial act legally established Translink as a separate entity from the GVRD, the two organizations were joined in many formal and, most important, informal ways. For example, members of the GVRD held twelve of the fifteen Translink board positions.[17]

The functional mandate of the initial Translink was to "plan and finance a regional transportation system that moves people and goods efficiently and supports the regional growth strategy, air quality objectives and economic development of the Greater Vancouver Regional District." Provincial funding for Translink's operations was approximately $545 million in 2000 and was to increase to over $1 billion by 2009. Translink was also given the ability to increase revenues through several other "taxation" instruments—though in many instances, such as a vehicle levy, it needed provincial assistance to collect much of this revenue. The initial Translink board's institutional image was one of an almost at-arms-length provider of management for the several subsidiary companies and programs it established under its jurisdiction. It described its role or management style as steering not rowing (Fershau, 2003, p. 77).

In creating GVTA/Translink, the province recognized that the needs of the Vancouver metropolitan region were different from those of all other regions in the province. BC Transit is a purely provincial entity under the supervision of the appropriate minister; Translink could be described as an addition to the family of local/regional governing bodies in metropolitan Vancouver because its board was controlled by indirectly elected GVRD members. With that change in structure came a corresponding change in function—in that the *Greater Vancouver Transportation Authority Act* moved responsibility for the Vancouver area's transport into the hands of locally elected regional officials. Financially, the capacity to levy a toll and tax—even if still needing provincial assistance on its collection in many instances—marked a change in the de facto financial power of those holding seats on the GVRD/GVTA as well.

In terms of efficiency and accountability, moving control over transit to a regional body continued the trend of decentralization begun in BC in 1997; this might be described as an attempt to unleash the innovational power of local officials and make transit more efficient. However, in terms of accountability this initial Translink authority created a new problem; it more fully empowered indirectly elected officials who were now two steps removed from their constituents. While the GVRD was primarily a forum where locally elected mayors and councilors can discuss and make voluntary agreements on issues such as regional growth, there was little need for them to be directly elected. But now that these same officials were vested with the power to make decisions over service provision and taxation with little provincial supervision, a stronger argument could be made for the need for more accountability such as through direct elections.

This was demonstrated late in 2000 when Translink attempted to use one of its new revenue-generating instruments to directly levy a vehicle tax. The proposed levy generated widespread public opposition from many different sectors and was ultimately abandoned when the province of British Columbia refused to collect the new tax—largely due to the politics around the issue. This underscored the fact that while GVRD/Translink now had the jurisdictional capacity to impose such charges, they often lacked the administrative and political capacity to collect such taxes. More important, the public outcry against the vehicle levy highlighted the ongoing regional accountability gap. This accountability gap became a ravine during the summer 2002 Vancouver bus strike, which lasted over several hot summer months, during which no one could find any accountable politician at Translink, which had turned management of its buses over to a subsidiary, Coast Mountain Bus Company Ltd. The absence of a clear accountability to match increased efficiency was very apparent.

This Vancouver metropolitan governance dilemma has had several impacts on linking provincial governmental policies and metropolitan initiatives. Perhaps two recent examples illustrate this best: (1) the senior (provincial and federal) governmental pressure to ensure regional building of a rapid transit airport-to-downtown Vancouver link—the Richmond–Airport–Vancouver (RAV—or Canada) line, as part of senior (federal and provincial) efforts for the 2010 Winter Olympics in Vancouver; and (2) the clash between the values of local initiatives/home rule included in the new BC Community Charter Act and subsequent provincial legislation, reasserting its jurisdictional ascendancy with the Special Projects Streamlining Act and legislative reform efforts to rein in the original Translink, the regional transportation authority, creating a New Public Management-South Coast BC Transportation Authority replacement body in 2008.

On the RAV line decision making, after considerable local lobbying to get transportation planning authority from the province, the GVRD finally achieved this goal in mid-1998. Coupled with the development of the land use-based LRSP in 1996 and now its SRI in 2002–8, and earlier efforts, such as the Long-Range Transportation Plan for Greater Vancouver (Transport 2021—a joint GVRD/BC project), which reported in September 1993, the intention was that metropolitan

Vancouver would be able to plan for both metropolitan land use and transportation aspects as the region saw fit.

The early twenty-first-century versions of a regional plan (the LRSP/SRI) were clearly set out—for both land use and transportation. It did not include a RAV link in the early stages—certainly not before one additional cross-regional link—and a subsequent spur to the northeast was completed. Then came the decision—promoted particularly by the provincial and federal governments—to award Vancouver the 2010 Winter Olympics bid. Both senior governments came offering additional funds for the RAV line, with provincial support tied to a P-3 (public-private partnership) option, unlike the two prior lines' public enterprise aspect. The funding offered by the senior governments was substantial, and it was tied to RAV going ahead of regionally defined rapid transit needs.

As a case study in multilevel governance, the RAV decision tells much about the relative lack of change in BC vis-à-vis other Canadian provinces. The new rapid transit "skytrain" RAV line addition was initially costed out at $1.5 billion. The federal government came to the table with between $300 million and $450 million, the province with $370 million, an anticipated private builder/operator and the region picking up the rest. In spite of the clear desire of both levels of senior jurisdiction to have the RAV line built in time for the 2010 Winter Olympics in Vancouver, the regional authorities (GVRD and Translink) had serious reservations about the proposal. Their concerns were threefold:

- the public-private partnership (or P-3) requirement imposed by the provincial government;
- the question of anticipated cost overruns—particularly for a planned tunneled section in the city of Vancouver—and the fact that these would have to be covered by metropolitan taxpayers. In the end, the project used a cheaper "cut and cover" method—like Boston's Big Dig—with significant attendant disruption and economic hardship to local businesses;
- the fact that the RAV line itself was not the top transit priority as identified by more than a decade of discussion within the Greater Vancouver region.

That combination of local/regional concerns led to a Translink decision (seven to five) on May 7, 2004, "not to precede work on the RAV line due to projected cost overruns." Provincial disappointment in the metropolitan authorities' decision led the premier to announce on June 15, 2004, that British Columbians collectively would cover any cost overruns as well as contribute $170 million to the RAV-delayed Northeast Skytrain connector. On June 18, 2004, Translink again defeated the RAV proposal with a six to six vote.

The province's transportation minister, Kevin Falcon, MLA for Surrey (Greater Vancouver's "second city," south of the Fraser River) announced that the provincial dollars were lost for RAV/Transit and would instead be used to twin suburban por-tions of the Trans Canada Highway and twin (i.e., build a parallel bridge) at the

Port Mann Bridge crossing of the Fraser River into the older inner suburbs and the city of Vancouver. This route was an area of considerable private auto congestion for the minister of transportation's constituents and those in government-friendly municipalities beyond. Such a proposal ran completely counter to more than a decade of land use and transportation planning by the region. The combination of senior (federal and provincial) governmental funding and overt political pressure resulted in an unprecedented third vote on the same issue. The result was that the senior governmental priorities trumped regional policy decisions—with a vote of eight to four. RAV is being built; it will be completed ahead of the 2010 Olympics, but regional priorities were substantially altered.

Continuing provincial pique over the RAV line process led the minister of transportation to order a "thorough governance review" of GVTA/Translink in 2007. Its March 2007 Report contained much of what regional government advocates had feared: the replacement of its indirectly elected, locally controlled board with a "stakeholders" board of professionals, under a Translink chief executive officer (CEO), both appointed through a "provincial" process largely excluding local control. A separate Mayors' Council was to be given some long-term planning and funding (something on the order of a ten-year time horizon) capacity, and a Translink Commissioner was to be appointed to oversee fare setting. In the 1980s, transit planning in the Vancouver region was sometimes called "the three-headed monster." The new structure legislated in November 2007 and running as of January 1, 2008, is "six-headed," including:

- Translink Board of Directors (professionals via a stakeholders' selection process—three from the downtown Vancouver business community),
- chief executive officer,
- commissioner,
- Mayors' Council,
- GVRD, and
- the province

There is little in the Greater Vancouver region's past to suggest that this setup will involve a happy marriage. It has been referred to as an assault on local democracy in the Vancouver city-region. Passed and approved by the BC Legislature in November 2007, the new Translink Board structure began to work as of January 1, 2008. They were selected by an appointed Board of Selectors made up of one provincial appointee, one collective mayors' selection, and three from the Institute of Chartered Accountants, the Vancouver Board of Trade, and the Gateway Council of BC—all three latter representing the downtown Vancouver business community. Between January and summer 2008, the board gave themselves an unannounced sixfold pay increase over the prior board (in February 2008), a new chief executive officer was appointed, a commissioner was confirmed, a real-estate arm (worth about $2 billion) was established, and the new Translink (currently serving Metro

Vancouver and some edge communities in the FVRD) has anticipated a significant short-term deficit on announced transit and transportation projects.[18]

The BC Community Charter vs. Special Projects Legislation

This tension between province and region is also highlighted in the clash between the relatively new Community Charter legislation and the Special Projects Streamlining Act. Here the juxtaposition of competing values is just as stark: the Community Charter Act (Bill 14) commenced January 1, 2004. It set out its purpose in language recognizable to all advocates of modest home rule; for Canadian urbanists, BC's Community Charter legislation also includes language that students of Section 92–8 of the Constitution Act, Canada, recognize as maintaining provincial juris-dictional oversight potential. American local governance observers might simply recognize this as Dillon's Rule Lite—or "Home Rule Extra Lite." This is clearest in the purposes of the new Community Charter.

Purposes of Act

Sec. 3. The purposes of this Act are to provide municipalities and their councils with:

a. a legal framework for the powers, duties, and functions that are necessary to fulfill their purposes;
b. the authority and discretion to address existing and future community needs; and
c. the flexibility to determine the public interest of their communities and to respond to the different needs and changing circumstances of their communities.

The principles of the act sound closer to local autonomy/home rule advocates' views. They reflect a stated desire to clarify both the municipal and the provincial components of the provincial-municipal relationship in British Columbia and, potentially, to add to local autonomy.

Under BC's Community Charter, certain key principles of municipal gover-nance are recognized: municipalities are recognized as an order of government; democratically elected, autonomous, responsible, and accountable by the will of the residents. The province commits to ensuring that municipalities have adequate powers and discretion, authority, and the ability to draw on adequate financial and other resources. The principles of municipal-provincial relations include respect for each other's jurisdiction, cooperation, and a commitment to harmonize provincial and municipal policies and programs. To ensure this, the province undertakes not to download responsibilities without provisions for resources to meet any new responsibilities, to consult on any legislative changes affecting municipalities. Any conflicts should be resolved by consultation, negotiation, facilitation, and other forms of dispute resolution (Leonard, 2003).

The legislative language hides as much as it illuminates, however. For example, despite talk of limiting interference by the senior provincial authority, should local governments under BC's Community Charter decide to raise local taxes—such as on businesses—rather than opt for more provincially preferred user fees and the like, the province reserves the right to impose limits on property tax rates— in direct contradiction of the Community Charter's empowering local autonomy intent. And under a redefined provincial-municipal relationship, the Community Charter reminds local governments that apart from acknowledging and respecting each other's jurisdiction, the legislative intent is to "work towards harmoniza- tion of provincial and municipal enactments, policies and programs." This may work in many instances, but not where a local government wishes to take a rather divergent policy tack. Here, the intergovernmental game becomes more perilous for local authorities.

The 1980s provincial dismissal of school boards in BC and the "over a weekend" order-in-council elimination of the GVRD's authority over the region's watershed when it tried to block provincial implementation of a natural gas pipeline through that regional watershed to Vancouver Island serve as historical reminders of senior provincial powers. The more recent provincial overturning of a local governmental (a Vancouver suburb of Delta) bylaw to limit the negative air quality impacts of large greenhouses by requiring them to utilize natural gas or propane versus wood waste, and the use of similar provincial powers (right-to-farm legislation) to pre- vent local coastal municipalities from using their bylaw powers to limit possible negative environmental impacts from fish farms and the provincial return of fines to fish-farm operators continue to serve as current reminders that constitutional authority does matter when significant policy differences arise between local and provincial players.

Perhaps most stunningly, given the principles enshrined in BC's Community Charter, was BC's Bill 75, the Significant Projects Streamlining Act, introduced and passed in just three weeks in November 2003; it allows the provincial government to override any local governmental opposition on any project deemed of significant provincial interest. Over half of the Union of BC Municipalities (UBCM) members passed motions condemning Bill 75. Then-minister of state for deregulation Kevin Falcon noted that the act was to "cut red tape," "remove unnecessary and costly delays," and "create new economic activities." Run out of the Premier's Office, the Special Projects initiative produced an official, highly critical UBCM response:

> The UBCM Executive is shocked by the degree of intrusion of this legislation into local affairs. It allows *any* Minister . . . to replace *any* local government bylaw, plan, regulation, policy, etc. to facilitate the approval or development of a "provincially significant project." Cabinet can make that determination without *any prior* notice to the local government or the community. The Com- munity Charter . . . promised us recognition as an independent, accountable

and responsible order of government. . . . The Community Charter touted public accountability and openness but Bill 75 replaces local, publicly developed plans (including those developed through public hearing processes) with fiats from the provincial Minister. We recognize there is a need to balance local and provincial interests. . . . This is just not the way to achieve it. The Executive is calling on the provincial government to remove local government from Bill 75.[19]

Similar school board experience in several of Ontario's largest cities in the latter period of the Harris/Eaves Tory rule of the 1990s mirrors these provincial-municipal lessons. If the test is in puddings, it would appear necessary to go back to basic recipe ingredients on local empowerment and accountability and start again in British Columbia. Provincial responses in the early twenty-first century seem as much push as pull.

Conclusions: Governance vs. Government in Metro Vancouver

BC's Regional District system has worked admirably for the past fifty years; it may well continue to provide a highly successful and flexible model of decision making for another half century in most regional districts in BC. Even in the capital region of Victoria, if Bish is correct, this may remain true for the province of Nova Scotia but not for the Halifax Region which is equivalent in size to Victoria's capital region. And in the 1990s Ontario—in Toronto, Ottawa, Carleton, Hamilton, Wentworth, Sudbury, and beyond—came to the same conclusion.

In metropolitan Vancouver, the crunch has come. Metro Vancouver and related regional authorities such as Translink increasingly lack the mandate to make regional decisions without an appropriate political accountability base. For twenty-six, and probably twenty-seven, of BC's regional districts, past is prologue. For Greater Vancouver, it is probably simply past. That leaves the question, "what next?" If not now, then very shortly, the Province of British Columbia and Metro Vancouver (and the GVTA and its successor the SCBCTA) will be forced to recognize that accountability concerns may overwhelm the considerable regional successes of the past century in BC's largest metropolitan district. It will be reactions to new regional charges/taxes for regional services that will tip the balance, or the lack of a regional policing capacity in the face of one of North America's major mass murders (sixty missing women in Greater Vancouver, with twenty-six confirmed murders). The tipping point may come with GVTA/Translink improvements. It may result from higher charges for the more traditional range of services such as water or parks or it might be precipitated by financial pressures toward regional policing (and other public safety) services. With a more neoliberal provincial government agenda, it could also be pushed by a substantial downloading of social service responsibilities as occurred in the 1990s in Ontario.[20] Whatever the back-breaking straw, the regional camel in metropolitan Vancouver will increasingly be under structural pressure and citizen scrutiny over its governance.

That should not seem surprising, whether in restructuring for new regionalism or more traditional forms of regional government. There is a central debate about accountability in public governance. On one side, the argument is made that accountability is half of an equation—the other side being efficiency. Governance theorists such as Peter Self have contended that the relationship between accountability and efficiency is zero sum; as you add to one, you subtract equally from the other. Self has further asserted that the relationship between accountability and efficiency is the central dilemma in public administration. It is also a dilemma that has grown considerably more complex with time. Certainly, all governments in the late 1990s and now the 2000s are under increased pressure on the efficiency side. For regional districts in large urban settings like metropolitan Vancouver, however, there is now also need for more accountability (Self, 1977).

The most obvious "what next" in terms of improving accountability for Greater Vancouver—the only regional district over 500,000 in population and the only region with multiple municipal units over 100,000—is democratic electoral and structural reforms. That might imply a shift to a new, directly elected Metropolitan Vancouver Authority. This has already been suggested. In the spring of 1998, a report on *Making Local Accountability Work in British Columbia* recommended "the creation of a Greater Vancouver Authority, with a directly elected Greater Vancouver Assembly and a Regional Mayor elected across the whole region." The report noted that "with . . . eleven municipal units of 50,000 and more than half of these at or over 100,000 population size, a shift to direct elections would appreciably enhance local-regional accountability."

Greater London, after Margaret Thatcher's *Streamlining the Cities* annihilation of the Greater London Council and six other Metropolitan County Councils MCCs, has had forms of regional authority reestablished—like the Greater London Authority. Part of the rationale is to provide a broader regional structure to compete more effectively internationally ("Who Represents 'London'?" vs. "Who Does What?"). For Metro Vancouver, the international dimensions of regional governance reform would be a significant collateral benefit. Britain's recent Blair/Labor government reforms creating a Greater London Authority suggest both regional *and* international benefits.[21]

Democratic reforms to Greater Vancouver could include other electoral notions as well. These might include broader electoral system changes including, if direct elections were introduced, some form of proportional representation; it might also include electoral expense/spending limit reforms; and it would involve a clearer disentangling of who does what. Bill 31, the Local Government Statutes Amendment Act (1998), recognized local government as an independent, responsible, and accountable order of government. Subsequent unilateral action by the province on cuts to municipal grants generally and on required skytrain technology in Greater Vancouver rather suggested a continued senior governmental paternalism versus legislative efforts to make local governments both more independent *and* accountable in BC. The late 1990s to early 2000s policy failures of NDP municipal affairs ministers on accountability reforms suggest more pessimism than optimism on this front. As (then) deputy premier Joy MacPhail said—to the agreement of NDP leadership colleagues in early 2000—on municipal accountability reform "we chickened out." The new Liberal administration has done no better. On October 2, 2004, Translink directors criticized the "province's unilateral approach to regional transportation planning." Their concerns reflected the stance of transportation minister Kevin Falcon to consult (the region), but then push ahead with the (highway/bridge twinning) project. This Gateway project to "freeway" Vancouver's suburbs into central Vancouver continues today. Certainly, equally important to international benefits of regional governance reform would be the accountability benefits of renewed Greater Vancouver governance.

Finally, it is arguable that with a clearer link to its regional citizenry, whatever form the regional restructuring of governing takes, metropolitan Vancouver might be better able to resist senior governmental pressures and blandishments—at least where these threats and inducements run counter to policies determined by, and for, the region itself. In its past, one of the great successes of local-regional interests and institutions in the Vancouver region has been the ability to anticipate and recognize the need for change. Failure to do so now and in its short- to intermediate-term future may threaten the longer-term prospects for another fifty years of regional planning and governance success in Metropolitan Vancouver.

Notes

1. The main exception for BC's Regional Districts was planning—a mandatory function between 1965 and 1983. On BC's Regional Districts and Local Governing, see Bish and Clemens (2007); see also Smith (1986, 1995, 1996, 1998).

2. Paul Tennant and David Zirnhelt (1973) first coined this phrase.

3. This name change required formal provincial government approval, in the fall of 2007 (Skelton, 2007, pp. B1, B4).

4. For more on the Fraser Valley portion of "metropolitan Vancouver," see "In Our Region"; available at www.fvrd.bc.ca/Pages/default.aspx/.

5. On the Georgia Basin, see www.gov.bc.ca/env or www.pyr.ec.gc.ca/GeorgiaBasin; and on the Puget Sound-Georgia Basin Environmental Initiative, see www.psat.wa.gov/shared/shared.htm (accessed July 1, 2008).

6. On BC's Gateway Strategy, see, for example, www.gov.bc.ca (accessed July 1, 2007).

7. On recent 2006 census of the population see Statistics Canada, "Canada's Population," *Daily,* September 28. Statistics Canada Ottawa: Statistics Canada, 2007, is available at www.statcan.ca/Daily/English/060927/d060927a.htm.

8. BC Stats, Canada, 2006 Census (Statscan: Ottawa, 2007), and www.bcstats.gov.bc.ca/data/pop.pop.htm (accessed August 13, 2008).

9. On the changes in the Metro Vancouver, Lower Mainland, and BC economies see Howlett and Brownsey (1992) and Smith (1994).

10. Stats, Canada, 2006 Census (Statscan: Ottawa, 2007), and www.bcstats.gov.bc.ca/data/pop.pop.htm (accessed August 13, 2008).

11. Unless otherwise indicated, material for this historical section is taken from Oberlander and Smith (1993).

12. For a more extensive discussion of this, on Vancouver, see Smith (1992) and Smith and

Cohn (1994). On the significance of the Port of Vancouver, see also Ginnell and Smith (2008).

13. North and Hardwick (1992); and "Case Three: Land Use Planning and Policy-Making," in Oberlander and Smith (1993, pp. 356–66).

14. Conflict over land use—between the provincial government and the LMRPB, and, at times, the LMRPB and local municipalities—contributed to provincial thinking on regional diffusion in the Lower Mainland, and on regional districts in general. See Oberlander and Smith, "The LMRPB and Regional Planning" (1993, pp. 358–59).

15. See *Statistics Relating to Regional and Municipal Governments in B.C.* (Victoria: Province of B.C., June 1989), p. 3, for a full list of these voluntary functions. Unless otherwise indicated, material for this historical section is taken from Oberlander and Smith (1993) and Tindal and Tindal (2000, pp. 123–24). More recently, Tindal and Tindal have noted the continued benefits of this flexibility but have argued that accountability concerns have increased in prominence: "The regional districts have proven to be a flexible structure for dealing with a variety of considerations. They have assumed direct responsibilities for . . . municipal services . . . in unorganized areas. They have also acted as the administrative agency for certain functions or projects which some of their member municipalities wished to pursue jointly. In addition, they have assumed responsibility for various functions delegated to them by their constituent municipalities. . . . (But while) the flexible structure of the regional districts allows diversity and preserves a sense of community, . . . accessibility concerns exist." (Tindal and Tindal, 2000: 5th edition, 142–43).

16. *Greater Toronto: Report of the GTA Task Force* (1996). (Toronto: Queen's Printer, January). Anne Golden (1996) and her Greater Toronto Area commissioners did note that differences in regional political culture helped explain the relative success of "consensual decision-making" in the Greater Vancouver case. The Task Force's general conclusions, however, were that such an approach was "weak."

17. Clive Rock, (then) Translink manager, Simon Fraser University presentation, February 2001. The other three board seats were provincial members of the Legislative Assembly (MLAs), appointed by the government; at the end of the NDP era (May 2001) these MLAs were not attending meetings and under the new Liberal government these positions were not filled.

18. On July 2, 2008, former NYC Subway VP/former Long Island Railroad president Thomas Prendergast was appointed CEO by the Translink Board. Martin Crilly, current BC Ferries commissioner was appointed Translink commissioner by the Mayors' Council, June 2, 2008. On anticipated deficits, see, for example, Luba (2008); the Transportation Authority anticipates a minimum $150 million annual deficit by 2012.

19. See Penner (2003). In this case, the suburban municipality of Delta had passed a bylaw to provide some local controls of large (e.g., eighteen-acre) greenhouse operations, in particular their use of less-clean fuel sources for heating. The BC government intervened when a grower challenged the bylaw, citing provincial right-to-farm legislation over the right of a municipality to legislate on local businesses. The province also argued that the local bylaw contradicted the provincial Waste Management Act, which exempts agricultural operations. Urban-rural issues of this sort are not new to Delta, a Vancouver suburb. In the late 1980s and 1990s, Delta held the longest land use dispute hearing in Canadian history over efforts to develop farmland for urban use. The debates over the so-called Spetifore lands near the Tsawwassen ferry terminal to Vancouver Island initially led to the Bill Bennett Social Credit government's abolishment of regional planning in 1983 when the GVRD prevented development plans by a Delta Social Credit supporter. The BC minister of Agriculture and Fisheries has since precluded use of local bylaws to prevent local regulation of coastal fish farms in BC as well. On such fish farms issues, see, for example, Anderson (2004, p. A6).

20. On the Toronto merger, see, for example, Golden and Slack (2007); on recent changes in Ottawa-Carleton see Andrew (2007).

21. On the Tony Blair regional governance reforms in the London region, see also Dunleavy and Margetts (1998).

References

Anderson, Charlie. 2004. "Auditor-General to Look into Return of (Fish-) Farm Fines after a Complaint by the Sierra Legal Defence Fund." *Province,* February 15, A6.

Andrew, Caroline. 2007. "Evaluating Municipal Reform in Ottawa-Gatineau: Building For a More Metropolitan Future?" In *Metropolitan Governing: Canadian Cases, Comparative Lessons,* ed. Eran Razin and Patrick Smith, 75–94. Jerusalem: Magnes Press, Hebrew University of Jerusalem.

Artibise, Alan, and Michael Seelig. 1991. *From Desolation to Hope: The Pacific Fraser Region to 2010.* Vancouver: University of British Columbia Press.

Bish, Robert L. 1990. *Local Government in British Columbia.* Richmond, British Columbia: Union of British Columbia Municipalities.

———. 2000. "Evolutionary Alternatives for Metropolitan Areas: The Capital Region of British Columbia." *Canadian Journal of Regional Science* 23, no. 1: 73–88.

Bish, Robert, and Eric Clemens. 2007. *Local Government in British Columbia.* 3d ed. Richmond: Union of BC Municipalities.

Bond, David. 1996. "Sustaining the Metropolitan Economy." In *Urban Solutions to Global Problems: Vancouver-Canada-Habitat II,* ed. Patrick J. Smith, H. Peter Oberlander, and Tom Hutton, 68–71. Vancouver: University of British Columbia, Centre for Human Settlements.

Davis, Craig, and Thomas Hutton. 1995. "The Two Economics of British Columbia." *BC Studies,* no. 89, 3–15.

Dunleavy, Patrick, and Helen Margetts. 1998. *Report to the Government Office for London: Electing the London Mayor and the London Assembly.* London: LSE Public Policy Group (June).

Fershau, Jonathon. 2003. "Muddling Through Urban Regionalism: Rational Actors, Arenas without Rules, and Transportation Governance in the Greater Vancouver Regional District." Master's Thesis, Department of Political Science, Simon Fraser University, Vancouver.

Ginnell, Kevin, and Patrick Smith. 2008. "Making Biggest Bigger: Port Vancouver's 21st Century Re-Structuring-Global Meets Local." *Canadian Political Science Review* 2, no. 4 (December): 76–92.

Golden, Anne. 1996. "Greater Toronto: Report of the GTA Task Force." Toronto: Queen's Printer (January).

Golden, Anne, and Enid Slack. 2007. "Urban Governance Reform in Toronto." In *Metropolitan Governing: Canadian Cases, Comparative Lessons,* ed. Eran Razin and Patrick Smith, 29–74. Jerusalem: Magnes Press, Hebrew University of Jerusalem.

Higgins, Donald. 1977. *Urban Canada: Its Government and Politics.* Toronto: Macmillan.

———. 1986. *Local and Urban Politics in Canada.* Toronto: Gage.

Howlett, Michael, and Keith Brownsey. 1992. "British Columbia: Public Sector Politics in a Rentier Resource Economy." In *The Provincial State: Politics in Canada's Provinces and Territories,* ed. Keith Brownsey and Michael Howlett, 265–95. Toronto: Copp Clark Pitman.

Jacobs, Jane. 1984. *Cities and the Wealth of Nations: Principles of Economic Life.* New York: Random House.

Leonard, Frank. 2003. Union of BC Municipalities. Press Release, November 7. Available at www.civicnet.bc.ca (accessed February 14, 2006).

Luba, Frank. 2008. "Translink Predicts Future Funding Deficit." *Province,* June 24, www.theprovince.com.

North, Robert, and Walter Hardwick. 1992. "Vancouver Since the Second World War: An Economic Geography." In *Vancouver and Its Region,* ed. Graeme Wynn and Tim Oke, 200–233. Vancouver: UBC Press.

Oberlander, H. Peter, and Patrick J. Smith. 1993. "Governing Metropolitan Vancouver: Regional Intergovernmental Relations in British Columbia." In *Metropolitan Governance: American/Canadian Intergovernmental Perspectives*, ed. Donald Rothblatt and Andrew Sancton, 329–73. Berkeley: Institute of Governmental Studies Press, University of California.

———. 1998. "Restructuring Metropolitan Governance: Greater Vancouver-British Columbia Reforms." In *Metropolitan Governance Revisited: American/Canadian Intergovernmental Perspectives,* ed. Donald N. Rothblatt and Andrew Sancton, 373–406. Berkeley: Institute of Governmental Studies Press, University of California.

Penner, Derrick. 2003. "Tomato King Cheers Right to Burn Wood: Court Overturns Bylaw that Restricted Growers Fuel-Delta Bylaw 'Set Undue Restrictions.' " *Vancouver Sun,* April 19, C1–2.

Sancton, Andrew. 1995. *Governing Canada's City-Regions: Adapting Form to Function.* Montreal: IRPP.

Self, Peter. 1977. *Administrative Theories and Politics.* Boston: Allyn and Unwin.

Skelton, Chad. 2007. "Goodbye GVRD, Hello Metro Vancouver." *Vancouver Sun,* August 3, 2007, B1, B4.

Smith, Patrick. 1986. "Regional Governance in British Columbia." *Planning and Administration* 13, no. 2 (Autumn): 7–20.

———. 1992. "The Making of a Global City: Fifty Years of Constituent Diplomacy—The Case of Vancouver." *Canadian Journal of Urban Research* 1, no. 1 (June): 90–112.

———. 1994. "British Columbia: Public Policy and Perceptions of Governance." In *Canadian Politics,* 2d ed., ed. James P. Bickerton and Alain-G. Gagnon, 506–26. Peterborough: Broadview.

———. 1995. "Governing Metropolitan Change: Public Policy and Governance in Canada's City Regions." In *Canadian Metropolitics: Governing Our Cities,* ed. James Lightbody, 161–92. Toronto: Copp Clark.

———. 1996. "Restructuring Metropolitan Governance: Vancouver and British Columbia Reforms." *Policy Options* 17, no. 7 (September): 7–11.

———. 1998. "Local Politics: An Introduction." In *The Puzzles of Power: An Introduction to Political Science,* 2d ed., ed. Michael Howlett and David Laycock, 393–403. Toronto: Oxford University Press.

———. 2008a. "Branding Cascadia: Considering Cascadia's Conflicting Conceptualizations-Who Gets To Decide?" *Canadian Political Science Review* 2, no. 2 (Summer): 57–83.

———. 2008b. "British Columbia Changes Metro Vancouver's Transportation Governance—A Re-Examination of Peter Self's 'Dilemma Thesis': Efficiency vs. Accountability." *Local Matters* (Auckland, NZ: Auckland University of Technology, Local Government Centre), Issue 2 (April): 2–4.

Smith, Patrick, and T.H. Cohn. 1994. "International Cities and Municipal Paradiplomacy: A Typology for Assessing the Changing Vancouver Metropolis." In *The Changing Canadian Metropolis: A Public Policy Perspective*, vol. 2, ed. Frances Frisken, 725–50. Berkeley: Institute of Governmental Studies Press, University of California.

Smith, Patrick, and H. Peter Oberlander. 1998. "Restructuring Metropolitan Governance: Greater Vancouver-British Columbia Reforms." In *Metropolitan Governance Revisited: American/Canadian Intergovernmental Perspectives,* ed. Donald N. Rothblatt and Andrew Sancton, 373–406. Berkeley: Institute of Governmental Studies Press, University of California,.

Smith, Patrick, and Kennedy Stewart. 2005. "Local Government Reform in British Columbia, 1991–2005—One Oar in the Water." In *Municipal Reform in Canada: Dimensions, Dynamics, Determinants,* ed. Joseph Garcea and Ed LeSage Jr., 25–56. Toronto: Oxford University Press.

———. 2006a. *Global Calgary: A Globalist Strategy for the City of Calgary.* Ottawa: Canadian Policy Research Network (April).

————. 2006b. "Local Whole-of-Government Policymaking in Vancouver: Beavers, Cats and the Mushy Middle Thesis." In *Canada: The State of the Federation 2004*, ed. Robert Young and Christian Leuprecht, 251–72. Municipal-Federal-Provincial Relations in Canada. Kingston: Institute of Intergovernmental Relations, Queen's University.

————. 2007. "Immature Policy Analysis: Building Capacity in Eight Major Canadian Cities." In *Policy Analysis in Canada: The State of the Art*, ed. Laurent Dobuzinskis, Michael Howlett, and David Laycock, 265–88. Toronto: University of Toronto Press-Institute of Public Administration of Canada Series in Public Management and Governance.

————. 2009. "British Columbia." In *Foundations of Governance: Municipal Government in Canada's Provinces*, ed. Andrew Sancton and Robert Young, Toronto: University of Toronto Press.

Steffenhagen, Janet. 2004. "RAV Foes Promote Light Rail Line." *Vancouver Sun*, June 21.

Tennant, Paul, and David Zirnhelt. 1973. "Metropolitan Government in Vancouver: The Politics of Gentle Imposition." *Canadian Public Administration* 16 (Spring): 124–38.

Tindal, Richard, and Susan N. Tindal. 2000. *Local Government in Canada*. 5th ed. Toronto: McGraw-Hill Ryerson.

14

Some Reflections on Metropolitan Governance in Contemporary Mexican Cities

Mario Bassols Ricardez

When we examine images of a city, such as Mexico City, from a helicopter, some of the criticisms about the severe problems of the main Mexican metropolis make more sense. Looking at some good-quality aerial pictures of the relevant locations is sufficient to confirm the seriousness of problems such as air pollution, vehicle congestion, urban poverty, or the lack of urban planning. The territorial structure of the city can also be seen, beginning with its traffic infrastructure (bridges, streets, avenues, main roads, and Metro lines, etc.). Large socioeconomic inequalities dividing its inhabitants are also observed, since the experience of living in the city is accentuated by dwelling units that are defined by many contrasts as well as by public spaces that give an identity to the city. Certainly, other critical issues cannot be captured by the lens of an aerial photographer, for example, increased crime and unequal access to the labor market, among other things. The picture captures the image of the moment, that is, an effect on the urban space that is perfectly observable. But the processes of power creation, the shaping of political institutions, and the influence of several social urban actors on them take a long time. Thus, they become the raw material for the formulation of more solid explanations about governability in this major Mexican metropolis.

The aim of this chapter is to analyze *governance*-possible constituent features by means of formulation and implementation of urban social policies in Mexico City and, correspondingly, to analyze some similarities and differences between Mexico City and Monterrey.[1]

Governability and Governance

We need to make some theoretical statements on the concept of governance. A first question relates to the change in federal state functions in the context of an emerging neoliberal economy in the 1980s. In losing its centrality and strength in the fields of economic relationships and the exercise of power, the national bureaucratic apparatus has suffered a considerable reduction in size. Under the new market economy oriented toward competitiveness, export, and flexible work, the focal point of the state-market and civic society relationship were redefined. In Latin America, this process has been accompanied by the fall of several military and authoritarian regimes; however, this has not been followed by a wave of overall democratization in the region, but of political reorganization, resistance, or incipient changes in local or state circles. It is a well-known fact that the end of that decade also meant the decline of socialism as a model, both for economic organization and the state.

Concepts such as *governability* and *governance* appeared in the literature on urban management and local government during the following decade. The first was widely disseminated in different forms in Latin American urban and political analysis and even now it is used in generalized and multiple ways. For most Latin American countries, this period was a time of economic stagnation, annual inflation levels higher than 100 percent, adjustments in the labor market, and capital flight. As a consequence, the state's ability to act as an intermediary in the growing conflicts became eroded and new regional forces that promoted political decentralization and economic deconcentration—until then mainly located in the big cities—arose.

Talking about governability in order to define the ability of governing a territory would then make sense. It was urgent to manage increasingly limited public resources effectively. In order to accomplish this, the Ford Foundation and the World Bank promoted several formulas and practices for "good government." Two types of governability were frequently mentioned: democratic and authoritarian. The latter emphasized the vertical exercise of power in strong governments linked to local oligarchies, and it made civic society groups highly corporate. Democratic governability promoted decentralization of decision making, citizen participation, and communitarian and autonomous management, among other issues.

Gradually, the stale concept of governability, at least in Mexico, sank into the hackneyed jargon of political speech just as the concept of "sustainability" did. It began to be replaced with alternative concepts such as governance. Although its translation into Spanish proposed the term *gobernanza* (strongly influenced by Barcelona's strategic planning model), it is not used by all the literature in Spanish as merely a translation.

Essentially, and for the purposes of this chapter, governance and *gobernanza* are assumed to be "synonyms" but, for operative reasons, we have decided to use the term "governance." The core idea lies in the importance given to the several actors that comprise urban management, their roles, and the search for new instruments promoting economic growth. There may be, as Le Gales notes (in de Mattos, 2005), two strategies: one that privileges a business-style growth and another that aims to avoid social conflict in the process of economic change. Therefore, governance can be directed by a model of urban regime, such as the well-known case of Atlanta (Stone, 1989) or by a model that considers a policy of social cohesion, where businessmen do not play a central role in decision making. In both cases, governance is exerted from a pattern other than the hierarchical one and is instead based on cooperation and interaction among the federal state and the nonstate actors (according to Mayntz, in Hernández Vargas, 2006).

As the above-mentioned concept has been disseminated and discussed, it has become more complex and refined, to the extent that its effectiveness must take into account several requirements such as goal setting, conflict resolution, account rendering, and process adaptability, among others. Thus, only a few cities are expected to exert real governance in their territory. So, the concept also loses some efficacy when it is classified in closed governance models.

In this sense, our approach states that the concept acquires significant analytic potential, provided that the specific models of urban governance are differentiated in order to identify the specific features or abilities of local governments so that they may respond effectively and legitimately to the social interests raised, through novel and creative public policies (Hirst, 2000).

A Look to Northern Mexico: The City of Monterrey

Monterrey is a city located in the north of Mexico, whose metropolitan area (see Map 14.1) includes almost 90 percent of the total population of the state of Nuevo León.[2] First, it is identified as a "typically industrial" city, even if at the dawn of the twenty-first century it has been transformed into a financial and commercial sector services city. Monterrey is the first Mexican city that, on the grounds of the former Fundidora Monterrey, which concluded its activities in 1983, shows off an "industrial archaeology" museum. Other studies have highlighted the influence on Nuevo León's political life historically exerted by businessmen (Cerutti, 2002; Vellinga, 1988). Therefore, it is possible to assert that the political history of Nuevo León's metropolis is closely linked to local business class development, to its ideology, and to its "city plan." As noted by Arzaluz (2006, p. 132), "in this city, more than in any other city in the entire country, there is deep interference of business actors in the composition of the local political agenda." As time went by, the powerful business class gathered into "holdings" that concentrated capital and work resources and also became leading actors in national political life, through, for example, their affiliation with the Coparmex (Confederación Patronal de la República Mexicana [Employers Confederation of the Mexican Republic]) and the Consejo Coordinador Empresarial [Business Coordinator Council], founded in 1975.

Later, businessmen from its ranks registered as mayoral and gubernatorial candidates on behalf of the Partido Acción Nacional [National Action Party] (PAN), which, to date, continues to split off some politicians that come from the main families of Nuevo León from the Partido Revolucionario Institucional [Institutional Revolutionary Party] (PRI) and the PAN. It could be said that in Nuevo León, and more specifically in Monterrey, politics is a "family business," due to the fact that

Map 14.1 **Metropolitan Zone of Monterrey, 2005**

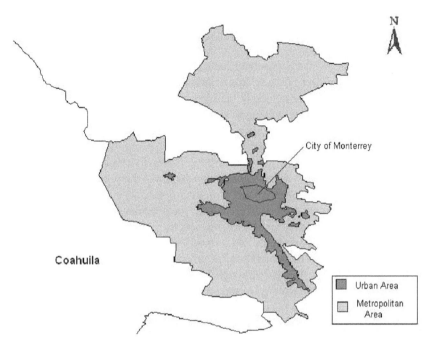

Source: Secretaría de Desarrollo Social (SEDESOL), Consejo Nacional de Población (CONAPO), Instituto Nacional de Estadística, Geografia e Informática (INEGI). *Delimitación de las zonas metropolitanas de México*, 2005.

these are more or less closed power spaces that exert their control on plans for the political life of the city.

Along with the business class, a working class also arose during the twentieth century, and large contingents of this class entered industrial production processes. They lived under business patronage that, in times of plenty, provided workers with supplementary goods and services. Moreover, given the ideological features of local businessmen and their growing separation from federal politics, they kept working organizations under control by means of "white unions" (Federación de Sindicatos Independientes [Federation of Independent Unions]), cut off the national workers' central union, the Confederación de Trabajadores de México [Confederation of Mexican Workers] (CTM). Nevertheless, the presence of unions and workers' organizations is important in local political life. For example, several of their members are representatives in councils of metropolitan municipalities (Arzaluz, 2006, p. 137).

However, the early 1980s crisis began to undermine the basis of capital accumulation and the privilege-granting model among Nuevo León's political and business elite. Industrial groups of Monterrey began to experience severe financial problems (based on external credit). The well-known Grupo Alfa—the largest private company in Mexico at that time (which, by 1980, numbered more than 150 companies)—was the clearest example of the decline of regional businessmen (Vellinga, 1988, p. 134).

Since then, the formerly powerful regional business groups lost strength and have been handing over space to transnational capital through the sale of their assets, capital mergers, or company bankruptcy. However, former elite families have retained most of their privileges, and new generations have diversified their business activities toward real estate, commercial, and educational sectors while keeping their sights on changes of direction caused by governmental action in urban space. Furthermore, Monterrey is a *business city,* in that it expresses a form of space organization and a style of urban management similar to the typical characteristics of an urban regime (Bassols, 2006).

Neighborhood organizations are among the social actors with some presence in the organization of urban space. Monterrey was the cradle of a powerful popular urban movement beginning at the end of the 1960s and continuing in subsequent years. There were large demonstrations of urban land *posesionarios* (people who acted as the owners of the land although they were not) established on irregular settlements who had the state government on the rack. Tierra y Libertad [Land and Liberty], Monterrey's most important movement, was the spearhead of the Coordinadora Nacional del Movimiento Urbano Popular [National Coalition of Popular Urban Movements] (CONAMUP), which had an important social basis in Durango, Cuernavaca, Acapulco, Mexico City, Tepic, and Chihuahua.

During the 1980s, the CONAMUP mobilized the urban masses, and then, in 1991, it disappeared. Many of its members became members of the new Mexican leftist party, Partido de la Revolución Democrática [Party of the Democratic Revolution] (PRD), created in 1989. Nevertheless, the old leaders of Tierra y Libertad formed their own party, the Partido del Trabajo (PT), a coalition with other political forces. Even though the urban movement is currently anchored in certain local, well-defined spaces, its presence in the creation of the city cannot be underestimated, particularly the part of the urban space that is not in the urban image conceived by the local elite. A tour along several Metro Rey stations illustrates that this part of the "built city" (around 50 percent) was developed within the past fifty years of Monterrey's urban history.

Nuevo León is now a highly segregated city, spatially fragmented into nine metropolitan municipalities and an urban management pervaded by the powerful influence of the state government on the metropolitan territory and the public works carried out there. Its government executes the great urban infrastructure works (the *urbanistic megaprojects,* as Garza [2003] has called them), while the mayors of metropolitan municipalities become mediators who struggle to gain access to financial resources (public and private) for their own municipalities. That is, intermunicipal competitiveness creates hierarchies in negotiation on several levels: geographical location, efficiency levels of local management, presence of political leaderships, or, simply, political empathy among mayors and governor (whether this empathy comes from party identity or from family or personal affinity).

In short, the metropolis's urban management model has two conflicting goals. The first aim is the historic overlap of the business class with local political power, since its strong linkages are reflected not only in the main municipal governments (Monterrey, San Pedro, San Nicolás de los Garza) but also in the state government and in the Nuevo León chamber of deputies. The second aim comes from the centralism that characterizes state public management, which de facto assumes, according to a well-known researcher, the functions of a "metropolitan government" (Garza, 2003).

It is worth noting that given this "structural environment," which defines the general guidelines of urban management in the whole metropolitan area of Monterrey (MAM),[3] it is important to pay attention to social actors and party forces that intervene in local politics in each municipality. This gives us a more complex picture of local and state forces that are struggling to gain access to resources and power spaces.

After this brief panorama of Monterrey's case, we now proceed to the interesting experience of constructing a "local government" that has a set of features close to governance, although sometimes far from it.

Mexico City and the Construction of a Local Government: Background

For approximately fifty years, Mexico City has engaged in a process of expansion beyond the political-administrative limits of the Federal District [Distrito Federal] (DF). First, it spread over the municipal territories of the State of Mexico, until, in recent years, it reached the territory of the State of Hidalgo, in the north of the Federal District. Thus, by 2000, the number of political-administrative units making up the Metropolitan Zone of Mexico City (ZMCM, by its Spanish acronym) included the sixteen municipal districts into which the Federal District is subdivided, four municipalities of the State of Mexico, and one municipality of Hidalgo, totaling 18 million inhabitants (see Map 14.2). This is almost one-fifth of the total Mexican population (Partida and Anzaldo, 2004, p. 197).

The strictly political processes of Mexico City's urban management have a historic explanation that is found in the overall model of the political regime the country had between 1929 and the last decade of the twentieth century. Its essential features were:

1. a federal government system whose basic tenet was a strong presidential system and a weak legislative one supported by the dominant party (the PRI), which governed the whole country on a nationwide scale and at different levels of government—federal, state, and municipal;

Map 14.2   **Metropolitan Zone of Mexico City, 2005**

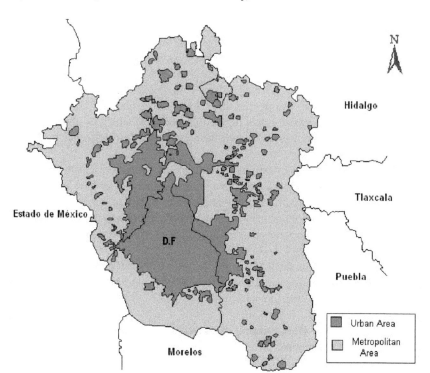

Source: Secretaría de Desarrollo Social (SEDESOL), Consejo Nacional de Población (CONAPO), Instituto Nacional de Estadística, Geografía e Informática (INEGI). *Delimitación de las zonas metropolitanas de México,* 2005.

2. a social domination pattern based on the sectoral structure of the PRI, which channeled worker, farmer, and popular demands through a "pork barreling or clientelistic" scheme and through traditional local leadership;

3. a boom in public works (including new roads, building of the system of collective transportation, the Metro [subways and railways], deep sewage system), as Mexico's economic growth consolidated around the mid-1940s, Mexico City's inhabitants also benefited from important subsidies to transportation and urban services;

4. the suppression, since 1929, of municipal government in Mexico City, which implied the disappearance of citizens' rights to elect their leaders; instead, the position of the city mayor emerged, who was directly assigned by the president of the republic from 1929 until 1997;

5. decision making on the organization and urban management of the city

that was centralized in two essential positions: the mayor of the capital city and, as Mexico City expanded across the territory of the State of Mexico, the current governor of that state;

6. the process of legitimization of the political system as well as the hegemonic (or "quasi-unique") party regime, which began to weaken as stability started weakening by the end of the 1960s, and especially because of the disaster provoked by the 1985 earthquakes;

7. subsequent political reforms that lessened this weakening slightly, but only delayed by a few years the spectacular fall of the ruling party and its local political elite during the 1990s;

8. the phenomenon of political alternation in the Federal District that began when the Congress approved a law proposed in 1988 by the Representatives Assembly of the Federal District, which has regulatory powers and is made up of sixty-six representatives[4] elected by citizen vote. A few years later it would transform itself into the Legislative Assembly as a local organism that would counterbalance the power of the capital government and its sixteen political districts;

9. a new political reform approving the creation of a local government in the Federal District, which is still pending;

10. advances on this matter that are summed up as: the substitution of the mayor of Mexico City for the chief of government of the Federal District, elected by direct vote since 1997; and the direct election of the sixteen district chiefs since 2000.

However, it has not yet reached the status of a local government with a legal system similar to that of the other Mexican federal entities (a total of thirty-two including the DF), since it does not have its own constitution. Instead, a government statute rules its actions.Thus, the National Chamber of Deputies (similar to the House of Representatives) and not the Legislative Assembly of the Federal District approves the annual income budget of this federal entity, as well as establishing the possible amount of indebtedness. It is obvious that given these restrictions, the Federal District's government depends on political criteria, whereby parties contend for several interests, both local and national. Likewise, the chief of government is subject to the ups and downs of national politics, due to the very fragility of the judicial statute of the DF, as was proved by the "impeachment" of the then chief of government, Andrés Manuel López Obrador, that was carried out by the Chamber of Deputies, which has the constitutional power to do so.[5]

These factors illustrate the interweaving of local and national interests that have an impact on the political structure of Mexico City's government and complicate its decision making.

In summary, the lack of democratic representation in local government since 1929 has been the main focus of attention and the central object of subsequent political reforms put forward in the Federal District, particularly since the 1980s.

Nevertheless, we cannot analyze the discussion processes and implementation of reforms separately. It is helpful to consider that the changes in the local political scenario have been accompanied by a series of social movements during the past twenty years that began with the movement of people affected by the 1985 earthquake. This moment in Mexico City's history constituted an era of urban conflict that underwent several periods of growth and decline of social movements, the emergence of new actors "made up relatively apart from the corporative populist pact" (Duhau, 1994, p. 57), and the implementation of social organizations' corporate policies in regulating urban conflicts. Thus, a gradual reform of the special Mexico City regime of government could be implemented without seriously eroding the foundations of local social and political order. It is worth mentioning that, simultaneous with this process, an urban planning system was consolidated that, in the midst of social conflict, became a regulatory body for organizing urban space. Finally, to deal with the presence of large irregular settlements in the metropolitan area, "mechanisms of land property regularization and financing of progressive housing programs, as well as of social policy" were implemented, and incorporated community participation in their designs (ibid., p. 58).

The Partido de la Revolución Democrática Government in the Federal District: 1997–2006

Given the legal restrictions on local government, has the new party in power in the Federal District had any impact since the first democratic election in 1997? To date, the PRD has been the party at the head of the government with the following people in charge: Cuauhtémoc Cárdenas (December 1997–May 1999); Rosario Robles (May 1999–December 2000); Andrés Manuel López Obrador (December 2000–March 2005), Alejandro Encinas (March 2005–December 2006), and Marcelo Ebrard, since December 5, 2006. The first government term resulting from the popular vote was restricted to three years in order to coordinate it with the presidential election in 2000. After that, six-year terms began. More than ten years of PRD government have passed since then. It seems to be a period reasonably long enough to draw some conclusions, even though they may be oversimplified and general.

The first point worth mentioning is that two of the elected chiefs of government did not complete their constitutional terms because they were public officers who replaced the local official in that position. That is, this was not a result of voting but of nomination or, if done by the party in power, an *appointment* and, more specifically, by the person leaving leadership: Cuauhtémoc Cárdenas designated Rosario Robles so that he could run for the official candidacy of his party for the presidential election of 2000; Andrés Manuel López Obrador played a similar role, nominating Alejandro Encinas as his substitute. In both cases, Robles and Encinas did not follow guidelines of politics and urban management that differed a great deal from those of their predecessors. Their terms of office were short, but

Rosario Robles's term as chief of government was slightly longer. Besides, in both cases, their previous office was as Mexico City's general secretary of government, a purely political position that requires the ability to handle local social and urban conflicts, as well as a special talent for keeping the relationships of other levels of government reasonable, both federal and district.

Mexico City's current leader, Marcelo Ebrard, began his term on December 5, 2006, so he has still a long time to serve—more than four years—as head of the capital city, but no one will be surprised if he declares himself as a candidate for president of the republic in the next general election.

The second point concerns the continuance of the PRD in power during that period. In other words, the replacement of the former party in power (the PRI) in the Federal District had as a distinctive element a process of limited alternation in which a sole party, the PRD, retained the political hegemony owned by the PRI during its better times. The spectacular fall of the latter party in the elections was far from predictable a few years before 1997. Certainly, this was the prelude to the presidential election three years later, even if in this case, the other party, the PAN, would benefit from the popular vote. The loss of a party's legitimacy in the government is not the result of merely circumstantial factors, but of years of accumulated problems that, in the atmosphere of the economic crisis initiated in the 1980s, eroded the foundations of power, fragmented the political class, and influenced the perception of citizens that the end of the "quasi-unique" party in power was close. In any event, the PRI's fall exceeded expectations. Therefore, during the first PRD government in the DF, the PRI obtained a majority of votes in only one of the forty electoral local districts within the Legislative Assembly. But in the 2000 election it did not get any of the sixteen districts at stake.

On the other hand, the PAN governed six districts in 2000 and became the second political force of the DF. Only in the intermediate election of 2003 would the PRI win a district (Milpa Alta), while the PAN maintained two district charges (Miguel Hidalgo and Benito Juárez). With these results, in 2000 the PRD lost some strength, while the PAN gained some because of the successful presidential campaign of Vicente Fox. The PRI, for its part, disappeared almost completely from the local political scene (Gómez Tagle, 2000, p. 664). Six years later, the PAN regained the two districts it had governed three years earlier, while the PRD kept the remaining fourteen, including the suburban district of Milpa Alta. That is, the ruling party in the Federal District has consolidated its power, and the Legislative Assembly comprises a party composition of a simple majority in favor of the PRD.

What interpretation can we offer about the permanence of an opposition party in the government of the main Mexican city that is also the nation's capital? By means of what kind of mechanisms and actions has Mexico City's government held power while applying newly coined social politics? Has it been possible to implement the objectives of political institutions' democratization and, therefore, the strengthening of citizen participation in the political processes of the city (Alvarado and Davis, 2003)?

To consider these questions, we must take into account the conditions under which an opposition party such as the PRD managed to consolidate itself in this political site, in spite of being in the "crossfire" of national and local interests that are permanently in dispute in the capital of the republic. Besides, it can be said that the success of its policies does not necessarily lead to very optimistic results regarding Mexico City's long-standing problems, such as crime, air pollution, deficient public transportation, and water shortage, among others. This brings us back to some aspects of Mexico City's recent political history.

Elements of an Evaluation

Our first area of analysis looks at the origin of the social basis constituting the political support of the PRD. As a young party, born in 1989 by means of the fusion of several Mexican left parties from that time, the PRD built one of its primary pillars of political electoral support on the structure of social organizations that mobilized after the 1985 earthquake in Mexico City. The earthquake victims' movement had its main territorial base in the historic downtown district and its neighboring areas. The Coordinadora Única de Damnificados [United Coordinating Committee of Earthquake Victims] constituted its primary platform of struggle during the subsequent years.

In the 1988 presidential elections, a significant number of social organizations supported the candidacy of Cuauhtémoc Cárdenas from the Frente Democrático Nacional [National Democratic Front] (FDN). In the DF this candidate officially received the majority of votes over the PRI candidate, Carlos Salinas de Gortari. Although Cárdenas did not achieve a national triumph, he served to announce the important presence of the opposition in the federal capital. This recognition was palpable in the negotiations undertaken by Manuel Camacho Solís during his five years as capital regent (1988–93), within the framework of his "social agreement" policy with the city's civic organizations.

By then, the PRI was completely discredited, so the newly formed Federal District Assembly of Representatives (ARDF) and the regent were in charge of negotiating a consensus policy. They defined a policy line that allowed "contained governance," that is, one that avoided greater social conflict even as the legitimacy of the capital city's government, whose head was still appointed by the national president, was severely questioned. Hence, the discussion and later approval of a new political reform (1993) and a citizen plebiscite (March 1993) appeared. The latter placed two issues on the table: the election of the local government head and the possibility of creating a thirty-second state of the republic.

The essential element of the 1993 political reform was not carried out,[6] due to the fact that during the early years of the last PRI national president, Ernesto Zedillo (1994–2000), the subject of a new political reform regained force and the Senate approved direct election of the local head of government in 1997, whose first term would last three years, and thereafter a six-year term would be instituted.

The position of city regent would be eliminated, and the possibility emerged that an opposition party could win the elections. Then, the PRD—under the still strong leadership of Cuauhtémoc Cárdenas—gained a victory that was considered "historic" for the Mexican left. Cárdenas won not only because of support from multiple urban-popular organizations—already incorporated into the core of the PRD—but also because he had the votes of a great part of the capital city's middle-class, university-graduate, intellectual, and educated electorate, who sympathized with the democratic ideas and values identified with him. The PRD's political operators had already begun to organize client-oriented citizen networks. It is worth mentioning that the Federal District contains most of Mexico's public universities and educational centers and most of the "critical mass" of intellectuals and artists, as well as the national press.

The PRD later reached out to another type of organization, once integrated within the now declining PRI: taxi drivers and informal-sector merchants, groups that had grown significantly in number and importance over the previous decade and that belonged to the PRI. Internal grievances and divisions undermined the PRI's presence in these organizations and contributed to increasing the political clientele of the new party in the capital city's government. Nevertheless, persisting since then is a *difficult* sector that objects to local governmental policies. This sector is composed of two strong "corporative" groups, both in membership and in their local actions: the Collective Transportation System Workers Union (SNTSTC-Metro) and the Federal District Government Workers Union (SUTGDF, by its Spanish acronym), both integrated into the PRI. Salary increases and collective bargaining negotiations tend to be very difficult, with the constant threat of labor strikes, especially in the subway system. This situation illustrates the tough aspects of a governmental agenda that has been unable to build an open and understanding policy with all urban social partners, regardless of their political leanings.

The first three-year period of the PRD in city hall constituted the starting point for the construction of "democratic governability." Arturo Alvarado and Diane Davis (2003) showed in their analysis that this governability is far from being consolidated in its fundamental features. The slogan "The City of Hope" was spread to identify the new government, and microregional planning was encouraged by the discussion of several partial plans for urban development in some areas of the city, where diverse neighborhood organizations were involved (Bassols and Arzaluz, 2002). Real efforts were made to promote an integral policy of metropolitan planning; however, it did not work due to political and operational difficulties arising from two different criteria of territorial action, one used by Mexico City's government and the other by the State of Mexico (Pradilla, 2004).

A second Citizen Participation Law was approved, although it was somewhat ambiguous with regard to the possibility of generating solid citizen organizations. In 1999, Neighborhood Committee elections were held in the DF, organized by the newly created Federal District Electoral Institute. Less than 10 percent of citizens registered on the electoral rolls turned out to vote. Both the procedure and its social implications were questioned. Nevertheless, this was the last time such elections were held in the DF. In spite of the fact that they are stipulated in the legislation itself, these elections have not been held during the terms of López Obrador and Alejandro Encinas. Neighborhood Committees' integration has shown citizens' lack of interest in this type of citizen representation structure, which was composed mostly of PRD's militants (Sánchez and Enríquez, 2006, p. 241).

Comparing the first two elected Federal District governments, important differences are clearly highlighted not only in the construction of the public image of the head of government but also in public works that were carried out. While at first Cárdenas's government attempted to mark its differences from the authoritarian governments of the recent past, López Obrador's administration no longer had a need to focus there and, instead, could implement its public works and social policies program with an orientation toward the construction of an electoral environment favorable to the local governor. While the first government lasted three years, the second would cover twice that many, a fact that allowed the possibility of developing long-term building works and an improved distribution of the public budget. In addition, López Obrador skillfully designed a strategy to create a close rapport with the media through his traditional morning press conferences, which caused the upper echelons of Fox's government to worry. Cárdenas did not have a defined media strategy, and when he left his post to launch his third presidential candidacy, his image was in decline and his performance in the 2000 electoral process marked the end of his leadership within the PRD.

Moreover, the Cárdenas-Robles government faced financial problems due to the withdrawal of federal funding to the Federal District and it also faced the highest rate of criminal activity until then in Mexico City. This situation, combined with the difficult problem of street hawkers and the ancient corrupt structure of police corporations, seriously undermined its credibility before public opinion, and it represented a challenge not overcome during the first PRD administration of the DF (Alvarado and Davis, 2003).

López Obrador's government was marked in a much more evident way by permanent confrontation with the federal government and its party, the PAN, both of which persisted in efforts to obstruct his path toward the 2006 presidential succession. Far from achieving that goal, they generated greater publicity for López Obrador in the national and even international media. In this respect, the impeachment case was PAN's biggest political mistake, even if former president Vicente Fox was its main instigator.

López Obrador's administration succeeded in building the image of an "honest and courageous" politician who knew how to confront his political enemies, carry out public works, and "help the people." However, the PRD's image was severely questioned after the "video scandals" disseminated in 2005 involving politicians who were very close to Mexico City's leader. Some, such as René Bejarano and Carlos Imaz, went to jail, but were later released. Bejarano, in particular, had distinguished himself as one of López Obrador's main political operators in the DF, but public opinion continued to view López Obrador, the politician from the state of Tabasco, as "something else." In any case, the 2000–2006 term served to consolidate a "solid vote" in the DF, strengthening the party's citizen networks in the delegations with a strong PRD presence. An exemplary case is that of Iztapalapa, a delegation with almost 2 million inhabitants—mostly low income—with serious water shortages, insecurity, and a deficient public services administration. Nevertheless, people were loyal to the PRD and, especially, to the presidential candidate.

One of the most important instruments used by López Obrador to increase and consolidate his electoral clientele was his social policy, which consisted of granting economic support to single mothers and elderly people (older than sixty-five) residing in the DF, as well as providing school supplies—such as pens, pencils, notebooks, books, rulers, and so on—to all children and young people in the city's public schools (elementary and high school).[7] It must be said that an increasing portion of the capital's population is older than sixty-five, therefore, the aim of the benefit was to win the sympathies of that sector—one usually neglected by state policies. Likewise, the number of single mothers is increasing, particularly adolescents and women younger than twenty-five. Therefore, the program had the popular support of thousands of families that saw in López Obrador a leader who "really fulfilled" his promises. These actions were the object of criticism by the opposition, which considered them a populist strategy for preparing the presidential electoral campaign; nevertheless, they were copied by politicians of the PRI in the State of Mexico. Thus, the political sensitivity of that leader brought him enormous popular support to the point that two public referendums were carried out to ratify his government, and favorable results were expected from the participating population. In fact, López Obrador used these new forms of citizen participation, the referendum and the plebiscite, to confirm citizen support for his government.

The second important action was a public works program that demonstrated what could be accomplished by the local government in just a few years. A "second floor" was built above the Periférico, a key city freeway that, by 2000, was saturated with vehicles practically all day. The project was conducted in two phases, the first one inaugurated by López Obrador in 2005 and the second by Alejandro Encinas and the secretary of environment, Claudia Scheinbaum, in May 2006. This project was submitted for public consideration, and although there was some resistance on the part of affected property and shop owners, it was finally carried out without any major obstacles.

This project required a significant investment of public funds for which the opposition unsuccessfully requested the total cost, an issue that has had some but not much impact on the presidential campaign. A complementary transportation work was also implemented: the construction of Metrobús stations along Insurgentes Avenue—a road characterized by its world-class buildings, shops, car dealers, and some luxury hotels—which was once considered glamorous and modern. With the Metrobús, the head of Mexico City's government chose to delegate exclusive public transportation rights to this system and to forbid small buses licensed by the government to private owners of one or more vehicles. Negotiations with the transportation sector were necessary, but finally they reached an agreement to eliminate the run of small buses. Urban policy was designed to benefit the middle classes, especially people living in the western section of the city. Essentially, the public works offered were oriented toward mega-projects of road infrastructure with the active participation of private capital, which was rewarded with fiscal incentives and exemptions for their companies (Pradilla, 2004, p. 58).

Regarding housing policy, since 1997 the PRD has developed a novel proposal for working with civic organizations. Specifically, the Habitat Coalition includes the most important associations dedicated to promoting state-subsidized housing in Mexico City, such as "Casa y Ciudad," CENVI, and COPEVI. A Dwelling Improvement Program and a New Housing Program for single-family dwellings were promoted (Sánchez and Álvarez, 2006, p. 226), where it was possible to work jointly with the Institute of Housing and to develop a vast housing program for sectors with low resources. However, during the term of López Obrador, the action of private real estate groups was strengthened, while the city government presented an increasingly pragmatist housing policy. Therefore, when the second PRD government concluded (December 2006), the DF experienced an unprecedented stock of new housing developed by private real estate companies. The promulgation of a government edict banning construction of new housing outside the perimeter of the four central districts of the DF reinforced this situation.

One more achievement of this government was the decisive intervention in the city's historic downtown to present a "beautiful" and "tidy" image of the city's core to national and foreign tourists, as well as an impetus toward generating greater private capital investments. The proposal was promoted in collaboration with the Mexican businessman Carlos Slim, who has become one of the world's richest men due to his investments in various telephone, stock market, and commercial ventures. This type of joint action between government public works and business ventures had never been seen before, and it demonstrated the enormous potential that a globalized city like the Mexican capital could offer to investors who viewed the city in the medium- or long-term perspective. It also constitutes an example of the possibility of generating public-private associations for the urban management of large cities. Therefore, López Obrador has had a margin of credibility and confidence among national and foreign investors. The construction of the Torre Mayor, the tallest building in Latin America up to 2006, and the renovation of Paseo de la Reforma Avenue, intended for international tourism and the highly specialized services sector, were possible using this approach.

Completing this set of governmental interventions that had promotional success among large segments of population, López Obrador encouraged the holding of free rock concerts and other cultural activities in the famous Zócalo (Mexico City's main square). Thus, he answered the demands of thousands of young people who had been asking for these spaces for a long time. As a consequence, the Zócalo reinforced its nature as the main public space for citizen expression, not only for conducting protest demonstrations but also for strengthening the civic and recreational culture of DF inhabitants.

Among the public works carried out during the first years of the twenty-first century, some new high schools and a university, the Universidad de la Ciudad de México, were built in the east of the city for young people with limited resources. Professors and researchers from the main DF public universities did not consider its creation appropriate, believing that it was better to support the existing infrastructure than to create new facilities. A short time later, this university gained its autonomy from the government of the Federal District, and it began an interesting integration process in the social and urban problems within the country's capital city.

A Summary Comparison of Monterrey and Mexico

The metropolis of Mexico City can undoubtedly be distinguished as a space where political institutions are in constant transformation. Through the subsequent political reforms experienced during the past twenty years, there have thus been changes in its local legislation or new political institutions have been created with the primary aim of achieving greater decentralization of the power previously exerted by the president of the republic. On the other hand, in Monterrey, the urban political regime has barely changed. The district council is still the same, the structures of local government remain almost untouched, and there is a certain regularity of the norms governing relationships between citizens and government.

Both metropolises have common features in growth patterns and spatial transformation, such as the urban sprawl toward peripheral municipalities, socioterritorial stratification, more evident in the Metropolitan Area of Monterrey (MAM) than in the Metropolitan Area of Mexico City (AMCM), a city based on the intensive use of private transportation (cars and taxis) and on a collective transportation system of buses and collective transports organized into powerful networks controlled by leaders affiliated with some of the political parties (the PRI, in the MAM; the PRD, in the AMCM).

Regarding party composition in local governments, there are some similarities due to the two-party nature of their territory. In Monterrey, power is basically shared between the PRI and the PAN, while in the country's capital city it is shared between the PAN and the PRD. In both cases, the third party (the PRD for the MAM; and the PRI for the AMCM) retains some political niches in metropolitan municipalities.

With respect to the more visible social actors, there are some remarkable similarities and differences. Private real estate groups continue to act in the central and peripheral spaces of each metropolis, producing an expansion of urban space. Moreover, the oldest neighborhood organizations (some were created at the end of the 1960s) have experienced a decline since the past decade, and they have concentrated themselves in well-defined local spaces of power. That is, they have lost visibility and strength. In both metropolises, and as an expression of the prevailing political society in Mexico, parties have become privileged political actors, each preserving its own logic of access to power and its own political spaces. Several citizens' and neighborhood organizations align themselves vertically and subordinately with them, even if there are others that maintain real autonomy from any political party. In Monterrey, businessmen are more visible actors than in Mexico City, because they are a prestigious and well-established group in local circles.

Nevertheless, it is worth noting a great difference between Mexico City and Monterrey. Mexico City maintains an indisputable nationwide supremacy on goods and services production (about 20 percent of national gross domestic product), in addition to being the location for global capital main offices in Mexico. Monterrey is the main site in the north of Mexico located in the North American Free Trade Agreement (NAFTA) corridor and therefore, the beneficiary of certain regional advantages that NAFTA offers. While Mexico City, and particularly the Federal District, is heir to a rich cultural history dating back more than 600 years, Monterrey arose during the Spanish colonial administration and had an early industrializing boom during the last third of the nineteenth century. This later allowed Monterrey to express itself as autonomous and apart from the country's main center of power. In addition, there is a difference in population size; while the AMCM[8] registered almost 18 million inhabitants in the year 2000, Nuevo León's main metropolis was six times smaller with only 3.2 million people.

Finally, it is noteworthy that, since 1997, the Federal District has a directly elected government. As has been pointed out, the PRD has won three consecutive times in the Federal District, turning it into a political bastion of that party. By its side, in Nuevo León, and specifically in the municipality of its capital city, Monterrey, the PRI has won that site in two consecutive terms (2003–6 and 2006–on) after being governed by the PAN during three consecutive terms (from 1994 to 2003). In both cases, there has been strong leadership: first Cárdenas, then López Obrador in the DF; and in Monterrey, the emergent figure of Natividad González Parás, as governor of the state of Nuevo León.

For a brief comparison of both styles of urban management, we have to emphasize that we are talking about two different models of city functioning, with specific social actors and political agents. In Mexico City, the explanation is more complex, but it can be said that in comparison with Monterrey, businessmen have a weaker presence in local political life. Economic and political elites are not as interwoven as they are in Monterrey. But we only refer here to a certain degree of *invisibility of businessmen,* which is not permanent. We thus summarize the planning of the cities in two different ways. On one hand, Monterrey, as national emblematic business city, which tends to adhere to the concept of urban regime, but where municipalities struggle in a considerable way for the access to public and private resources. On the other hand, Mexico City, a metropolis divided among the Federal District, State of Mexico, and partially, the State of Hidalgo, besides being the site of federal activity, has very different traits. In particular, the DF serves as a symbolic space for Mexican leftists and as the central point of confluence of their ideological expression. However, when compared with Monterrey, half of the metropolitan territory has no municipalities. Instead, it has sixteen political districts, which are not autonomous and cannot compete with the central power of the Federal District Government (GDF). Thus, the competitiveness observed among the municipalities of Nuevo León or, among those of the State of Mexico, is not the same in Mexico City's case.

Although Mexico City has made more "progress" in building an urban *governance* than Monterrey has, negotiation with local actors does not seem very different. Nevertheless, it is necessary to distinguish dissimilar forces. As we will soon see, a leftist government in the Federal District has not succeeded in radically changing the traditional ways by which agreements on urban projects have been produced. That is, a policy of social cohesion under the parameters of urban corporatism practiced by the former party in power, the PRI, is taken into account.

Governance: Some Conclusions from the Case of Mexico

With these first brushstrokes on recent public action in the DF, few doubts remain about the enormous popularity achieved by López Obrador in his term of office, upon which he capitalized in his national presidential campaign. One thing left behind is whether the above-mentioned activity actually meant the construction of new elements of governance—in other words, whether it is possible to identify a special ability of the local administration to respond efficiently and legitimately to the interests of the majority through novel, creative public policies that promote social participation (Hirst, 2000).

The PRD administration in the Federal District has succeeded in building its own image of strong local government, with leadership capable of addressing certain citizen needs and demands (Alvarado and Davis, 2003). Therefore, the decentralization of public administration is an evident fact, although political district governments are still weak and dependent on the DF central government.

There was a sensitive change in López Obrador's style of governing, more oriented toward a pragmatic policy, separate from a territory's rational planning. We are not able to establish the existence of a broad process of citizen participation in urban policy design. Far from it, the citizens passively supported the policies of López Obrador, who knew that whatever the case, he would have their backing or, at least, the acknowledgment that Mexico City was changing under his administration. We must also take into account the fact that the Federal District has been a very important part of the national political scene. In this sense, local and national interests frequently interact and disagree with each other, in either the legislative or executive arenas. Thus, debates in the Legislative Assembly of the DF have been intense in the face of the Projects of Law issued by the local executive power, while it has not always counted on the party majority to approve them.

Additionally, the media have played a fundamental role in influencing the building of a leader's public image. Hence, López Obrador, compared with Cárdenas, wisely used the press and the media to project his own image, despite criticisms from some of his closest collaborators.

It is also important to recognize the intense labor of PRD's political operators in the DF, although it has entailed some dishonest actions that have already been subjected to the judgment of public opinion. The old clienteles of social organizations from PRI's CNOP (Confederación Nacional de Organizaciones Populares, PRI's popular sector) have changed stripes and are now loyal followers of the local government party, in spite of the fact that it is not a part of serious urban planning policy.

The city still needs an integral organization of street hawkers, small-bus routes proliferate without a general transportation and traffic-flow plan, and transportation sector groups continue to aggressively oppose any attempt to regulate routes and to improve the service. Massive irregular land invasions have indeed ceased, although Iztapalapa and other city districts still reflect the inheritance of that history; therefore, the capital city administration has yet to satisfy infrastructure demands in certain areas that form part of a metropolis that remains spatially segregated and socially divided by well-defined social classes and strata.

In the sphere of government–civic society relations, there are difficulties with respect to achieving a more fruitful dialogue—first, because the Federal District Government (GDF) has a complex, highly centralized administrative structure. So, in spite of an initial approach expressed by means of a policy of negotiations with civic organizations, the practical outcomes have often been scarce (Sánchez and Álvarez, 2006, p. 220). In terms of *urban governance,* there is a weak initiative to start new administrative practices promoting dialogue and the implementation of public policies in order to facilitate citizenship decision making. The practice of getting favors in exchange for support has not yet been overcome in the PRD because this constitutes a social basis for supporting local government policies. In this respect, the creation of urban governance in Mexico City is a process that only began during the first directly elected government since 1929 (date of closure of the local government), whose party, the PRD, aimed to democratize local political institutions. However, the new networks built among groups of street hawkers, taxi drivers, settlers of irregular settlements, and other social organizations conformed to a political coalition very similar to the one that the old PRI had through the CNOP in former times. Hence, some of the main leaders have obtained public positions in the local government (Alvarado and Davis, 2003, p. 160), and it is still happening in the current six-year term of Marcelo Ebrard because of the presence of social forces supporting López Obrador's political campaign in 2006.

Urban governance is also limited by the presence of other emerging groups such as organized crime at several scales of operation ranging from the action of groups involved in "narco-menudeo" (retail narcotics traffic) to those involved in importing illegal merchandise (smuggling) into the country or selling "pirate" cybernetic products (CDs, videos, software). In this case, the PRD government's political rhetoric faces a dilemma because, usually, the search for "capos" in houses and neighborhoods is made in zones with a strong cultural identity, such as Tepito. As a consequence, each public action has a popular reaction, often orchestrated by interest groups entrenched in those zones.

The "structural environment" surrounding the local administration since 1997 has undergone two phases that draw the outlines of local governance. The first one begins with the Cárdenas government that explicitly aimed to mark a clear differentiation from federal government neoliberal policies. Ernesto Zedillo, then president from the ranks of the PRI, could not stop intergovernmental relationships from being conflictive. This had never happened before during the long period of regencies of the capital. But, in the needed division between both levels of government, there were frictions as well as legislative and financial obstacles that prevented the Cárdenist administration from performing better. Likewise, some private enterprise groups disagreed with the ascension of Cárdenas to the city government because of his leftist ideology, although this did not lead to a critical rupture. It was simply that public works during the times of Cárdenas were not accompanied by large private investments, and the city seemed to enter into clear decadence, falling behind in the network of cities connected to the global market in some aspects such as tourism and services infrastructure.

With the first alternation of federal government, headed by the PAN and former PRD leader López Obrador leading the GDF, the structural environment changed slightly. First, the new local leader set out to differentiate himself from his predecessor and, thus, had more pragmatic policies regarding capital, strongly encouraging private investment in the city. On the other hand, from the outset, the relationship between the GDF and the federal government became increasingly difficult. Many of López Obrador's statements to the press during his famous morning "press conferences" were addressed to federal government actions, or they were references to the national political scene, and so, he was already running as the PRD's possible candidate for the presidency of the republic. The critical point was the leader's impeachment, which revealed the severe fissures among power groups and levels of government. This news was taken up in the international press, which essentially brought to light the structural weakness currently faced by the Federal District local government, under pressure from national forces and interest groups.

It clearly is too soon to pronounce the existence of urban governance in Mexico City. One primary reason is that it incorporates only one half of the population and the territory of its metropolitan area.

A second point stands out beginning in December 2006, with Marcelo Ebrard as head of the GDF and Felipe Calderón in the national presidency. The level of conflict has decreased during the first months of both governments, but nothing allows us to suppose that when the "electoral environment" of the next election becomes heated, pressures will not restart and the Federal District, like a "pressure cooker," will burst open once again.

The difficulty in reaching long-term political agreements with the main social actors as well as with the main national and local (federation–state–municipal) political institutions is the final point about the characteristics of urban governance in Mexico City. Social accords cannot be reached by means of top management or corporative agreements, since these do not promote discussion and involvement of the population in decision making on large urban projects. Maybe we are talking about *tropicalizing* urban *governance,* that is, a governance that cares about the local components of civic society, its available resources, and its political culture on the part of both leaders and the citizenry.

Before ending this discussion of governability and governance, it is worth emphasizing that the main Mexican metropolis requires regional and negotiated intervention among the different levels of government. Problems such as pollution, transportation, water, or urban land have to be tackled by means of metropolitan public policies that warrant the future sustainability of the metropolis and its region. That has already been discussed broadly and in detail by those dedicated to its study or those who know the government's technical and operational aspects. Reinforcing urban governance in Mexico City implies, at first, the definition of a long-term government agenda, the strengthening of intergovernmental relationships, the transparency of public works, and the decentralization of decision making to the political districts without encouraging the spatial fragmentation that could accompany it.

The near future brings, as in other parts of the world, the need for thinking about governments or authorities with metropolitan character and thus projecting a metropolitan governance which, like the cases of Madrid, London, Montreal, or Tokyo, in developed countries, or Sao Paulo, Caracas, Buenos Aires, or Quito, in Latin America, are better preparing themselves to build more solid and coordinated city plans (Lefèvre, 2005). Nevertheless, in order to achieve this metropolitan governance, the Federal District still requires new political reform granting, once and for all, the juridical status that it deserves as an integral part of the existing federal pact among the thirty-two states of the Mexican Republic.

Notes

1. For Monterrey's case, see Bassols (2006).
2. The remarks on the case of Monterrey are based on Bassols (2006). Refer to this paper for more detail.
3. The Metropolitan Area of Monterrey (MAM) included, in the year 2000, nine municipalities: Monterrey, Guadalupe, San Nicolás de los Garza, Santa Catarina, San Pedro Garza García, General Escobedo, Apodaca, Juárez, and García, and it represented almost 85 percent of the total population of the state of Nuevo León.
4. Forty of them are directly elected by DF citizens and twenty-six as a result of a statistical formula of proportional representation, depending on the votes obtained in the forty local electoral districts.
5. The impeachment was a result of a long dispute following a demand of the Department of Justice (PGR), based on the charge of contempt of court by the chief of government to a judicial order regarding roadwork in the western zone of the city. López Obrador was substituted for some days as the head of government, while the media reported the process step by step, winning the then leader great popularity in the wake of the 2006 electoral

process. With the boomerang effect against it, the PGR withdrew the charges and the chief of government returned to his position convinced of having obtained a better political platform for his subsequent postulation as presidential candidate of the Partido de la Revolución Democrática (PRD) and the Partido del Trabajo (PT), within the Alianza por el Bien de Todos. The bitter election of July 2006, in which the IFE declared the panista Felipe Calderón Hinojosa winner of the presidential election, was proof of both the political leadership obtained by López Obrador and the relevance of the place that the Federal District had acquired in the national political scenario.

6. In fact, it was an indirect mechanism to elect the DF's next governor, so designed because of President Salinas de Gortari's insistence on not allowing local elections to be held in 1994.

7. Actually, the package was broader, and consisted of the following programs: (a) free transportation for elderly people; (b) health care for elderly people; (c) rescue of housing units of social interest (for an evaluation of this program, see Sánchez and Álvarez, 2006).

8. Mexico City, composed of the sixteen DF districts, fifty-eight municipalities of the State of Mexico and the municipality of Tizayuca, within the State of Hidalgo, is, along with Sao Paulo, Brazil, one of the two biggest metropolises in Latin America, surpassed in population only at the worldwide level, by the Tokyo-Yokohama agglomeration.

References

Alvarado, Arturo, and Diane E. Davis. 2003. "Participación Democrática y Gobernabidad en la Ciudad de México: el reto del PRD en la Transición Política." In *Revista Estudios Sociológicos de el Colegio de México* 21, no. 61 (January–April): 135–66. Mexico: El Colegio de México.

Arzaluz, Socorro. 2006. "Gobierno, Empresarios y Gestión Urbana." In *Explorando el Régimen Urbano en México. Un Análisis Metropolitano.* 125–65. Mexico: El Colegio de la Frontera Norte, UAM-Iztapalapa, Plaza y Valdés Editores.

Bassols, Mario, ed. 2006. *Explorando el Régimen Urbano en México. Un Análisis Metropolitano.* Mexico: El Colegio de la Frontera Norte, UAM-Iztapalapa, Plaza y Valdés Editores.

Bassols, Mario, and Socorro Arzaluz. 2002. "Avatares de la Planeación Urbana en el DF." In *Ciudades,* no. 53 (January–March) 33–40. Puebla: Red Nacional de Investigación Urbana.

Cerutti, Mario. 2002. *Propietarios, empresarios y empresa en el norte de México.* Monterrey: de 1848 a la globalización. Mexico: Siglo XXI Editores.

De Mattos, A. Carlos. 2005. "Gestión Territorial y Urbana: de la Planeación a la Governance." In *Ciudades,* no. 66 (April–June) 2–9. Puebla: Red Nacional de Investigación Urbana.

Duhau, Emilio. 1994. "Gobierno y Gestión de la Ciudad de México. Los Dilemas de la Transición." In *Gestión Metropolitana y Política,* ed. Augusto Bolívar, René Coulomb, and Carmen Muñoz, 53–88. Mexico Programa de Reencuentro de Dos Ciudades; México-Santiago de Chile/El Cotidiano/UAM-Azcapotzalco, Mexico.

Garza, Gustavo. 2003. *Políticas Urbanas en Grandes Metrópolis: Detroit, Monterrey y Toronto.* Mexico: El Colegio de México.

Gómez Tagle, Silvia. 2000. "Elección de Jefe de Gobierno, 1997." In *La Ciudad de México en el Fin del Segundo Milenio,* ed. Gustavo Garza, 658–66. Mexico: Gobierno del Distrito Federal/El Colegio de México.

Hernández Vargas, José Guadalupe. 2006. "Crisis y Transformación de Formas, Estructurales, Procesos y Mecanismos de Gobernabilidad Económica Global." In *Entelequia, Revista Interdisciplinaria,* no.1. Available at www.eumed.net/entelequia.

Hirst, Paul. 2000. "Democracy and Governance." In *Debating Governance Authority, Steering and Democracy,* ed. Jon Pierre, 13–35. New York: Oxford University Press.

Lefèvre, Christian. 2005. "Gobernabilidad Democrática de las Areas Metropolitanas. Experiencias y Lecciones Internacionales para las Ciudades latinoamericanas." In *Gobernar las metrópolis,* ed. Eduardo Rojas et al., 195–261. Madrid: Banco Interamericano de Desarrollo, Universidad de Alcalá de Henares.

Partida, Virgilio, and Carlos Anzaldo. 2004. "Escenarios Demográficos y Urbanos de la Zona Metropolitana del Valle de México." In *Procesos Metropolitanos y Grandes Ciudades. Dinámicas Recientes en México y Otros Países,* ed. Adrián Guillermo Aguilar, 189–218. Mexico: Instituto de Geografía-UNAM/Miguel Ángel Porrúa.

Pradilla Cobos, Emilio. 2004. "Ciudad de México: Los Cambios de la Privatización de lo Urbano." In *Ciudades,* no. 64 (October–December) 57–62. Puebla: RNIU.

Sánchez Mejorada, C., and L. Álvarez Enríquez. 2006. "Participación y Cambios Recientes en la Relación Gobierno-Sociedad en un Gobierno de Centro Izquierda: el Caso de la Ciudad de México (1997–2003)." In *Espacio Metropolitano, Población, Planeación y Política de Gobierno,* ed. María Soledad Cruz Rodríguez, 202–46. Mexico: Red Nacional de Investigación /UAM.

Stone, Clarence. 1989. *Regime Politics: Governing Atlanta, 1946–1988.* Lawrence: University Press of Kansas.

Vellinga, Menno. 1988. *Desigualdad, Poder y Cambio Social en Monterrey. Mexico:* Siglo XXI Editores.

About the Editor and Contributors

Editor

Don Phares is professor emeritus of economics and public policy at the University of Missouri-St. Louis. He is the author of the books *Who Pays State and Local Taxes?* and *State-Local Tax Equity: An Empirical Analysis of the Fifty States;* co-author of *Municipal Output and Performance in New York City;* and editor of *A Decent Home and Environment: Housing Urban America* and *Metropolitan Governance without Metropolitan Government?* He also has written more than seventy articles and book chapters and scores of technical and government reports. He has consulted for and done research with the federal government, numerous states, local jurisdictions, research organizations, businesses, foundations, and universities. He has also served as an expert witness in legal cases pertaining to state and local taxation; the projection of future income; and the analysis of social, demographic, fiscal, and economic trends. He has done numerous economic and fiscal impact studies for both public and private organizations. His administrative experience includes positions as chairperson of a department of economics, director of a public policy research center, dean of a college of arts and sciences, and vice chancellor for a university campus. He received his BA from Northeastern University and his MA and PhD from Syracuse University.

Contributors

Wasim al-Habil is a doctoral candidate at the Maxine Goodman Levin College of Urban Affairs. His research in public administration focuses on governance and the building of indigenous local government systems in emerging democracies. His dissertation involves a design of new local government structures for the Palestinian Authority.

John Stuart Hall is a professor of public affairs at Arizona State University. He received his PhD in political science from the University of Oregon in 1973. He is the author or co-author of numerous books and articles about urban regional and intergovernmental politics and governance. As a founder and former director of Arizona State's School of Public Affairs, Center for Urban Studies, and Urban Data Center and as project director of many large-scale funded public policy research projects, he has specialized in linking the university to pressing community public policy and governance issues. He served three four-year terms as an elected member of the Board of Directors of the National Civic League, and has served on several civic and public policy panels including All American Cities Juries, the Phoenix Futures Forum policy committee, Arizona Employment and Training Counsel, and the Arizona Commission on Tax Reform and School Finance. As co-principal investigator, he is now at work on a large interdisciplinary urban regional research project, supported by a $2.2 million grant from the National Institute on Aging, to understand urban resilience and its impacts on health and well-being in diverse social areas of the Phoenix region.

E. Terrence Jones is professor of political science and public policy administration at the University of Missouri-St. Louis. He is the author of *The Metropolitan Chase: Politics and Policy in Urban America; Fragmented by Design: Why St. Louis Has So Many Governments;* and *Conducting Political Research.* He is also the co-editor of *St. Louis Metromorphosis: Past Trends and Future Directions.* He has served as a consultant to more than sixty governmental and nonprofit agencies and, for twenty years, was co-director of the Leadership St. Louis program. He was dean of arts and sciences at UM-St. Louis for fourteen years.

Dennis R. Judd is a professor in the Department of Political Science and Fellow in the Great Cities Institute, University of Illinois at Chicago. He has published numerous books and articles on urban political economy, urban economic development, national urban policy, and urban revitalization. Recently he has pioneered scholarly research on urban tourism. As part of this continuing research program, he co-founded the International Tourism Research Group and co-edited *The Tourist City* (with Susan S. Fainstein; Yale University Press, 1999), *Cities and Visitors* (with Lily M. Hoffman and Susan S. Fainstein; Blackwell, 2003), and edited *The Infrastructure of Play* (M.E. Sharpe, 2003). From 1985 to October 2001 he served as editor of the *Urban Affairs Review.* Currently he is working on a book that examines the postwar campaign to revitalize the downtown in St. Louis, and a book on the building of the tourist infrastructure in Chicago. In 1998 he received the Career Achievement Award from the Urban Politics Section of the American Political Science Association.

David Laslo is research assistant professor and the director of the Metropolitan Information and Data Analysis Services (MIDAS) of the Public Policy Research Center (PPRC) at the University of Missouri-St. Louis. The current applied public policy research focus of the MIDAS section is on workforce development and the implementation of a biannual, statewide labor demand survey and a Web-based Workforce Information System. Recent applied research has included an economic and fiscal impact study for the City of Creve Coeur, a study of philanthropy in the St. Louis region and trends impacting it for the United Way of Greater St. Louis.

He is also chair of the Research Committee of the United Way and is a member of the Community Advisory Board for the *St. Louis Post Dispatch.* Prior to joining PPRC, he was a senior research associate for the City of St. Louis's Planning & Urban Design Agency where he was involved in a wide range of applied public policy research. His academic research has focused on the patterns and politics of urban economic development with recent publications in the *American Behavioral Scientist* and a chapter in the *Infrastructure of Play,* edited by Dennis R. Judd. Additional recent publications have focused on the demographic trends of the St. Louis metropolitan area, the changing demographics of the St. Louis labor force, and an assessment of recent workforce planning efforts. Current research includes a case study of postwar St. Louis focusing on the evolution of strategies used to create the necessary civic capacity to revitalize the downtown.

Suzanne M. Leland is an associate professor in the Political Science Department at University of North Carolina at Charlotte, where she teaches state and local politics, urban politics, and intergovernmental relations. She has published articles in *Public Administration Review* and *Public Administration Quarterly.* She is also the co-author of *Case Studies of City-County Consolidation: Reshaping the Local Government Landscape* with Kurt Thurmaier (M.E. Sharpe, 2004).

Rob Melnick is associate vice president for economic affairs and public policy at Arizona State University (ASU). He also serves ASU as the chief administrator of Arizona's oldest "think tank," the Morrison Institute for Public Policy. He has worked extensively as a policy analyst for government agencies, corporations, foundations, and school systems nationwide. He is the principal author of the books *Urban Growth in Arizona* and *Visions of the Future* and co-author of *Teaching and Media.* Prior to working for ASU, he was a senior research fellow at the Hudson Institute. In 1985, he was elected vice president of Hudson Institute and named the first director of Hudson's Center for Education and Employment Policy. He has managed and/or contributed to nearly 200 funded policy studies on topics including economic development, education reform, urban growth, quality of life, and workforce development. His work has been supported by Fortune 100 corporations, national philanthropic organizations, and both federal and state government agencies. He has been the director of the Morrison Institute since 1987 and was appointed ASU's associate vice president for economic affairs and public policy in 2003. He is a research scientist in the School of Public Affairs. He received his BA from Dartmouth College and his MA and PhD from Arizona State University.

Donald F. Norris is professor and chair of the Department of Public Policy and director of the Maryland Institute for Policy Analysis and Research at the University of Maryland, Baltimore County (Baltimore, Maryland). He is a specialist in urban politics, public management, and the use of information technology in public organizations. He has written extensively on the subject of metropolitan governance. His works in this and other scholarly areas have been published by a number of presses and in several scholarly journals. He holds a BS in history from the University of Memphis and both an MA and a PhD in government from the University of Virginia.

Mario Bassols Ricardez has a master's degree in sociology and a doctor of town planning from the National Autonomous University of Mexico (UNAM). He has been a full-time professor in the Department of Sociology at the Metropolitan Autonomous University (UAM) campus in Iztapalapa since 1988. He has been a member of Urban Research National Network (RNIU) in Mexico since 1989, and Researchers on Local Government of Mexico (IGLOM) since 2006. He is a member of the Technical Committee, Habitat Prize, SEDESOL/CIDE, and editor of Polis, Department of Sociology, UAM-Iztapalapa, since 2007. He is the author of Urban Politics in Aguascalientes (1968–1995), Instituto Cultural de Aguascalientes/UAM-Iztapalapa (Mexico, 1997; in Spanish); Exploring the Urban Regime in Mexico. A Metropolitan Analysis, ed. El Colegio de la Frontera Norte/UAM-Iztapalapa (Mexico, 2006; in Spanish); and "Urban Sociology: In Search of Its Identity?" a chapter in Latinamerican Treatise of Sociology, ed. Enrique de la Garza, Anthropos/UAM-Iztapalapa (Barcelona, 2006; in Spanish).

Mark S. Rosentraub, PhD, is a professor of urban affairs at the Maxine Goodman Levin College of Urban Affairs Cleveland State University. His research interests focus on urban redevelopment, economic development and change, tourism management for economic development, and the economic and intangible value of sports, the arts, and other amenities for urban centers. He has helped numerous cities and institutions with the assessment of the economic value of museums and sports events and facilities. He has worked with the Children's Museum of Indianapolis, the Indianapolis Motor Speedway, the Indianapolis Colts, and the San Diego Padres as well as with venues in numerous other cities. The author of more than ninety articles and book chapters, his most recent book is *The Economics of Sports: An International Perspective,* which he co-authored with Robert Sandy and Peter Sloane. In 1997 he published *Major League Losers: The Real Cost of Sports and Who's Paying For It.* A second, revised edition was published in 1999. His op-ed editorials on these and related topics have appeared in the *New York Times, Wall Street Journal, Cleveland Plain Dealer, Indianapolis Star,* and many other newspapers and business journals. His research and books have been reviewed by more than 100 newspapers and discussed as features on *Nightline* and ABC's *20/20.* His forthcoming book *Major League Winners* focuses on cities that have successfully used sports for revitalization and development and complements *Major League Losers* (1997, 1999), which focused on the abusive sports subsidy system and its impact on cities.

Andrew Sancton, a native of Montreal, received his doctoral degree in politics from Oxford University in 1978. Most of his academic career has been spent at the University of Western Ontario in London, where he is a professor in the Department of Political Science. He was chair of the department from 2000 until 2005. He is now director of the department's Local Government Program, which offers undergraduate and graduate education in public administration for municipal managers. Many of Canada's senior municipal officials have attended these courses. From 1998 until 2000 he was president of the Canadian Association of Programs in Public Administration and a board member of the Institute of Public Administration of Canada. He is the author of many publications relating to Canadian local government. His most recent book is *Merger Mania: The Assault on Local Government* (McGill-Queen's University Press, 2000). His work on the relationship between municipal amalgamations and cost savings won the 1996 J.E. Hodgetts award for the best English-language article in the journal *Canadian Public Administration.* In recent years he has been both a consultant and an expert witness. He acted in these capacities in the debates about municipal amalgamation in Toronto and Montreal.

Hank V. Savitch is the Brown and Williamson Distinguished Research Professor, School of Urban and Public Affairs, University of Louisville, Louisville, KY. He is a former president of the Urban Politics Section of the American Political Science Association. He has published ten books or monographs on various aspects of urban development, public policy, and regional governance. His most recent co-authored volume, *Cities in the International Marketplace* (Princeton University Press) received the best book award in the urban field by the American Political Science Association. His more than seventy-five articles have appeared in leading journals, collected works, and research outlets. He has received numerous awards both in the United States and abroad. He has been the recipient of two Fulbright Scholar Awards (France), he served as a visiting scholar at the London School of Economics (United Kingdom) as well as being named a Lady Davis Fellow at the Hebrew University of Jerusalem (Israel). He has also served as a consultant to former mayor of New York City David Dinkins, the U.S. Department of Housing and Urban Development, and the Mayors' Urban Summit. He recently completed *Cities in a Time of Terror: Space, Territory, and Local Resilience* (M.E. Sharpe, 2007). He and his co-author Ron Vogel have been monitoring metropolitan governance and development in Louisville for about two decades. They are currently working on a book that compares the rescaling of cities in Europe, North America, and Asia.

Patrick J. Smith (PhD, government, London School of Economics) is a professor of political science/urban studies and director of the Institute of Governance Studies, Simon Fraser University, Vancouver, BC. He is the author/editor of such books as *The Vision and the Game: Making the Canadian Constitution* (Calgary: Detselig,

1987); *The Almanac of Canadian Politics,* 2d ed. (Toronto: Oxford University Press, 1995); *L'Alannach Politique du Quebec* (Montreal: Editiones Americaines, 1997); *Ties that Bind: Voters and Parties in Canada* (Toronto: Oxford University Press, 1999); *Continuities and Discontinuities: The Political Economy of Social Welfare and Labour Market Policy in Canada* (Toronto: University of Toronto Press, 1994); and *Urban Solutions to Global Problems: Vancouver-Canada-Habitat II* (Vancouver: UBC/Centre for Human Settlements, 1996). He has written more than 100 articles, book chapters, and reports on local government, multilevel governance, global cities, Cascadia, international city-regions, planning and community economic development, local/urban/regional and metropolitan governance, municipal intergovernmental relations, Canadian political parties, elections, electoral reform, Aboriginal issues, accountability, open government, affirmative action, labor market policy, public sector ethics, ombudsmania, antiterrorism legislation, and human rights. He has served as consultant to Canadian provincial and local governments provided expert testimony for provincial and federal governments in Canada, served as department chair/institute director at Simon Fraser University, and as a member of the national boards of the Canadian Political Science Association and the Institute of Public Administration of Canada.

Carl W. Stenberg is professor of public administration and government at the School of Government, University of North Carolina at Chapel Hill, and director of the Master of Public Administration Program. He also serves as faculty director of the school's Public Executive Leadership Academy. He previously held academic positions as dean of the Yale Gordon College of Liberal Arts at the University of Baltimore and director of the Weldon Cooper Center for Public Service at the University of Virginia. His experience as a practitioner includes positions as executive director of the Council of State Governments and assistant director of the U.S. Advisory Commission on Intergovernmental Relations. He is former chair of the Board of Directors of the National Academy of Public Administration and past president of the American Society for Public Administration. He is co-editor of *Managing Local Government Services: A Practical Guide,* published by the International City/County Management Association in 2007.

Mark Tranel is director of the University of Missouri-St. Louis Public Policy Research Center. He has served as principal investigator on over fifty applied research projects in the past decade. He has taught public administration in the UM-St. Louis Department of Political Science and public policy analysis in the Public Policy Administration Program. Before he joined the center staff, his experience included positions as director of real estate development, Economic Council of St. Louis County, which was responsible for industrial development sites and the small business incubator program; and manager of Neighborhood Preservation and Community Planner, Normandy Municipal Council. He has been responsible for housing, and community and economic development programs in twenty municipalities. He is on the board of directors of several St. Louis nonprofits. His has a PhD in public policy analysis and administration from St. Louis University.

Ronald K. Vogel is professor of political science and urban and public affairs and chair of the Department of Political Science at the University of Louisville. He is currently a Fulbright Scholar at the University of Hong Kong and heads the Comparative Urban Politics related group in the American Political Science Association. He is co-author of *Political Change in the Metropolis* (with John Harrigan, 8th ed., 2007), editor of the *Handbook of Urban Politics and Policy* in the United States (1997), co-editor of *Regional Politics: America in a Post-City Age* (with H.V. Savitch, 1996), and author of *Urban Political Economy: Broward County, Florida* (1992). Savitch and Vogel have been monitoring metropolitan governance and development in Louisville for about two decades. They are currently working on a book that compares the rescaling of cities in Europe, North America, and Asia.

Robert K. Whelan is visiting professor in the School of Urban and Public Affairs at the University of Texas at Arlington. He is co-author of *Urban Policy and Politics in a Bureaucratic Age,* and he has authored and co-authored many book chapters, articles, and papers. He has also written on Montreal's urban governance structure. He was a professor at the University of New Orleans for twenty-four years. He served the College of Urban and Public Affairs as acting dean, associate dean, and MPA coordinator. He chaired the Planning and Zoning Commission in the city of Slidell, Louisiana. He conducted a study evaluating the Houma, Louisiana-Terrebone Parish consolidation. He received his BA from Columbia University and his PhD from the University of Maryland-College Park.

Lin Ye is an assistant professor of public administration in the Department of Political Science and Public Administration, Roosevelt University, Chicago, IL. His research interests include public administration, urban development, and planning issues. He has published articles in *Journal of Urban Affairs, Journal of Planning Literature,* and *China Public Administration Review.* His research on housing studies has appeared in several chapters in edited volumes and in research reports. He also conducts research on various comparative urban issues in China and the United States. Lin Ye received his MPA and PhD degrees from the University of Louisville.

Tonya Zimmerman is a PhD candidate in public policy at the University of Maryland, Baltimore County. She is currently working on a dissertation about the impacts of state anti-predatory lending laws with an emphasis on the impacts on certain borrower populations. She received a BA from Albion College and an MA from Temple University.

Index

For Product Safety Concerns and Information please contact our EU
representative GPSR@taylorandfrancis.com
Taylor & Francis Verlag GmbH, Kaufingerstraße 24, 80331 München, Germany